FIRST-YEAR TEACHER'S
Survival Kit

Ready-to-Use Strategies, Tools & Activities for
Meeting the Challenges of Each School Day

JULIA G. THOMPSON

JOSSEY-BASS
A Wiley Imprint
www.josseybass.com

Published by Jossey-Bass
A Wiley Imprint
989 Market Street, San Francisco, CA 94103-1741   www.josseybass.com

Many of the illustrations are reproductions from Art Explosion, Nova Development Corporation.

Jossey-Bass books and products are available through most bookstores. To contact Jossey-Bass directly call our Customer Care Department within the U.S. at 800-956-7739, outside the U.S. at 317-572-3986 or fax 317-572-4002.

Jossey-Bass also publishes its books in a variety of electronic formats. Some content that appears in print may not be available in electronic books.

Library of Congress Cataloging-in-Publication Data

Thompson, Julia G.
    First-year teacher's survival kit / Julia G. Thompson.
      p. cm.
    ISBN 0-13-061644-3 (paper)
     1. First year teachers—Handbooks, manuals, etc. 2. Teacher orientation—Handbooks, manuals, etc. 3. Teaching—Handbooks, manuals, etc. I. Title.

LB2844.1.N4 T52   2002
371.1—dc21   2001058358

Printing 10 9 8 7 6

High Praise for
First-Year Teacher's Survival Kit

"I can't think of anything this *Kit* doesn't have! It's common knowledge that the first year of teaching presents endless challenges and a plethora of questions. Thompson's *First-Year Teacher's Survival Kit* will prove to be an invaluable tool for new teachers. Seasoned teachers will love it for its new and innovative ideas. I would have one available for each teacher on opening day!"

Gloria Smith, Early Childhood Staff Developer
District 7, Bronx (NY)

"Julia Thompson is a hero among teachers. She has skillfully created an invaluable survival kit for new teachers that is filled with a wealth of expertise and wisdom. *First-Year Teacher's Survival Kit* has successful strategies that will help navigate new teachers through virtually every problem or situation they may encounter. With this resource at their side, new teachers will be better prepared, more effective, more efficient, and more positive educators. Every new teacher of the 21st century should have and read this book!"

Sherry Cameron, Resource Teacher
Richard B. Wilson K–8 School (AZ)

"I found Julia Thompson's *First-Year Teacher's Survival Kit* to provide it all. She has written a remarkable guide that any teacher will enjoy having. The ideas and suggestions she has gathered provide a 'compass' of usable and practical information. This *Kit* will help keep new professional educators focused on what is most important: the mutual positive development of their students and themselves."

Dr. David E. Hutt, Superintendent
Buellton Union School District (CA)

"First-year teachers—and veterans, too—will find an abundance of resources in this well-stocked survival kit. Julia Thompson's down-to-earth ideas are based on years of classroom experience, seasoned judgment, and a strong sense of professionalism. This book is like having a personal mentor to guide new teachers through the demanding process of becoming educators. Experienced teachers will also find fresh insights that can transform effective instruction from instinctive to intentional."

Elisabeth H. Fuller, Coordinator of Grants, Budget, and Resources
Isle of Wight County Schools (VA)

"Julia Thompson earns an A+ for her practical and comprehensive *First-Year Teacher's Survival Kit*. The veteran educator skillfully provides effective classroom-tested strategies to guide the new teacher through the possible problems and potentially stressful situations often encountered during that memorable first year of teaching. This valuable resource provides a wealth of useful information that will help the teacher remain upbeat, confident, and motivated. *First-Year Teacher's Survival Kit* should be required reading for all new teachers!"

Jack Umstatter, English Teacher
Cold Spring Harbor High School (NY)

"*First-Year Teacher's Survival Kit* offers a true insight into handling the challenges of our profession. As a university supervisor with student teachers for over 12 years, I would make Julia Thompson's book mandatory reading for beginning teachers. Her approach to planning and classroom management is very relevant to today's students. This book will enable the new teacher to have a foundation for a stable, rewarding first year."

Pamela J. Edwards, Supervisor, Teacher Education Services
Old Dominion University (VA)

"The *First-Year Teacher's Survival Kit* is a comprehensive guide filled with practical advice for new teachers. From detailing how to work effectively with students, colleagues, and parents to maintaining balance in personal life, this *Kit* covers virtually every concern and problem a new teacher may have. It even includes numerous helpful resources, such as online forums and education databases. The *First-Year Teacher's Survival Kit* can help new teachers not only survive but flourish, setting the stage for a successful and rewarding career. It should be required reading for all new teachers."

Gary R. Muschla, former Sixth-Grade Teacher
Appleby School (NJ)

"I wish I had this *Kit* when I was starting out as a first-year teacher. It offers new teachers as well as experienced teachers a wealth of numerous tips and strategies, from managing time to creating a user-friendly classroom. There are suggestions for specific activities on how to start on that first day, including ice-breaking activities. I also like the practical advice for relating to students, including the difficulties involved in being a 'popular' teacher, ways of gaining your student's respect, and ways to deal with rudeness in the classroom. The author's friendly voice speaks directly and clearly—you know that she wants every first-year teacher to succeed."

Cynthia Stowe, Consulting School Psychologist
Eagle Mountain School (MA)

"This survival kit is one of the best that I've seen for new teachers. This experienced teacher knows firsthand what new teachers will encounter that important first year in the classroom. She provides practical strategies and ready-to-use materials to make sure that the common pitfalls of discipline, organization, time management, lesson planning, grading and assessment, working with other teachers, and job burnout are avoided. Julia Thompson also knows that teaching is one of the most challenging as well as one of the most rewarding jobs in the world. From what I've read, her mission is to keep talented new teachers in the classroom and not pursuing other careers. Thank you for writing this book!"

Darlene Mannix, Special Education Teacher
Crichfield Elementary School (IN)

"Julia Thompson's *First-Year Teacher's Survival Kit* offers new teachers a variety of paths to help them not only survive but thrive. Her high professional standards are translated into clear, concise strategies written in a way that makes the challenges of teaching more manageable. The self-assessments throughout the sections help readers to evaluate their knowledge and attitudes and to plan changes. Her central message is about students, the profound role that teachers play in their lives, and the exuberance of a well-spent day with them. Because I can think of no higher praise than I'd want Ms. Thompson to teach my daughters, I am pleased that her hard-earned wisdom is available to new and experienced teachers."

Dr. Margaret Hallau, Director, National Outreach, Research,
and Evaluation Network
Gallaudet University (Washington, DC)

"What an extraordinary book! With this one resource, Julia Thompson addresses the needs of all beginning teachers. Elementary, middle, and high school teachers—both new and experienced—can find beneficial information on every page. Not only are there tips on how to manage the 'science' of education—seating charts, lessons plans, daily routines—but also on how to master the 'art' of this profession with sections devoted to classroom management, motivation, professional expertise, and learning how to be part of a team of professionals. Beginning teachers need this valuable resource. Certainly, in my early years of teaching, I could have benefited immensely from having this book on my desk."

Pam Leigh, English Teacher
Spotswood High School (VA)

Acknowledgments

I am grateful to my editor, Susan Kolwicz, for her hard work, guidance, and insight in the preparation of this book.

Thanks to Gloria Fuzia for her patient suggestions and improvements thoughout each section.

Special thanks to the following veteran teachers who took the time to offer advice to first-year teachers:

Paige Adcock	Kelly Mansfield
Denise Boyer	Rebecca Mercer
Dawn Carroll	Patty Muth
Sandra Councill	Donna Nelms
Melinda Cummings	Ken Pheifer
R. K. Gach	Yann Pirrone
Edward Gardner	Carole Platt
Kim Marie Hogan	Kristen Sanderlin
Verna Jones	Rick Shelton
Joyce Kennedy	Sabrina Smith
Barbara Knowles	Marlene Stanton
William Lee	Sarah Walski
Stephanie Mahoney	

About the Author

JULIA THOMPSON received her B.A. in English from Virginia Polytechnic Institute and State University in Blacksburg. She has been a teacher in the public schools of Virginia, Arizona, and North Carolina for over twenty years. She has taught a wide variety of courses including freshman composition at Virginia Tech, all of the secondary English grades, mining, geography, reading, home economics, math, civics, Arizona history, physical education, special education, graduation equivalency preparation, and employment skills. Her students have been diverse in ethnic groups as well as in age, ranging from remedial seventh graders to adults. Ms. Thompson is currently teaching English at Windsor High School in Isle of Wight County, Virginia.

About This Kit

Welcome to the other side of the desk! For years you have sat on the student's side completing assignments, working with your teachers, and learning. Now, on the teacher's side of the desk, you will design and deliver those assignments, work with students as well as other teachers, and, best of all, continue to learn.

If you are like other first-year teachers, you probably feel a mixture of excitement and uncertainty as you face each new school day. You know what you and your students are supposed to achieve, but you are not sure how to proceed. One class period may find you catching the interest of every student in your class while the same technique fails to engage students in the next class. Some days increase your confidence in your teaching skills while others test your dedication.

Take heart. Almost everyone begins a teaching career with the same emotions. Many veteran teachers also suffered through the tough days when they didn't know what to do and gloried in the days when they were able to engage every student in the magic of learning. The daily barrage of pressures on first-year teachers can be so exhausting and defeating that some eventually choose another career that is not as difficult . . . and not nearly as rewarding.

On the other hand, the first years of your teaching career can be immensely satisfying ones. Your first years as a teacher can be ones of dynamic professional growth and personal fulfillment as you achieve your own dreams while helping your students achieve theirs.

Helping you find success in the first years of your career is the goal of this *Kit*. The suggestions and strategies in these pages can help you develop into an skillful classroom teacher who remains enthusiastic about the possibilities in every student. For instance, you'll find:

- Instructional strategies that will enable you to turn textbook theories into a classroom reality
- Helpful ways to efficiently manage paperwork and other time robbers so that you can focus on teaching
- Guidance as you translate your curriculum guides into interesting and useful lessons that will engage all of your students
- A wide range of motivational strategies that will help you involve every student in learning activities every moment of class

- ▸ Assistance in identifying your professional responsibilities and establishing personal priorities to accomplish them
- ▸ Guidance in mastering workplace skills and becoming part of a supportive network of professional educators
- ▸ The tools you need to examine your current teaching skills and establish achievable goals for your professional life
- ▸ Inspiration, insight, and practical advice from successful veteran teachers
- ▸ A wide variety of innovative and time-tested classroom management activities, strategies, and techniques to help you create a positive learning environment
- ▸ Confidence in your ability to find the satisfaction that a career in education can bring

The *Kit* is designed to help you meet the challenges that each school day brings. Inside these pages you will find the answers to the most common "how-to" questions that many first-year teachers have:

Section 1:   How can I develop into a successful professional?

Section 2:   How can I master the workplace skills that I need?

Section 3:   How can I begin my career with confidence?

Section 4:   How can I develop a successful professional relationship with my colleagues?

Section 5:   How can I develop a meaningful relationship with every student?

Section 6:   How can I plan lessons that will meet the needs of my students?

Section 7:   How can I deliver instruction that will engage my students in the learning process?

Section 8:   How can I assess my students' progress accurately and fairly?

Section 9:   How can I motivate my students to succeed?

Section 10:   How can I help my students develop study tools to become independent learners?

Section 11:   How can I use every minute of class time so that my students are on task as much as possible?

Section 12:   How can I prevent discipline problems from disrupting the positive learning environment that I want to establish?

Section 13:   How can I manage discipline problems once they occur?

Section 14:   How can I cope with some of the more common problems that can happen in any classroom?

Section 15:   How can I meet the needs of each child in my diverse classroom?

Section 16:   How can I deal with the stress that my new career will bring?

What is the most effective way to use this resource? The answers to this question are as varied as the teachers who use it.

- ✔ You could browse through it section by section, gathering ideas to enrich your classes and strengthen your teaching skills. This method allows you to pick and choose as you adapt the practical advice and activities you'll find included here.

- ✔ When you become familiar with the format and contents, you can use it as a desk top resource. You can use the table of contents and the index to quickly look up solutions for specific problems that are of immediate concern.

- ✔ Work through a section at a time: learning, applying, practicing, and adapting the information as you go. While you can't learn how to be an excellent teacher all at once, you can benefit from this systematic approach.

- ✔ When you find that you have had a discouraging day at school, look over the advice from experienced educators who offer tips and insights to help you keep your problems in perspective, or use the journal entries as a guide to self-reflection.

However you choose to use this book, it is designed to be an interactive experience. Use a pencil to take the assessments, set your goals, and make notes as you read each section. Highlight. Underline. Dog-ear the pages. Place bookmarks in the sections that appeal to you at the moment. As you go through the process of learning the intricacies of your new profession, refer to this book for assistance with the daily problems that can rob even the most stalwart educator of confidence.

The most effective use of the information in these pages, however, is to help you become the confident and knowledgeable educator that you dreamed of being when you chose your new career. From the first day of school to the last day, you can be one of the greatest assets that our nation can have—*a successful teacher*. With patience and practice, you can realize your own professional dreams. Your first years as a teacher can help you achieve the satisfaction that only a career in education can bring.

Julia G. Thompson

Contents

SECTION THREE: BEGIN THE SCHOOL YEAR WITH CONFIDENCE   57

SECTION FOUR: BECOME A VALUABLE TEAM PLAYER 83

SECTION SIX: DESIGN EFFECTIVE INSTRUCTION　153

SECTION SEVEN: DELIVER EFFECTIVE INSTRUCTION   183

SECTION EIGHT: EVALUATE YOUR STUDENTS' PROGRESS   221

SECTION ELEVEN: MAKE THE MOST OF YOUR INSTRUCTIONAL TIME   317

SECTION THIRTEEN: HANDLE BEHAVIOR PROBLEMS EFFECTIVELY 369

SECTION FOURTEEN: SOLUTIONS FOR SOME WIDESPREAD PROBLEMS   399

Your New Vocation

The alarm rings too early. Sleepily he heads for the shower and then pulls on his new school clothes wishing that he could just wear his old jeans. His school shoes pinch after a long summer of sneakers.

He forces himself to face the most important meal of the day: coffee. After his second cup, he checks out his lunch box. Wrapped neatly inside it is a peanut butter and jelly sandwich, his favorite. Less sleepy now, he starts packing his new book bag. When the "Back to School" signs went up last month, he was one of the first in line to get his new school supplies. He drops his binders, pens, pencils, and paper into the book bag. He adds the extra supplies that he knows some students can't afford. He was surprised to see how many other teachers were also out buying supplies for their students. He can't really afford to buy school supplies, but he is determined his students will have what they need.

He adds another dog-eared teacher's edition of one of the textbooks his students will be using. He has just about memorized it, hoping to always be ready when someone asks a tough question. Finally, he fits in his grade book, trying to close the stuffed bag.

Another school year, another first day. He's still just as apprehensive as he was when he was waiting to catch the bus to his first day of kindergarten. Only this time, he's the teacher.

"Value truth. Value professionalism."

—Barbara Knowles, 36 years experience

"Welcome Back!" Those signs up all over schools across the nation apply to teachers, too—especially new teachers. As a first-year teacher, you will have an exciting and memorable year. You will face new challenges and have lots of fun with your students.

Fun? Yes, teaching is fun. Lots of teachers have fun every day at school, contrary to what most people think. Thinking that teaching can't be fun is just one of the many misconceptions many people have about teaching. As a new teacher, you will join millions of others in a profession that is probably the most universally misunderstood one in the world.

The rest of the world thinks that teachers enjoy short hours and long summer vacations . . . that they must have taken courses in how to answer seemingly endless questions with unflinching patience . . . that they enjoy eating in a cafeteria with two hundred children who left their table manners at home . . . that they must like wearing clothes stained with red ink, crayon, and chalk.

The rest of the world doesn't know that teachers spend their evenings, weekends, and summer vacations grading papers, making bulletin boards, writing lesson plans, and taking classes for recertification . . . how hard a teacher tries to find the right words to chide, comfort, explain, and inspire . . . how teachers worry over their students as if they were their own children . . . how teachers weep when a school erupts into violence because they know that it could have been theirs.

Your life as a new teacher will be a paradox. You will have to be strict and loving at the same time. You will be exhausted and exhilarated. Best of all, you will receive more than you can ever give, no matter how generous you are.

As a teacher, you will never be rich, even if your district has the wisdom to offer you a signing bonus. However, you will be rewarded over and over because you will help students achieve their dreams, and in so doing, you will achieve your own. Teachers don't just "touch the future," as the bumper stickers promise. Education is far more than that. Teachers face the future every day in the students who sit in their classrooms, whose papers they grade, whom they discipline and reassure and try to keep securely on the right path. Teachers see the promise of the future in the unruly present.

It's not easy being a teacher. You will need to develop heroic qualities: the stamina of an Olympic athlete, the diplomacy of a head of state, the courage of a soldier, and the charisma of a pop star. It sounds like a tremendous challenge, but other teachers have done it, and so can you. After all, someone had to teach those other heroes. Olympic athletes, heads of state, soldiers, and pop stars aren't just born that way. Standing behind them—behind every hero—is another hero: a teacher.

Welcome to your new vocation.

Your Teaching Career: The Good News

"You're a teacher? Boy, I don't see how you do it. I could never be a teacher." Perhaps you have already heard this several times since you announced that you signed a teaching contract. Media reports are full of grim news about the teacher shortage, embarrassingly low teacher salaries, controversies over standards and standardized testing, and, worst of all, school violence.

While these reports are not exaggerations, there is a great deal of good news about education that never gets reported. Day after day, good children go to school and learn what they are expected to learn, and even exceed expectations. The many positive aspects to being a teacher include the following.

You are part of a large supportive team of caring professionals.

The good news about being a teacher today is that you are not alone. Teachers are members of a team of supportive adults who care about and work with all students in a school. Depending on the size of your school and your district's guidelines, you may be called on to work with social service workers, support committees, student mentors, parole officers, counselors, and other adults.

You have access to an increasing amount of educational research.

Since the 1970s, there has been an amazing increase in the amount of educational research. Because of the research we can better understand students' differing needs. We can quickly find solutions to many of the problems teachers face every day. And because of this research, we know now that school plays a much more important role in shaping students' futures than was once thought. An even more amazing factor of this research increase is that much of it is available to any teacher online or through conferences, professional organizations, or in bookstores.

You have access to technology that can connect you and your students to the world.

One of the best things about being a teacher in the new millennium is the technology available for educators. Not only do we have access to sophisticated technology, but so do our students. Even if there is a shortage of equipment in your school, there are remedies to this problem. (See Section Two for some ideas on how to make sure that your students have the technological advantages that they need.) Along with the advances in equipment, there are countless education resource sites on the Internet, and you have access to hundreds of thousands of other teachers who are just a keyboard away and who are willing to share ideas. You can visit Web sites, join listserves, enter chat rooms, and find all sorts of innovative lesson plans and materials online.

You can rise to the challenge of standards and standardized testing.

One of the most controversial education topics in recent years is the increase in standardized testing and the accountability measures that accompany them. Although media coverage of this issue tends to be sensational and negative, there is much that is good about standards and standardized tests. School districts, teachers, and students are all under enormous pressure to improve academic performance, and although standards and standardized tests are not yet perfected, they are reasonable measures of achievement. Standards provide guidance, and students and teachers who rise to the challenge imposed by standards and standardized tests can only be enriched by their efforts.

Today's teachers reach out to all students.

In years past educators reflected the social climate of their times by not fully including all children in the education process. Students were discriminated against because of many factors, including gender, race, ability, and national origin. Today teachers include

3

all students in their instructional efforts. We even teach the children who make it clear to everyone around them that they are not interested in an education.

The best reason to teach is the simplest: children.

Although the preceding five examples of the recent news in education are positive ones, they are not the best feature of your new career. The very best news about the teaching profession is that you get to be with children all day long. Whether the children in your class are eighteen-year-olds with severe cases of senioritis, second graders who just can't settle down, or eighth graders with an acute case of insolence, they are still the best reasons to go to school each day.

> *"In order to teach children effectively, you have to keep their welfare in the forefront. You have to rid yourselves of the mistaken idea that all learning must be fun. Learning requires hard work and perseverance. The fun, or joy, comes from having learned how to do something and then being able to do it again independently."*
>
> —Elizabeth Crosby Stull, 30 years experience

New Problems (and Some Old Ones) All Teachers Experience

Given the purpose of your work and the diverse personalities, needs, and backgrounds of your students, problems are inevitable. Every day that you teach, you will have problems. Some will be simple to resolve, others will take longer, and still others will not have workable solutions.

On the days when your life as a teacher seems beset with serious problems, take comfort in knowing that you are not alone. *All* teachers have problems. First-year teachers, experienced teachers, teachers at every grade level and every ability level have to cope with problems . . . no matter how ideal the school situation.

The following are just some of the problems all teachers experience. Anytime you feel overwhelmed, remember that all teachers have had to deal with what you're going through.

- Stacks of tedious paperwork
- Fatigue and burnout
- Frequent class interruptions
- Difficulty in contacting parents
- Not enough equipment or materials
- Students with overwhelming family problems
- The threat of school violence
- Uncertainty about the right course of action to take
- Unsupportive and uncooperative parents
- A culture or generation gap with students
- Not enough productive time with students
- Lack of practical solutions to discipline problems
- Too much to do in too short a time
- Overworked and unsympathetic administrators
- Overcrowded classrooms

Figure 1.1

Below you will find some of the most common assumptions that many first-year teachers have about teaching.

- ✔ Put a check in the box beside each statement that you think is valid.

- ✔ Then check the key at the end to see how much you really know about your new profession.

☐ 1. I will have weekends and summers off.

☐ 2. It's important that my students like me.

☐ 3. My students will relate to me better if I'm dressed casually.

☐ 4. The advice more experienced teachers have been giving me makes sense: "Don't smile until Thanksgiving."

☐ 5. I should return graded papers to my students within a week.

☐ 6. It's important to bond with my students by having lots in common with them.

☐ 7. Lawsuits happen to other teachers.

☐ 8. Rules and seating charts will only restrict my students' individuality.

☐ 9. If I agree to sponsor at least three after-school activities, I will have a better evaluation than teachers who don't.

☐ 10. School won't interfere with my social life.

☐ 11. Paperwork is not a problem. Grading papers and keeping my roll book straight doesn't take much time.

☐ 12. Tests and homework inhibit students' creative expression.

☐ 13. Profanity in the classroom is okay. After all, students hear it everywhere.

☐ 14. Most of my students will come from broken homes with busy parents who don't take an active interest in what's happening at school.

☐ 15. All year will be as tough as the first semester.

Key

1. **I will have weekends and summers off.** True. You do not have to report to school on weekends or during the summer unless you have to hold Saturday school, or attend summer classes, or teach summer school, or attend a sports event or sponsor a club, or . . . Aside from that, your weekends and summers will be free after your lessons plans are done, all those homework and test papers and graded, and you've called those parents you promised yourself you would call.

2. **It's important that my students like me.** We all want our students to like us. However, as a teacher you will often have to ask students to do things that they might not want to do and to enforce the rules they must follow. It is not your role to be a student's well-liked friend. It is important that students respect you and your role as a teacher, too. Work to maintain a balance between students liking you and respecting you.

3. **My students will relate to me better if I'm dressed casually**. If "casually" means multi-hued spikes, numerous piercings, and ragged jeans, you should rethink your casual dress. Teachers are not supposed to be mistaken for students' peers. Dress professionally, and take your cue regarding an appropriate dress code from the other teachers in your school.

4. **The advice more experienced teachers have been giving me makes sense: "Don't smile until Thanksgiving."** Why shouldn't you smile? No one likes a grouch. Besides, students will not respond any better or behave any better if you show no sense of enjoyment in teaching them and being with them. Balance the need to be strict with a cheerful presence.

5. **I should return graded papers to my students within a week.** A week is too long. Students need immediate feedback to effectively learn. Resolve to grade and return papers as quickly as you can.

6. **It's important to bond with my students by having lots in common with them.** You should build bridges to your students based on common interests. Keep in mind, however, that if your common interests are not ones that you would be very comfortable discussing in front of the school board, you would be better off not sharing them with your students, either. It is acceptable to share an interest in a local band with your students; it is quite another matter to be seen intoxicated at a club where the band is playing. And although having common interests with your students can be helpful, always be discreet about what you reveal about yourself to your students.

7. **Lawsuits happen to other teachers.** Lawsuits are one of the hazards of modern life and teaching is not exempt from the threat. Don't be lulled into thinking that a lawsuit can't happen to you. You can protect yourself by keeping your documentation records in perfect order and by being professional in your conduct at all times.

8. **Rules and seating charts will only restrict my students' individuality.** All students need boundaries, and rules and seating charts provide boundaries, not barriers.

9. **If I agree to sponsor at least three after-school activities, I will have a better evaluation than teachers who don't.** Don't allow your initial enthusiasm for your new position to cause you to misjudge your time and the amount of work you can do well. You will be asked to take on many assignments because you are new. Use good judgment about what you are capable of doing—and doing well.

10. **School won't interfere with my social life.** If your social life involves the public consumption of alcohol, tobacco, illegal drugs or other behavior that conservative parents could object to, school *should* interfere. Further, because your new responsibilities will take up so much of your time, you'll find that you'll have less of it for socializing.

11. **Paperwork is not a problem. Grading papers and keeping my roll book straight doesn't take much time.** Grading papers and keeping a roll book straight are just some of the paperwork duties that teachers have. You need to be efficient about completing all paperwork promptly and accurately.

12. **Tests and homework inhibit students' creative expression.** Even among motivated students, tests and homework are two of the biggest complaints about school. Neither one has to inhibit creative expression if the assignments and tests are designed to be more than rote recall exercises.

13. **Profanity in the classroom is okay. After all, students hear it everywhere.** School is not the world of popular entertainment and should not be a place where profanity is accepted. While you and some of your students may think that it is acceptable to swear, many other students and their parents don't. Don't allow profanity in your classroom and don't be tempted to use it yourself.

14. **Most of my students will come from broken homes with busy parents who don't take an active interest in what's happening at school.** While many of your students will come from one-parent households, many will not. Besides, very few parents are too busy to help teachers who are interested their child's welfare.

15. **All year will be as tough as the first semester.** The first few months of any job are the most difficult ones. The first semester of your teaching career will be the same. Every day of your first semester and first year—and every year if you are lucky—will be an opportunity for you to learn and grow, and although neither activity is always comfortable, before long you will be handling your role as a teacher with confidence and ease.

"Sometime in that first spring, you will begin to notice things you 'should have done.' You will wish you could start a new year off right then with a fresh bunch of students and wonderful new procedures. Relax, I guarantee the new year will come soon enough."

—Kelly Mansfield, 2 years experience

YOU ARE THE SOLUTION

According to media reports, schools are hotbeds of social, behavioral, and academic problems. You are the solution to those problems. While it is exciting to think of the powerful influence that you can have on your students, it is just as unnerving to accept the challenges that accompany your importance.

Countless studies have proved that teachers are the most significant factor in any student's schooling. And although you may be tempted to think that sports, peer pressure, physical environment, or books have more influence than you do, consider the many ways in which you play a role in your students' lives, including the following.

- Inspiring students to have goals and dreams and to know they can achieve them
- Keeping defenseless students safe from bullies
- Encouraging a lifelong interest in learning
- Guiding to students to build a better life
- Offering comfort and guidance
- Teaching someone to read, to write, to think
- Modeling how to be a good citizen and a successful adult
- Helping students believe in themselves
- Encouraging students who get little encouragement elsewhere
- Patiently mentoring students who are stretching their wings
- Extending gentle kindness and endless patience even when reprisals would seem reasonable

A teacher's influence in the lives of students is often subtle and immeasurable, but if you doubt your importance in the lives of your students, think for a moment about a teacher who inspired you, who offered you a glimpse into the world of adults, and who made it clear that you had the power in you to succeed.

"Be yourself. Remember that in the eyes of the community you are a professional all of the time, even away from school."

—Edward Gardner, 36 years experience

10 Excellent Choices to Make Right Now

Teaching is a deliberate act! A successful career in education, just as in all other ambitious undertakings, does not happen by chance. It requires effort, attention to detail, planning, and reflection.

Each day that you teach you will make choices that affect not only your life but also the lives of the students in your care. Because of the serious responsibility and tremendous power teachers have over the lives of young people, you must carefully think through the choices you make. Just as it is common to make resolutions to celebrate a new year, you can also make resolutions as your new school year begins. You can choose to act in a positive and career-enhancing manner each day. The following resolutions are some that you can adopt as you begin a new school year.

1. **Resolve to cope with the daily stress that you will face as a teacher.** If you don't plan how you will manage your stressors, you will soon be a candidate for burnout. (See Section Sixteen for more on stress management.)

2. **Resolve to prevent discipline problems from disrupting your class.** You are in control of your class. Early intervention strategies are far more effective than having to cope with the aftermath of a discipline problem.

3. **Resolve to be as professional in your school life as you can be.** Let your dress, demeanor, and speech reflect your commitment to be an excellent educator.

4. **Resolve to listen more than you speak.** Instead of presenting routine lectures, ask questions that will lead your students to discover new knowledge and the excitement that comes with learning.

5. **Resolve to attend to paperwork quickly and accurately.** Get organized. Learn to manage your time well. Education is a profession that generates a great deal of paperwork; attend to your paperwork efficiently before it overwhelms you.

6. **Resolve to accept your students for what they are.** You can choose to determine what your students don't know and proceed from there or you can choose to spend months bewailing your students' ignorance, lack of preparation, and general ineptitude.

7. **Resolve to plan exciting and creative lessons.** While you do not have to entertain your students every moment, you also do not have to offer uninteresting lessons, either. Even the driest subject can been enlivened by an enthusiastic teacher. If you do not know where to begin, try one of the many lesson plan sites on the Internet.

8. **Resolve to be friendly, fair, and firm in your dealings with students.** While you do need to connect in a positive way with all of your students, you also need to be a strong force in your classroom. This means that you must be decisive about how to handle discipline issues.

9. **Resolve to give 100 percent while you are at school.** Spend your school days on school matters. Make a deliberate choice to focus on your students and their learning from the time you arrive at school until you leave.

10. **Resolve to take time to enjoy your students.** When you have papers to grade, meetings to plan, and phone calls to make, it is very easy to lose sight of how much satisfaction there is in looking over a classroom of excited students chattering about a topic you have just introduced. Take time every day to simply enjoy being in your classroom with students.

A Teacher's Daunting Daily Responsibility

Your "To Do" list is three pages long. You have a time-consuming meeting after school, twenty minutes of lunchroom duty, three phone calls to make, a class set of papers to grade, and fifty records to search during planning. As pressing as these duties are, they are not as important as your primary responsibility: *teaching every child in your class every second of the day*.

What does this mean to you? Everything that happens in your classroom should be designed to lead to the successful transfer of knowledge. You are a teacher, the adult in the classroom. This means you must be emotionally in control of yourself, prepared for class, and focused on teaching.

The following list contains some examples of circumstances that may lead to decreased learning time for some or all students. Resolve that you will avoid such interference in your classroom. There is space at the end of the list for you to add examples of your own. Let this list serve as reminder to yourself to fulfill your responsibility daily.

- In the middle of class you suddenly remember that some equipment that you need is still in the trunk of your car and send a student to bring it in.
- You are tired and allow your students to sit idly for the last few minutes of class.
- You have a lesson plan that is not working and you don't change it.
- An unpleasant incident in your first class ruins your day. You take it out on the rest of your students.
- You hold a few students at the end of class and make them late for their next one.
- You allow a small disruption to grow until it ruins class for a significant number of your students.

- _____

  _____

- _____

  _____

- _____

  _____

10

Figure 1.2
HOW WILL YOU RATE AS A TEACHER?

Examine some of the qualities of a good teacher. See where your strengths lie and which qualities you need to develop further by following these steps.

1. Put a check in the box before each characteristic in the preceding list that applies to you *every* day that you are at school.
2. When you are finished, total the number of checks that you have.
3. See the rankings at the end of the test to see how you rate.

Before you begin, remember that good teachers are not just born that way; instead, they make deliberate choices to become the teachers that they are. You can do the same. As a first-year teacher, you should commit yourself to developing as many of the following qualities as you can as fast as you can.

Good teachers:

- ☐ Enjoy their students
- ☐ Act like adults and not like children in class
- ☐ Inspire their students to want to know more
- ☐ Return papers promptly
- ☐ Use a variety of interesting activities in a lesson
- ☐ Keep students engaged in meaningful work all class
- ☐ Make sure students know how to do an assignment well
- ☐ Know their subject matter
- ☐ Are reliable role models
- ☐ Maintain orderly classrooms
- ☐ Are prepared to teach every student every day
- ☐ Do not have favorites
- ☐ Spend time after school helping students who need it
- ☐ See themselves as part of a team
- ☐ Are polite to everyone all of the time
- ☐ Commit themselves to professionalism
- ☐ Make their students feel capable
- ☐ Handle paperwork efficiently
- ☐ Stay open-minded
- ☐ Have a great sense of humor

Check mark total: _____

Key:

18–20: You are definitely on the right track! Keep up the good work!

16–18: Begin by choosing one or two qualities to improve. Make a plan, set your goals, and work to develop all the attributes of a successful teacher.

15 and lower: Remember that improving your performance as a teacher takes time and deliberate choices. Begin by selecting the qualities that are most important to you right now. Set your goals to develop each one.

Mistakes You Can Avoid

One of the most interesting aspects of a teaching career is that teachers have many opportunities to learn from their mistakes. New teachers, in particular, can expect to make many mistakes because of the overwhelming number of issues they will be facing for the first time. Mistakes novice teachers make often stem from the best of intentions, often arising out of a desire to avoid some of the unpleasant experiences that they may have had in their own school days, and leading to either an overly strict or overly lenient disposition toward students.

> *"Teaching is not your hobby! It is your job and your are paid for an eight-hour-a-day stint. You must be prepared to face your class every day. Your first year will be the most difficult year since you will be working way over eight hours per day!"*
>
> —Stephanie Mahoney, 24 years experience

As a first-year teacher you will make many mistakes. While this is an unavoidable part of your learning process, there are some mistakes that should be easy to avoid with a bit of foreknowledge, common sense, and planning. Keep these pointers in mind and avoid many first-year errors.

Mistake 1: You find it easy to be over-familiar with students. Maintain your role as friendly adult toward your students and don't be tempted to be "one of them." Although it is important that students see you as an accessible adult, you must still maintain the dignity of your position as their teacher.

Mistake 2: You try to bluff your way through material for which you have not carefully prepared. Set aside plenty of time to read, design lessons, prepare handouts, and gather other materials. Many teachers, experienced and novice alike, set aside preparation time on the same day each week by noting this on their calendars at the start of the year. This is a good practice that will help you avoid being caught unprepared for a lesson.

Mistake 3: You are not as well-rested and ready for school as you should be. Make a commitment to yourself to arrange your personal life so that it does not interfere with school.

Mistake 4: You are uncertain about rules, policies, and what to do about discipline problems. While experience will make this mistake easier to avoid, it is important that you carefully read the faculty handbook and ask for clarification and help.

Mistake 5: You lose your cool and punish a student in anger. Resolve to never make this mistake, because students will come to see you as harsh and punitive. By remaining calm you will win over your students much more easily than if you lose your temper. If you find your blood pressure rising during an incident with a student, back off, cool down, and think the situation through before acting. Tell the student, "I see that we disagree. We will discuss this later."

Mistake 6: You establish a class routine and rarely ever vary it. Change the pace! Shake students up and keep them alert by designing creative and engaging lessons. Don't let routine get in the way of students' enthusiasm and motivation.

Mistake 7: You overlook small behavior problems until they disrupt class. Keep small problems that way by taking the necessary action before they grow out of control. Call parents, consult with a guidance counselor or administrator, and enlist students— especially those at the center of the problem—in finding a workable solution. (See Section Twelve for more on this topic.)

Mistake 8: You believe that your students will connect with you better if they see you as you really are: a free-spirited person who is up-to-date with the latest clubs, bands, slang, body art, fashions and other bits of popular culture. No one asks you to give up your identity, but as the teacher, you must separate yourself from your students and maintain a professional demeanor and persona. Besides, not all of your students will think that you are appropriate in your relationship with them if you act like a student instead of they way they think a teacher should act. And parents and guardians surely won't appreciate your free-spirited lifestyle. Keep your personal life separate from your professional life.

Mistake 9: You are comfortable teaching by telling stories, jokes, and entertaining your students. Although the occasional joke or story enlivens class, be careful not to overdo it. Your students are not an audience for you to entertain. They are there to learn, and your job is to teach them. You can keep students engaged through dynamic lessons and not with shallow entertainment.

Mistake 10: You call in sick when you're not. Don't be tempted to use up all your allotted sick days. Your students need you. Use your sick days for times when you may really need them and avoid needlessly disrupting your students' learning.

Mistake 11: You try to relate to your students by speaking non-standard English and sometimes even mildly cursing. If you do this, then you are not teaching your students how educated and professional adults behave in the workplace. Even though they may not always show it, students want their teachers to speak in a correct and dignified manner.

Mistake 12: Your lesson ends before class is over. This can easily happen to any teacher. Avoid this problem by planning for more than you will ever be able to cover in a class period.

Mistake 13: You don't agree with some of the school rules and don't enforce them. You send a very negative and confusing message to students when you ignore certain school rules and then try to enforce others. Everyone benefits when all teachers and students abide by the same rules.

Mistake 14: You don't want to bother busy teachers or appear foolish, so you avoid asking for help and advice. Don't isolate yourself this way. Experienced teachers know many of the answers that you need and are more than willing to help a new teacher.

Mistake 15: You confront a misbehaving student in front of the rest of the class. When you do this, you not only embarrass the student, but also run the risk that the rest of the students will side with their classmate in sympathy.

Mistake 16: You hold students back to make them tidy up the room or talk over a problem. Keeping students after class for any reason interferes with and disrupts the instructional time and plans of other teachers. Plan to end your class in a timely and organized manner.

Mistake 17: You find yourself taking problems home and feeling more and more stressed. Plan your stress management strategies now and remain as objective as you can in confronting problems. (See Section Sixteen for more help with this.)

Mistake 18: You like to sit at your desk or stand at the front of the class while students are working. Monitor your students by circulating throughout the room all class period. Many behavioral and interpersonal problems can be prevented through teacher proximity.

Mistake 19: You have high expectations, but for some reason your students are not reaching them. While having high expectations for your students is a vital part of what you should be doing at school, it is not enough. It is your job to help all students reach your expectations. Start teaching with material that is familiar to your students and gradually increase the difficulty until everyone succeeds.

Mistake 20: You make a mistake and try to keep it under wraps. If this is a mistake that an administrator is likely to hear about from someone else or one that you need help to keep from repeating, admit your error right away and ask for help from an administrator or mentor. Even the best teachers make mistakes—own up to yours while there is a chance that the situation can be rectified.

How to Be the Best Teacher You Can Be

How can you develop into the kind of teacher that you want to be? The answer is simple: *act like a student again.*

Just as you worked hard for years to be a good student, so you will now have to work to be an excellent teacher. Both endeavors require the same skills. Study, concentrate on your objectives, believe in yourself, seek help, do your homework, work well with others, take notes, and, above all, pay attention to the excellent teachers all around you!

> *"The best advice that I can give is that new teachers need to understand that they are the adults in charge in the classroom."*
>
> —Ken Pfeifer, 28 years experience

10 Common Sense Steps to Boost Your Confidence

As you go through the first year of your new career, it is really easy to lose confidence in yourself and in the choice that you made to be a teacher. This lack of confidence is not only stressful, but can make you begin considering other, less rewarding professions.

There are many things that you can do to feel self-assured about teaching and about how well you are adjusting to the changes a new career can bring. Follow these suggestions for boosting your self-confidence and enjoy the rewards that they will bring.

1. **Dress the part.** If you look like a veteran educator, then your professional image will speak for you in the moments that you are too shy, overwhelmed, or uncertain to think of just the right things to say.

2. **Be prepared for class.** There is a great sense of accomplishment in knowing that you are prepared for questions, have the correct number of handouts, and know just what to ask to interest your students in the day's lesson.

3. **Listen more than you speak.** This does not mean that you should never speak up; it just means that the veteran teachers around you have a great deal to offer to those novice teachers who listen to what they have to say.

4. **Keep it simple at first.** Do not plan elaborate class activities such as lengthy collaborative learning exercises or overnight field trips until you've gotten to know your students well enough and have enough experience and support from administrators to ensure that the activities will be successful.

5. **Pay attention to your successes.** It is very easy to dwell on your failings at work. Make a conscious effort to focus on the improvements you make in your first year. Keep a list of the things that you did correctly each week or reward yourself when you have mastered a professional goal.

6. **Seek support from your colleagues.** Novice and veteran teachers all can offer encouragement and advice. Often it is just comforting to know that other teachers are experiencing the same problems that are bothering you.

7. **Set professional goals for yourself.** By setting goals for yourself, you will not only improve your teaching skills, but you will also give yourself a psychological boost because you will feel a greater sense of control over your professional life. Keep your goals manageable and track your progress.

8. **Stay organized!** When you are organized at work, you will avoid many stressful situations because you will be in control of your physical environment. You won't lose papers or other materials. You will not have to cope with an unpleasantly messy desk. You won't waste precious time looking for your keys or other belongings.

9. **Smile and act as if you've got things under control.** Your students do not need to know that you are having a bad afternoon. They just want to have a teacher who is ready for class. By being poised even in difficult situations, you and your students will benefit because the classroom environment will be more controlled.

10. **See opportunities instead of disasters.** You will need to develop an optimistic and resilient attitude to feel confident as a teacher. Instead of dwelling on your mistakes or on what went wrong during the day, see such occasions as they really are: opportunities to learn and grow.

Keep a Journal and Grow Professionally

Education is a paradoxical profession. As a teacher, you spend your days surrounded by energetic young people who demand that you focus your attention outwards. In order to do this well, you need to turn inwards. Being introspective is a vital component of your growth as an educator.

Teachers are notorious for writing little notes to themselves on odd scraps of paper, on self-sticking note pads, on the handouts they receive at faculty meetings, in the margins of textbooks, and especially all over their lesson plans. Using writing as a tool to keep organized—mentally, emotionally, and physically—is an important skill for all teachers. Just as your students learn through reflection, so can you. In order to become the kind the teacher that you want to be, you should develop the habit of using a teaching journal to reflect on your day.

The purpose of a journal is to allow you to record your thoughts as your experiences help you grow professionally. A teacher's journal is a tool for thinking, processing, and planning. It can help put the events of the day in perspective for you.

Your entries don't have to be lengthy, spelled correctly, or even very detailed to be of benefit to you. You should, however, try to write consistently each day. This habit will make the process meaningful and worthwhile as your entries begin to accumulate and you can see the progress you make over the course of the school year.

There are two problems with keeping a teacher's journal; however, both can be easily managed. The first one is finding the actual journal that you want to use each day. Although there are many, many styles and types of journals on the market, it is easiest to begin simply. Purchase a spiral notebook or use loose leaf paper and a three-ring binder.

The second problem with keeping a teacher's journal is not as easy to solve: finding the time to write each day. The sensible solution used by many professionals is to allow no more than ten to fifteen minutes at the end of the day. Many experienced writers keep their journals by their beds so they can quickly write as they prepare for bedtime.

What should you include in your journal? You should record the date, of course. After that, there are many topics to include in your journal. At the end of each section of this resource you will find a list of journal topics that can help you explore your thoughts about the topics covered in that section. Of course, there are countless topics to cover, many of which will arise out of the specific events of your day.

Some other ideas for journal entries that will help you as you experience your first year as a teacher include the following.

- Advice you've received
- A brief summary of your day
- Funny things you hear or see
- The emotions you experienced
- New ideas
- Mistakes you will not repeat
- A solution to a problem you've encountered
- Ideas for teaching a new unit of material
- An activity or event that went well
- An activity or event that did not go well

- Your feelings about an event
- Cause and effect in the classroom
- Something new that you learned
- Procedures that you need to change
- Something you did well
- Kind things someone did for you
- What you would like to remember about the day
- Problems that you can solve quickly

- Where to turn for help with problems you can't solve alone
- Plans for the upcoming days or weeks
- Your ideas about a school issue
- Complaints
- Your goals
- Things you find yourself having to say too often
- Impressions of other teachers, students, or school events

Figure 1.3

SAMPLE JOURNAL ENTRIES THAT PROMOTE BETTER TEACHING

Here are three sample entries from a first-year teacher's teaching journal to guide you in writing your own entries.

September 9

Today we began a new chapter in math. I was surprised to see how few of my students did not have the background that I thought they should have to understand even the problems on the first page. The smart thing I did was pass out scraps of paper and ask students to look over the chapter and tell me what they already have been taught. I should have done this last week. I spent time during plan period deciding how to bring everyone up to speed.

January 30

It started snowing today right before lunch. It made me remember how much I used to love snow days when I was in school. I switched lessons to include something about snow and we spent some time together enjoying the snow and learning at the same time. I will definitely do this the next time it snows. I have already started a "Snow File" of activities that we can do when it is snowing.

March 30

They were wild today! Everyone seemed keyed up and not at all interested in learning anything. I didn't know how tough it would be to try to teach serious lessons the week before Spring Break. I kept things under control, but need to rethink this time of the year. For tomorrow, I plan on having students do worksheets that should be engaging for them.

Journal Entries About Your New Vocation

Here are a few entry suggestions about the topics in this section that could spur your professional development. Explore these in your journal as a way to help you grow in your role as an educator.

- List fifteen people who have shaped your life. Choose the three most important and explain how they influenced you to be a teacher.
- Complete this statement: "I teach because . . ."
- Complete this statement: "I accept as my responsibility . . ."
- When have you experienced the most growth as a teacher? What did you learn?
- Write about your favorite teacher. What have you learned from this person?
- What beliefs do you share with your students? What else do you share with them?
- What beliefs about teaching do you share with your colleagues? How do your beliefs differ? How can you learn from each of your colleagues?
- Under what conditions would you quit teaching? What can you do right now to make your career more satisfying?
- What kind of teacher would you like to be? What steps do you need to take to become your ideal?

Develop Your Professional Expertise

She sat in the crowded auditorium waiting for the keynote speaker to begin. At her feet lay a souvenir bag stuffed with brochures, business cards, trial software, sample textbooks, pens, and memo pads.

Her excitement faded as she looked around at other teachers in nearby seats. They seemed so confident and knowledgeable. She was sure that their students always did their homework and probably even raised their hands to be called on. These teachers made teaching seem easy. She knew it wasn't.

She made so many mistakes. Just last week she had irritated the entire faculty when she jammed the photocopier. Sighing, she looked at the self-assured speaker. "I'll bet that he never jammed a photocopier," she thought, "or finished a lesson with twenty minutes of class time still left."

She picked up one of the souvenir pens and began taking notes. Perhaps the speaker could help her become as confident and successful as the teachers around her.

*J*ust as in any profession, a teacher's first years are certainly the most difficult ones. In addition to the problems any novice professional faces, beginning a teaching career is difficult because of other factors, too. The following is a brief list of some of the reasons that your first few years as a teacher might be difficult ones. Some of these probably will sound familiar to you.

- You have too much work to do in order to do it well.
- You don't know how to teach and handle non-instructional duties at the same time.
- You may have unrealistic expectations about your students, your responsibilities, or even your chances for success.
- Everything is overwhelmingly new.
- There is a great deal of crucial information that you must master immediately.
- It is hard to know how to prioritize when you are not sure what is most important.

- ▶ You may not be sure about the best course of action to take in every situation.
- ▶ You sometimes feel isolated physically and emotionally from experienced teachers.
- ▶ You may not have enough materials, equipment, or resources.
- ▶ You don't know how to handle the physical and emotional exhaustion that you are experiencing.

Take heart. The first years of the teaching profession are indeed difficult ones. However, millions of teachers have survived them and gone on to help their students realize their dreams. They did this by developing their professional expertise.

What is the professional expertise that will make your school life successful? It can be as simple as not losing your class keys and as complicated as working well with a mentor. Having professional expertise means developing the skills and attitudes that competent educators have. It is reflected in many tangible ways, such as how you dress, organize your materials, grade papers . . . Students and colleagues can tell at a glance that you are in control of your situation and of yourself. However, the hallmarks of professional expertise are mostly intangible ones such as time management, efficient use of technology, good work habits, and, most of all, how skillfully you convey a seriousness of purpose about your new career.

As you face the hardships of the first years, take them as opportunities to learn and overcome challenges. Retain your sense of humor, expand your sense of adventure, work hard, and develop into a professional educator. Even the most seasoned experts have to begin somewhere. Soon you will find that the demands of your new profession will first become manageable and then will become rewarding as you develop into a professional educator.

> *"You can never be too professional. Shake hands, make eye contact, introduce people properly. Bring a pad and pen to meetings and take notes. Do this especially when people are being difficult to deal with. Being emotional, outwardly angry, or rude will always haunt you later."*
>
> —Kim Marie Hogan, 9 years experience

The Good News About the First Years

While it is true that a teacher's first years can be difficult, there is much about this time in your career to appreciate. Here are five important advantages that novice teachers have that experienced teachers do not. Take advantage of them!

1. **You have up-to-date training.** You have probably recently finished your teacher training courses or taken courses designed to help you earn a teaching license. This gives you a tremendous advantage over faculty members who may not have been in a classroom as a student in several years and who are not aware of some of the recent trends and changes in education.

2. **You have enthusiasm.** If you ever have shared planning time with a teacher who has lost enthusiasm for teaching or even being with students, you will really appreciate the fact that your inexperience allows you to be enthusiastic about things that some jaded teachers may no longer find interesting. Don't lose your enthusiasm and let it be infectious! If you can always carry it in your heart, your success as a teacher will be assured.

3. **You have not yet developed poor work habits.** You're starting with a clean slate. Now is the time to develop the good work habits that will lead to successful teaching. Use this time in your professional life to learn how competent teachers accomplish their teaching objectives successfully.

4. **Your colleagues will be generous to a new teacher.** The experienced teachers that you work with can recall their own difficulties during the first few years of their careers and will likely be generous in offering you the help you need. As a new teacher you will find that others will offer you materials, supplies, advice, equipment, and support.

5. **Others will be more understanding of your mistakes.** Simply because you are a new faculty member, others will not expect you to have the same level of knowledge or expertise that more experienced teachers have. This doesn't mean that you should not work as hard as you can to become a competent teacher; rather, it means that other staff members will be understanding when you don't know some things that they take for granted. Enjoy this small perk and remember to return the favors when you are an experienced teacher.

Your Classroom Responsibilities

Education is a complex undertaking. It differs from many professions in the multitude and variety of daily tasks teachers must accomplish. As a teacher you not only have to master the art of interacting successfully with others at all times, but you also face a wide range of other duties, from creating lesson plans, to grading papers, to meeting with administrators and parents. One of the most difficult tasks that you face as a new teacher is learning how to manage all of your duties successfully. In order to accomplish this, you should first focus on your classroom responsibilities. Here are some suggestions to help you with this crucial task.

1. **Become thoroughly familiar with the content of the course that you are teaching.** You must be the authority on this material in the classroom. If you do not know the material, then your students can't learn.

2. **Quickly develop and maintain a positive relationship with every child.** This is a sure way to a successful school year for students and teachers alike.

3. **Develop interesting, innovative strategies for teaching the material that your students need to know.** You should include a variety of activities to meet the needs of every student every day.

4. **Establish clear objectives for your students.** Having clear objectives will focus your instruction and allow your students to concentrate on what is important in each lesson.

5. **Learn to deliver instruction effectively.** You can and should learn to speak with poise and precision in front of a class. (There is more advice for you on this topic in Section Seven.)

6. **Teach your students the strategies that they need in order to do their work well.** Teachers who teach students metacognitive activities such as note taking, summarizing, using organizers, and successful time management empower their students to become responsible for their own learning.

7. **Recognize and address the diverse needs of students in each of your classes.** Students have different skill levels, ability levels, preferred learning styles, and previous knowledge. You should pay attention to each student's needs in these areas.

8. **Provide appropriate, helpful, and timely feedback to your students.** Make it your goal to return graded papers to your students within three days and to provide helpful, not critical, comments.

9. **Provide an orderly and safe environment where courtesy is the order of the day.** Classroom management is your responsibility and requires careful planning and consistent effort on your part. It does not happen by chance.

10. **Accept your role as classroom leader.** You are the primary positive force in your classroom and in the lives of many of your students. When you accept responsibility for what happens in your class, all of your students benefit.

Figure 2.1

MANAGE YOUR CLASSROOM RESPONSIBILITIES

It can be difficult to know how to begin meeting each of your many classroom responsibilities. You can avoid many problems in your workday if you create strategies for accomplishing each responsibility that you face. Use the chart below to organize your thoughts as you plan for a successful school year.

Classroom Responsibility 1: Become familiar with the course content

Strategies:

1. _____

2. _____

3. _____

Classroom Responsibility 2: Develop a positive relationship with every child

Strategies:

1. _____

2. _____

3. _____

Classroom Responsibility 3: Incorporate innovative teaching strategies

Strategies:

1. _____

2. _____

3. _____

Classroom Responsibility 4: Establish clear goals for students

Strategies:

1. _____

2. _____

3. _____

Classroom Responsibility 5: Deliver instruction effectively

Strategies:

1. _____

2. _____

3. _____

Classroom Responsibility 6: Teach metacognitive techniques
Strategies:

1. _____

2. _____

3. _____

Classroom Responsibility 7: Address the diverse needs of students
Strategies:

1. _____

2. _____

3. _____

Classroom Responsibility 8: Provide appropriate feedback
Strategies:

1. _____

2. _____

3. _____

Classroom Responsibility 9: Provide an orderly and safe environment
Strategies:

1. _____

2. _____

3. _____

Classroom Responsibility 10: Accept responsibility as classroom leader
Strategies:

1. _____

2. _____

3. _____

How to Make Educational Theories a Classroom Reality

One of the most frustrating issues about your first years as a teacher is the gap between what you know should be happening in your classroom and what really does happen. Part of the professional expertise that you will develop early in your career is how to bridge the gap between the intriguing theories that you have learned in your education classes and the reality of your classroom.

You know, for example, that students learn best in a productive, focused, orderly environment. However, it is one thing to know that this is the expected norm for a successful classroom and quite another to try to maintain such a classroom. Have confidence! It is possible to make the theories that you learned as you trained to be a teacher into reality. Here are three ways to begin: 1) learn from colleagues, 2) read and research, and 3) *practice, practice, practice.*

LEARN FROM COLLEAGUES

The first way to learn how to create the teaching experiences you have learned about and want for your students is by learning from other teachers. You will learn more from your colleagues than from any other source.

The following tips offer ways in which you can take advantage of your colleagues' expertise to create the kind of classroom reality that you want.

> *"Always ask for help when you need it, or do not understand a student or an administrative directive."*
>
> —Joyce Kennedy,
> 11 years experience

- Observe other teachers as often as you can. Even if you don't stay for an entire class or have a specific agenda for observing, you will learn something new every time you watch other teachers teach.

- Ask questions. Other teachers can answer most of the questions you have. Ask them for help.

- Have other teachers observe you. The more teachers who can watch you teach and offer constructive criticism, the better. This will also have the added benefit of helping you quickly grow accustomed to being observed and making you more comfortable with an administrator's observation.

- Join a group on the Internet through a listserve or chat room. An advantage of this method of learning from other teachers is that you gain a sense of the shared successes and problems that all teachers face, no matter where they live or the district in which they work.

- Establish a local support group. You will learn a great deal from other teachers if you can meet regularly to discuss problems and solutions. (You will find more suggestions for how to establish such a group in Section Sixteen.)

- Seek your own mentors even if your school has a working mentorship program. You will find suggestions for how to do this later in this section.

LEARN THROUGH READING AND RESEARCH

The next way that you can turn educational theories into a classroom reality is through reading and research. Here are some suggestions for using these techniques to your advantage.

- Visit a library near your home. Public libraries and college libraries abound with useful materials for teachers. Even if you do not formally belong to a particular library, you can still take advantage of the materials it offers by just dropping in to take notes.

- Use the extensive resources on the Internet. There are thousands of sites on the Internet devoted to education and teaching issues. Visit them!

- Read professional journals. Professional reading will not only broaden your knowledge of educational issues, but will also provide you with up-to-date information and teaching strategies. Many professional journals also have Internet sites.

- Join professional organizations. Whether you join your local teaching association or one devoted to the subject matter or grade level that you teach, you will benefit from the association that you have with other professionals.

- Review your college textbooks. Your perception of the material in your texts and notes has changed now that you have your own classroom responsibilities. Review your texts and notes with a fresh perspective.

- Take a class. Reading and researching are intrinsic components of many education classes. Now that you are a teacher, there may be a class that you did not take while you were enrolled in school that you would now find beneficial. Some districts even offer monetary incentives for teachers who take certain courses.

PRACTICE, PRACTICE, PRACTICE

A final way that you can turn those educational theories into a classroom reality is through practice. Here are a few practical suggestions to help you begin.

- Remember that being successful at any task will take time. Practice being the best teacher you can be every day and, in time, teaching will be easier.

- Plan what *you* are going to do in class each day. Even though this might seem obvious, it can easily be overlooked. Don't just plan what you intend for your students to do, but plan how you will use your time, as well.

- Set goals for yourself and work to achieve them. Without the focus that goals provide, you will not achieve success quickly.

- As you approach various tasks during the school year, take time to reflect on how you will accomplish them, and—after you've completed them—how you've done. Record data that supports or refutes what you believe about a certain teaching practice. Think things through!

- Don't give up if you try an activity that fails. Analyze what went wrong and see if you can adjust it for greater success.

⬥ Proceed with steadfast confidence in yourself. Teaching is not for the faint of heart. You can be a successful teacher if you proceed with deliberation and have enough self-confidence to sustain you through tough times.

Develop Your Own Philosophy

At some point in your job search, you may have had to answer a question that intimidates even the best-prepared candidate: "Tell us about your personal philosophy of education."

The popularity of this question comes not from its ability to weed out teacher candidates with the wrong philosophy, but rather from what it reveals about how prepared the person answering the question is. Prospective teachers who have not yet thought about what they believe about teaching are not as well prepared as those who have.

Just as many businesses today use a mission statement to guide their actions and help them meet their objectives, many schools also have mission statements that exemplify the beliefs of the staff. Mission statements are one form of expressing educational philosophy.

It is important that you establish your personal framework of beliefs about education. Even though you may change your beliefs, you should formulate your own ideas about teaching and how you and your students can be successful together. You should create your own mission statement that will guide your actions throughout the school year.

As a novice teacher, where do you begin to formulate your personal philosophies about teaching? Draw on your previous training, your school district's philosophy, and your previous experiences—both positive and negative—in school.

Use Figure 2.2 to guide your thinking in the process of developing your philosophy.

5 Proactive Attitudes for Success

Although there are many aspects of your teaching career that you will never be able to control, you do have jurisdiction over the most important key to success: your attitude. Use it as a tool to become a successful teacher. Take control of your attitude from the moment you sign your teaching contract.

To help you become a successful educator, there are many positive attitudes that you can adopt. Here are five attitudes that you can adopt today that can immediately have a positive effect on your teaching success.

1. **Be a team player.** You are now part of a team of professional educators. Although teachers have never worked in isolation, this sense of teamwork has never been more necessary than in recent years. Students are served by many adults, such as family, past and present teachers, other adults in the community, and school support staff, all working on their behalf. As a member of this team, you must cooperate with all other members of the team for the mutual benefit of the students in your care.

Figure 2.2

DEVELOP A REALISTIC WORKING PHILOSOPHY

To develop your own educational philosophy, commit your thoughts and ideas to paper. Begin by looking over this list and jotting down what you believe about each of these topics as they relate to school, students, learning, and achievement.

1. School rules _____

_____

2. Class rules _____

_____

3. School procedures _____

_____

4. Class procedures _____

_____

5. Successful discipline practices _____

_____

6. Lesson planning _____

_____

7. Motivation _____

_____

8. Time on task _____

_____

9. The purpose of education _____

_____

10. Appropriate goals for teachers _____

_____

11. Quality of work _____

_____

12. Self-discipline _____

_____

13. Your role as a team member _____

_____

14. Professionalism _____

_____

15. The importance of what you teach _____

_____

16. Learning styles_____

_____

17. Diversity _____

_____

18. The teacher as role model _____

_____

19. The importance of ability _____

_____

20. Students' rights _____

_____

After you have written your thoughts on each of the topics above, use what you have written to guide you as you begin to formulate your philosophy in a brief mission statement. Begin by asking yourself what you believe to be true about education.

_____

_____

_____

_____

Reminder: Check your personal mission statement and your list of thoughts every few months to see if you have had any permanent shifts in your beliefs that affect your philosophy. Expect this to happen regularly during your first years as a teacher.

"Stay away from the negative people. Gravitate toward the positive.
Do this for your students."

—Rebecca Mercer, 25 years experience

2. **Become a lifelong learner.** Now that you are a teacher, you have entered a new phase in your own education. One of best things about being a teacher is that there are so many opportunities for growth. Choose to take control of your career by resolving to become a lifelong learner. Seize the opportunities that you will be offered at school each day to grow and learn.

3. **Believe that all children have the ability and the need to learn.** If you truly believe that all children can succeed in school, then your career will have substance and depth that will lead to success—for yourself and your students. When educators approach their professional responsibilities with this attitude, their school days have meaning and purpose that students respond to with enthusiasm for learning.

4. **Accept responsibility for what happens in your classroom.** If you waste time blaming students, the media, other teachers, and society for the problems that you and your students experience, then you are not working to solve them. Accept responsibility for what happens in your class and your students will flourish.

5. **Teach one day at a time.** Forget the negative experiences that you may have had in the past and don't obsess about problems that you may have in the future. Focus on improving your skills in the present and the future will take care of itself.

Develop Good Work Habits

Your life experiences have taught you how to accomplish complicated tasks with a minimum of fuss. The teaching tasks that you face now require the same good habits that have helped you through your college training and in other areas of your life. You will need to be self-directed, accurate, and thorough in your professional work just as you have been in the past when studying for tests, writing papers, or finishing long-term projects on time.

The problems that you may experience with work habits can be caused by your inexperience with those tasks. You can overcome this problem with just a bit of effort.

As teachers grow in their career experience, they develop some key work habits that serve them throughout their careers. Below are some of the work habits that successful teachers have mastered. Getting into these good habits will make your professional life much easier.

- Be prompt to school and other appointments.
- Use a calendar to keep track of important information.
- Prioritize the tasks you need to complete.
- Arrive at school early enough to make sure that your classroom is set for the day's work.
- Leave your desk clear at the end of each day.
- Carry class sets of papers to be graded with you so that you can grade them when you have a spare moment.
- Store papers waiting to be graded in color-coded folders.

- Be efficient when you photocopy. Don't use the photocopier as a work area for preparing documents you need to copy. For example, when you need to cut and paste a document, move away from the copier so that others may use it.

- Photocopy items at least a week in advance. Plan for extra copies to make sure you will have enough.

- Avoid accumulating tall stack of papers waiting to be filed. File all papers on the same day you receive them.

- Keep a supply of passes, forms, pens, and other materials on hand.

- Use "To Do" lists to keep yourself on track.

- Maintain a folder for each student so that you can easily access all information relating to that student.

- Document each phone call, parent conference, or other contact right away.

- Delete your e-mail messages as soon as you have acted upon them.

- Learn to use overhead projectors, video players, computers, and other school equipment competently.

- Return all phone calls within twenty-four hours.

- Put attendance information, report card information, the grading scale, and other pertinent information in your grade book for easy reference.

- Take the time to do a task correctly the first time so you will not have to waste time repeating it.

- When you plan lessons, list the materials and tasks that you will need on your calendar and "To Do" list so that you will have what you need to teach a lesson successfully.

- Don't grade every paper. Occasionally assign work that is just for practice.

- When you have to grade a set of assignments or tests with more than one sheet, check all copies of one page before switching to the next page.

- Set up a rubric or a grading sheet when you make an assignment.

- Update your grades weekly.

- Lay out your clothes and pack your school materials at night.

- When you receive a notice that you are supposed to post, post it right away.

- Maintain a recycling box for reusable paper in your classroom.

- Keep all supplies that you use frequently near at hand.

- Keep a calendar, pen, and note pad near the phone or computer.

> *"Create back up of your electronic grades weekly. I save to diskette or zip drive and print out hard copies. I keep the hard copies at my desk and will often write myself notes in the margins."*
>
> —Stephanie Mahoney, 24 years experience

Figure 2.3

ASSESS YOUR STRENGTHS

What is the current state of your professional expertise? Below you will find a brief list of some of the positive attributes that teachers need to be successful. Use the following three-point scale to see how well you're doing.

> **1 = I need to develop this attribute.**
> **2 = I have some experience with this attribute, but need to work on developing it more fully.**
> **3 = I have mastered this attribute.**

___ 1. I believe that being a professional educator is a worthwhile endeavor.

___ 2. I have established several professional goals.

___ 3. I value the differences among my students.

___ 4. I want each of my students to have a positive attitude about school.

___ 5. I am interested in independently researching topics related to education.

___ 6. I have a positive outlook about my success as a teacher.

___ 7. I learn something new about teaching each day.

___ 8. I am developing strong time management skills.

___ 9. I am an organized person.

___ 10. I am in charge of my class.

___ 11. I see myself as part of a team of dedicated professionals.

___ 12. I can handle almost all of the problems that I face at work each day.

___ 13. I can successfully prevent many discipline problems.

___ 14. I know how to cope successfully with most discipline problems.

___ 15. I promote the belief that learning is enjoyable.

___ 16. I have a thorough knowledge of my content area.

___ 17. I prioritize my school responsibilities.

___ 18. I control my attitude about work.

___ 19. I have a supportive group of people to whom I can turn for help.

___ 20. I believe that courtesy is important for smooth professional relationships.

___ 21. I want my classes to be dynamic and enjoyable.

___ 22. I encourage students to be cooperative with each other and with me.

___ 23. I see problems as challenges rather than obstacles.

___ 24. I allow enough time to manage my career and personal responsibilities.

___ 25. I believe my students are worthwhile people who can learn and succeed.

- First identify all the areas in which you scored a 3 and be proud of yourself for your current strengths as a teacher.

- After you have examined your successes, turn your attention to the areas where you are not as strong, areas in which you only gave yourself a 1 or a 2. These scores indicate the attributes that you can work on as your career progresses.

Figure 2.4
WHAT GOOD WORK HABITS DO YOU ALREADY HAVE?

Here is a chance to assess the quality of your work habits. Below you will find ten of the many tasks that teachers tackle each week. First, write out your own way of tackling each task. When you have finished, check the key at the end to see if you have left out an essential step in managing each task well.

1. Write your lesson plans for next week.

_____

_____

_____

2. Check attendance.

_____

_____

_____

3. Create, administer, and grade a test.

_____

_____

_____

4. Hold a successful parent conference.

_____

_____

_____

5. Phone six parents about a class disruption.

_____

_____

_____

6. Administer a career interest survey to your students.

_____

_____

_____

7. Attend a faculty meeting.

_____

_____

_____

8. Show a film to all of your classes.

_____

_____

_____

9. Hold a successful after-school detention conference with a disruptive student.

_____

_____

_____

10. Photocopy two quizzes, a test, and a syllabus.

_____

_____

_____

Key

Although each of the tasks that you have been asked to plan can be accomplished in a variety of ways, there are some essential steps necessary for each one. Below you will find just three of the many essential steps that you should consider when planning how to accomplish your school tasks efficiently. Remember: Good work habits can make each workday a successful one.

1. Write your lesson plans for next week.
- Check the school calendar to see if there is an event scheduled that would affect your plans.
- Check the availability of the resources you want to use.
- Allow for individual student needs and learning styles

2. Check attendance.

- Use your seating chart to determine who is absent.
- Record the necessary information before the end of class.
- Report the information to the staff member responsible for attendance.

3. Create, administer, and grade a test.

- Determine what essential knowledge you will test.
- Create an answer key or rubric.
- Set aside enough time to grade the papers promptly.

4. Hold a successful parent conference.

- Write out a list of the points that you want to cover in the conference.
- Assemble the student's work or other information that you will need.
- Arrange the meeting area so that there will be no interruptions.

5. Phone six parents about a class disruption.

- Have students fill out an information sheet early in the term with phone numbers and other data that you need for contacting parents or guardians.
- Before you call, jot down the facts of the disruption and the role that each student had in it.
- Decide the purpose of the phone call. Are you arranging another conference, asking for help, or just informing them of the situation?

6. Administer a career interest survey to your students.

- Review the directions for administering the survey. Ask for clarification if necessary.
- Plan for the time that you are to administer the survey.
- Label a folder and organize the surveys so you can promptly submit them to the proper staff member.

7. Attend a faculty meeting.

- Make a note of the meeting time on your personal calendar.
- Be sure to bring a pen and paper to take notes.
- Even if you are tired, adopt a positive attitude.

8. Show a film to your classes.

- Preview the film for suitability.
- Teach your students the behavior that you expect from them during a film presentation.
- Create an assignment for your students to do before, during, and after the film.

9. Hold a successful after-school detention conference with a disruptive student.

- Notify parents or guardians of the date, time, and purpose.
- Set a goal for the conference. What is your desired outcome?
- Write notes of the points that you would like to cover.

10. Photocopy two quizzes, a test, and a syllabus.

- Allow a sufficient block of time for photocopying a few days in advance of the dates you will need the copies.
- Organize your papers so that you can complete this task quickly once you have access to the photocopier. For example, do any cutting, pasting, and removing of staples ahead of time.
- Prioritize your papers so that you copy the most important ones first.

Figure 2.5
HOW GOOD ARE YOUR WORK HABITS?

Look over this brief list of questions about work habits for professional educators to see how well you are doing and to identify areas in which you'd like to improve. Answer each question by writing *Yes*, *No*, or *Sometimes* in the space before each question.

1. _____ Do I keep my absences to a minimum and do I get to school on time?

2. _____ Do I listen to more experienced faculty members more than I speak?

3. _____ Do I observe school rules?

4. _____ Do I meet deadlines promptly and with accurate work?

5. _____ Do I dress in a professional manner?

6. _____ Do I respect others' work space and time?

7. _____ Do I share materials and information with other staff members?

8. _____ Do I treat everyone I meet with courtesy?

9. _____ Do I ask for help when I need it?

10. _____ Do I conduct professional business at school and my personal life at home?

Ask yourself the following questions about any work habit to which you answered *No* or *Sometimes*.

- Why is this habit not as good I want it to be?
- What is keeping me from developing it fully?
- What actions must I take to change this into a positive work habit?
- How can I begin to change?

School-Wide Policies and Procedures You Need to Know

There is a great deal of nuts-and-bolts information that all teachers are expected to learn quickly—as early as the first day of school in many cases. Most of this information is available to you in handouts, memos, your faculty manual, and through initial faculty meetings at the start of the school year.

Keep track of your mastery of school policies and guidelines. Examine each school-wide policy listed below as you learn about it. If there is a policy listed here that is not covered in your other sources of information, ask a colleague or a mentor about it.

- Acceptable student behavior
- Attendance procedures
- Audio-visual aids procedures
- Behavior rules for common areas
- Bell schedules
- Children with special needs
- Chronic attendance problems
- Class parties
- Class schedule
- Detention policies and procedures
- Discipline procedures
- Dismissal procedures
- Early dismissal procedures
- Emergency safety codes and procedures
- Faculty attendance procedures
- Faculty committees
- Faculty handbook information
- Family vacations
- Field trips
- Fire drills
- Food in the classroom policies
- Guest speakers
- Handling serious teacher injuries

- Handling student injury
- Homework policy
- How late you may stay in the building
- Janitorial concerns
- Lesson plan format and reviewing
- Library use policy
- Lost textbook policy
- Lunch procedures
- Parent conference procedures
- Professional organizations
- School organizations
- School staff members
- Supplies
- Support staff procedures
- Student absentee procedures
- Substitute teacher procedures
- Tardiness policies
- Teacher duties and responsibilities
- Technology use policies
- Textbook distribution procedures
- Tornado drills
- Withdrawal from school procedures

Professional Policies and Procedures You Need to Know

In addition to being part of a school community, you are, of course, also part of larger educational communities, including your local school district, your state board of education, and of course, the national State Department of Education.

The policies and procedures of these larger professional communities are very important and affect your school life every day. The policies that will have the most immediate bearing on your school life are those of your local and state districts. Here are some of the district and state policies and procedures that all teachers should learn quickly. Use the check boxes to track your mastery of each one. To keep abreast of education issues of national importance try this Internet site for the U. S. Department of Education home page: www.ed.gov/

- ☐ Areas covered by the school district
- ☐ District curriculum guidelines
- ☐ The district's mission statement
- ☐ Emergency school closing procedures
- ☐ Grading policies
- ☐ Inservice meeting schedules
- ☐ Insurance policies
- ☐ The location of the district offices
- ☐ The location of other schools in your district
- ☐ The local school calendar
- ☐ The members of the local and state school boards
- ☐ The names of key staff members
- ☐ Payroll department personnel and location
- ☐ Reporting periods and procedures for grades
- ☐ Retention and promotion policies
- ☐ Staff attendance policies
- ☐ Staff evaluation policy and procedures
- ☐ Standardized testing schedule
- ☐ Tenure policies
- ☐ When and where the local school board meets

> *"Take a computer class from your district or from a community college if you do not know how to use a computer. Learn to surf the Internet. There are many fantastic teacher sites that will help you with daily lesson plans. Join a listserve for your subject or grade level."*
>
> —Stephanie Mahoney, 24 years experience

Become an Efficient Teacher

No messy classroom. No missing papers. No forgotten phone calls . . . As a novice teacher you may be tempted to think that the art of teaching is intrinsically more worthwhile than the numerous details that lead to being an efficient teacher. Not so. Both are essential for a successful professional educator.

Being an efficient professional simply means that you can handle your numerous non-instructional responsibilities in the most efficient manner. It means you don't lose papers, you don't miss deadlines, and you are competent and in control.

With so many new responsibilities you need to develop a system to manage them. Although this may seem like common sense, in the daily press of starting a new career, many new teachers do not take the time to plan how to accomplish the many tasks they face every day. The result is wasted time, unfinished work, and stress. If you find yourself overwhelmed by the new responsibilities you have to juggle, remember that other teachers have figured out solutions to the problems that confound you and before long you will be able to handle those problems like a pro, too. In the meantime, turn to your colleagues for support. Ask them how to set up a work calendar, store materials, or get the most out of a planning period.

Tips on Eliminating Procrastination

Follow these suggestions to learn how to eliminate procrastination, organize your materials, and manage your time.

- **Identify the problem.** Quickly jot down the tasks that you tend to put off. Some of the ones common to many teachers include setting up parent conferences, phoning parents about problems, filing handouts, writing out lesson plans, keeping up with attendance, photocopying, grading papers, and dealing with problems they may have with a colleague.

- **Ask yourself why you procrastinate.** You don't procrastinate because you are lazy. Maybe you lack the supplies to get the job done well. Maybe you don't know how to do the task. Maybe you need a specific deadline. Maybe you need to find ways to make the chore more enjoyable and rewarding. Whatever the reason for your procrastination, address the problem. (Do it today.)

- **Realize that you can break the procrastination habit with just a bit of consistent effort.** It is not an innate life force, just a habit that you control.

- **Before you begin a job, break it into smaller parts.** You can then see how easy it is to accomplish the job one step at a time.

- **Just begin.** Remember the old proverb, "A journey of a thousand miles begins with one step." Often just the act of beginning to work on a project will break the inertia that has caused your delay (and guilt and stress).

- **If you have a due date for a project, give yourself an earlier due date.** Sometimes this simple trick will encourage you to work at a task until it is complete.

- **Prioritize your responsibilities.** A "To Do" list can help you with this and can help you ensure that you accomplish tasks in a timely fashion.

- **Get in the habit of doing your work NOW.** If you spend too much time thinking about something you have to do and why you aren't doing it, the task becomes increasingly onerous. Instead, if you have something to do, do it *now*.

- **Reward yourself once you have accomplished a burdensome task.** While the accomplishment may not seem important to others, you know how hard you worked to get it done. Take time to recognize your achievement with a long walk, a snack, or an hour of leisure.

Tips on Organizing Materials and Supplies

1. Take the time at the start of the term to actually clean your file cabinets, closets, and desk. Begin your organizing tasks with a sufficient amount of clean storage space and the materials you will need to keep your supplies in order.

2. To begin the process of getting organized, make sure you have the following supplies on hand.
   - Cleaning supplies
   - Scissors
   - Boxes of all sizes
   - Rubber bands
   - Clips
   - Labels
   - Tape
   - File folders
   - Markers
   - Cans and other recycled containers
   - Resealable plastic bags

3. If you have inherited a classroom crammed with old and out-of-date materials, check with your supervisors first to make sure that nothing is vital, then clean out the clutter.

4. Set up your own system for storing materials so that they are easily accessible.

5. Store similar materials together: paper in one area, crayons in another, oversized books in yet another area, and so forth.

6. Clearly label in large, dark letters any materials that you have stored in a box that you can't see into.

7. Set up a folder or binder for each day of the week; a color-coded one for each day is very efficient. In each folder keep the materials that you will need for that day: lesson plans, handouts, and any other resources.

18 Tips for Managing Your Time

1. Prioritize! You can't do everything all at once! Keep a list of what needs to be done and put the things you need to do in the order that you need to do them.

2. If a task will take less than three minutes, do it now.

3. Establish a routine for how you perform various tasks.

4. Use a calendar to plan. Record specifics such as what, where, when, and any other necessary information.

5. Don't just plan for a day, but for the week, for the month, for the semester, and for the year.

6. Use the spaces on your calendar to record tasks, appointments, and other information that you need to remember. Keep you calendar in an easily accessible spot. Make it a habit to refer to it often.

7. Prioritize your planning time so that you won't have to make three trips to the office when one would do.

8. Arrange a time during your planning period to handle the routine paperwork that you face each day.

9. Say "no" when someone asks you to give time that you can't spare.

10. Don't waste all of your planning time just visiting with other teachers. You should make it a point to use your time at school as efficiently as possible so that you can have more free time at home.

11. Remember to use your biological clock whenever you can. If you are not a morning person, then setting aside time in the morning to accomplish detailed work will not be as productive as if you were to stay after school and work more efficiently.

12. Follow the old business rule: Touch each sheet of paper only once.

13. When you are at your mailbox, deal efficiently with mail. Act immediately on items that need to be responded to in writing. Throw away or recycle junk mail. File catalogues for later.

14. Create a binder to file e-mails, memos, and other directives that you will need to refer to at various times in the school term.

15. Keep a file for each student. In this file, make sure each child has given you important information you need to contact his or her parents or guardians. Use this file to store all documents relating to that student.

16. Color code as many files and other papers as you can for quick reference.

17. Consider keeping a binder in which you store your lesson plans, handouts, tests, notes, assignments, and other material for each class. If you have this all together, it is much easier to see what you and your students have accomplished during the term and what you have yet to do.

18. Delegate as much as you can. Even very young students can accomplish many routine tasks such as putting up posters or keeping the supply cabinet clean.

8. Place a folder, tray, or box on your desk to contain items that you need to handle during your planning period.

9. Keep extra copies of all forms that you use frequently—hall passes, detention notices, tardy slips, lunch counts, and attendance sheets, for example—in a clearly marked folder at the front of a file drawer so that you can find them quickly.

10. Make organizing your materials and papers a daily task. Allowing your room to become messy with overflowing papers and incomplete projects robs you of your peace of mind and sends a negative message to your students.

Manage Those Stacks of Paper with Ease

One of the most difficult things about being a teacher is the heavy paperwork load. In fact, paperwork is one of the leading causes of stress for teachers. Like many other professionals, teachers have to document actions, keep track of progress, write out plans, handle correspondence, and keep accurate records. And like other professionals, teachers complain about the proliferation of stacks of paperwork. In the last few decades, the amount of paper that all professionals have to handle has multiplied. Even though computers will some day create a paperless society, that certainly hasn't happened yet. To the contrary, the hundreds of computer printouts teachers have to cope with are a new and large part of the paper problem.

Paperwork is one of the leading causes of stress for teachers. And no wonder. During the course of just one school year, the average teacher will have to handle more than *ten thousand* student papers. (For more tips on how to grade papers efficiently, see Section Eight.) When you consider the notices, memos, pamphlets, directives, reports, agendas, calendar items, printouts, purchase orders, letters, notes, forms, catalogues, flyers, newsletters, and publications that we receive each day, the amount of paperwork that confronts a teacher is staggering.

How can you manage this paperwork? First, you need a plan. Your plan should be a personal one designed to help you cope with the special needs your paperwork responsibilities. Here is a three-step one to use as a model.

Step One: Recognize that the only way to cope successfully with paperwork is to create an efficient and useful system to manage it.

Step Two: Set up your system. Use the flow charts below to help you set up your own plan for the successful flow of paper in your classroom.

Step Three: Be consistent in how you use your system. If a part of it doesn't work for you as well as you would like, then adjust it. And keep in mind that even the most fine-tuned system won't work unless you use it consistently.

The following flow charts are designed to help you set up your paperwork management systems.

Flowchart One: All papers

You should:

1. Act on them,
2. File them, or
3. Throw them away.

Flowchart Two: Student papers

1. Have students place them in designated collection area.
2. Place them in a color-coded folder to be graded.
3. Grade them.
4. Record grades in grade book.
5. Return them to students.

Flowchart Three: Correspondence. Divide your mail into categories as you retrieve each piece from your mailbox.

Category One: Urgent papers

1. Take immediate action.
2. Document your action if necessary.

Category Two: Papers that can be briefly delayed

1. Place in designated box, folder, or tray.
2. Handle during planning.
3. Document your action if necessary.

Category Three: Junk mail

Place in trash or recycle bin.

Category Four: Reference materials

1. Place in designated box, folder, or tray to await filing.
2. File catalogues, articles, and other resources in designated areas.

Category Five: Memos

1. Place tasks on your "To Do" list or calendar.
2. File memos in a binder or folder for directives.
3. Follow directives on memo.

Use Small Blocks of Time Wisely

One of the frustrating aspects of a teacher's life is that there is never enough time to accomplish everything. While the general shortage of extra time seems to be a problem, large blocks of time are in especially short supply. A teacher's days are filled with interruptions and frequent schedule changes.

You can cope successfully with this by learning to be an expert at accomplishing many items in small moments. This is possible with determination, preparation, and practice. Those minutes add up.

Still not convinced? Here are just some of the things that a focused teacher can accomplish in just a few minutes.

In fifteen minutes you can:
- Grade the objective portion of a set of test papers.
- Create a quiz.
- Create a review sheet.
- Answer e-mail.
- Find a Web site with information for the next day's lesson.
- Create anticipatory sets for the entire week.
- Photocopy a worksheet.

In ten minutes you can:
- Call a parent.
- Write a lesson plan.
- Grade some essay questions.
- Average grades.
- Skim tomorrow's lesson.
- Check homework papers.
- Make a transparency.

In five minutes you can:
- Create a dynamic closing exercise.
- Collect homework.
- List key words on the board.
- Write a positive note and send it home.

- Use the hole punch on a set of papers.
- Write a positive comment on at least five papers.
- Review key points in a lesson.

In three minutes you can:
- Revise your "To Do" list.
- Record grades.
- Drill your students with flashcards.
- Remind a class of the homework assignment.
- Put stickers on a set of papers.
- Praise a class for good behavior.
- Have students write an evaluation of the day's lesson.

In one minute you can:
- Straighten your desk.
- File a set of papers.
- Erase the board.
- Display a cartoon about the day's lesson.
- Have students tidy the room.
- Select the student of the day or week.
- Write an inspirational message on the board.

Figure 2.6
CHECKLIST: FIND THE TIME

Although chronic time shortage is a problem for most educators, you can add valuable minutes to your day with just a bit of organization and effort. Here is a checklist of timesaving tips that will help make your workday a more productive one. Check off those that you have already mastered, and work on the others.

You save time when you:

- ☐ Never lose your keys because you keep them in the same location each day.
- ☐ Always file student papers in large folders grouped by class.
- ☐ Keep your desk neat and organized.
- ☐ Create assignments for student viewing when you preview films.
- ☐ Have an up-to-date set of emergency plans ready—just in case.
- ☐ Maintain a file of alternative lessons for students who finish early or need enrichment or remediation.
- ☐ Keep a folder with paper and pen nearby to make notes when you make phone calls.
- ☐ Use a daily "To Do" list you keep on your desk in a bright, easy-to-see folder.
- ☐ Keep your grade book in the same location.
- ☐ Keep your grade book up-to-date rather than having to average hundreds of grades the night before grade reports go home.
- ☐ Teach class routines for restroom breaks, tardiness, handing in papers, sharpening pencils, and trash disposal.
- ☐ Set up audio-visual equipment early just in case there are problems with the equipment.
- ☐ Give clear directions to your students so that you don't have to repeat them.
- ☐ Keep the supplies that you need on hand.
- ☐ Maintain order in your classroom so that you don't have to spend time dealing with behavior problems.
- ☐ Schedule a specific time to work at home.
- ☐ Learn how to use school equipment efficiently.
- ☐ Use a checklist or rubric to grade papers quickly.
- ☐ Set aside the last two minutes of class for students to tidy their work area and pack their materials.
- ☐ Don't arrive too early or too late to meetings or duty assignments.
- ☐ Keep on hand receipt books and the other materials you need to collect money.

Arrive a Little Early, Leave a Little Late

One of the biggest mistakes that many new teachers make is to arrive at school just in time to sprint to class, drop a brief case, and begin teaching. While students chat idly, their stressed-out teacher rushes to take attendance, turn on computers, find the grade book, and put the assignment on the board.

In the afternoon, the same inefficient work habits can hamper those teachers who race from the building the minute that the last bus pulls away from the curb. The stress from arriving late and leaving early builds until many teachers suffer significant distress. There are better ways to begin or end your school day.

While you don't have to spend hours of extra time at school, experienced teachers will be the first to tell you that it is important to get the day off to a good start and to leave your classroom in good shape for the next day's classes. If you are tempted to race in late or leave early every day, there is a better way to handle your school responsibilities.

Plan your arrival time so that you can be in your classroom at least fifteen minutes early. Use this time while your students are not yet in the room to organize yourself for the day. If you also plan to stay after school for just a few extra minutes every day, you will also save yourself distress. You can finish any extra work that you don't want to complete at home, leave the room ready for the next day, and complete any of those pressing tasks that are always waiting.

You can also save yourself stress if you plan to stay after school on the same day each week so that you can provide extra help for students who need it, help students make up missing work or even just work on projects, or hold detention conferences.

Make Every Minute Count

Remember, you don't have to spend hours of extra time if you use just a few extra minutes before and after school to keep yourself organized and stress-free. Teaching is a career that requires more than eight hours a workday on most days. Using the time that you have wisely will earn you increased student success and decreased stress.

Here are just some of the activities that you can do in just a few minutes either before or after school.

- Grade papers
- Schedule a parent conference
- Check you calendar
- Write receipts
- Return phone calls
- Record grades
- Preview a video
- Check e-mail and voice mail
- Write lesson plans
- Straighten file cabinets
- Plan a field trip
- Write a warm-up or the assignment on the board
- Arrange papers and materials
- Find resources for lesson plans
- Write or respond to a reminder notice
- Organize your desk
- E-mail colleagues
- Attend to urgent business in your mailbox
- Photocopy
- Write a quiz

Your Teacher Binder

Many teachers have found that staying organized is easier if they organize all of their daily tasks in a combination of calendar, planner, and address book similar to the daily planners that other professionals use. Although you could purchase and use a planning system designed for executives, you can organize your responsibilities in a simple binder.

There are many different organizational systems on the market. Make sure you select the tools and organizing ideas that suit the demands of your life. Here are the directions to help you set up your teacher binder so that all of the important information that you need is right at your fingertips during the day.

Materials You Will Need:

A sturdy three-ring binder with pockets	Writing pads
Divider pages	Self-adhesive notes
Paper	Pens and pencils
	Calendar

The Outside:

Make sure that the binder you purchase for the task of keeping you organized all year long is sturdy enough and big enough (at least two inches) to hold all of your important papers. Try to select one that is easy to carry and immediately recognizable.

On the outside, use a permanent marker to label it with your name, school, and room number so that it can be delivered to you if you misplace it. If you select a binder with a clear pocket on top in which you can slip a sheet of paper with identifying information, make sure the paper that you use is very bright so that you can easily find your binder.

The Inside:

Pockets:

- Use the pockets to store note pads, pens and pencils, adhesive notes. You could even store computer disks here if you need to.

Divider pages:

- Insert divider pages to keep your calendar, "To Do" lists, professional goals, grade book, and address lists separated from each other so that they are easy to use.

Calendar:

- Find a calendar that has spaces large enough to record information comfortably. School districts often offer these at the start of the new school year, or you can purchase or even make one yourself.
- Your school district will issue a calendar of the year's holidays, PTA meetings, sports events, and other important dates at the start of the term. Use your calendar to record these unchanging items in ink.
- When you record information on your calendar, write legibly and be very specific. For example, don't just scrawl "meeting." Instead, jot down what the meeting will be about as well as when and where the meeting will be.

- Consider using pencil for items that may be changed or canceled. Use ink for items that you know will be permanent.

- Use colored ink for items that you want to highlight. For example, you could use red ink for reports that are due in the office, green for phone calls, and purple for conferences.

- Use adhesive notes to help you recall vital information. Use small ones that you can slip over a calendar block to help you stay on track.

- Make it a habit to check your calendar several times each day. At a minimum, you should check it when your day begins, at the start of your planning period, and right before you leave for the day.

- Using a calendar to plan your professional life is an important skill to model for your students. Talk with them about the importance of planning and about how you plan your work as you teach them to take the same organized approaches to their school work.

Address Lists:

The first address list you need is one that includes the addresses, e-mail information, and phone numbers of the teachers and administrators that you need to contact when you will be absent or when you have questions about school. Be sure to include your mentor in this list.

The second address list should include the phone numbers, e-mail information, and addresses of your students' parents or guardians so that you can quickly contact them from school or from your own home. You can create a spreadsheet with this information or you can just photocopy the student information sheets you find in Section Three.

Grade Book or Grade Printouts:

You may want to slip your grade book or a printout of your students' grades into your binder so that you have easy access while you speak with parents or guardians.

Professional Goals:

Your professional binder is a perfect place to store a list of professional goals because you will be able to check your progress as you work. (To find out more on setting your personal goals, see Section One.) Staying focused on your goals will be easier if you have easy access to your list.

"To Do" List:

You will find a sample "To Do" list on page 49. Adapt it for your own use or photocopy the one provided here, and use one for each school day. Use it to plan your day and to keep a record of what you did each day, too. This will be invaluable if you forget to document a parent conference and need to refer to the date later in the year. You will be able to quickly find the information you need by reviewing your "To Do" lists.

© 2002 by John Wiley & Sons, Inc.

Figure 2.7
A TEACHER'S "TO DO" LIST

Date _____

Phone Calls Concerning Students

Student   Parent Number   Reason   Time

_____

_____

_____

_____

_____

Other Phone Calls

_____

_____

Parent Conferences   **Other Meetings**

Student   Outcome   What   When   Where

_____

_____

_____

_____

After-School/Duty Responsibilities

_____

Items to Duplicate

_____

Lesson Plans/Projects to Complete

_____

Notes/Reminders/Errands

_____

_____

_____

_____

_____

Web Sites to Help You Stay Organized

In addition to using a teacher's binder to keep yourself organized, there are numerous Web sites you can turn to for ideas to help you become a more organized person. Check out some of the following:

- www.webnow.com/theorganizingspecialists
- www.clutterhelp.com
- www.dailydrill.com
- www.organizetips.com
- www.e2do.com
- www.digitaldaytimer.com
- www.learn2.com
- www.123sortit.com
- www.putsimply.com
- www.daytimer.com

Find Your Mentors at Work

In recent years, partly in response to the high dropout rate of new teachers, many school districts have established formal mentorship programs. In these programs, experienced teachers serve as trusted advisors to novice teachers. When the relationship works well, new teachers gain skills and confidence from the wisdom of the mentor. When teachers adjust quickly to their new profession, everyone benefits: novice teachers, mentors, and, most of all, students.

Many of these formal programs are very successful for a variety of reasons; however, some schools do not have formal mentoring programs and still others have programs that are just not as successful as they could be. If your district does not offer a formal mentorship program, don't be discouraged. Every school has successful, approachable teachers who can function as mentors, and you can find one to serve as yours.

To find a mentor, begin by looking for competent teachers who have high standards for themselves and who are comfortable about being observed by other teachers. An effective mentor is one who will be patient with your efforts to learn, is eager to share ideas with you, and who is good-humored, tactful, and knowledgeable. In short, look for a mentor who is enthusiastic with teaching, about students, and about helping you learn to be a better teacher.

WHAT TO ASK OF YOUR MENTOR

What should you ask of a mentor? While there will obviously be a wide variety in the needs that novice teachers have, even within the same school, there are some common concerns that all teachers share. These usually can be divided into two levels of questions that you will discuss with your mentor.

The first is the practical level: the daily concerns that are so difficult to manage at first. Here are just a few of the *day-to-day concerns* that you could ask a mentor about.

- Planning procedures
- Goals for the semester or year
- Curriculum issues
- Time management
- Where to find materials
- How to work with parents
- Where equipment is stored
- How to group students successfully
- How to handle standardized tests
- Planning for emergencies
- What's expected of teachers in your school

"College will never, ever prepare you for real teaching. Find a mentor, someone your respect, and stick to that person like glue. No question is too silly for a first-year person to ask."

—Paige Adcock, 4 years experience

The second level of help you should ask from a mentor focuses on more complex issues. After you have settled into the school term and mastered the general information that you need to manage a class, you will be able to expand the focus of your concern to the art of teaching. You will no longer need help with the "how-to" questions, but will shift your concern to larger issues such as classroom management, teaching styles, or the best ways to connect meaningfully with your students.

Some of the *complex issues* that your mentor can discuss with you include:

- Solving common problems
- Helping students with special needs
- Increasing student motivation
- Handling diverse classrooms
- Managing group discussions
- Evaluating students fairly
- Anticipating student reactions
- Incorporating a variety of teaching strategies
- Collaborating effectively
- Enhancing student self-esteem
- Communicating well with others

One of the biggest problems that people involved in a mentorship program have is the lack of time to work together. You and your mentor should plan to meet on a regular basis if you are going to find the kind of success you need as quickly as you need it.

While it is not always easy to find the time to work together, here are a few suggestions for coping successfully with this problem.

- Use e-mail.
- Call each other in the evening.

- Set aside time each week by writing it on your calendar.
- Write notes to each other.
- Eat lunch together.
- Visit a bookstore or teachers' supply store together.
- Arrange to share a meal together outside of school.
- Share rides.
- Arrange to observe your mentor's class during your planning period.
- Collaborate on a project.

School, Technology, and You

On days when you finally unfreeze the computer only to find a notice that the server is down again, technology in the classroom doesn't seem like such a good idea. There are and always will be many problems associated with technology in schools. Three long-term problems are:

1. There will never be enough functioning equipment for every student's needs to be adequately met.

2. It will always be a challenge for teachers to find the best ways to help students use the technological resources available to them.

3. Teachers themselves will have to become more proficient at a variety of technological tasks.

One of the biggest advantages that you have as a novice teacher is that your recent training probably exposed you to more technology than many of the experienced teachers in your school have had. Many teachers are still hesitant to incorporate technology into lessons just because they don't really understand how to manage the combination of resources and students.

Some school-related technology is simple to use and very effective. Many schools now use voice mail, e-mail, homework hotlines, digital cameras, computer labs, Internet services, and the old standbys of video and audio equipment. We even have access to electronic grading systems that outdate the calculators that used to be state-of-the-art technology in many classrooms.

As a new teacher, you should be comfortable with the technology that you do have. Start small and gradually add to your repertoire. Here are some of the basics that you will need to know how to use:

- Calculator
- Internet access
- Word processor
- Computer presentation device
- Computer
- Overhead projector

- Grade book program
- Audio equipment
- Video equipment
- Printer
- Digital camera
- Television monitor

There are many ways to use technology in your classroom; however, when you begin to combine students and technology, there are some special considerations that you should think about. The following tips can help you overcome many obstacles.

▶ Make sure you have a clear purpose for using technology, then communicate this purpose to your students.

▶ Make sure the equipment is working and that you know what to do if it isn't. It never hurts to have a back-up plan in case of equipment failure.

▶ Try the activity yourself to see just how difficult it will be for students.

▶ Monitor students carefully. For example, if you have students researching a topic on the Internet, make sure that everyone is on task and no one is checking e-mail or visiting off-limit sites.

▶ Make sure that you follow your school's guidelines for disk use. You do not want to be responsible for infecting your school's computers with a virus that a student brought from home.

▶ Make sure that the lesson that you teach has an end product so that you can more easily keep students on task. If they have to hand you a report or even a disk, students are more likely to stay focused.

▶ Set clear rules, procedures, and expectations for your students when you have them working with computers or other equipment. Make sure that students know how they are supposed to behave.

▶ If students will be printing documents, make sure that the printer is working and that you have enough paper and time for everyone to finish printing.

While there are many problems with technology in the classroom, there are also many solutions. If you are resourceful, determined, and observant, you can certainly overcome technology problems. For example, as mentioned earlier, one of the most common problems is a shortage of equipment for students to use. There are many possible solutions to this problem. Try these.

▶ Put computers on carts and move them from class to class.

▶ Have students work in teams.

▶ Stagger deadlines.

▶ Have students rotate among tasks.

▶ Allow more time to complete a task.

▶ Scale down assignments that necessitate computer use.

▶ Involve the PTA, parents, and the community to purchase more equipment.

▶ Allow students to work on home computers.

▶ Have students work before or after school.

▶ Share with other teachers.

▶ Have students sign up for computer time.

30 Ideas for Using Technology in Class

Below you will find some project ideas to incorporate computers and other technology into your lessons. Use these or adapt them to suit the needs of your students.

1. Make a slide show presentation.
2. Research a project.
3. Find a Web site of the week or of the day.
4. E-mail pen pals.
5. Drill and review presentations.
6. Word process documents.
7. Create graphs.
8. Create spreadsheets.
9. Write letters.
10. Produce a class newsletter.
11. Create multiple versions of a test.
12. Draw vocabulary definitions.
13. Reproduce digital photos.
14. Make a video.
15. Create a class CD.
16. Play music.
17. Maintain your grade book.
18. Give students tests.
19. Chat with a discussion group.
20. Research vocabulary words.
21. Extend your blackboard space.
22. Scan photos to enhance textbook.
23. Create graphic organizers.
24. Open class with interesting trivia.
25. Simulate a situation.
26. Fill in the blank stories
27. Check the weather.
28. Check up-to-the-minute news.
29. Assess online encyclopedias.
30. Create a Web page.

USING THE INTERNET AS A TEACHING RESOURCE

As anyone who has ever "surfed the net" for a report knows, the Internet is a fascinating and useful tool for finding information. Millions of dollars are poured into school-oriented Web sites each year.

When you begin to use the Internet to find educational resources, don't do it by yourself. Find a colleague who is already experienced at using the Internet for educational research and who can share ideas.

Here are other useful strategies for learning to use the Internet to find resource materials.

▶ Bookmark or keep a list of sites that appeal to you. It is almost impossible to retrace your path after a few days or weeks have gone by and you need to revisit an appealing site.

▶ Take a class on using the Internet. Your school district may offer one or you may be able to enroll through a local community college or university.

▶ Take advantage of the free tutorials offered online. Some of the sites mentioned below will guide you to these.

▶ Try instructional research first at a large clearing house or resource center such as AskEric (askeric@ericir.syr.edu).

10 Tips for School E-mail

1. Use your school's e-mail only for school business. Your rule of thumb for downloading material should be to never download materials that you would not be comfortable having on top of your desk for all to see.

2. Log on to check your e-mail outside of class time. Would you stop class to phone a friend? During class you should be teaching.

3. Be very careful to respect the confidentiality of your students. Never mention a student's last name in e-mail communications.

4. Keep in mind that just because you can delete messages with the click of a few keys, it doesn't mean they're truly erased. The messages are permanently stored on the server and can be used against you in court. Be careful about what you write.

5. Just because you can answer instantly, you should not answer impulsively. A common mistake is to react to a message without completely thinking it through. Think carefully before you send any message.

6. Although e-mail has a more informal tone than a personal letter, don't take that to mean you can be sloppy or use unprofessional language. Use spell check and carefully proofread your e-mail correspondence. Don't use chat room communication styles for school business. Do not use emoticons, all capital letters, or foul language.

7. Keep all replies businesslike and to the point, but not terse. Use a salutation, a closing, and sign your name.

8. Keep messages to parents, especially working parents, brief and informative. Request a phone call to discuss problems rather than going into detail by e-mail.

9. It is legal for a network administrator to read your e-mail. Keep this in mind when you are tempted to use school equipment for personal business.

10. Don't violate copyright laws. If you download protected material for your own use, then you are within the limits of the law. If you make copies for work, then you are violating copyright laws. For more information on copyright laws, try: www.pitt.edu/~skvarka/education/copyright/.

Below is a list of just few of the thousands of Internet sites devoted to education. As anyone who has ever surfed the net for hours know, one site will lead to a related site and another and another, so you need to be careful to use the time that you spend online wisely.

When you're just getting started, the following Web sites are a good place to gain a quick overview of some of the information available to you.

Emergency lesson plans: www.jjohnnypress.com

Worksheets: www.rhlschool.com

Science lesson plans: ousd.k12.ca.us/~codypren/lessons.html

Core knowledge lesson plans:
www.coreknowledge.org/CKproto2/resrcs/index.htm

All subject lesson plans: www.nytimes.com/learning/teachers/lessons
Professional development: www.ascd.org/frametutorials.html
Professional development: school.aol.blackboard.com
Using Power Point in the classroom: www.actden.com/pp
Using Power Point in the classroom: www.teach-nology.com
Using the Internet at school: www.nsglobalonline.com
Using the Internet at school: www.riverdeep.net
Using the Internet at school: www.virtualblackboard.com
Using the Internet at school: www.mff.org/edtech
Using the Internet at school: connectedteacher.classroom.com
Using the Internet at school: www.getnetwise.org

Journal Entries to Help You Develop Your Professional Expertise

▶ Describe your school organizational skills. What do you need to change? How can you make this change?

▶ How are you a trustworthy faculty member? Which colleagues do you find trustworthy?

▶ Explain this statement: "You must teach in order to learn."

▶ What education theories are you eager to try? How are you going to do this?

▶ What is the real business of a teacher?

▶ What are the most important professional qualities that teachers can develop? How can you develop them?

▶ What policies and procedures do you feel confident about? Which ones do you still need to master?

Begin the School Year with Confidence

They filtered in a few at a time, nervously glancing at her face and then looking quickly away. She showed each one where to sit and stood by the door as she waited for the bell to ring. Her palms were sweaty. "This is ridiculous," she told herself. "They are just little kids. How bad can this be?"

Pretty bad, she figured. Her new shoes already hurt. She had left her lunch at home. At least she hadn't forgotten the class rosters. They were here—somewhere.

Yesterday some older teachers had gone over her rosters and told her terrible stories about her new students. She hoped they had been joking.

She had expected to be excited and a little nervous, but not completely afraid. Could teachers suffer from stage fright?

She moved to the front of the room and tried to speak. She cleared her throat. All eyes were now glued to her face. No sound would come out. Not even a squeak.

She tried again. Still nothing. She thought that she was afraid before. She was terrified now.

This was awful.

"Miss? Miss? Are you okay? You look kinda funny. Zeke, go get the teacher some water."

She sat down. Put her head between her knees. Right there in front of her class.

They were up and out of their seats now, crowding around her. Patting her back, fanning her face, handing her a glass of water. Anxiously waiting to see if she was going to be okay.

And suddenly, she knew she would be. These were not just little kids. They were her little kids.

*T*he first few days and weeks of school are exciting and stressful . . . and crucial. The rest of the year hinges on how well a teacher manages the start of the year. The hardest part of starting your first new school term is that you are expected to do the very same work as veterans with years of experience at opening the school year. You are expected to do it just as well as the veterans even though you don't have the resources or the experience.

It is no wonder that many first-year teachers sleep poorly at the start of a new term. They suffer from nightmares of endless rows of desks to be moved and "To Do" lists that ceaselessly grow longer. They spend restless nights worrying if they will ever be ready for school to begin; if their students will like them and what they'll do if they don't.

In spite of these stressful days and nights, somehow teachers always manage to get it done. Take heart! For years and years now, dedicated teachers have gotten their students off to a good start. You can, too.

> *"Until students get to know you, they don't care what you know, they want to know that you care."*
>
> —Edward Gardner, 36 years experience

Questions You Need to Answer Before the Term Begins

There are many questions to which you will have to find answers before the term begins. After all, your students will expect you to have the answers to every question they have just as soon as they walk through the door. Unfortunately, so will everyone else.

The trickle-down effect of not knowing something at school can be formidable. For example, if you do not know how to report attendance during the first week of school, the attendance clerk will have to stop work, contact you, interrupt class to obtain the information, correct any previous report, and contact the clerk at the district office to explain why the report is not on time. Can you imagine the confusion if several teachers didn't report attendance correctly? What if you didn't know how to report a lunch count? Or set up your grade book? Or manage the fire drill that you can expect during the first week of school?

Ask questions! If you are shy and don't want to bother lots of people with questions that you are afraid may be "dumb," think again. Experienced teachers know that the few minutes they will spend answering your questions will save them hours of having to help you straighten out problems later.

- Along with asking experienced teachers, try getting answers from your faculty manual. Take notes.
- Pay attention in meetings. Take more notes.
- Ask your grade level chairperson or department head.
- Make a list of questions and ask your mentor.

Figure 3.1

WHAT DO YOU ALREADY KNOW ABOUT BEGINNING A SCHOOL TERM?

✔ Put a + in the blank beside each item that you have already completed to begin a new term.

✔ Put a – in the blank beside each item that you need to complete to begin a new term.

___ You have memorized your daily schedule. You know when each class begins and ends and what each bell means. You know what your duty assignment is.

___ You have already written your plans for the next few weeks. You have also scheduled the resources you will need.

___ Your handouts for the next few weeks are ready.

___ You have checked your calendar against the district one. You have scheduled your lessons around important holidays and other events.

___ Your substitute folder is complete, even down to class rosters and seating charts.

___ You have filed away copies of the forms you will need: attendance, lunch counts, discipline, etc.

___ You have purchased, collected, or picked up the supplies you will need.

___ You have familiarized yourself with your faculty handbook and any other information from workshops and meetings.

___ You know what to do in an emergency, in a fire drill, and during a lockdown drill.

___ You can recognize the key people in your building and in the district. You understand what their jobs are and how each one affects you and your class.

___ You know how to do routine tasks such as entering grades in your grade book, reporting attendance, and scheduling resources.

___ Your classroom is decorated, all desks are in place, your own desk is organized.

___ You have enough copies of the textbook for everyone. You also have the teacher's editions and resource materials that you will need.

___ You know where to turn for help.

___ Your personal life is organized so that you can manage your hectic schedule over the next few weeks as you adjust to a new term.

How did you do? If you have more plusses than minuses, then you are well on your way to starting the new school year right. Of course, your goal should be to have as few minuses as possible.

"Seating charts are a must!"

—Sandra Councill, 17 years experience

The following are some key areas that you will need to ask questions about. As soon as you have learned the information, you can check it off the list.

District Information

- ☐ Contracts
- ☐ Health benefits
- ☐ Investment information
- ☐ Certification information
- ☐ Pay periods
- ☐ Who's who at the district level
- ☐ The school calendar
- ☐ Leave policy
- ☐ Curriculum guidelines

School Information—Non-instructional Issues

- ☐ Who's who at the school level
- ☐ How to join PTA
- ☐ How to pay hospitality/friendship dues
- ☐ How to collect money
- ☐ What to do with a child who becomes ill
- ☐ What to do when there is an accident in your class
- ☐ How to contact an administrator for help
- ☐ How to schedule movies, the computer lab, other resources
- ☐ What to do in case of violence
- ☐ What to do in a fire drill
- ☐ What to do in a tornado or other disaster drill
- ☐ Whom you should contact when you will need a substitute
- ☐ What extra duty assignments you will have
- ☐ What office equipment can you use and how to use it
- ☐ Where you can find equipment for your classroom
- ☐ Where various areas of your school are located
- ☐ When the building will be open for teachers
- ☐ What committees you will be on
- ☐ How to report attendance

School Information–Instructional Issues

- ☐ How to obtain your teachers' manuals
- ☐ How to obtain textbooks

© 2002 by John Wiley & Sons, Inc.

- ☐ How to gain access to student folders
- ☐ Which of your students have special needs
- ☐ What the class schedules and bell schedules are
- ☐ How to report grades
- ☐ When special school events are going to be
- ☐ How to find school-level curriculum materials
- ☐ If there is a school-level homework policy

Figure 3.2

A "To Do" List to Ensure a Smooth Start

Because there are so many tasks that all teachers have to complete in the few weeks and days before the beginning of a term, it is very easy to be overwhelmed.

If you are hired some months before the start of a new term, then you obviously will have an advantage over teachers who are not as lucky. If you have been offered your position just a few weeks or even days before school begins, you will have much to do to catch up. Either way, the list below will help you prioritize your responsibilities and avoid being overwhelmed with too much to do in too little time.

A month before the term begins:

- ☐ Hit the back–to-school sales for supplies.
- ☐ Make sure you have a wardrobe that will reflect your professional status.
- ☐ Order any supplies your district allows.
- ☐ Gather the other supplies that you may need.
- ☐ Pick up your curriculum guides.
- ☐ Pick up the school calendar for your school district.
- ☐ Pick up teachers' editions and supplementary materials.
- ☐ Begin reading and studying the course materials.
- ☐ Create your professional goals.

Three weeks before the term begins:

- ☐ Schedule events from the school calendar on your own planner.
- ☐ Join at least one professional organization.
- ☐ Create a course overview for the year.
- ☐ Create semester plans.
- ☐ Decide on the resources you will need for each unit of study.

Two weeks before the term begins:

- ☐ Create a syllabus or planner for your students.
- ☐ Make sure the equipment in your room works well.

- [ ] Brainstorm a list of classroom management solutions.
- [ ] Create your class rules and procedures.
- [ ] Put together materials in case you need a substitute.
- [ ] Put your classroom in order.
- [ ] Set up your desk and files.

The last week before the term begins:

- [ ] Obtain the school forms that you will need.
- [ ] Ask any last minute questions.
- [ ] Master the material in your faculty manual.
- [ ] Be prepared for emergency drills.
- [ ] Create a daily routine for attendance.
- [ ] Write a letter to parents or guardians introducing yourself.
- [ ] Photocopy anything your students will need as early as possible.
- [ ] Write out your first three weeks of daily plans.
- [ ] Devise a workable system for textbook distribution.
- [ ] Study your class rosters so you can be familiar with names.
- [ ] Create an alphabetical seating chart.

The day before school starts:

- [ ] Finish any last minute tasks.
- [ ] Make a final curriculum and room check.
- [ ] Exercise, eat well, get enough rest.

Establish Routines and Procedures

All students have some characteristics in common. One is the need for structured time. From energetic kindergartners to sophisticated seniors, students need routines in their school days to keep them on track. While the particulars of these routines will vary from teacher to teacher and from grade level to grade level, there are certain "business operations" that teachers and students must adhere to for harmonious classrooms.

The following are classroom routines and procedures that you should decide how to handle before school begins.

- Beginning class
- Ending class
- Tardies/absences/make-up work
- Handing in work
- Keeping the work area clean
- Formats for written work
- Asking questions
- Emergencies and drills
- Going to lockers/restroom/nurse/office
- Materials needed for class each day
- Homework
- Class interruptions
- Class discussions
- Coming to attention
- Testing procedures

Organize Your School Life

You can always tell the well-organized teachers in a school; they are the ones who waltz serenely through each school day with unhurried ease. They never lose student papers or misplace their grade books. They never have to ask their students, "When did I tell you that report was due?" Meanwhile, disorganized teachers alternate reading articles on stress management with classified ads for employment in foreign countries.

Organized teachers enjoy school. Disorganized teachers don't.

You can become an organized teacher with just a bit of time and effort. When you organize your school life, you should think in terms of organizing your time and your environment. Because every teacher's day is unique, there is no set plan that can suit all teachers. Instead, you will have to tailor the time you have available to meet the demands of your day.

ORGANIZING YOUR TIME

There are many time factors that you can control with certainty at school. These are the factors that you should organize first. Here's how.

Begin with a calendar with large blocks for the days of the week. Block off the time that you must be in direct contact with your students. Because you must put your students first, you can't allot any of this time to other chores with any hope of consistent success. Next, block off time that you know will be taken by standing appointments such as faculty and committee meetings, hall duty, etc.

Now that you have determined the time that you have to successfully complete your other tasks, you should figure out how much time each one will take. Write down each task on your calendar as you decide just how long it will take and when you intend to accomplish it.

Now, make the commitment to yourself that you will stick to your calendar and you will reap the benefits of effective time management.

ORGANIZING YOUR ENVIRONMENT

You will find that it is easier and probably less time-consuming to organize your physical environment than it is to organize your time. Try these quick tips to organize your work space for maximum efficiency.

Your Desk

1. You will need to actually clean your desk before you put your personal belongings in it. This is not part of the custodians' job.

2. Keep the top of your desk as free of clutter as you can. Make sure that what is on your desk top reflects your personality, of course, but also keep it businesslike. Some of the things you should have on top of your desk include the following.

   - Trays for folders and papers
   - A calendar
   - Pens/pencils
   - Note pads
   - Stapler (labeled "Teacher Use")
   - Paper clips
   - Tape dispensers

Plan Your Time

Here is a quick list of some of the routines that you should be able to predict and organize successfully. In the blank beside each one, estimate how long it should take you daily or weekly.

_____	Checking e-mail	_____	Photocopying
_____	Phoning parents	_____	Creating lesson plans
_____	Holding after-school conferences	_____	Staying late after school
_____	Handling voice mail	_____	Arriving early to school
_____	Grading papers	_____	Making trips to the office
_____	Recording grades	_____	Checking your mailbox
_____	Averaging grades	_____	Researching material
_____	Filing papers	_____	Other: _____

3. If your desk is a space allotted for your use and for you to keep your own supplies, you should discourage students from taking items from it. Set up a student work center at a spot near the door for students to use. In this area, place a stapler (labeled "Student Use"), a hole puncher, a trash can, a recycled paper bin, and a tray to collect student papers and other work.

4. Do not place scissors, knives, liquid paper, thumb tacks, markers, glue, or any sharp object on the desk top. If something could harm a student or be used as a weapon, it should be stored inside your desk.

Student Materials

1. You will need two areas for this. The first will be for storing materials that are not currently in use; the second will be for materials that your students will use during class. You will save time if these two areas are near each other and if you teach your students how you want items returned at the end of class.

2. Keep similar items together. For example, all of the glue sticks should be stored together, all of the construction paper should be in another spot, and so on.

3. Label the bins or boxes that you use for storage with large, dark letters.

The Rest of the Room

1. You will need a calendar for your students to refer to. Post it in a conspicuous place.

2. You will need a working clock that both you and your students can see. If you can, you should purchase an inexpensive battery operated clock for the back of the room, so that you will be able to maintain a constant check on the time while you are speaking to your students from the front of the room.

3. You will need a safe place to store your personal belongings. You should be able to lock away your purse. (Experienced teachers seldom have cash or credit cards at school.)

4. Detailed information for setting up a file cabinet follows later in this section.

Create a User-Friendly Classroom

Setting up a classroom takes time and physical effort. You will need plenty of both if you want to arrange things just the way you want them to be. If you have friends or family members who can help you shove desks and hang posters, ask for their help. You'll save hours of time that you could use to write lesson plans or complete some of the stacks of other paperwork that first-year teachers need to finish before the start of school.

When you arrange your room, you should try to minimize any negative conditions that your students will have to overcome. If your room is seriously overcrowded, for example, you will need to arrange desks in such a way that students don't bump into each other. Further, you should strive to create an an appealing environment where your students feel welcomed and able to succeed.

When you consider how you want to arrange your room, there are three important considerations: your personal space, traffic flow, and the physical arrangement of desks.

YOUR PERSONAL SPACE

1. One mistake that many teachers make is to put their desks in the front of the classroom in front of the board. This is not the best place; the back of the room is. If your desk is in the back of the room, you can monitor your students' activity easily from there. You can have personal conferences with students without the entire class as an audience and you will not block the view of the board.

2. If possible, your file cabinet and other personal storage areas should be set up near your desk so that you can quickly find what you need. If you have a computer that your students do not use, it should be in this area, also.

THE TRAFFIC FLOW

The flow of traffic in your classroom is more important than many novice teachers realize. For example, if you place your trash can near the door, the stapler on your desk, and a tray to collect completed work near the front, students will wander all over your room after a test just to throw away scrap paper, staple their papers, and turn in their tests. Carefully consider the routine activities that your students will do before you set up your room so that you can minimize distractions and interruptions. Some of these routine activities could be:

- Entering class
- Checking posted material
- Working on the board
- Passing in papers
- Speaking with you privately

- Using a computer
- Picking up supplies
- Disposing of trash
- Sharpening a pencil
- Using a stapler

65

You should plan the most efficient ways for your students to move around the room. Think about what they have to do and put the equipment that they need for each task near enough together so that they complete each one with a minimum of bother. For example, if a student needs to go to the library, he may have to speak with you privately, sign out on the computer, and pick up supplies before leaving the room. If all of the areas are located near each other, no other student need be disturbed.

THE PHYSICAL ARRANGEMENT OF DESKS

Arranging student desks so that your students can focus on their work is important for their success. Although you will change the arrangement of desks several times during the term as your students work in groups of various sizes, to arrange student desks for an optimum effect, keep these pointers in mind.

1. You must be able to see every student's face, and every student should be able to see you with no difficulty.

2. Begin the year with traditional rows if you can. This sends a message that you want your students to focus their attention on you and not on each other.

3. You must be able to move freely around the room. You should be able to walk behind every row of desks.

4. Keep desks away from attractive graffiti spots such as bulletin boards, window ledges, or walls.

5. Avoid placing desks near distractions such as a pencil sharpener or computer monitor with an interesting screen saver.

USE A SEATING CHART FOR MAXIMUM ADVANTAGE

Your first seating chart, which you should make as soon as you receive your class rosters, will be based on the alphabetical order of your students' last names. This is also a good way to learn every student's name quickly.

In a week or two, after you get to know your students, you should make up a more permanent seating chart based on other factors. Begin by drawing a diagram of your room with each desk represented by a rectangle. Make plenty of copies. Next, take your class roster and pencil in the names of your students. Begin with the students that you know must sit in a certain area of the room due to medical issues or the terms of their Individual Education Plans or 504 Plans. After you have taken their needs into consideration, move on to those students who misbehave in their current seat. Place them where they can focus on you and their work rather than on having fun with their classmates. Finally, move the rest of your students. Do your best to find each student a seat that will be comfortable for his or her size and temperament.

66

The Benefits of Seating Charts

No matter what age your students may be, seating charts are necessary. Teacher arranged seating charts solve many problems and prevent many more, for the following reasons.

- Students from the same neighborhood won't sit next to each other in an obvious ethnic separation.
- Timid students will have the same seating opportunity that more aggressive ones do.
- Students will not argue with each other over which desk belongs to whom.
- You can move your less motivated students from the back of the room to a spot where you can more easily engage them in lessons or offer them assistance.
- You can seat easily distracted students where they can stay on task.
- Students with special needs can be seated where their needs can be met with a minimum of fuss.
- You can accommodate students with medical problems.
- Taller students will not block the view of smaller ones.
- You send a clear message that you are the person in charge of the class.

Set Up Your File Cabinet

You will have to set up a filing system for the paperwork that will flood your desk as soon as school begins. If you have a system in place before the term begins, you will save yourself much frustration and time later.

Setting up a file cabinet is not a complicated task. Once you have a file cabinet, clean it out and lubricate any stuck drawers.

Next, go shopping or searching for file folders. Begin your search by letting it be known that you can use any folders that anyone in your building is about to toss out. The main office and the guidance office are particularly good places to look for old folders. After this initial search, you will have learned the importance of recycling folders. If your school has allotted money for you to spend on supplies, be sure to spend some of it for materials for your file cabinet. Purchase hanging files for as many drawers as your budget permits. In addition to hanging files, you will need folders, labels, and permanent markers.

Organize your filing cabinet as follows:

- Set aside one file drawer for student business. Here you will keep documentation, student information, progress reports, report cards, copies of parent correspondence, and other paperwork related to students.
- Set aside another file drawer for general business. Here you will store your substitute folder, detention forms, and other general paperwork such as memos from the

office. Make sure you also file all paperwork related to your contract, certification, and recertification.

▶ In the other drawers, you should file material such as unit plans, handouts, tests, and paperwork related to your curriculum by alphabetical order.

---

9 Tips for Creating a Useful File System

After you have completed the basic steps in setting up your file system, the following refinements that will make your system much more efficient and easy to use.

1. Label the front of each drawer in large bold letters so that you can tell at a glance what's inside.

2. Neatness counts! File material according to subject in alphabetical order. Make a special effort to maintain orderly files.

3. Label everything. If you can color code your labels, it will be even easier to find what you need quickly.

4. Don't stuff a file drawer so full that it's almost impossible to move files around to find what you are looking for.

5. In the front of each drawer, create an index folder to hold an index of the files in that drawer. If you do this, then you will be able to find the paper you are looking for even if you have filed it under a name that is not easy to recall.

6. When you add paper to a folder, add it to the front so that you have a chronological order to your paperwork.

7. Stagger the tabbed labels on hanging files and the file folders within them so that you can see what's in the file drawer at a glance.

8. Use big, bold letters and a heavy marker to label each file.

9. Use color coding whenever possible. Even if you can't color code the entire file, use a colored dot on the tab to group like files together.

Set Up Your Computer Files

Chances are that the more technologically advanced your district is, the more confusing it is to keep up with all of your pass codes, screen names, and voice mail access protocols—to say nothing of the procedures for using all of the technology that is supposed to make your school life easier.

One efficient way to manage all this information is to create a folder just to store the handouts you will receive on the equipment in your room. Keep this folder handy as you work your way through all of the equipment you have to learn to use.

4 Steps to Managing E-Files

Now that you have the business of how to operate the technology in your classroom under control, take time to devise a system for storing computer documents in such a way that you can quickly find them again. Try these steps:

Step 1: Think of each disk, or CD, or zip drive, or whatever storage tool you use as a large file cabinet.

Step 2: Create folders for each class or unit of study.

Step 3: Make sure that you assign simple and logical names for all your folders and documents. Store all documents related to a class or unit of study in its folder.

Step 4: Back up all your work. Once you have finished a document, back it up by storing it on a disk, CD, zip drive, etc. It is less painful to lose a single document in a computer crash rather than a semester's worth of work because you had not yet gotten around to saving each document.

Equipment You Will Need to Operate

Depending on your college and previous work experience, you may not have had much practice with school equipment. Some school districts will provide crash courses in using equipment, but most will not. You will have to ask someone to show you how to operate much of the equipment that you will have to use. Here are a few tips to help you learn how to use some of the most common machines with ease and efficiency.

Photocopier

- Plan what you need to copy well in advance of when it is due. Find the time of day when there are not many people using it. This is hard to do at the start of the year and right before big projects or final exams are due.

- Take time to learn how to use it. Ask questions, and find out whom you should notify when the copier needs repairs.

- Make sure that your originals are dark enough to copy well.

- Learn about copyright laws *before* you copy, not after.

Overhead Projector

- Pick up a supply of transparency sheets as early as you can. They tend to disappear early in the year.

- Clean your machine. Dust affects the quality of what you want to project.

- Print or use a large size font so that your students can read the text clearly.

- Cut down on glare by cutting off some lights in your room; however, don't darken the entire room.

⬧ Make sure that the area on which you are projecting the images is clear of any distractions and is located high enough so that everyone can see it without moving.

⬧ If you have to use an extension cord, tape it to the floor so that no students can trip over it.

Your Supply List

Even if you teach secondary students, you will need more than just pens and paper to reach your students. Unfortunately, many schools do not provide teachers with enough money to pay for the supplies that they need. Teachers everywhere have learned to adjust to tough economics by recycling, asking parents or businesses for help, and making good use of the supplies that they have.

Here you will find a list of some supplies that you may find useful as you go though the year. Included in this list are plenty of recycled and "found" items.

- Pens—blue and black
- Colored pens for grading
- Pencils
- Colored pencils
- Baby food jars
- Plastic margarine tubs
- Calculator
- File folders
- Tissues
- Hole punch
- Duct tape
- Boxes—especially cereal and shoe boxes
- Cardboard pieces
- Display boards from old science fair projects
- Newspapers
- Poster mounting putty
- Cotton from pill bottles
- Old clothes, hats, sunglasses (for role play)
- Mints
- Thank you notes
- Overhead transparencies
- Liquid paper
- Overhead pens
- Rubber bands
- Reward stickers
- CD or tape player
- CD or tapes (check them out from a public library)
- Crayons
- Glue
- Transparent tape
- Computer disks
- Computer paper
- Printer cartridges
- An easy-to-find key ring
- Get-well cards
- Pencil sharpener
- Envelopes
- Note cards
- First aid kit
- Staplers (one for students and one for you)
- Paper clips of all sizes
- Index tabs for your grade book
- Labels
- Scissors
- Three-ring binders
- Needle and thread
- Stackable trays
- Packing peanuts
- Scraps of fabric
- Yarn
- Dental floss or fishing line (great for hanging things from the ceiling)
- Board erasers
- Safety pins
- Discarded books from libraries
- Board games and puzzles

Just What Are Your Students Expecting?

As soon as you have your room set up and your lesson plans in order, you need to give lots of thought to how you can make sure that you convince your students that you are the best teacher they will ever have.

As you do this, keep in mind that your students are probably anxious that they will not have a good teacher or a good year. Your first-year jitters may be bad, but theirs are worse!

Because it is so important that the first day of school goes well, you must present yourself to your students in as positive a manner as possible. This will be easy for you if you focus your energies around the following four important priorities. Following each, you will find three quick tips to help you put it into practice.

PRIORITY 1: TAKE CHARGE OF YOUR CLASS

1. Even if you are overcome by stage fright, you must conquer your personal feelings and pretend to be confident and self-assured. Sometimes, by pretending to be confident, you convince yourself that you are.

2. Have a seating chart ready so that you can show students to their seat and get them started on their opening exercise at once. Write an assignment on the board or give students a handout as they enter the room.

3. After you have made up your class procedures, rules, and established other expectations, have a friend videotape you as you present them. You could really have fun with this if you film your presentation at the beach, on a boat, or even in your own backyard. When school starts, instead of standing in front of class after class going over the same material, pop in the video, and hand your students a handout of the class expectations to fill in as they watch and listen.

PRIORITY 2: CALM YOUR STUDENTS' FEARS

1. Stand at the door and welcome students to your class. Wear a bright name tag. Make sure your name and the room number are prominently displayed so that students and their parents can be sure that they are in the right place.

2. Look cheerful and happy to see every child. Greet each one pleasantly; use their names if you can. Assume the best from each one.

3. Teach that first lesson as if it was the most important lesson you plan to teach all year. In many ways, it is. Your students should feel that they not only learned something interesting, but that they will continue to learn something in your class every day.

PRIORITY 3: ENGAGE YOUR STUDENTS' MINDS

1. Give each student a written assignment. This will keep them busy and allow you to complete any record keeping you need to do. It will also give you an opportunity to assess their readiness for the class and general work habits.

2. Plan to run out of time. Students should never go home bored on the first day of school. Give them fast-paced lessons from the time they sit down on. Include a brief homework assignment to reinforce the day's work and to get them back into the habit of doing homework.

3. Appeal to a variety of learning styles in that first lesson. Involve some critical thinking skills. Don't attempt group work unless your students are older and very mature.

PRIORITY 4: BEGIN TO TEACH THE CLASS ROUTINES

1. Teaching acceptable school behavior is part of what teachers do and is certainly part of what students expect from their teachers. When it is time for students to turn in the written assignment, show them the procedure for passing in papers that you expect to see them follow from now on.

2. If students lack supplies to do the assignment, lend them what they need for class and gently remind them that they will need to have paper and pencils in the future. Keep any reprimands very low key. Stick to gentle reminders instead.

3. When the time comes to dismiss class, remind your students of how you expect them to leave the room from now on. Spend time showing them how you will dismiss class. Hold a brief practice session if you see the need.

> *"Establish the structure and routines in your classroom the first day of school. Make sure students know that you mean business and then you can relax a little."*
>
> —Paige Adcock, 4 years experience

Overcome Those First-Day Jitters

There are many things that you can do to handle the jitters that beginning a new career can bring to even the most self-assured and well-trained professional. To calm yourself, try an assortment of tips and techniques from this list.

- Accept the fact that you will feel nervous and excited on the first day of school. Many veteran teachers do, also. Denying your concerns will not help you deal successfully with them.

- Boost your confidence by dressing well. Teachers traditionally dress up a bit on the first day—even the ones who slouched around the before-school workshops in jeans.

- Pack a good lunch. Force yourself to eat it. Avoid too much caffeine for breakfast.

- Get your classroom ready before the first day of school. If you can come in on the first day without having to worry about hanging posters or moving desks around, you will be much more relaxed.

▶ Ride to work with a colleague if you can. Car pooling on the first day will give you a chance to share your fears and provide mutual support.

▶ Pack your book bag the night before and leave it by the door so you can just grab it as you leave.

▶ Look over the list of your students' names one last time the night before school starts. You'll feel better if you can pronounce them correctly.

▶ Plan interesting assignments for your students. Plan more than you ever believe that they can accomplish, then plan some more work. It is truly terrifying to run out of work for your students on the very first day of school.

"Motivate, initiate, demonstrate, rather than entertain. Education and entertainment do not equate."

—Barbara Knowles, 36 years experience

▶ Relax! The chances of major behavior disruptions are slim. Students tend to be on their very best behavior during the first few days. Enjoy the honeymoon.

▶ Try the video approach mentioned earlier. If you are too nervous to speak well, the video will show your students a happy and relaxed teacher. Your students will be involved in the assignment and you won't have to worry that you have covered everything.

▶ Have extra supplies so that every student can complete the assignments with no trouble.

▶ Prepare a seating chart. One easy way to do this is to number each student's name on the roster, then place a number on top of the desk or on the seat. As you greet students at the door, ask their names and direct them to find the seats with the correct numbers. You will also match faces to names quickly this way.

▶ Smile, even when you feel stressed. Sometimes just acting in a confident manner will help you find the confidence you need.

▶ Arrive early. You don't have to be so early that you help the custodians unlock the building, but you should be early enough that you aren't rushed to finish any last minute chores.

▶ Keep in mind that the most stressful part of your day will be over sometime in the first half hour of class when you realize that your students are cooperative and pleasant and *depending on you*.

15 More Activities for the First Day

In addition to the lesson that you should teach and the class expectations that you will have to go over on the first day, there are lots of other activities that you can include to keep students engaged in meaningful work all class long. When you are trying to decide just what you want your students to do on the first day, consider some of these activities.

1. Fill out forms together. When you explain your expectations, your students should fill in the information on a handout you have prepared rather than just take notes.

2. Photograph students in their new school clothes. This is a good way to begin your class scrapbook.

3. Show examples of the supplies that they need.

4. Pass out scraps of paper and ask everyone to tell you what they can contribute to make the class a better one for everyone.

5. Issue textbooks and have students complete the textbook survey form you'll find later in this section.

6. Have students work with a partner, telling that other person one thing that they can do well and one thing that they would like to learn how to do. Have partners introduce each other to the class by sharing this information.

7. Ask students to write you a note telling three things that you need to know about them so that you can teach them well.

8. Place a large sheet of paper on the wall. Hand students old newspapers and magazines and have them tear out words and photos that describe their strengths and talents. Focus on what students have in common. Glue the photos and words in place to create an instant decoration that will be interesting to every student.

9. Have students jot down what they already know about the subject you are teaching and then share this information with the class.

10. Have students fill out one of the Student Inventories. (See Section Five.) Select the one that is most appropriate for your students.

11. Send students around the room to find out what they have in common. Some areas to explore could be hometowns, hobbies, favorite movies, pets, goals, and sports.

12. Have students create bookmarks with inspirational messages for younger students.

13. Ask older students to retell a memory from their earlier first days of school.

14. Put a quotation or unusual word related to the day's lesson on the board and ask students to tell you what they think about it.

15. Have students write exit slips explaining what they learned in class on their first day.

Student Information Records

Ask students to provide you with up-to-date information as close to the first day of school as you can. You will need this information all year long. Adapt or use as is the form on page 76 to meet the needs of your students. There is much that you can add, but keep in mind that the purpose of the form is to allow you quick access to contact information.

Even young students can complete many portions. It is also a good idea to ask younger students to take the form home to have adults help them fill it in.

Learn Your Students' Names Quickly

Learning how to correctly pronounce and spell your students' names is one of the most important tasks that you'll have to master as the school year begins. Being able to call all of your students by name is an important step in getting to know them as people and in assuming control of your class.

The depth of resentment that mispronouncing or misspelling a student's name can cause is often surprising to first-year teachers. Although teachers may think of it as a small mistake, students tend to view teachers who don't call them by the right name as uncaring and insensitive.

Learning all of your students' names on the first or second day of school is not very difficult if you use some of the strategies listed here. These quick tips will make it possible for you to go home on the first day of school confident that you know the students in your class well enough to get the term off to a good start.

- Put in some preliminary work! Organize your seating charts, study class rosters, and prepare name tag materials.

- Make sure your students sit in their assigned seats for the first few days so you can more quickly associate their names and faces.

- Have students wear name tags for the first day or so until you get to know everyone. If students seem reluctant to do this, ask them to name some professions that require identification badges. Stressing that this is a businesslike approach to the problem should help your students' hesitation vanish.

- Make sure that you have students fill out an information form similar to the one on page 76. When you get home or have time during your plan period, read what your students have written and mentally match up faces to the information in front of you.

- When students are working on an opening-day writing assignment, walk quietly around the room checking the roll. Ask each child to say his or her name for you. Repeat it as you study the child's face.

- Mark pronunciation guides for yourself on your roll. Also make notes to help you recall them. For example, you can write "big smile" or "very tall" next to a student's name. These little clues will help you when you are struggling to recall a name on the second day of school. Make sure you pay attention to characteristics that are not likely to change, such as height or hair color.

Figure 3.3
STUDENT INFORMATION FORM

Your full name: _____

What you want me to call you: _____

Your home phone number: _____

Your e-mail address: _____

Your birthday: _____

Your age: _____ Your student number: _____

Your brothers and sisters: _____

_____

What are your goals for the future? _____

What hobbies do your have? _____

What sports are you interested in? _____

Name your parent(s) _____

or guardian(s):_____

Which parent or guardian would you like me to contact if I need to call home?

_____
   (Title)   (First name)   (Last name)

Please tell me the occupation, business phone, and e-mail of each of your parents or guardians.

Mother _____
   (Occupation)   (Business phone)   (E-mail address)

Father _____
   (Occupation)   (Business phone)   (E-mail address)

Guardian _____
   (Occupation)   (Business phone)   (E-mail address)

Guardian _____
   (Occupation)   (Business phone)   (E-mail address)

What is your address?

_____
(Street address)   (City)   (Zip code)

- Use any bits of information that students reveal about themselves to help you connect faces and names.
- When you can't recall a child's name, admit it and ask for help. When you hear it again, write it, repeat it, and try again until you can recall it.

How to Get to Know Your Students

It goes without saying that getting to know your students as quickly as you can is one of the most important tasks you will have as the school year starts. Although getting to know each child well will take time, there are many ways to learn the background information you need.

"My advice is that new teachers must be very secure about who they are. The new teacher can't go into the classroom looking for a 'fight,' trying to set an example the first day because if that is what he is looking for, he will find plenty of them, and he will nearly always lose."

—Ken Pfeifer, 28 years experience

One way to get information is to review students' records. Be sure to follow the correct procedures and confidentiality regulations for this. You may want to jot quick notes on each student as you scan their folders.

When you make a positive phone call to a student's parents, you have a wonderful opportunity to ask parents about their children. Likewise, when you send home an introductory letter, you can add a section asking parents and guardians to tell you information about their child. You can also learn a great deal about your students from writing assignments where students write responses to classroom issues and from student inventories. (See Section Five for sample inventories.)

Your students' former teachers may be another good source of information. However, the drawback to this is that you may sometimes get information that is not completely objective and that may bias your view of a child. Ask about former students only of teachers who strike you as fair-minded professionals. If you find yourself listening to unfair horror stories about how much the student misbehaved in previous years, then you should excuse yourself from the conversation.

One of the best ways to get to know your students, however, and to help them get to know each other, is to assign ice-breaker activities. As you watch them interact with each other, you will learn a great deal about them. In addition, icebreaker activities will give your students an opportunity to learn to value each other's contribution to the class.

10 Ice-Breaker Activities

1. Have students work in pairs or triads to fill out an information form for each other. Include questions that will cause them to learn interesting and usual details about each other. For example, having students list their favorite performer or a pet peeve would make a good conversation starter.

2. Try playing a silly chaining game where students try to recite everyone's last name without having to stop to think. You can even offer a small reward for the first student who is able to do this.

3. Pass around a large calendar for students to record their birthdays. Pass around a map for students to mark their hometowns, also.

4. Create a class newsletter during the first week of class. Have students share a variety of ideas as they interview each other for articles in the newsletter. You can include almost anything you and your students would enjoy, including interviews with parents or administrators, predictions, advice, cartoons, and study skill tips.

5. Create a duty roster for the classroom tasks that students can manage well. This will encourage students to work together to take ownership of the class.

6. Take photographs of your students and post them. Ask students to bring in photographs from when they were much younger and post these, also.

7. Make it a point to focus on your students' strengths by asking them to reveal what they do well. Share these with the class when appropriate.

8. Put students in groups to determine just what they have in common. Go beyond the obvious to focus on mental traits, goals, and successful attitudes.

9. Have each student research a quotation about school success and bring it in. Post these around your classroom to inspire all of your students.

10. Don't forget that as your students are learning about each other that they need to learn a bit about you, too. While you should not be overly personal, they need to see that you have a human side, also.

"Do something fun the first day of class. Rules need to be established, but should children do rules all day? If you teach secondary classes, think about what kids will be doing in other classrooms when you prepare your lessons for the first day of class."

—Stephanie Mahoney, 24 years experience

First Week Priorities

Look at the following list of priorities for the first week of school. Some will take several days to accomplish while others will take only a day or two, depending, in part, on you. The better organized you are and the more efficiently you complete your paperwork responsibilities, the more successful you will find that your first week of school will be.

- Make every student in your class feel confident, successful, and motivated to learn more.

- Learn all of your students' names as quickly as you can.

- Establish, teach, and enforce school and classroom rules.

- Be accurate with paperwork and other records. Modify your paperwork organization system if you need to.

- Help students new to your school orient themselves to new rules, procedures, and classmates.

- Have students set both long-term and short-term goals for themselves.

- Teach lessons that are directed to meeting the objectives of your state and local curriculum guides.

- Establish, teach, and enforce classroom routines and procedures.

- Make sure that all students have the supplies they will need for class.

- Issue textbooks and other school-issued materials in an organized and efficient way.

- Include motivation techniques in every lesson so students will want to learn more.

- Reach out to every child. Make the connection that lets each student know that you value him or her.

- Take action to keep discipline concerns from disrupting class. Focus on prevention.

- Assess your students' readiness and previous learning.

- Set up your grade book, grade program, voice mail, homework phone line, computer use forms, attendance records, and all other record keeping, documentation, or paperwork procedures that you can.

- Send a letter home with each child introducing yourself.

- Cope with the increased demands on your time in a proactive way by using effective stress management techniques. (See Section Sixteen.)

What You Must Accomplish During the First Week

The first week of school is, in many ways, the best week of the entire year for your students. The workload isn't overwhelming and they haven't failed any tests; they remember to bring their books and pencils to class; and they are still on their best behavior because they are unsure of you and of their classmates. For teachers, too, the first week is an exciting one. After the initial nervousness has passed, you will find that you can manage your students, and that the rush, rush, rush of the week of before-school preparation has slowed down considerably. Nevertheless, the first week of school has plenty of difficult moments for both teachers and students. Everything you teach is new and you and your students are still unpredictable strangers to one another. When the first week ends, both teachers and students are usually glad for a weekend break.

Analyze Your Students' Readiness

The analysis you make of your students at the start of the school year is different from the assessments of prior knowledge that you will make as you begin a new unit of study. At the start of a term, you need to learn as much as you can about your students' readiness for success in your class. You can do this in a variety of ways: informal writing assignments, pre-tests, permanent record checks, and talks with parents and previous teachers. However you decide to determine your students' readiness for the demands of your class, you should consider several issues. Answer these questions as well as you can about each of your students in order to determine his or her readiness at the start of a term.

- Has the student been successful in the past?
- What do his or her parents say about their child?
- Has the student attended other schools? What types of instruction were offered?
- What deficiencies can you notice right away in the student's general academic and social skills?
- What interests does he or she have?
- How quickly does the student work? Is he or she easily drawn off task?
- What do previous teachers say about this student?
- What does the student say about his or her own readiness for success in your class?

> *"Always remember that you used to be on the other side of the desk. I've always found that students are more receptive to the ideas of a teacher who makes a true effort to respect and understand them."*
>
> —Krissy Sanderlin, 5 years experience

Create a Group Identity

Unless you create a positive identity for your students as a class, they can take your smallest misbehavior correction and interpret it to mean that you think of them as a troublesome class. This will happen even more quickly if you teach a class with students who have struggled with school in the past. Once a group starts thinking of itself in a negative way, it is almost impossible to change a the group's self-perception into a positive one.

Be proactive! You know that it is important that you not only connect with each child in a meaningful way, but that you also shape the group's image into a positive one. Think of a positive label or two for each class and use these labels frequently. Each of your classes should believe that they have a special place in your heart.

There are many positive labels that you can use with even the most difficult classes. Here are a few that your students should hear you use at the start of the year as you talk about their class.

- Energetic
- Caring
- Motivated
- Interested
- Interesting
- Kind
- Intelligent
- Well-prepared
- Successful
- Upbeat
- Practical
- Compassionate

- Friendly
- Helpful
- Deep thinkers
- Organized
- Self-confident
- Cooperative
- Thoughtful
- Polite
- Serious
- Studious
- Goal-oriented
- Alert

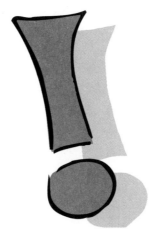

Journal Entries to Help You Begin with Confidence

▶ Think back over this school week and fill out this statement in as many ways as you can: "When I see_____ I think of _____."

▶ Describe the environment of your new classroom. What changes do you need to make?

▶ What kinds of skills do you wish your students had? What can you do to help them acquire these skills?

▶ List the primary events of your first school day. How did you react to them? Think about what you did well and what skills you need to develop.

▶ Finish the following statement, "When I think about my first days with my new students, I am thankful for . . ."

▶ What would it have been like to have been your student today?

▶ What kind of relationship do you want to have with your class?

▶ What kind of relationships do you want to have with each of your students?

▶ How do you want your students to feel about themselves as learners?

Become a Valuable Team Player

She hadn't been this nervous in a long, long time. The dreaded phone call had come out of nowhere. "We would like to arrange a conference."

She only hoped that she hadn't done anything wrong. She was as anxious as she had been the day her own parents had marched off to a parent conference. Her hands were shaking. Maybe her student's parents were upset about the detention last week. They hadn't written anything on the notice, though. She had been late to school last Monday. Could that be why they called? No, that was silly. Maybe they thought she gave too much homework. She just hoped that they wouldn't be too difficult for her to handle. She had asked about them at lunch and had found out that they were "really involved" and could be "difficult to handle." She wondered what that meant. She hoped it wouldn't be bad. She took a deep breath. It was supposed to calm people down. It didn't.

She moved chairs into place and got her papers in order. She practiced looking confident and professional. She gave up.

Suddenly there was a light tap on the door. Two very nervous parents and their even more nervous son waited there. Her first parent conference was about to begin.

"Give at least three compliments every day, especially to colleagues."

—Barbara Knowles, 36 years experience

For many people, it comes as no surprise that the primary reason that many employees are fired is not poor job performance, but the inability to work well with others. Schools are like other organizations in that there, too, employees must learn to work well with others.

Teamwork Skills

Schools are much more complex than many organizations. Each school is an ever-changing mixture of young and old, cheerful and cranky, competent and struggling individuals. Teachers work in large communities of young people and the adults who care for them. In many school districts, there are clerks, custodians, technical assistants, school nurses, counselors, psychologists, coaches, media personnel, paraprofessionals, teaching assistants, police liaison officers, and computer wizards as well as teachers, their students, and their students' families. These complicated communities extend far beyond the boundaries of the school yard. The challenge for teachers is to get along with every single member of that community with whom they come in contact.

10 Teamwork Skills That Build Success

According to an ancient Japanese proverb, "None of us are as smart as all of us."

Teams make the workload easier and the task more pleasant only if all of the team members have the skills to work well together. But just what does it take to be a good team member? The following ten teamwork skills are a good place to start.

Teachers who are good team members . . .

1. . . . build bridges of understanding and connectedness to their colleagues and students.

2. . . . treat all people in their work community with courtesy.

3. . . . listen to all other opinions before making decisions.

4. . . . are reliable and can be counted on to keep their promises.

5. . . . commit themselves to the good of the school.

6. . . . are quick to celebrate the hard work and success of others.

7. . . . are prepared to compromise when a group decision depends on it.

8. . . . cheerfully offer help to other colleagues when needed.

9. . . . are cheerleaders for their school.

10. . . . are sensitive to the needs and feelings of others.

Figure 4.1

RATE YOUR CURRENT TEAMWORK SKILLS

Below are several scenarios of school situations that will test your teamwork skills.

✔ Read each one and circle the letter of the response that best matches your own.

✔ Check your answers against the key at the end.

1. A colleague comes to school terribly upset about an argument with a car dealer over expensive car repairs that he believes were not correctly done. He wants to talk with you, but you have to finish getting the assignment on the board before class starts. What do you do?

    a. Stop and listen
    b. Tell him you have to get your work done
    c. Arrange to meet at lunch so you can hear all about it.

2. There is a school rule that you just don't think is needed. It is a hassle to enforce and students don't like it either. What should you do?

    a. Enforce it anyway.
    b. Ask others how they enforce it.
    c. Enforce it, but form a committee to speak to the principal about the rule and why it should be abolished.

3. Your school has a voice mail system that you are supposed to use as a homework hot-line, but it is really complicated to use and takes a long time. What should you do?

    a. Spend some time after school practicing so you can use it more efficiently.
    b. Ignore it. You've heard that no one else uses it anyway.
    c. Suggest that the school system adopt a voice mail system that is easier to use.

4. Your principal calls you in for a conference and tells you that your teaching performance is poor. You are upset and angry. What should you do?

    a. Wait until you cool off and then send an e-mail defending yourself.
    b. Go to the lounge and find a shoulder to cry on.
    c. Remain calm and professional and ask your principal for specific ways you can improve your performance.

5. You had a bit too much to drink at a faculty party. It wasn't really a problem until you notice that conversation ceases when you enter the lounge. What do you do?

    a. Resolve to never attend a faculty party again.
    b. Be very careful to limit your alcohol intake at future parties.
    c. Resolve to stay out of the teachers' lounge for a long while.

6. You are walking in the hall and notice bits of scrap paper lying near some student lockers. What do you do?

    a. Pick it up and throw it away.
    b. Find the nearest student and make her throw it away.
    c. Ignore it because the custodians will get it later.

7. You and another faculty member become romantically interested in each other. Soon you are dating. What is the best way to handle this?

    a.   Let other teachers know that you are dating, but keep it secret from students.

    b.   Keep your relationship on a professional level while you are both at school.

    c.   Try not to let your students know, but answer their questions honestly.

8. You are too shy to face the cafeteria and the crowd at the teachers' table each day. What should you do?

    a.   Stay in your room and eat. You can catch up on some work, too.

    b.   Force yourself to go anyway.

    c.   Find a friend or two to eat lunch with you in your room.

9. The teacher next door asks you to keep the noise down during a fun activity with your students. What do you do?

    a.   Tell your students that the activity is over because of a complaint.

    b.   Switch to another activity that isn't as loud. Plan to reteach the rules for noise levels before trying that activity again.

    c.   Count to ten before telling the teacher that her students are always too loud.

10. One of your students needs more time to finish a test, but it's time for your lunch break. What do you do?

    a.   Ask a teacher who has a plan period then to come to your room to watch the student so that you can eat.

    b.   Tell the student that he has to turn in the test.

    c.   Miss lunch and monitor the student. You can grab a snack later.

Key

1. **c** Your colleague needs to talk to you, but the time isn't right. If you arrange for a more relaxed and private time to chat, you will be able to be a good friend and an effective teacher at the same time.

2. **c** A school rule is one that should be enforced. Rules, however, should be reviewed periodically. Forming a committee to discuss the rule and its usefulness is a sensible alternative.

3. **a** Practice until you can use it well. Parents need to have access to your voice mail.

4. **c** Asking for specific ways to improve your teaching performance is not just professional behavior, but is an approach that will ultimately lead to better evaluations.

5. **b** You can't undo the mistake you made, but you can avoid repeating it. Resolve to limit your drinking at future parties. Make sure your school behavior is above reproach until the gossip about you fades away.

6. **a** The custodians are part of the school team, too. Be careful to do all you can to help them keep the school tidy. Picking up scrap paper will only take you a few seconds and will set a better example for students than if you were to ignore the litter in the hallways.

7. **b** Focus on your teaching responsibilities and keep your relationship as discreet as you can.

8. **b** Although you may feel uncomfortable at first, you need to socialize and connect with other teachers.

9. **b** It's often difficult to judge just how loud an activity will be. Be sensitive to the classroom situations of the teachers near you and always have a back-up plan ready in case an activity does not work out.

10. **c** Your student is your responsibility and you should do what is necessary to help him succeed, even if it means a slight inconvenience to you.

Figure 4.2

SET GOALS TO IMPROVE HOW WELL YOU WORK WITH OTHERS

The first year of your career is a terrific time to improve how well you work with others. You have a new relationship with all the teachers in the building—even those you may already know well. Take the following steps to get off to a good start by establishing goals to improve your working relationships with others.

- ✔ Look over the list of teamwork skills below. See each one as a goal to work towards.
- ✔ Determine the steps you need to take to achieve each of these goals. Make sure that the steps you decide to take are achievable and geared to your success.
- ✔ Write the steps down on the lines provided.
- ✔ Set about being the best team member you can be!

Goal 1: Connect to colleagues and students.

Steps I can take to achieve this goal:

_____

_____

Goal 2: Treat all people in the building with courtesy.

Steps I can take to achieve this goal:

_____

_____

Goal 3: Listen to all other opinions before making decisions.

Steps I can take to achieve this goal:

_____

_____

Goal 4: Establish a reputation for being reliable.

Steps I can take to achieve this goal:

_____

_____

Goal 5: Be committed to the good of the school.

Steps I can take to achieve this goal:

_____

_____

Goal 6: Be quick to celebrate the hard work and success of others.
Steps I can take to achieve this goal:

_____

_____

Goal 7: Be willing to compromise when a group decision depends on it.
Steps I can take to achieve this goal:

_____

_____

Goal 8: Cheerfully offer help to other colleagues when it's needed.
Steps I can take to achieve this goal:

_____

_____

Goal 9: Be a cheerleader for my school.
Steps I can take to achieve this goal:

_____

_____

Goal 10: Be sensitive to the needs and feelings of others.
Steps I can take to achieve this goal:

_____

_____

On-the-Job Courtesy

Now that you have minded your manners long enough to make it though the initial interviews that resulted in your new career, it is time to develop the business manners that will guarantee your success. Follow these suggestions to present yourself as a courteous professional.

- Refer to other adults in the building by their title and last name in front of students.
- Greet absolutely everyone you meet with a pleasant smile.
- Do not allow your students to complain to you about another teacher.
- Pay attention during faculty meetings.
- Be known as a punctual person.
- Plan ahead so that you don't have to ask to cut in line at the photocopier.
- Be extra careful to say "please" and "thank you." Take extra care to remember this during stressful times.
- Don't repeat gossip.
- Leave your work area clean. If you use the paper cutter, pick up scraps; if you spill food at lunch, wipe up the mess.
- Answer the phone or respond to the intercom message in a businesslike manner.
- Be very polite to all cafeteria staff members and expect that your students will do the same.
- If you are having a disagreement with a colleague, be careful to remain calm and professional. Never raise your voice. Absolutely never stage such a disagreement in front of students.
- If you see another teacher struggling with books, papers, or any of those other packages that teacher lug around, offer to help carry a couple of items or hold the door.
- If you borrow it, return it.
- Keep the noise level in your class down so that you don't disturb other classes.
- Meet your students at the door with a friendly word.
- Share your materials, supplies, and other resources.
- Respect the class time of other teachers. Unless there is an emergency, try not to interrupt another teacher's instruction.
- Do not make students late to another teacher's class or ask that they be allowed to miss another class to come to yours instead.
- Share the phone lines. There will never be enough phones in a school, so be careful to limit your phone conversations to business matters.

"Make a schedule of what you need to do and when you plan to do it."

—Verna Jones, 27 years experience

Figure 4.3

COURTEOUS BEHAVIOR IN 3 DIFFICULT SITUATIONS

How would a courteous teacher handle these problem situations? After each, you will find some suggestions for the best way to handle the situation.

1. **You are having a great day until you accidentally overhear two other teachers discussing you. They are very uncomplimentary. What is the best course of action to take?**

   Let the teachers who are discussing you know that you have heard them. Defuse the awkwardness of this situation with a calm and open approach. Be very calm even if you are angry. If they apologize, be gracious and let the matter drop. Remain gracious even if they don't apologize. One thing you should not do is indiscriminately spread your version of this event.

2. **A group of other new teachers invites you to join them every Friday afternoon at a local bar. You enjoy their company and accept the invitation. The problem is that you realize that the conversation about school in this public place is very indiscreet. No one else seems to care. What should you do?**

   Speak up! Indiscreet public conversations, especially in a place where alcohol is served, are not just unprofessional, but a violation of privacy laws. Before you go out with this group of teachers again, speak to one or two of them about your concern. Be clear that you enjoy the company, but are worried about the unprofessional conversation. Enlist their support in encouraging the group to police itself. If the situation does not improve, suggest that everyone move to a less public place. You can also choose to not attend or only stay for a little while.

3. **You witness a heated argument between the principal and another teacher. Neither one realizes that you are there. What should you do?**

   Do not allow yourself to give in to the temptation to eavesdrop. Make your presence known at once and offer to come back later. Respect the privacy of the two other people involved and resist the desire to spread the news of what you have witnessed.

Diversity in the Workplace

Many people who are familiar with the expression "global classroom" may think that it only refers to the access that teachers now have to other classrooms and resources all over the world through the Internet. Not so.

One of the most intriguing trends in American education in recent years is the push to hire teachers of differing cultures and ethnic backgrounds in more and more schools. Many school districts, partially in response to the teacher shortage, even actively recruit and hire teachers from other countries. As a first-year teacher, the chances are excellent that if you look around at your opening faculty meetings, the faces you see will not look like yours. Other teachers will probably have very different backgrounds from your own. The benefits that a multiethnic faculty offers a school are limitless. A culturally diverse faculty is a ready-to-use resource that gives students (and other staff members) an opportunity to learn first-hand information about other cultures. Stereotypical thinking, dangerous to members of any society, can be replaced with informed ideas. Everyone can benefit from exposure to a faculty that values the contributions of other cultures. However, the benefits of a diverse workplace can't be realized unless all members of the school community agree not to just tolerate or accept each other's heritage, but to value and embrace it. All members of a school community should be aware of how easy it is to create an unfriendly work environment. Suspicion, misunderstandings, and fear of rejection are all problems that can affect any workplace, especially a diverse one.

What is your role as a first-year faculty member in a diverse workplace? While the parameters of your workplace will dictate the specific actions that your school will take to include all faculty members in the common goal of educating students, the following guidelines will assist you in finding a way to become a team player in the "global classroom" in your school.

1. Keep an open mind. Realize that you can learn a great deal from people whose backgrounds are very different from yours. Work with your students to help them learn to value people from other cultures. Everyone benefits when a diverse workplace is a successful workplace.

2. Make sure that your language is appropriate. Be aware that the names you use and the things that you may criticize when referring to people of other cultures are very real reflections of your own thinking. Make sure that your language is reflective of an open-minded, well-educated person who values people of other cultures.

3. Reach out! If you sometimes feel ill at ease in your school environment, think how much more difficult it is for teachers of other cultures. Be friendly to everyone. Show a genuine interest in and respect for another person's culture.

For more information on how to thrive in a diverse workplace, check out the following organizations.

The Multicultural Alliance
Box 857
Ross, California 94957
(415) 454-3612

U. S. Department of Education
Office of Bilingual Education and Minority Language Affairs
600 Independence Avenue, SW
Washington, D.C. 20202
www.ed.gov/offices/OBE/MCA

National Alliance of Black School Educators (NABSE)
2816 Georgia Avenue, NW
Washington, D.C. 20071
www.nabse.org

Working Well with Your Supervisors

The supervisory staff of your school district and your school building depend on faculty members to make things run smoothly for every one. While it is only natural that not everything will go smoothly in a school, it is up to you to do all you can to work well with your supervisors.

There is a certain hierarchy of supervision in any school. It is likely that you will have a department head, lead teacher, or grade level leader to whom you report and who serves as a liaison between a group of staff members and administrators. Assistant principals make up the next level. At the top of the hierarchy in your school is the principal, who is the instructional leader of your building. At the district level, your supervisors may differ in their titles, but will include curriculum coordinators and assistant superintendents who report to their supervisor (and yours), the superintendent of schools. The hierarchy does not end there. All employees, including the superintendent, are supervised by the school board.

If you want to establish a positive relationship with your supervisors, you will need to take positive action. Don't just hope that no one will notice you because you are a first-year teacher. In fact, you are particularly noticeable just because you are a first-year teacher!

Follow these suggestions to establish a positive working relationship with all of your supervisors.

- If you work in a large school, you will probably work with a large number of administrators. Get to know each one as well as you can as quickly as you can.

- Behave in a professional manner at all times. This will win you the support of administrators not only because it will make their jobs easier, but also because a solid reputation will make it easier for an administrator to support you when you make mistakes.

- Take time to familiarize yourself with the information in your faculty manual. This will help you avoid mistakes that may lead to negative interaction with your supervisors.

- Your administrators are responsible for the entire school and you are responsible for only a very small part of it. If you can achieve this mind set, you'll find that it is easier to understand some of the policies or decisions that you might otherwise find confusing.

- Accept the fact that you are not always going to agree with the decisions and actions of the administrators with whom you work, but public criticism of their actions can seriously damage your professional reputation. Think before you voice criticism in public.

- Don't threaten to send your students to the office instead of independently resolving the problem using other, more successful methods of discipline. Maintain control of your classroom, so that when you have to send a child out of class, the action will have meaning—to students as well as administrators. (You can find tips on classroom management in Sections Twelve, Thirteen, and Fourteen.)

- Once you have referred a student to an administrator, you may disagree with an administrator's discipline decision, but you should not publicly criticize that action. Instead, make an appointment to discuss the situation with the administrator.

▶ Remember to always be professional in your dealings with administrators. Always present a calm and competent image, not an image of a furious teacher lacking in self-control.

▶ Regardless of your personal feelings toward a supervisor, always model the respect that you want your students to show towards your supervisors.

▶ When you make mistakes, be truthful in discussing it with your supervisors. And if you can do this before they find out the bad news from someone else, you should do so.

▶ Share your successes with your supervisors. Help them create successful public relations for your school by letting them know about noteworthy positive news about your students.

20 Mistakes No Teacher Should Ever Make

Although the culture of your school and the preferences of your administrators will determine a great deal of what is considered acceptable behavior for teachers, there are certain behaviors that are just not acceptable for any teacher at any time. Below is a list of twenty mistakes that no teachers should ever make.

1. **Drug use.** This means avoiding illegal substances at any time, and alcohol and tobacco at school or when they bring negative attention to you. This also means not overlooking these problems when you find them in your students. In addition, most teachers are not allowed to dispense medication to students, even cough drops or other seemingly harmless over-the-counter medications.

2. **Lying.** Not being truthful to your colleagues, to your supervisors, to parents and guardians is clearly not acceptable in the workplace. In addition, do not be tempted to lie on your job application.

3. **Inappropriate physical contact.** This can range from having a sexual relationship with a student to touching that a student may find inappropriate.

4. **Engaging in illegal or criminal behavior.** Breaking the laws of your community or state is clearly not acceptable for a role model. You are required to report arrests to your school division.

5. **Inadequately supervising students.** You should not leave your students unsupervised or unattended at any time. Further, you should take steps to keep students from becoming out of control.

6. **Neglecting special needs students.** Do not ignore the directives of a student's Individual Education Plan or 504 Plan. For more information on these, see Section Fifteen.

7. **Using foul language.** Using even mildly foul language around students or allowing students to use it around you is not acceptable in any place in a school.

8. **Maintaining an unprofessional appearance.** This includes your personal dress, your language, and even the way your classroom is arranged.

9. **Tolerating harassment.** Ignoring student bullying or harassment can create an unhealthy environment where learning is difficult and where victims may resort to extreme acts of violence to solve the problem.

10. **Failing to report neglect or abuse.** Teachers are required by law to report cases of suspected child neglect or abuse.

11. **Violating a student's right to privacy.** It is not acceptable to criticize one student to another child or another parent or guardian. It is also not acceptable to post students' grades or to share a student's grade with the rest of the class.

12. **Cheating.** Offering inappropriate assistance on tests, especially standardized tests, is not only unethical, but is also an offense that is now against the law in many states.

13. **Discriminating against students.** Treating students in a biased manner or making derisive remarks about them is never acceptable, and when it is based on a student's race, gender, or disability, it is also illegal.

14. **Keeping sloppy records.** Not keeping accurate and up-to-date attendance and grade records is a serious mistake. Your students and their parents rely on you to grade them fairly based on accurate grade and attendance data. Further, some teachers have had their records subpoenaed when a student has been called to court.

15. **Refusing to enforce school rules.** Ignoring school rules and policies will not endear you to your colleagues. Further, you will have to deal with the behavioral problems that will result from your lax enforcement of the rules.

16. **Showing disrespect for colleagues.** Criticizing another school employee to students or allowing students to do so is unprofessional and inappropriate.

17. **Ignoring students' safety.** Not safeguarding your students' health and well being is not only unprofessional, but often it's also grounds for a lawsuit.

18. **Having poor attendance.** Being late to or absent from school, class, or meetings without good reason is an offense that will result in a reprimand or, if persistent, can cause you to lose your job.

19. **Neglecting to intervene.** Overlooking behavioral or academic problems until they become serious is not acceptable to your supervisor and does not serve the best interests of your students. Intervene early and take the necessary actions, including contacting parents, to avoid this problem.

20. **Wasting instructional time.** Your students should be engaged in meaningful work while they are in your class.

The Evaluation Process

Just like other professionals, teachers are evaluated on a variety of criteria every year. There are several components to the evaluation process. First, you can expect one of your supervisors to talk to you in a pre-observation conference where you will discuss your goals and progress so far that year. This is a good time to mention any particular problems that you are having and to solicit advice.

Some time after your pre-observation conference, your evaluator will make a planned classroom observation. At this point, the evaluator will be looking for your strengths and weaknesses as an educator. You will probably just want to get through this nerve-racking time without forgetting your own name.

After the observation, you will meet with your evaluator again in a post-observation conference. At this conference, the evaluator will talk with you about the lesson that you taught and about your strengths and weaknesses as a teacher. There will be other observations in the course of the year, also. The number varies from school district to school district. Expect to have many informal visits from administrators over the course of your career, but especially during your first few years when you don't yet have tenure.

At some point near the end of the school year, you will have a final evaluation conference. This conference will involve more than just the formal classroom observations that you have had throughout the course of the year. It will address your overall effectiveness as an educator. There should be no surprises with regard to your final evaluation. If your supervisors believe that you are not an effective teacher, you would certainly receive some indication of that before the final meeting.

PREPARING FOR AN OBSERVATION

In many ways, the informal visits that evaluators make are much easier to get through than the planned, formal observations. You don't have time to worry and build up anxiety about an unannounced visit, whereas knowing that an administrator is going to observe you in a few days leaves plenty of time to worry about everything that could go wrong. Taking steps to prepare for the observation can help you feel confident, both before and during the observation.

6 Steps You Can Take to Prepare for an Observation

Step 1: Be proactive. Make sure you ask for a copy of the observation form if a copy is not in your faculty manual. In fact, you should do this as early in the term as you can. Study the form so that you know what the observer will be looking for as you teach.

Step 2: Clean up your room. This will give you a psychological boost as well as a positive mark on your form.

Step 3: Plan a lesson that is interesting and not very complicated. Do not plan a test or a video. The observer wants to see you and your students interacting. Keep your lesson simple so that you can do it well. Experimenting with a class skit or a first time collaborative grouping are not activities that will showcase your confidence and skill early in your first-year.

Step 4: Tell your students what is going to happen. Tell them that there will be a visitor in your classroom and that you would appreciate their cooperation. Don't bribe them for good behavior.

Step 5: Write out your lesson plan and collect a copy of all handouts, textbooks, or materials that you need for this lesson. Select a non-intrusive place for your visitor and place this material there. Be ready to show all of your lesson plan books as well as your grade book.

Step 6: Now, prepare to take the most important step in your preparation: getting control of your anxiety. If you are prepared, and have a well-planned lesson, you do not have to worry. Expect to be nervous and to feel stressed, but also expect to do well. Have confidence in yourself!

Figure 4.4
HOW OBSERVERS WILL EVALUATE YOU

When you are evaluated during a classroom observation, your observer will make notes on a form that has been approved by your school district and that should be available to all employees. While these forms vary from district to district, there are certain items that are common to most of them. These include:

- Demonstrating that you follow the district's curriculum
- Having an objective for the lesson
- Making the objective of the lesson clear to students
- Delivering accurate and appropriate information
- Showing a depth of understanding of the material
- Making use of all available class time
- Keeping students on task
- Providing for transition times between activities
- Using a variety of teaching strategies
- Demonstrating effective questioning skills
- Creating a student assessment instrument for the lesson you are teaching
- Motivating students to succeed
- Establishing the relevance of the lesson
- Providing timely feedback
- Monitoring students effectively
- Encouraging and assisting students
- Interacting in a positive way with students
- Maintaining an orderly classroom
- Minimizing any disruptions that might occur
- Giving preferential seating to students who require it
- Incorporating critical thinking activities in assignments
- Having classroom rules posted
- Enforcing classroom rules
- Demonstrating that procedures for routine tasks are in place
- Delivering clear instructions
- Projecting a professional image

"Help them look within themselves for answers."

—Barbara Knowles, 36 years experience

MAKE EVALUATIONS WORK FOR YOU

Evaluations throughout the year can either be of enormous benefit to you or they can turn you into a nervous wreck. The difference is in your attitude. If you want to grow as a teacher, then adopt the attitude that your evaluators can only offer you suggestions and advice in areas that you need to improve that you had not yet thought about. And remember: *No teacher is perfect, and every teacher has areas of performance that can be improved. One way to identify those areas is through evaluations.* You can suffer through the process or you can benefit from it. The choice is yours.

TURN CRITICISM INTO A POSITIVE EXPERIENCE

Hearing negative things about yourself is never pleasant. Hearing them from your supervisor is even less so. The following are a few things you can do as a first-year teacher that will help you turn the inevitable criticism that you will hear into a positive experience instead of a negative one.

- Go into your post-observation conference or any other evaluation conference with paper, pen, and an open mind. Be prepared to hear negative as well as positive comments about yourself.

- Listen objectively. Most of the criticism is likely be about issues that you are already aware of and have already started to address yourself. Before you allow yourself to become defensive, stop and make the effort to remain objective.

- Listen more than you speak. During an evaluation conference, ask for advice and suggestions for improvement, then listen carefully, write them down, and follow them.

- Ask a mentor for suggestions regarding how you can handle specific criticism.

- Release your negative emotions in your teacher's journal and not in the lounge.

- After the conference, when you have had an opportunity to correct some of your weaknesses, keep the administrator up-to-date on your progress in following his or her suggestions.

THE IMPORTANCE OF SELF-EVALUATION

If you are already in the habit of evaluating yourself there will be few surprises for you when an observer is in your classroom. Many experienced teachers do this on a daily basis in a variety of informal ways. Here are three techniques you can use to develop this habit.

1. Use your teacher journal to reflect on your day. Pay attention to what went wrong and what went well and exactly what you did to cause both outcomes.

2. Elicit feedback from your students. This does not have to be a lengthy or elaborate process to be effective. Many teachers have found that simply asking students to jot down what they liked about class at the end of the day is a useful indicator.

3. Videotape yourself in class, then watch the tape with the evaluation form that follows near at hand. If taping yourself is too distracting to your class, complete the form based on your recollection of the class. Try to fill out the form as soon as you can after the class you targeted is over so that you can have accurate information.

Figure 4.5

EVALUATE YOURSELF AS AN OBSERVER MIGHT

Rate your performance on each of these positive qualities by circling the number that best fits your assessment of your own skills in teaching a particular class. Use this scale:

1 = I had no problems.

2 = I only have a few problems.

3 = I really need to work on this skill.

1	2	3	I followed the district's curriculum.
1	2	3	I had objectives for the lesson.
1	2	3	I made the purpose of the lesson clear to my students.
1	2	3	I delivered accurate and appropriate information.
1	2	3	I showed a depth of understanding of the material.
1	2	3	I made use of all available class time.
1	2	3	I kept all of my students on task.
1	2	3	I provided for transition times between activities.
1	2	3	I used a variety of teaching strategies.
1	2	3	I demonstrated effective questioning skills.
1	2	3	I had an assessment instrument for the lesson.
1	2	3	I motivated my students to succeed.
1	2	3	I established the relevance of the lesson.
1	2	3	I provided timely feedback.
1	2	3	I monitored my students effectively.
1	2	3	I encouraged and assisted students.
1	2	3	I interacted in a positive way with my students.
1	2	3	I maintained an orderly classroom.
1	2	3	I minimized any disruptions.
1	2	3	I gave preferential seating to my students who require it.
1	2	3	I incorporated critical thinking activities in today's assignment.
1	2	3	I had classroom rules posted.
1	2	3	I enforced classroom rules.
1	2	3	I made sure that procedures for routine tasks are in place.
1	2	3	I delivered clear instructions.
1	2	3	I projected a professional image.

Develop a Plan to Correct Weaknesses

Now that you have begun the process of self-evaluation, it is not enough to just make yourself aware of your weaknesses. You must plan how to correct them. Here's how.

Step 1: Choose three of the areas that you intend to work on and list them on a sheet of paper or in your teacher's journal.

Step 2: Brainstorm as many ways as you can to improve these weaknesses. Remember that brainstorming works best when you keep generating ideas past obvious solutions.

Step 3: Let your list of ideas rest for a day or two while you mull over the solutions that appeal most to you.

Step 4: Go over your list again and decide on the steps that you need to take to correct your weaknesses. Write them down.

Step 5: Put the list in your teacher binder or in another conspicuous place so that your personal improvement plan is accessible.

ASK A COLLEAGUE TO OBSERVE YOU

Another evaluation technique that will improve your teaching performance is to ask a colleague to observe you. Tell the observer one or two specific problems that you know you have and ask that person to offer suggestions. Be prepared for the constructive criticism that will come your way. Don't be defensive, just be appreciative that someone would take the time to help you.

Whenever you have the opportunity to observe another teacher or to substitute in another teacher's classroom, you should take advantage of the chance to learn more about teaching and how other teachers are successful.

The Importance of Working Well with Colleagues

The largest group of people with whom you will have to learn to work well are your colleagues, which includes all of the adults in the building. One of the best ways to work well with others is to be a person on whom others can rely for help.

One of the most important facets of your professional reputation—one that you should establish as quickly as possible—is that you are a dependable teacher. Good teachers are known as the people upon whom other staff members can rely for big and small tasks. The rewards of this reputation are priceless.

5 Rules for Establishing a Reputation as a Dependable Educator

As a first-year teacher, there are many actions that you can take to establish a reputation as a dependable educator. Apply the following rules to your school situation and you will reap the benefits of a successful working relationship with your colleagues.

Rule 1: Develop professional relationships with your colleagues. Learn the roles that various people play in your school and how they contribute to the overall picture. By doing this you will be able to be supportive when they need your help.

Rule 2: Keep your promises. Because this is so important, be very careful not to make promises that you can't keep. It is very easy to become caught up in the enthusiasm of a moment and agree to something that you may regret later. Take your time and ease into your new responsibilities.

Rule 3: Make sure that your written work is neat and accurate. If you produce just one class newsletter that contains several misspelled words, your reputation is damaged, no matter how many accurate papers you produce the rest of the year.

Rule 4: Keep an attendance and punctuality record that you can be proud of. Let it be known that you are aiming for a perfect record.

Rule 5: When you are assigned to work in teams, on committees, or in informal groups, be the person who takes notes for the group. By doing this you will not only force yourself to pay attention, but you will also be confident that you know what to do and can share that information with others.

ALL STAFF MEMBERS ARE YOUR COLLEAGUES

As a new teacher you will have to learn many new faces and names as quickly as possible. While it is sensible to first learn the names of other teachers and administrators, it is a mistake to think that those are the only people in the building who are your colleagues.

A school community is composed of many different people in many different positions, and each of them deserves your cooperation and respect, because they all work toward the same goal that you do: the common good of all children in the school.

There is much that you can do to encourage a spirit of teamwork with your colleagues. Here is a brief list of just some of the actions that you can take right away to treat all staff members as colleagues.

➧ Find out the names of the support personnel in your school as quickly as possible. Greet each by name when you meet. Treat each person in the building with the same courtesy that you would like to receive.

◗ Encourage your students to respect the work of support personnel by modeling that respect yourself. Speak courteously to the cafeteria staff. Make sure your students leave their work area clean. Let them see you picking up bits of trash in the hall.

◗ Realize that if a work order you placed is not completed as quickly as you would like, it does not mean the custodial staff is ignoring your request. Requests for repairs have to be approved by several levels of administrators in many school districts. Be patient.

◗ *Never* make a disparaging comment about the work of support staff members around students. This courtesy means that you should go so far as to avoid making unkind remarks about the food served in the cafeteria, the media ordered by the school librarian, or the computer glitches that the technicians just can't solve quickly.

◗ Be as cooperative as possible. If a colleague is in a position to request that you hand in reports, grade sheets, attendance information, or other paperwork, respond promptly and accurately.

◗ Respect all your colleagues' time, equipment, and other resources. If the school secretary asks that you not tie up an outside line, even though you may have a very important phone call to make, respect that request.

◗ Over the course of your first year, spend a little bit of time learning about the duties of all of the people in your building. In your beginning years as a teacher, don't just focus on your teaching responsibilities; take time to understand the "big picture" of how schools work.

PROFESSIONAL BEHAVIOR AT MEETINGS

No matter how friendly and informal the atmosphere in your school, faculty meetings are serious business. If you've never had a job where staff meetings were routinely scheduled to work out problems or share information, adjusting to professional faculty meetings may be difficult for you at first. And while you may quickly become bored with information that you believe you have already heard many times, do not give in to the temptation to act on this feeling.

THE TEACHERS' LOUNGE

When you were a student, the teachers' lounge was probably a mystical place where your teachers vanished when you had recess or lunch. Your idea was not far from the truth. A teachers' lounge is a mystical place and teachers do vanish into it.

Because of economic measures and overcrowding, many newer schools don't have a special room where teachers can gather to eat, relax, and share information. If you are fortunate enough to work in a school with a teachers' lounge, take advantage of the opportunities it offers, but be sure to avoid its pitfalls.

Staff Meeting Etiquette

Here are a few rules for presenting a professional image at meetings.

- Be on time. Faculty meetings are not optional. Many administrators take attendance. Even if no one calls roll, you can be sure that your absence will be noted.

- If your school has a set time for meetings, mark them in advance on your calendar so that you can plan appointments around them.

- If you have to be absent, contact the person in charge of the meeting to let him or her know that you will not be there.

- Arrange for a friend to take notes and collect any handouts for you.

- Sit near the front and take notes. Make sure you bring along a paper and pen. Many experienced teachers take a spiral notebook or three-ring binder with them expressly for the purpose of recording meeting information.

- Pay attention to the speaker and follow along on your agenda. Do not chat while the speaker is leading the meeting. This is not only rude to the speaker and to the people around you who are trying to hear, but it marks you as a rude person to your colleagues.

- Even though you may have a tall stack of tests to grade, it is still rude to grade papers or do other paperwork in a meeting.

- Turn off your beeper or cell phone so that the meeting is not interrupted by ringing from your book bag.

A teachers' lounge offers a haven for teachers who want to take a break and still be in the company of others. In a lounge you can enjoy a rare opportunity to socialize with your colleagues during the school day. You can also share ideas and solicit suggestions for solutions to problems you may be having with your classes.

The pitfalls of a teachers' lounge involve two key areas: shared space and students. The shared space of a lounge is not for intense work requiring concentration and quiet unless everyone in the room agrees to this. If you are in a rush to grade some papers and do not want to be interrupted, the teachers' lounge is not the place to accomplish this. It is also not the place to share the intimate details of your weekend with a colleague who is also a close friend. If you want to talk over a personal matter, then you should do so in private, not within earshot of everyone else who may happen to be in the teachers' lounge.

"Find out about colleagues'—not your students'—lives and interests in the teachers' lounge."

—Barbara Knowles, 36 years experience

The second pitfall of a teachers' lounge involves student intrusions. Students should not be in the lounge. Do not send students to the lounge to collect papers that you left behind, or to purchase a snack, or for any reason. Respect the privacy of other teachers who may be there for a break from the demands of their students. You should also never discuss students in the lounge. This is an unprofessional practice.

A final caveat: Gossip of any kind—about other teachers and especially about students—is never acceptable in the lounge. Do not allow yourself to initiate or participate in this unprofessional practice.

> *"Do not gossip at work. Find a friend to confide in, but keep a positive attitude."*
>
> —Stephanie Mahoney, 24 years experience

WORKING WELL WITH DIFFICULT COLLEAGUES

People in all professions have to learn to deal with difficult colleagues, and teachers are no exception—even first-year teachers. Some of your colleagues may be so difficult to get along with that you find it very challenging to work with them.

Many people make up a school community. You may form close friendships with some, and never quite hit it off with others. To be a successful professional educator and part of an effective team, *you have to work well with every colleague*. This may not always be easy to accomplish.

The best guideline you can follow to work well with difficult colleagues is to recognize that you share a common goal: the education of the children entrusted to your care. With this common goal, you have little choice but to work well together, because the alternative could result in failure, for students and for you.

How to Maintain a Private Social Life

Watch what you reveal about yourself to your colleagues and to your students. If you are indiscreet about sharing details of your personal life, expect to have the details not only gossiped about in homes all over your school district, but wildly embellished. Be very careful what you reveal about yourself to your colleagues and even more so about what you reveal to your students.

Follow these guidelines to keep your social life private.

- It is not a sensible idea to purchase alcohol, tobacco products, or other very personal items in a place where you could run into your students, their family members, or unsympathetic colleagues.

- If you eat out in a restaurant, limit your alcohol intake. In fact, to avoid hearing rumors of how you were publicly intoxicated, avoid purchasing alcohol in places where you could meet someone connected to your school.

- Avoid sharing too much information about your personal life at work. It is one thing for your colleagues to learn that you have a new puppy; it is quite another for you to tell about how the puppy accompanied you and your new boyfriend on a romantic weekend adventure.

Tips for Working with Difficult Colleagues

The following tips will help you learn to work well with colleagues you find difficult.

- Don't rush to judgment. If you meet someone at the start of the term, you are most certainly meeting a colleague with too much to do and who is significantly stressed as a result. Be patient and wait until you know the person better before making a judgment.
- Look for the good traits in your colleagues. Just as everyone has irritating personality quirks, so do they have appealing ones. Be on the lookout for these positive traits in everyone you work with.
- Do not gossip about a person you find difficult. If you are really unsure of what course of action to take with a difficult person, quietly and privately ask a close colleague or a mentor for advice.
- The best way to handle a colleague who is a bully is to use the same technique you probably learned in grade school: Stand up for yourself. Don't try to argue with a bully, just make your point firmly.
- Negative people are that way for many reasons. The chief harm that they may do is encourage you to be negative, too. Because it is almost impossible to cheer up people who are determined to be negative, avoid them.
- Make sure that you are not one of the difficult people in your school! Listen more than you talk and be as tolerant of others as you can.
- Realize that you can't always avoid every colleague whom you find difficult. Keep your common goal of educating students in mind and you will find it easier and worth the effort to learn to not just cope, but work well, with everyone.

- Do not make personal phone calls or send personal e-mails at school. The phone calls may be overheard and school e-mail is not private.
- If you decide to date a staff member, keep your relationship as private as possible. Your students should have absolutely no idea that you are involved with a fellow staff member.
- The less you say about the details of your personal life to your students, the better. Instead, model acceptable and mature behavior. Before you reveal anything about your personal life, ask yourself, "Would I be comfortable revealing this if a school board member were in the room?"

"Keep time for yourself and your family. Exercise at least three times a week. You will need this time for your brain to function at its best. You will also need plenty of sleep and a good diet."

—Stephanie Mahoney, 24 years experience

Working Well with Parents and Guardians

All parents have the right to remain informed about their child's behavioral and academic progress. Not only is it their right, but you will find that your job will be much easier when you take a teamwork approach with your students' parents and guardians. They can be enormously helpful to you. After all, these are the people who know more about your students than anyone else. And these are also the people who want their children to be successful and look to you for help in achieving this success.

Without a doubt, parental support has a major impact on students' attitudes about school. When students know that the important adults in their lives present a united front, then they are less likely to misbehave and more likely to strive for success. It is your responsibility to reach out first to your students' parents. Although this means extra demands on your time, this is time that is well spent. Always remember to treat parents with careful respect even if you disagree with their opinions and how they express their concern for their children. Working well with the parents and guardians of your students is simply good sense if you want to create a positive learning climate in your classrooms. If you make the effort to work successfully with the parents and guardians of your students, you will find them more willing to support you as you work with their children.

HOW TO FOSTER A TEAM APPROACH WITH PARENTS AND GUARDIANS

Follow these suggestions to create a strong connection with the significant adults in your students' lives.

- Be careful to make the first contact with your students' parents and to make that first contact a positive one. A good example of an initial contact would be to send home a letter containing information that they need to know in order to help their children adjust to school. (You can find a sample letter later in this section.)

- If there is a crisis in a student's family, express your concern and offer what assistance you can. For example, if there is a death in the family, send a condolence note.

- Encourage parents to drop by your classroom often. They could volunteer or be guest speakers.

- Some experienced teachers send out monthly newsletters or have a web page for their class. You could involve parents in both of these projects.

- Take the time to make positive phone calls at the start of the term. Send home positive news as often as you can. Parents who hear good news from you will be more willing to work with you when a problem develops.

- Return phone calls to parents or guardians as soon as possible. Make it a rule to call within twenty-four hours.

- Take the time to be a good listener when you talk with parents. Together you can work out many problems while they are still small ones.

- When you talk with parents, realize that their own past negative experiences with school may affect their perception of you. Be as positive and professional as possible to help them overcome their negative feelings.

- Don't give out your home phone number. Keep your relationship with parents on a businesslike and professional level. You have a right to protect your privacy at home.

- Notify parents and guardians as soon as you begin to notice a problem developing. Many parents complain that teachers wait too late to call.

- When you call parents at work, ask if they have a moment to talk instead of just plunging in with an account of the problem. This small courtesy will enable them to focus on the conversation with you.

- Avoid becoming confrontational with parents even when they are unpleasant and confrontational with you. Continue to show your concern and caring.

- Never discuss another person's child with a parent. This violates the child's privacy and is unprofessional.

- It is acceptable to compliment the parents or guardians of a child to other people and you should feel free to do this; however, it is not acceptable to criticize them.

10 Ways to Be Positive with Parents and Guardians

1. Call at the start of the term to relate a positive message.

2. Send home positive updates as often as you can. (You can find a sample later in this section.)

3. Have parents sign papers with good grades as well as bad ones.

4. Create a newsletter to relate the good things that happen in your class.

5. Compliment parents to other people. Don't hesitate to let students know that you think highly of their parents.

6. Make it a habit to thank the parents and guardians of your students whenever you see them.

7. Call or e-mail with good news.

8. If you have school voice mail, record a positive message to parents and guardians.

9. Hold a "Thank-a-Parent Day" at your school and encourage students to join in.

10. Send home a thank-you note after a conference.

THE FIRST CONTACT: OPEN HOUSE

Your school district will probably arrange several opportunities for parents and teachers to meet during the course of the school year. You may have a "Meet Your Teacher Day" before school starts so that parents and students can introduce themselves to you. Often some parents may just stop by your classroom to introduce themselves, especially at the start of the term or if their children have special needs.

While these opportunities are helpful to students, parents, and teachers who want to work well together, they don't have the impact of the "Open House." Open House is the time when parents can come to school and meet the teachers that they have been hearing about since the term began. In some places this event is referred to as "Back to School Night." No matter which term your district uses, this meeting can generate lots of good will for you all year long.

Open House can be stressful for teachers. You will have much to do in preparation and you will be on display for several hours. Both of these can be exhausting when you consider that they must be accomplished at night after you have already put in a long day. However stressed you may feel about Open House, it is your chance to really connect with parents and guardians in a positive and professional way. It is a good way to build a strong team of support for your students and an excellent opportunity to generate the good will that will sustain you in the days ahead, particularly when some of your students will need extra help and guidance from you and from their parents.

A Few General Guidelines

▶ At the open house you should expect to meet many parents or guardians. The number will vary with your school population and how successfully your school district has advertised the event.

▶ You will have to give a brief presentation that should be ten to fifteen minutes long.

▶ You must avoid talking about specific students and their concerns; instead, you will have to set up appointments for later times for those parents who want to discuss their children or your class policies or procedures in more detail.

How to Prepare

▶ Clean up your classroom! Parents and guardians want to see a spotless room that shows that you are a well-organized professional who is in control of your environment. You may not be able to do anything about graffiti from previous years, but you should make the room as attractive and clean as possible.

▶ Plan and practice your presentation. Rehearse what you are going to say. This is not the time to try your skill at "winging it."

▶ Start collecting student work on the first day of class and display it on the walls of your classroom. Parents expect to see their child's work on display, no matter how old the child is. You can find more information about displaying student work in Section Three and in Section Five.

▶ Take photos of your students as they work. If you use a digital camera, you can run a continuous computer slide show or Power Point presentation featuring your students.

▶ Use the overhead projector to display your rules and procedures. You could even cover the main points of your presentation in an overhead transparency or on the board.

▶ If you have the technical skill and the equipment, videotape your students at work. Edit the tape so that it is brief and interesting.

- You could also have samples of student work saved on disk so that parents can access it during Open House.

- Prepare a handout with general information about the course, homework, important dates, your policies, and contact information.

- Have copies of the text available.

- Prepare a sign-up sheet for conferences and place it near the door. Make a column for the student's name as well as one for adults so you will know which child's parents you will be seeing at the time of the conference.

- Dress in your professional best so as to present yourself as a competent professional educator.

What to Include in Your Presentation

- Tell parents what general topics you will cover in class before the end of the term. Give a quick overview so that parents will not be surprised about what their child is learning.

- Explain your class rules, policies, and procedures.

- Inform parents of any major projects and approximately when they will be assigned. Parents and guardians should have advance warning about projects such as major term papers, class trips, or science fairs.

- Ask for parents' support and for them to contact you if a problem arises. Make sure you give out your voice mail, e-mail, and school phone numbers. Avoid giving out your personal e-mail address or phone number.

Present a Professional Image

- Meet parents and guardians at the door. Show them to their seats. Pleasantly greet any latecomers.

- Begin your presentation promptly.

- Be upbeat, enthusiastic, and very positive.

- Do not mention specific students. If parents try to talk with you about specific concerns regarding their children, arrange a conference for a later time. The purpose of Open House is to present yourself and your class to a wide audience, not hold a parent conference.

- Be very careful not to mention problems that you are having with specific students. Protect their privacy and do not embarrass their parents and guardians.

- Plan to run out of time. Create a presentation that will last the entire time that you have to speak. If you open the floor for questions, you can run into a sticky situation where parents can attack you for reasons that you may not be prepared to defend in a large group.

Plan for a Successful Open House

One Week in Advance
- Send home Open House announcements
- Display student work
- Begin preparing presentation
- Make up handouts
- Photocopy handouts

Three Days Before
- Make up computer presentation
- Create transparencies
- Make up sign-in sheet

Two Days Before
- Begin practicing presentation

One Day Before
- Practice again—you can't be polished enough
- Begin straightening room
- Get enough rest for the long day tomorrow

On the Day of Open House
- Dress professionally
- Adopt a positive attitude
- Tidy the classroom one final time
- Make sure all equipment is working
- Put sign-in sheet near the door with a pencil nearby
- Have textbooks and handouts out

BECOME A GOOD LISTENER

To build good working relationships with your students' parents and guardians, it is important that you develop good listening skills. Try these simple but very effective suggestions for improving your listening skills and you will reap the benefits of improved communications.

- ▶ Stop talking. Allow the other person to speak without fear of interruption from you.

- ▶ Give non-verbal cues that indicate that you are paying attention. Nod your head, look the person in the eye, lean forward in your seat, or prompt with questions.

- ▶ Jot notes so that you can recall what is being said. Before you begin, tell the other person that you are going to do this to help you recall the conversation.

- ▶ Make sure that you fully understand what the other person says by asking for clarification. Say, "I am not sure I understand what you are saying. Do you mean. . . ?" or "I think I hear you saying . . ."

ASSISTING PARENTS AND GUARDIANS WHO DON'T SPEAK ENGLISH

At some point in your career, whether you teach in a very small town or in a large city, you will have to communicate with parents or guardians whose primary language is not English. This situation can be awkward and confusing for everyone if you are not prepared to offer assistance. Although it is likely that your school district became aware of the situation when the student enrolled and made efforts to provide assistance, there may be situations in which there are no other speakers of that language in your area who are also proficient in English, then it is up to you to find a way to communicate effectively.

One solution is to have the student translate. This is effective if the child is trustworthy and old enough to handle the task. Another solution is to involve an older sibling of the student if that person is also up to the task and responsible.

You can also access the world of technology for help with this problem. There are many Internet sites available to help you translate what you need to communicate to parents and guardians. Some are so helpful that you can type in what you want to say and it will be immediately translated into another language. Of course, you need to avoid slang expressions and other idioms that would be confusing when translated literally into another language. Two sites that you may find helpful in assisting parents or guardians who don't speak English are www.systran.aol.com and www.rivendel.com.

GRACEFUL ACCIDENTAL MEETINGS

There are few situations as awkward as making a quick trip to the grocery store dressed in your rattiest clothes and hearing, "Look mom, there's my teacher!" Or to be on the beach in your cute new bathing suit and hear, "Do you remember me? We met at my son's Open House." The collision between your personal life and your professional life can be unsettling. How can you handle such meetings gracefully? Try these suggestions.

- Be friendly and poised. Act glad to see the parent.
- Make the necessary introductions of friends who may be accompanying you. Try to avoid introducing your friends by the role they play in your life. For example, instead of, "This is my girlfriend, Jill Smith," simply say, "This is Jill Smith."
- Keep the meeting friendly and brief. Move on as quickly as you can without appearing desperate to get away.
- School business should not be discussed in public places where others can overhear your conversation. Instead, arrange another time to discuss specific concerns.
- If you are in a potentially embarrassing situation—with a grocery cart full of beer when you suddenly realize that the PTA president is ahead of you in the checkout line, for example—be prepared for the embarrassment that you will feel. You should also brace yourself for the potentially damaging gossip that will result.
- The best way to keep accidental meetings as graceful as possible is to avoid situations that could make you appear less than professional in public.

The Importance of Keeping Contact Records

By now you are probably convinced that you will spend all of your free hours at school documenting something that you took for granted in your own student days. There are forms for just about every interaction that you will have with your students, and all of them need to be filled out accurately.

It is just sensible to keep accurate records of when you have contacted the parents and guardians of your students. At some point in any education career, even the very best teacher can be called on to provide proof that he or she did all that could be done to help a particular student. Every year there are countless cases where frustrated parents sue teachers in an attempt to find a simple cause for a complex problem. Although it may be

Figure 4.6

DOCUMENTATION RECORD: CONTACT LOG

Student_____ Parent_____

Date and time of contact_____

Person who initiated the contact _____

Type of contact:

_____ Phone call   _____ Note home

_____ Letter   _____ Home visit

_____ E-mail   _____ Detention notice

_____ Open House/Meet the Teacher   _____ Informal meeting

_____ Meeting with administrator   _____ Other: _____

_____ Meeting with counselor

Topics discussed:

_____

_____

_____

Steps parent will take:

_____

_____

_____

Steps teacher will take:

_____

_____

_____

Additional notes:

_____

_____

_____

"When you write home to parents, keep it short. Exclude your emotions but include your concerns. Emphasis should be placed on your desire to be helpful. You may be the first person who has offered to help."

—Kim Marie Hogan, 9 years experience

upsetting to think that this could happen to a dedicated teacher, it does happen.

Fortunately, you can begin to protect yourself with just a few minutes of planning and paperwork. You can enhance your professional reputation and provide proof quickly when an administrator asks for proof that you have contacted parents as often as you should.

Keeping a record of parent contacts does not have to be time-consuming. Photocopy or modify the sample documentation form on page 111 and keep plenty on hand so that you can fill out one each time you contact a student's parent or guardian. Fill out the form and file it in a folder or binder with the other paperwork that you have for that student.

MAKE A GOOD IMPRESSION WITH EFFECTIVE CORRESPONDENCE

If you thought that your English teachers in high school were quick to catch your grammatical errors, you have not yet experienced the embarrassment of sending home a note with a misspelled word. With a bit of careful effort, you can spare yourself this humiliation.

When you send home a note, e-mail, or letter, it represents your effectiveness as a teacher to the people who receive it. The correspondence you send home should be businesslike. It should reflect your professional competence and expertise.

Follow these suggestions for making a good impression with effective correspondence.

- When e-mailing, before going into detail about an incident at school, consider phoning the parent instead. Much confusion can be cleared up quickly with a friendly phone call.

- Make sure that what you write in a letter is accurate. Verify the dates, times, and other details before you make photocopies for everyone to take home.

- Be brief, but not brusque. Cover your points quickly. Use bulleted lists or other businesslike writing techniques to make you letters easy to follow.

- Appearance counts! Photocopy with clean edges and with enough ink or toner to make clean and clear copies. Avoid cute graphics or unusual fonts whenever you can. Use letterhead stationary.

- Grammar and word usage matters a great deal in letters home. Have a colleague proofread your correspondence before you send it out.

- When you send home handwritten notes, write legibly. Use a dark ink for readability and take the time to proofread your work.

- Never give in to the temptation to fire off an angry e-mail or send a hasty note home. Cool off before you contact a parent.

In the next few pages you will find several samples of letters that you can adapt for your own situation so that the letters that you send home are as professional as possible.

Figure 4.7
Sample Letter: Introduce Yourself

Dear Parents and Guardians,

With this letter I would like to introduce myself as your child's English teacher this year. I am originally from Southwest Virginia and I graduated from Virginia Tech.

On September 23, I would like to welcome you to the PTSA Back-to-School night. I am looking forward to meeting you and showing you our texts and classroom. Please attend if you have the opportunity to do so.

This year will be an exciting one for my students and me. We will study literature, usage, grammar, study skills, vocabulary, and writing. I have planned many activities that I hope will encourage my students to succeed.

Many parents ask about homework assignments. While there may be times when long-term assignments will take lots of time, there is a routine that I try to follow as closely as possible to insure that students benefit from their homework assignments. You can expect to see your students doing homework for this class every night from Monday through Thursday. I try to avoid assigning homework on weekends. The assignments are listed on the syllabus that students are required to keep in their notebooks.

If you have any questions or if any problems arise, please contact me at school. The number is 555-2400. I will be glad to speak with you if you just give me a call or send in a note.

I look forward to working with your child this year. I also look forward to meeting you and learning how I might be of assistance to you and your child.

Sincerely,
Ms. Thompson

Figure 4.8
SAMPLE LETTER: OPEN HOUSE INVITATION

Dear Parents and Guardians,

Our school's annual Open House will be held this year on Thursday, September 22 from 7:00 until 8:30 p.m. We will meet first in the auditorium for a brief PTA meeting and then will adjourn to the classrooms.

I am looking forward to visiting with you and sharing some of our class's routines and activities. Please attend if you can possibly do so.

Please let me know if you plan to attend by signing the appropriate note at the bottom of this sheet.

I am looking forward to our visit!

Sincerely,

Ms. Thompson

_____ I plan to attend Open House on Thursday, September 22 from 7:00 until 8:30 p.m.

_____ I do not plan to attend Open House on September 22 from 7:00 until 8:30 p.m.

Parent or Guardian Signature: _____

Figure 4.9
SAMPLE LETTER: CONFERENCE CONFIRMATION

(Although you have probably arranged a conference over the phone, it is polite to send home a letter as a reminder with special information that may make the parent or guardian more at ease.)

Dear _____,

Our conference will be Wednesday, May 13, at 3:15 in Room 16. You will find plenty of visitor parking places in the parking lot directly in front of the school at that time. Please stop by the front office and pick up a visitor's pass.

The office staff will call me and I will come and escort you to the classroom. I look forward to meeting with you.

Sincerely,

Ms. Thompson

Figure 4.10

SAMPLE LETTER: POSITIVE POSTALS

(Although you may have other formats to choose from to notify parents of student achievements, it is best to keep them simple. Adapt this format to your own situation. You could brighten it with a colorful graphic or you could even personalize it by using your computer graphics skills.)

To the Parents or Guardians of _____:

    I am writing to let you know how pleased I am with your child's recent success in my class. You will be proud to know that_____

_____

_____

    I know you are as proud of this effort and achievement as I am. Thank you for your support.

                       Sincerely,

                       Ms. Thompson

MAKE TELEPHONE CALLS WITH CONFIDENCE

Phoning parents when there is a problem is one of the most unpleasant tasks that teachers face. Even experienced teachers can dread the occasional angry parent who makes phoning home a negative and upsetting experience. However, as disagreeable as this task can be, phoning a parent or guardian is a necessary and often helpful action. There are several strategies that you can adopt to make phoning parents easier. Follow some of these suggestions to make this a manageable task.

- Use the contact information that you have collected from your students early in the term to save time searching database records in the office.
- Plan what you want to say and what information the parent needs to know in order to work together to solve the problem.
- Take a pen and the notes that you have made about the situation with you.
- Find a phone at school where you can make the call with at least some privacy and with a chance that you won't be interrupted.
- Don't hesitate to call a parent at work. If you do, be very careful not to reveal too many details to the parent's colleagues. Protecting their privacy is a good way to help parents be cooperative when you ask for their help.
- If you do call while parents are at work, begin the conversation by asking, "Do you have a few minutes right now?" so that they can set their work aside long enough to really listen to you.

115

▶ Keep in mind that the purpose of the phone call is not for you to vent your frustration on the parent, but rather, to solve a problem by working together.

▶ Begin with a positive statement about the student and express that you would like to enlist their help in solving a problem, "I had a problem with Jim today and wonder if you could help me?"

▶ Be very specific about the problem. Don't just say, "Jim is acting odd today." Try, "Jim laughed out loud six times at inappropriate moments today and fell asleep right before lunch."

▶ Next, state what you have done to correct the problem. Be very specific again and give the result of your actions.

▶ Ask for their help. Listen while parents explain what they know about the situation. Make sure that you listen carefully and clarify any point that you do not understand.

▶ Never lose sight of the fact that you and the parent are *working together* to solve the problem. A teamwork approach to solving the problem is the best one to take.

▶ Finish the call with a positive statement expressing your appreciation and your confidence that a solution has been devised.

▶ Before you go on to your next task, complete a contact log sheet about the phone call so that you have a record of the conversation and what each party decided to do.

> *"Thank parents. Praise parents loudly and sincerely whenever you see them around school."*
>
> —Kim Marie Hogan, 9 years experience

Conduct a Successful Conference

Parent conferences can produce high-level anxiety for everyone involved: students, parents, and teachers. In spite of the anxiety they produce, face-to-face meetings are a very effective way to solve problems.

Teachers who want to communicate well with parents or guardians realize that parents want to be reassured that their child is doing well and can succeed in school. Even though this may not be what is happening at the moment, parents want teachers to work with them to help their children. Making a strong connection with your students' parents and guardians is achievable if you make sure that your goals for a conference are clear. There are five goals you should have for every conference.

1. You should present yourself to your students' parents as a friendly and knowledgeable teacher who has the child's best interests at heart.

2. You should strive to create an atmosphere of cooperation, support, and teamwork.

3. Parents should leave a conference with all of their questions answered and all of the points that they wanted to discuss covered.

4. Both parties should have a sense of mutual respect and an understanding of each other's problems and viewpoints.

5. A workable solution to the problem should be agreed upon and everyone involved should agree to work together to help the student.

> *"When a parent requests a conference, allow the parent to begin with the answer to your question: 'How can we help you and your child?' "*
>
> —Barbara Knowles, 36 years experience

Actions You Should Take . . .
. . . <u>Before</u> a Conference

- Make sure you have a clear purpose for the conference and a clear understanding of the outcome that you would like.
- Plan the points you want to cover. Write them down.
- Gather samples of student work or other evidence that you would like to show parents in the conference. Include progress reports and other information related to grades.
- Make sure that you review a student's cumulative record and report card information to avoid any unpleasant surprises.
- Make a rough estimate of the student's strengths and weaknesses as well as any other special information that you would like to present.
- Anticipate a parent's reactions and questions and jot down notes to answers that you may be too nervous to recall in the conference.
- Create a seating arrangement that will be comfortable for adults. Arrange chairs around a table or desks large enough for adults in a circle. Do not sit behind your desk.
- Make sure you have pen and paper for yourself and for parents.
- Mentally draft an agenda.
- Make sure you remain calm before, during, and after the conference. Nothing will be gained if you lose your cool.
- Make a neat "Do Not Disturb" sign and post it on your door so that you and the parents can meet without distractions.
- Meet parents and escort them to your room.

. . . **During** a Conference

- Be prompt and prepared to begin. Do not make parents and guardians wait while you shuffle papers.
- Begin by expressing your appreciation for the fact that the parents came to the conference. Try to establish a tone of goodwill and friendly cooperation as quickly as you can.
- Use language that will make parents comfortable. Do not use educational jargon.
- Begin with positive remarks about the child. Talk about the student's aptitude, special talents, improvements, and potential. Focus on strengths even if the problem is a serious conduct one. Never lose sight of the fact that the child is very important to the parents.
- Convey the attitude that the child's welfare is your primary concern.
- State the problem in simple, factual terms and express your desire to work together for a successful resolution.
- Discuss specific examples of the problem. Show examples of work that illustrates it, or give details of behavior situations.
- Always allow upset or angry parents to speak first. After parents have had the opportunity to say all of the things that they planned while they were driving to the conference, then and only then, can they listen to what you have to say or begin to work on a solution to the problem.
- If this is a problem that you have discussed before, let the parents know of any improvement.
- Be sure to state what you have done to correct the situation.
- Listen! If you want to solve the problem, give them your full attention throughout the entire conference. Your non-verbal language is crucial for success. Be friendly and attentive.
- End the conference gracefully by recapping the points that you have covered.
- Determine what you will do to follow up on the conference and keep in contact with them.
- Express appreciation again for their concern and the time that they have spent with you in the conference.

. . . **After** a Conference

Immediately complete your notes and the documentary evidence of what was discussed and the decisions that were made. Spend enough time on this so that your records are complete. Should you need to refer to this material later, you may not remember details accurately if your notes are not complete.

7 Conference <u>Don'ts</u>

1. Don't put parents on the defensive by becoming angry or by asking questions that are too personal.

2. Don't talk about other students or compare their child to theirs.

3. Don't try to outtalk parents. You may make your point, but the parents will not listen to you. Do not give in to the temptation to interrupt.

4. Don't forget to document the conference and to file your notes.

5. Don't neglect to follow through on the decisions that you and the parents made.

6. Don't divulge any confidential information that you have learned.

When Parents or Guardians Are Uncooperative

Sometimes no matter how hard you try, parents or guardians will not be as cooperative as you would like. Sometimes this will be a result of your interactions with them, and at other times, the lack of cooperation will have nothing to do with you. Regardless of the reason, it is unpleasant to deal with uncooperative parents or guardians.

The best way to avoid this situation is to prevent it by intervening early, following procedures and rules, maintaining accurate records, presenting yourself as a professional, and by making sure that parents are kept informed about their child's progress from the beginning of the year onward.

If you find yourself in a confrontation with a hostile parent, it is up to you to assume control of the situation. The following are some steps that you can take to accomplish this successfully so meetings with parents will result in productive outcomes instead of heated words.

▶ Listen to what angry parents or guardians have to say without trying to interrupt or correct them. Don't try to present your side of the disagreement until they have had an opportunity to express themselves.

▶ Show your interest by asking questions about specific details. Often a misunderstanding is the cause of the problem. Find out exactly what is bothering the parents.

▶ Make sure that you restate the problem so that the other person can be reassured that you do understand. Try, "I think you're saying . . ."

▶ Explain the problem from your viewpoint as objectively as you can. Be specific about what was expected of the child, what the child did that was not appropriate, and how you responded.

▶ Make it clear throughout the confrontation that you want to work together for the child's welfare.

➧ Remain calm throughout the confrontation. It can only harm you in the eyes of the parents and your supervisors if you act upon your natural desire to justify your actions in a loud tone or by returning insults.

➧ You do not have to accept threats or abuse from a parent. If, after you have sincerely tried to solve a problem, the parent or guardians remain upset, suggest that you call in an administrator.

➧ If you suspect that a parent plans to contact an administrator, you should make the contact first. It is never wise to surprise your supervisors with bad news. Instead, see an administrator, present your point of view, and ask for assistance.

Journal Entries to Help You Become a Valuable Team Player

➧ Are you a trustworthy faculty member? Explore ways in which you can enhance this attribute.

➧ Who among your peers supports your growth as a teacher? In what ways can you benefit from this support?

➧ What is the best piece of advice about education you have ever received? Explore ways in which you apply this in your role as an educator.

➧ What keeps you from listening? How does this affect your role as a teacher? What steps can you take to become a better listener?

➧ What strengths have you developed as a teacher? What strengths have you observed in your colleagues? How can you learn from them?

➧ As a first-year teacher, it is often difficult to fit into the school environment. What roles do you play in that environment right now? What roles can you anticipate that you will play in the future?

➧ What are some of the contributions that you make to your school? What do you add to a friendly and professional atmosphere? What contributions can you make in the future? How will you go about this?

➧ What are some of the negative comments that you have heard in an evaluation conference? How can you benefit from those comments? How do you plan to use constructive criticism to improve how you teach?

➧ What emotions do you feel before a parent conference? What emotions do you imagine that the parents feel? How do you imagine students feel? How can you deal with those emotions successfully so that everyone benefits?

➧ What unexpected courtesies have you noticed at school lately? What problems could these courtesies have prevented? How can you add unexpected courtesies to your school environment?

Connect with Your Students

The room was packed. He had chosen this workshop because of its title: "How to Connect with Your Students." Apparently, there were plenty of other teachers who wanted to know how to do this, too.

The first exercise that the workshop leaders had assigned was pretty easy. They had asked the workshop participants to write down the name of a teacher who had been important to them. He didn't have any problem selecting his high school physics teacher, Mr. Green.

The next exercise was not as easy. He had to write down a complete description of what the relationship between Mr. Green and his class had been. He hadn't really thought about that class in terms of a relationship between teacher and student before. Still, with some thought, he was able to do this exercise, too.

The third exercise was much more difficult. The workshop leaders had asked him to list the specific techniques that Mr. Green had used to connect with his students. Techniques? He had thought that somehow it was a natural connection, just like making friends with someone, and that Mr. Green was just charismatic, a natural.

The idea that Mr. Green had used certain techniques to reach his students was odd. But, now that he thought of it, the idea did make sense. He had just never realized that a good relationship with his students was something that would require work.

Still, he wanted to have a good relationship with his students. What teacher wouldn't? The idea that there were specific things that he could do to bring this about was appealing. It somehow took the mystery out of teaching.

School boards everywhere seem to be dealing with many of the same problems: over-crowded classes, out-of-date equipment, and school repairs, to name a few. As important and as unpleasant as these problems can be, very few teachers leave the profession because of them.

You are far more likely to feel stress caused by the fallout from a poor relationship with your students than you are from any other cause. Many factors can negatively affect this relationship, but only you can make sure that it is a viable one. As the adult in the classroom, you are in charge of making sure that each of your students feels connected to you. This connection must be a strong one if you and your students are to have a successful school term.

You will have to be the one who builds the bridge, who reaches out to your students, who inspires them to do their best. A successful relationship with your students will be just like the other meaningful relationships in your life: it will require patience, work, and commitment.

What Your Relationship with Your Students Should Be

As a first-year teacher, you may struggle to determine the relationship that you want to have with your students. How friendly should you be? What if your students don't like you? What if they won't listen to you? How strict is too strict?

As a teacher, you are responsible for just about everything that can happen in a class. You will determine the relationship that you have with each student. While this is a daunting responsibility, it is also empowering. If the type of relationship you have with your class is under your control, then you can make it a strong bond. This will require deliberate planning on your part.

A strong relationship with your students will require that you develop several characteristics that inspiring teachers have in common. Here is a brief description of five characteristics that teachers with healthy relationships with their students share, and that you will need to develop. You will find a few blank lines below each one to jot down the ideas that you have for how you can develop this characteristic for yourself.

> *"Students need adult listeners. They need direction. Like them because they often don't like themselves."*
>
> —Barbara Knowles, 36 years experience

1. **You should show that you care about your students.** Your students want you to like them and to approve of them even when they misbehave. Sometimes it is easy to lose sight of this very human need when you have so many demands on your time. It is crucial that your students feel that they are important to you and that you care about their well being. Get to know them as people as well as pupils you have to instruct. Don't be afraid to let your students know that you are interested in what they think and feel.

_____

_____

_____

2. **You should have a thorough knowledge of your subject matter.** Knowing your subject matter may not seem to have much to do with developing a successful relationship with your students, but it does. If you are not prepared for class, you will be focused on what you don't know instead of what your students need to know. The worst result of a faulty knowledge of your subject matter is that your students will lose respect for you and will not trust your judgment. Make sure that you are prepared for class each day.

_____
_____
_____

3. **You should take command of the class.** If you do not assume the leadership role in your class, others will. Often there will be a continuing struggle as students try to dominate each other. While you should not be overbearing, your students need for you to be in command of the class. You can and should allow your students as many options and as strong a voice in the class as possible, but never lose sight of your role as the classroom leader. Your students won't.

_____
_____
_____

4. **You should act in a mature manner all of the time.** This doesn't mean that you can't enjoy your students and have fun with them; however, if having fun with your students means indulging in playful insults, then you are not acting in a mature manner. Here are a few of the other immature behaviors that will destroy your relationship with your students.

- Being sarcastic
- Losing your temper
- Not being truthful
- Being unprepared for class

- Ignoring students
- Playing favorites
- Allowing students to bully each other

_____
_____
_____

5. **You should maintain a certain emotional distance between yourself and your students.** Being a teacher is much more than being a friend to your students. They have peers for friends. You are a teacher and not a peer. Good teachers know that they will be better able to help all of their students if they see themselves as their students' teachers instead of friends. The emotional distance that you keep between yourself and your students will enable you to make choices based on what students need instead of what they want.

_____
_____
_____

How Much of Yourself Should You Share?

"Do you smoke?"
"What kind of beer do you like?"
"What's your real hair color?"

It's only natural that your students will be curious about you. After the first few days of school, they will become comfortable enough around you to ask personal questions. Because they are young, your students, even if you teach seniors, do not always know what is appropriate to ask and what is not.

While you should not answer every personal question that your students ask, you will need to be prepared to handle them with tact. Your response to personal questions will help determine the type of relationship you will have with your students, their families, and with your colleagues.

Keep in mind that, in general, your students will only know what you tell them about yourself. To help you determine if information that you are tempted to reveal is appropriate ask yourself these two questions:

1. Would I be comfortable revealing this information to a class if the principal or another administrator were present?

2. Would I be comfortable revealing this information in front of my students' parents or guardians?

If the answer to either of these questions is "no," then be prepared with appropriate responses to possible student questions so that you won't be taken by surprise.

Here are a few other pointers to help you reveal only what you want your students to know about you.

Plan how you will answer student questions. It's not easy to deflect student interest, so you will have to think carefully about what you want to reveal about your personal life. You can expect to be quizzed on a variety of issues, so you will have to prepare what you want to say when they ask. If you can plan what you want to reveal about each topic before your students ask, then you won't be caught off guard. Remember to be careful not to lie to your students. Here are a few areas of your personal life that you can expect your students to be curious about.

Your social life	What you do in your free time
Where you live	Your pets
Who you live with	Your family
The kind of car you drive	What you think of other teachers

Forestall questions by giving some information out in advance. Your students should see your human side. If you share some innocuous information about yourself with your students, you will curb their curiosity and they will be less tempted to pry. For example, at the beginning of the year, you should tell your students about where you went to college and how hard you had to study. Or, you can tell them about your family while asking about theirs. By offering information in advance, you can build on your common interests and prevent them from asking questions that are too personal at the same time.

Let your answers show that you are serious about teaching. There are many ways to answer questions that will not only discourage unwanted curiosity, but also encourage your students to see you as a serious teacher. Here are two examples of answers that will satisfy student curiosity and promote good citizenship at the same time.

Instead of . . .	Say . . .
"I was always bad at math in school."	"I had to work hard to do well in my math classes. You should stay for tutoring. It helped me."
"Yes, I smoke."	"You know, I hate to see kids your age start that bad habit. It's against the law for under-aged people to smoke, too.

Keep students too busy to ask personal questions. Another technique that experienced teachers have found valuable in limiting the information that they reveal about themselves is to structure class in such a way that there is little free time for unstructured questions. If your students are busily engaged in learning all period long, then they will not have time to speculate more than necessary about your personal life.

What's Appropriate and What's Not?

Below is a list of personal topics that your students may want to know about you. As you read the list, put a check in the box beside the ones that you believe are appropriate for teachers to share with their students.

You can use the key on the next page to check your responses.

You can feel comfortable telling students about:

☐ 1. Your favorite sports
☐ 2. Your favorite candidate in the next election
☐ 3. Your serious romantic relationships
☐ 4. Your favorite book
☐ 5. Your public speaking fears
☐ 6. Your sinus headache
☐ 7. Your home phone number
☐ 8. Your problems with certain subjects in school
☐ 9. Your birthday
☐ 10. Your alma mater
☐ 11. Your favorite color
☐ 12. Your disagreements with another faculty member
☐ 13. Your vacation plans
☐ 14. Your pet's name
☐ 15. Your favorite music

Key

1. It is acceptable to let students know your favorite sports. This could be an interest you share.

2. You should not reveal your personal political views. Your students, no matter how sophisticated, will be influenced by what you say. Be unbiased. If pressed, you can remind students that ballots are secret.

3. You should not discuss your romantic life with your students. Would you be comfortable revealing this to students if an administrator were present?

4. You should reveal what you like to read. Students need good role models who encourage them to develop good habits such as reading for pleasure.

5. You should reveal that public speaking is something that makes you nervous only if you also can reveal the ways that you deal successfully with this problem. Knowing the tips that their teacher uses to fight stage fright will encourage your shy students.

6. You should tell your students if you do not feel well. This will prevent them from misinterpreting your behavior. You can also ask for extra support and understanding. Most of your students will want to help you.

7. You should not reveal your home phone number. You should keep your private life separate from your professional life. If you have e-mail at school or a voice mail there, offer it instead.

8. You should talk about your own problems in school only if you can help students overcome theirs. For example, sharing that you always hated math class is not helpful. Instead, offer study skills that helped you overcome your problems with math.

9. You should not reveal your birthday to your students if the date is upcoming. Students may be pressured to hold a party for you. If the date has already passed, you can reveal it without feeling that you are putting your students on the spot. This question is easy to deflect if you just ask students to reveal their own birthdays instead.

10. You should reveal where you went to college. Stick with the less sensational parts of your college career when you talk about this time with your students. Use this time to encourage students to plan their own futures.

11. You can reveal your favorite color to your students.

12. Your disagreement with another faculty member should not be obvious to your students. It would be unprofessional to speak ill of another faculty member or to allow students to do this in front of you.

13. You can reveal your vacation plans only if they are ones that you would be comfortable talking about if an administrator were in the room.

14. You can reveal the name of your pet. Sharing a common interest in pets is a good way to connect with your students.

15. If your musical tastes include songs that are vulgar or have violent lyrics, you should not include these in a discussion with your students. Remember that you are a role model.

You Are a Role Model

For several decades, social scientists have been concerned about the scarcity of positive media role models for young people. Too many children lack the direction that they need to keep themselves safe from harm.

While there may not be many media heroes, there are plenty of teachers who readily assume the task of guiding students through their youth. You are a role model to your students every day that they are around you whether you want this responsibility or not.

Your students, even when they are misbehaving, look to you for guidance. It is not always easy to have the right answer, to make the right decision, or to say the right thing even though your students expect all of these from you. When this burden seems to be a heavy one, ask yourself this question, "If I'm not a role model for my students, then who will be?"

Being a role model means that you are a caring adult who helps your students make good decisions. For many students, you are the only person in their lives who routinely stresses the importance of hard work and good character. Depending on the grade you teach, your role-model tasks could include making sure that your students wash their hands properly, have lunch money, learn about the dangers of using drugs, or get those college applications in the mail on time.

"I think the most important thing is to really enjoy the kids that you work with. If you are having fun they will have fun learning. Look for crazy moments and things that only kids could say."

—William Leigh, 11 years experience

Be a Positive Influence

Your actions will influence your students even when you are not aware of it. It can be an overwhelming responsibility, but you have chosen a profession with a profound impact. You can be a positive influence on your students when you:

- help students manage their anger appropriately.
- attend after-school events involving your students.
- show your appreciation for other staff members.
- are patient and never sarcastic.
- dress professionally.
- stay organized.
- are prompt.

- show sympathy and concern.
- handle misbehavior professionally.
- have high expectations.
- share common interests with your students.
- can laugh at yourself.
- accept criticism well.
- treat parents and guardians with respect.
- show an interest in your students.

Create a Professional Image

Just as actors create characters when they are at work, you will need to develop a strong image of yourself as a teacher. This means that you must separate your personal self from your professional self.

Many successful teachers have found ways to cope with the discrepancies between their personal selves and their professional lives. For example, there are many fearless teachers who are also too timid to speak publicly outside of their classrooms. Others drive too fast or stay up too late—both activities that they would not encourage in their students. Some teachers even have children of their own who misbehave at home in ways that they would not tolerate in their own students.

If you can create a strong image of yourself as a professional educator, then your school life will be much easier for you. You will realize that when your students are critical of you, they really do not know *you* at all. They are only reacting to your professional self—a person who has to set limits and correct mistakes.

Creating a professional image takes deliberate thought and planning. Begin by looking into the future. What would you like for your students to say about you ten years from now? How can you achieve this? After you have thought about the long-range effect you want to have on your students, jot your ideas down. Tape this in a conspicuous place to help you remember what you want your image to be.

LOOK THE PART

One of the most important ways that you can establish a satisfying relationship with your students is by paying attention to your appearance at school. You do not have to dress in primary colors or wear ties with the alphabet on them to maintain a professional appearance. Instead, you should strive to appear as professional as the other teachers in your school do. When your appearance is professional, others will take you more seriously. Since different schools have different dress codes, pay careful attention to any information that comes your way about how you should dress for your school. Teachers who insist on extreme individualism in their appearance often find that they are the target of unkind comments made by their students and their families, as well as colleagues. The following are some of the fashion errors that you should avoid when you prepare for school.

- Smelling like alcohol or tobacco
- Bad breath or unpleasant body odor
- Dirty and/or unkempt hair
- Distracting makeup, perfume, or jewelry
- Chewing gum
- Dirty or wrinkled clothing
- Missing buttons or broken zippers
- Clothing that doesn't fit
- Violating the student dress code

WATCH YOUR LANGUAGE

The words that you use when you speak with your students are one of the most important ways that you have to create a strong bond with them. Kind words spoken in a gentle voice make it much easier for your students to connect with you. If you say something unkind to a student, it will hurt even more than an insult from a peer because it's coming from you, someone the child should be able to count on.

There are very few set rules about how you should speak to your students. Often, what you say will have to be guided by the age and maturity level of your students. For example, while it is usually a serious offense in an elementary classroom for a teacher to tell students to "shut up," this phrase is not usually considered as anything other than rude when used around high school students. You should avoid using it, however, because there are many more effective ways to ask students to stop talking.

The one language mistake that you should not make is to swear around your students. When you do this, whether deliberately or in anger, you cross the line of what is acceptable and what is not. If you are ever tempted to swear around your students, remember that teachers have been fired for swearing at students. As a first-year teacher, it is possible that you may forget and swear in class. For example, a swear word may slip out as you close a drawer on your finger. In this case, you should immediately apologize to your students, let them know that you are embarrassed, apologize again, and then continue with class. After your class is over, you should speak with a supervisor and explain your side of the situation as soon as you can and certainly before your supervisor hears about it from an angry parent.

While swear words are clearly not something you should say around students, there are other language issues that you should also pay attention to. Make sure that your own words are ones that help your students and don't hurt them. Never make negative or insulting remarks about any student's:

- Race
- Religion
- Family
- Friends
- Gender

- Nationality
- Clothing
- Neighborhood
- Body size
- Sexual orientation

- Ability
- Disabilities
- Age
- Appearance
- Love life

> *"Never belittle students when you are talking to them. You lose any respect that the students have for you when they believe you are looking down on them."*
>
> —Melinda Cummings, 1 year experience

129

The Problem with Being a Popular Teacher

It's natural to want to be well liked. It's a wonderful experience to be in a mall or a restaurant and hear a young voice joyfully calling your name or to look out over a classroom full of students who are hanging on your every word. The problem with being a well-liked teacher is that it is sometimes such an exhilarating feeling that you are reluctant to give it up, even when you should. It's much more pleasant to hear your students cheer when you tell them that there will be no homework than to hear their groans when you give a tough assignment. Choices like this one make up a teacher's day. As a teacher, you should base your decisions not on what your students want at the moment, but on what they need in the long run. Students are shortsighted; you should not be.

There are many legitimate reasons for your students to like you. Are your classes interesting? Do you treat everyone with respect? Do you encourage their creativity? Are you inspirational? Unfortunately, there are many other reasons for your students to like you that are seductive traps that you must avoid by continuing to think of your students' needs. If you ever overhear your students say any of the following statements about you, then you should know that you are becoming popular for the wrong reasons.

- She never makes us do real work in that class.
- He always shows lots of movies.
- She's an easy grader.
- He never calls home no matter what I do.
- She doesn't make us take notes.
- He really likes to joke around.
- She doesn't care if we use swear words.
- He's just like us.
- She doesn't care about the dress code. We can wear what we like.

> *"When dealing with students, always remember what is was like on the other side of the desk. Try to put yourself in their shoes, and then treat them the way you would have wanted your teacher to treat you."*
>
> —Kristin Sanderlin, 5 years experience

Handle Student Crushes with Care

Although on television sitcoms a student's crush on his teacher is funny (and overcome by the end of the show), in reality, there is nothing funny about a student who has a crush on a teacher. If you are successful as a teacher, then every student in your class will feel special. However, some students can be confused by the feelings that a loving teacher inspires.

Although student crushes are natural and certainly understandable, they are not trivial for the student or the teacher. If you discover that a student has a crush on you, take steps to protect yourself as well as the student's feelings. Never allow yourself to be alone with a student who has a crush on you. If you do, you may be accused of serious misconduct by the student, and you will have no defense against the accusations.

If you ever are in a position where you have to confront a student directly about a crush, handle the student's feelings with the utmost sensitivity. Be aware that a scorned student is certainly capable of lashing out at you in anger over hurt feelings. If you don't handle the situation with delicacy, a student can accuse you of things that you did not do. Be extra careful to avoid situations where a student with a crush on you can express those feelings to you.

Discourage students from acting on their crushes by bringing you gifts or defending you to other students. Tactfully refuse the gifts if you can. Make sure students understand that you are clear about your role as a teacher even if they are not. Be sure that your behavior to all students is fair, friendly, and has the necessary emotional distance your students need from a teacher. Make sure that you don't inadvertently encourage a student with a crush into thinking that you are treating him or her in a way that is different from the way you treat other students.

If you find that your actions to discourage a crush are not working, then speak with your mentor or a supervisor. Ask for advice. Sometimes inexperienced teachers are reluctant to ask for help in dealing with student crushes, but you should not underestimate the potential for serious problems. If you enlist help from other professionals when you are first aware of the situation, then you have valuable allies should you need more assistance with the student later.

"Sometimes it is an obstacle because when students feel that because you look young they are on the same level. I have had to pull girls and boys to the side and explain to them that I am their teacher and not their peer and that they have to treat me with the same respect that they would any other adult. After I told a few of my students this, they knew I wasn't playing and made a major change for the better."

—Sabrina Smith, 2 years experience

"Are You Old Enough to Be a Teacher?"

It's not easy to have a baby face and be a teacher. You will have to withstand comments about how you look just like a kid yourself. Teachers on duty will ask you for your hall pass. You will have to tactfully deal with parents who are not certain that you are old enough to teach their children. Looking young is not always an asset to a teacher.

You can overcome the problems caused by a youthful appearance without having to wait for wrinkles to appear. You must be as professional and serious at school as you can be. If your conversation and dress are serious, people will soon take you seriously. This does not mean that you should wear spectacles or dress in drab colors just to pretend to be older than you really are. Instead, let professionalism be what people notice about you instead of your age.

When parents or colleagues remark that you don't look old enough to be a teacher, accept this as a compliment and laugh about it. Over time, your commitment to your students and to your profession will override the effects of your youthful appearance.

The Importance of Having Perfect Attendance

When you were a student, you may have been tempted to play hooky from school from time to time. At worst, you then had to spend extra time making up the work you missed. As a teacher, when you miss school, the problems caused by your absence are much more serious because so many other people are affected by it. Even the best substitute teacher is only a substitute for the real thing. Your students need for you to be in class with them.

Striving for perfect attendance benefits you and your students. You will avoid having to make lesson plans that you only hope a substitute teacher can follow, and you will avoid having to cope with the behavior problems that can happen when even your most mature and well-behaved students are on their own with a substitute teacher.

Your students benefit when you are present in class because they do not lose any instructional time. You also serve as a good role model for students who would like to miss school, but who have a teacher who cares enough to show them that it is important to come to school.

While you should not attend school if you are ill, there are plenty of times when you may be tempted to miss a day of school when you are not really sick—just like when you were a student. Be careful not to abuse your district's leave policy. If nothing else, you can never be sure of when you may need to use the sick days that you should be saving. A serious illness or an accident can erode years of banked leave time. Try to save those days for when you will really need them.

WHAT TO DO WHEN YOU HAVE TO MISS SCHOOL

If you do have to miss school, there are several things that you must do. Some of these will probably be required by your school district and others are just common-sense ways to make sure that the day goes smoothly without you. Here is a timeline of what you should do when you find out that you will need to miss a day of school.

Inform the Right People

▶ Make sure that you contact the people who are responsible for hiring a substitute teacher for you. Try to do this as quickly as you can so that they can be sure to hire the most competent sub for you. This will be easier for you if you make a note of the phone numbers at the beginning of the year and then keep them handy. You should *never* neglect to notify the school when you are going to be absent.

- Call a colleague and ask for assistance. Ask that person to look in on your class during the day and make sure that the substitute knows what to do.

- Contact an administrator. Do this at school if you know in advance that you will be out on a particular day. Ask the administrator to also look in on your classes from time to time throughout the day.

- If you think that your students will not take advantage of the situation, you should tell them that you are going to be out. Use this time to ask for their cooperation and to talk about any problems that may arise with a substitute teacher. Stress the importance of maintaining the daily routine even if you are not there. Many experienced teachers have found that students who are prepared for a teacher's absence react better than those students who arrive at school, find out that there is a substitute, and then goof off.

Leave Good Lesson Plans

- You should not ask a substitute teacher to interpret your lesson plans as they are written in your plan book. Instead, give a class by class description of what you want your students to do.

- Your plans should be based on written work that your students can do independently. Write out clear directions on the work so students can complete it without having to talk with others or ask the substitute to interpret.

- Don't show movies or ask a substitute teacher to take your students to the library or to the computer lab.

- Don't allow group work when there is a substitute teacher in charge.

- Students should not use computers when you are not there to supervise them.

- Let your students know that they are not just doing busy work. Make sure they know that the work will be collected at the end of class and that you intend to grade it.

- If the work involves handouts, photocopy them in advance and clearly label them so the substitute can find them quickly.

- The most common complaints that substitute teachers have is that teachers do not leave enough work for students to do. You should plan more work for your students than you would expect them to do if you were there. Always have extra work for those students who finish early.

Essential Information for Your Substitute

In addition to lesson plans, you should leave a folder of information for your sub. Because most of this information is not as apt to change as your daily plans, you should make up this folder early in the year and then update it as often as you need to. Your sub folder should include the following.

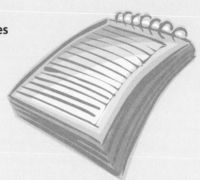

- An updated seating chart for each class
- A class roster
- Attendance procedures
- Your daily schedule
- The names of helpful students
- The names and room numbers of helpful colleagues
- A pad and pen for notes to you
- Class rules
- Class routines and procedures
- Where to find supplies and extra texts
- A map of the school
- Your home phone number
- Fire drill or other emergency information
- Information about students with special needs
- Referral notices and information
- Extra work for students to do if they finish everything else
- A thank-you note from you

How to Handle Behavior Problems When You Return

Make sure that your students know that you expect good behavior from them while you are absent. However, if your students have misbehaved while you were out, don't rush to punish. First, have students write out their version of the events of the class. You can even have them do this anonymously. Read these and think about what you are going to do before you punish an entire class based on what a substitute teacher has told you. If you have to deal with misbehavior problems after you have gathered the facts from the sub and from your students, then do so promptly.

Let Your Students Know You Care

You can have the most fascinating lesson plan in the world, but it won't work if your students think that you don't care about them. A good teacher-student connection will make everything in your class run smoothly. Without it, nothing will.

Students of all ages need to feel that their teachers like them and approve of what they do. This may be hard to communicate at times, particularly with a student who regularly misbehaves. In such cases, it is not always easy to find the time between reprimands to show your approval and caring. Most of the time, however, you will find that there are lots of ways that you can show your students that you care about them.

Consider adapting the following strategies when you want to strengthen the connection with your students.

> *"If you can find a connection, you get your foot in the door. Then, be honest, consistent, and listen to what the students say. Be as fair as possible, but be consistent."*
>
> —Rick Shelton, 3 years experience

- Set responsible behavior limits for everyone and be fair when you enforce these limits.

- Agree with your students as often as you can.

- Use a kind voice when you speak with your students.

- Listen to all of your students. Don't assume that your students are at fault when there is a problem.

- Make sure to say each student's name at least once in a class period.

- Take the time to get to know your students as people.

- Notice and compliment changes in your students' personal appearance even if those changes are not to your personal taste.

- If one of your students is featured in the paper for doing something good, clip out the article and display it.

- Stress the things that you and your students have in common: goals, dreams, and beliefs.

- When a student speaks to you, stop and listen.

- Maintain a birthday calendar for your students. Celebrate birthdays with birthday messages on the board.

- Attend school events. If your students are playing a sport or performing in a concert, go and show your appreciation for their hard work.

- Focus on your students' strong points and not on their weaknesses.

- Use good manners when you deal with your students and insist that they do the same.

- When students confide in you, follow up. For example, if students have told you that they were worried about a test in another class, take the time to ask about how they did.

- Be very clear with your students that you want to help them achieve their dreams.

- Ask about a student's family. If you know that someone is ill, show your concern.

- Create opportunities for success every day.

- Give your students plenty of opportunities to share their ideas and opinions with you.

- Show your sense of humor. Laugh when funny things happen in class—particularly when they happen to you.

- Speak to every student each day. Leave no one out of class discussions.
- Write notes to your students. Use plenty of stickers and write positive comments on their papers.
- Be generous and tactful in your praise.
- Pay attention to your students' health. If students need to go to the clinic, send them. When students have to miss several days because of illness, call to see how they are doing or send a get-well card. Be prompt with homebound work.
- Use this sentence to convey your concern: "What can I do to help you?"
- Talk with students when you notice a change in their behavior. For example, if normally serious students seem to be neglecting their work, find out why.
- Take the time to tell your students what you like about them.
- Take photographs of your students and display them.
- Stay after school once each week and offer extra assistance to your students who may be struggling.
- Take the initiative to be friendly to your students. Speak to them when you see them in the hall or in the neighborhood.

Promote Trust

You and your students need to trust each other. Much of what happens at school is based on mutual trust. These tips will help you and your students make trust a vital part of your relationship.

- Talk about trust with your students. Make it part of the conversations in your classroom. Have students share their ideas. Use banners and posters to call it to their attention.
- Be a model of trustworthiness. Talk about issues such as plagiarism or accurate record keeping and show how you avoid mistakes in these areas.
- Adopt a "we" attitude. Talk about trust as a mutual responsibility. Make every student feel important and necessary to the smooth functioning of the class and many of the problems that occur with distrust will vanish.
- Don't promise what you can't deliver. If a student confides in you, don't promise not to tell anyone else as a condition of the confession. Some things must be shared with counselors and parents.
- Avoid situations that will destroy your students' fragile trust. Don't leave your personal belongings or answer keys where students can be tempted. Situations such as these can destroy months of patient trust-building in a few seconds.
- Don't be a pushover. If students see that you believe every false excuse that their classmates offer, they will not feel that they can trust you to make good decisions.
- Accept that some students will take a long time to trust you. Be patient and persistent.

> *"The teacher who knows some little detail about his or her students that is beyond the subject area is the one who relates well to kids. That teacher will find ways to bring that little detail into the relationship with students and will make each child feel important."*
>
> —Patty Muth, 9 years experience

How to Empower Students and Not Lose Control of Your Class

When you give students a say in class decisions, you empower them with your trust and confidence. Many teachers, both experienced and inexperienced, are not comfortable allowing students a strong voice in the class. They may have tried to allow students to make decisions, but found that the choices that their students made were not sound. You can overcome this concern and still empower your students by offering them a limited choice. For instance, if you were to ask your students if they wanted homework on weekends, the answer would certainly be a resounding "no." Instead, if you asked them if they prefer to do the problems on page 6 or page 7 for weekend homework, then everyone wins. You will have the homework that your students need to do and your students will have had a voice in a class decision. Even younger students can make simple decisions. For example, should a project be due on Monday or Tuesday? Should there be three or four essay questions on a test?

There are many successful choices that your students can make for themselves when you give them the guidance that they need to make sound decisions. If you want to experiment with this, begin with small issues. Be sure to give plenty of guidance and do not consider allowing students to make decisions that make you uncomfortable.

Creating a Student-Friendly Classroom

In a student-friendly class, your clear vision of what you want for your students, a positive attitude, and the effort that you make to help them achieve their dreams will create a strong connection with your students. After all, you will all be working toward a common goal. A student-friendly classroom is not one where students are in charge. You are still a powerful driving force. However, your role now is that of collaborator and coach.

With careful planning, you can have an inviting atmosphere in your class from the first day of school. Begin by making sure that you know the answer to the question, "Why do we have to know this?" Your students should feel comfortable knowing that if they ask this question, you will have a thoughtful answer based on their immediate and future needs.

Another important hallmark of a student-friendly class is that your students do not sit passively listening to you deliver instruction. They do more talking than you do because they are finding answers to important questions that you ask. They also should feel that their opinions are valued.

10 Ways to Create a Student-Centered Classroom

1. Decorate your classroom with student work. Students feel a sense of ownership and pride in a class where their work is displayed. Be sure to display everyone's work. If you hang only the best work, you can be accused of favoritism, which will only cause harm.

2. Keep a supply of recycled paper, construction paper, crayons, markers, and other supplies on hand to help your students create work for display. Some of the items that would make interesting displays include projects, group-generated lists, homework assignments, cartoons, "sponge" activities, posters . . . anything that your students would be proud to display.

3. Have a sense of humor, particularly about yourself. If you make a mistake, admit it graciously. Don't be one of those teachers who never laugh with their students and never admit when they are wrong.

4. Give your students a voice in how some of the procedures of the class should be managed. They need to assume responsibility for running some of the class routines if they are to feel that what they do matters to you and to their classmates.

5. Teach your students how to work together well. This will take time and patience, but it is worth the trouble. Students who have the support of their classmates are not afraid to speak up or try new activities.

6. Your students crave success and approval. Create opportunities for this to happen by designing lessons that are challenging, but achievable. When students succeed, reward them. Keep lots of small, tangible rewards such as stickers on hand.

7. Make sure that your students are in touch with school events. Maintain a bulletin board with items about schedules, lunch menus, upcoming events, and other important information.

8. Promote courtesy and respect for school and classroom rules. Make sure that you model the behavior that you encourage from your students.

9. Encourage students to share their opinions and ideas. Teach them to value each other's creativity by encouraging and accepting their ideas.

10. Survey your students periodically so that you can make sure that the student-friendly classroom you think you've created really is. Surveying your students is a terrific way to find out what they think and to improve the way you manage your class.

How to Set Up a Shared Supplies Bank

Off-task behavior and discipline problems are just two of the things that can go wrong when students come to class unprepared. Keeping extra supplies on hand will help you avoid many problems.

Try to have three extra textbooks on hand to lend to students if they forget theirs. When you lend a book to a student, make sure that the student writes his or her name on the board or another safe place so you have a record of where your books are. You could also assign a responsible student to be in charge of issuing and collecting borrowed texts.

If missing pens or pencils are a problem, set up a system where students can borrow from a shared bank of supplies. Here's how.

- Select one or two students to be in charge of the supplies bank.

- Ask every student to donate a new ink pen, pencil, and a few sheets of paper.

- Mark the pens and pencils with a number.

- When students need to borrow a pen or pencil, the students who are in charge of the bank can record the number and the name of the student who borrowed it.

- The students who distribute the supplies are also the ones who should remind the borrowers to return them at the end of class.

Get to Know Your Students

You will prevent many problems by getting to know your students as quickly as you can. In fact, this should be a priority during the first few days of school. There are many ways that you can find out about your students. Two of the traditional ways are to check records and contact parents. Both of these are very time consuming.

Another traditional way that many teachers find out about their new students is to ask other teachers about them. However, there are some serious drawbacks to this practice. Students who misbehave for one teacher do not always misbehave for others. Because you are new to the school yourself, you can't determine if the information that you receive from other teachers is really accurate. Finally, students do mature and do deserve to be given a fair chance with you regardless of mistakes that they have made in the past. One way to tactfully handle this situation is to insist that teachers who want to tell you about your new students only tell you positive things. You will still have useful information that you can use to your advantage. For instance, you might tell a student a positive comment that you heard. Your new student will be flattered by your interest.

Another very effective way for you to get to know your students is to observe them as they get to know one another. Don't let them tell you that they all know each other well. You will be surprised at how many students do not know something as basic their classmates' last names. Your students need to know about each other and what each can contribute to the success of the class. While they are busily engaged in this, you can use your powers of observation to learn as much as you can about your new students. If you want to learn about your students as they get to know more about each other, try some of these activities.

- When you have your students fill out a student information form (see Section Three), include a section with questions designed to reveal interesting information. You could ask students to tell about their favorite classes, hobbies, strengths, weaknesses, goals, and dreams. You can ask them to describe a past success they have had in school or at another activity. You could even ask them to give you advice on how to be the best teacher they will ever have.

- Ask your students to list twenty things that they do well. You will be surprised at how difficult this will be for many students. Too often students focus on their weaknesses and not on their strengths. You will be surprised at the human side of your students that this exercise will reveal.

- Ask students to create a time capsule about their new class. You can all agree on a date when you will open it. Include photographs of your students, letters, videotapes, and other objects that will reveal what your students are like at the beginning of the term.

- A good way to break the ice is to put students into small groups and hand each group a bag with several common objects in it. You can have these objects all relate to your discipline if possible. Ask students to combine these objects in a new way. They can then name their invention and create a marketing plan for it. The point of this exercise is not just to learn about your students, but to have them work together in a way that also forces them to use their creative-thinking skills.

- Group students into teams and have them create a cartoon panel that illustrates a school-success topic. They can use stick figures to tell the story. They should also generate a story line that uses the members of the group as characters.

- Give your students the supplies that they need to create posters with wise advice on it. You can display these inspirational posters all term.

- Place students into pairs and have them interview each other. A twist that makes this old assignment interesting is to give each student an object and ask what he or she has in common with it. When your students present their findings to the class, you will learn lots about them as they reveal how they are like small rocks, bookmarks, tissue boxes, and other commonplace objects.

- During the first few days of the term, create a class newsletter. You can include students' interviews with each other, suggestions for successful study habits, cartoons and student art, or any other information limited only by the age and ability of your students. Keep the tone upbeat and stress the value of working together as your students complete the newsletter.

- Ask your students to bring in magazine pictures and words that indicate things that are of value to them. Combine these images and words into a giant class collage. Your students will see that, while each one is unique, they are all part of a large group.

- Ask students to write descriptive paragraphs about each other. Photocopy these paragraphs and bind them into booklets for all students. This will be the most intently read document that you will give your students all term.

- Put your students into pairs and have them determine ten things that they have in common. Insist that they go beyond the obvious to discuss topics such as shared past experiences, attitudes, goals, or other appealing topics.

- After you have met with your students for a few days, create permanent study teams. These students will work together all year and will watch out for each other. This strategy is limited only by the tasks that you think that they can handle as a group. They can take notes for absent members, share study tips, and call each other with reminders about work. If you notice that the chemistry in a group is not working, move students into a more cooperative grouping.

Student Inventories

Student inventories are a good way to learn information about your students that you just don't have time to learn in a class discussion or in a conference after school. Many teachers ask students to fill out an inventory during the first few days of school. Still others find that if they wait a few days, their students will feel secure enough to reveal more information. Whenever you decide to use an inventory, be sure to give plenty of time for students to answer thoughtfully.

Following you will find three inventories that you can reproduce for your students. You can also add or delete questions to adapt the information here to create an inventory suitable for your students.

Figure 5.1

STUDENT INVENTORY (FOR ELEMENTARY STUDENTS)

Name _____ Date _____

My birthday is _____

My family members are

_____

_____

_____

When I grow up I want to be _____

_____

My favorite things to do at home are _____

_____

My special friends are _____

_____

My favorite things to do at school are _____

_____

The subjects I do best in are _____

_____

The subjects I need help in are _____

_____

If I could change anything about school, it would be _____

_____

This year I am looking forward to learning about _____

_____

I like it when my teachers _____

_____

I would like to know more about _____

_____

I am happiest when I am _____

_____

Figure 5.2

STUDENT INVENTORY (FOR MIDDLE SCHOOL STUDENTS)

Name _____ Date _____

My birthday is _____

My family members are

_____

_____

_____

When I grow up I want to

_____

My closest friends are

_____

My favorite things to do are

_____

_____

Here are my favorites

    Radio stations _____ Magazines _____

    Sports _____ Hobbies _____

    Books _____ Movies _____

    Music _____ Clothes _____

One thing people don't know about me is

_____

A skill I have is

_____

A person I admire is _____ because _____

_____

Something I would like to learn to do better is

_____

I appreciate it when a teacher

_____

My previous teachers would tell you this about me

_____

I am proud of myself when I

_____

_____

Figure 5.3
STUDENT INVENTORY (FOR SECONDARY STUDENTS)

Name _____ Date _____

My birthday is _____

My family members are

_____

_____

_____

After graduation I plan to _____

_____

My greatest asset is

_____

I am an expert on

_____

One thing people don't know about me is

_____

My teachers last year will tell you that I am

_____

I have trouble dealing with

_____

My favorite class is _____ because _____

_____

The most influential person in my life is _____ because

_____

It was difficult for me to learn

_____

It was easy for me to learn

_____

I want to know more about

_____

Three words that describe my personality are

_____

One lesson I had to learn the hard way is

_____

Earn Your Students' Respect

One of the heavy responsibilities that novice and experienced teachers share equally is the task of earning their students' respect. Respect does not depend on how long you've taught or how much you know. You can plan fascinating lessons and have every procedure in place, but you will be a failure without the respect of your students.

Although respect is the touchstone of a successful relationship with students, there is no single action that you can take that will guarantee that every student will respect you. It is not even easy to know if they do respect you.

Respect lies in the small actions you take. It requires that you successfully manage a constant and delicate balance among the many roles that you have at school: disciplinarian, advisor, lecturer, role model, and motivator.

"Shake hands firmly and insist that students do the same."

—Barbara Knowles, 36 years experience

When your students respect you, they will see that you are not just another friendly adult. Instead you will have met their ideal of what a teacher should be. Many first-year teachers mistake affection for respect. Your students may like you for many reasons, none of which earn their respect. They may think that you don't assign too much work or that you relate to them well on a personal level. This type of affection fades when problems arise or at the end of the term when students realize that although they enjoyed your class, they did not really learn very much.

There are many other ways that you can lose the respect of your students because you have lost sight of what your role as a teacher should be. Some of these ways will be obvious to you and others will be subtle. Here are just a few of the mistakes that are easy for an unaware teacher to make.

- Failing to be a good role model
- Being unprepared for class
- Treating students unfairly
- Assigning insufficient or inappropriate work
- Being inflexible
- Refusing to admit that you have made a mistake
- Losing your temper
- Ignoring students who need help
- Being uncaring

15 Ways to Earn Your Students' Respect

Below is a list of statements involving practices that are geared to earn your students' respect. As you read over the statements, judge yourself as your students would judge you.

1. I engage every student in all assignments each day.
2. I know the material that I am supposed to teach.
3. I use a variety of discipline techniques to establish a positive class atmosphere.
4. I am willing to be flexible when necessary.
5. I use a variety of strategies to keep my students interested and on-task.
6. I respect my students' differences and encourage them to do the same.
7. I encourage a teamwork approach with my students and their families.
8. I am a good listener who is available to my students on a regular basis.
9. I focus my energies on preventing behavior problems through an assortment of techniques instead of having to deal with the serious consequences caused by misbehavior.
10. I make sure that my students know that I care about their welfare.
11. I practice being a patient and understanding person.
12. I teach my students how to do their work.
13. I make sure that my students know the benefits of doing an assignment so that they will want to do their work well.
14. I make a special effort to enforce rules consistently.
15. I use a wide variety of assessment techniques to evaluate student progress.

As with so many other aspects of your new career, earning your students' respect is something that will require time, patience, and persistent effort on your part. You will have to work consistently to gain and then keep the gift of respect from your students. Millions of other teachers have done it and you can, too.

Mutual Respect, Mutual Courtesy

No one wants to teach a room full of obnoxious children who alienate everyone they come into contact with. The goal of most teachers is to work with pleasant students who work together as a community of learners. Your dream of a good relationship with your students should be based on mutual respect and courtesy.

Unfortunately, the dream will not happen unless you make it so. Not all of your students will have had much exposure to polite society before they arrive in your class. They may have family members or previous teachers who have not been able to make them understand the importance of manners. Certainly, your students will not pick up the social skills they need from watching late night cable television or sitcoms.

Teaching courtesy is a task that you will have to assume if you want to have a smoothly running classroom. You will have to not only teach your students the social skills that they need to function well in your class, but you will also have to enforce those skills by insisting that they treat each other and you with courtesy.

You can do this if you keep in mind that the rewards for such efforts are great. The bond with your students will be a strong one and discipline problems in your classroom will be reduced. Here are a few suggestions for teaching social skills in your class.

"Get to know your students' dogs, cats, fish, iguanas—anything that can connect you to their whole day."

—Sandra Councill, 17 years experience

Make sure that everyone understands what's courteous and what isn't. Not all of your students mean to be rude when they shout insults at each other, interrupt, or put their heads down on their desks when you are talking to them. Social rules, particularly those in schools, vary widely. For example, some teachers tolerate behavior that others find very offensive. This confuses children of all ages. Be direct, specific, and clear about what you expect. Do this early in the year so that you can prevent mistakes.

Reward good behavior. Offer little treats and lavish words of praise when a class has been courteous. This is especially important at the start of a term when students are still not sure of their boundaries. When you see a student or a group of students being courteous, take notice. Point it out so that everyone else can see what you mean when you talk about being polite.

Exploit the power of peer pressure. You can steer students in the right direction by making sure that being courteous is something that everyone in the class is comfortable doing. When this happens, the student who is discourteous will see that there is no peer support for bad behavior and your role as enforcer will be lessened because students will police themselves.

Encourage students to accept each other's differences. Many of the negative behaviors that happen in a class can be eliminated if you encourage students to be tolerant of each other. You can do this by modeling acceptance and respect for each of your students, particularly the ones who struggle with their social skills. Allow your students plenty of opportunities to express themselves without fear of ridicule from you or from their classmates.

Model the respect that you want to receive. Rules are useless if you don't model the behavior that you want your students to show you. If you are rude to your students, you can be sure that they will be rude to you. You have hundreds of opportunities to show your students how to be polite each day. Take advantage of them. Being able to show that you are a respectful person is a powerful tool. For example, when a student slams a book while you are talking, ask the child, "Do I slam a book while you are talking?" "Then please don't slam a book while I am talking." Your request has authority because you are a good role model.

Your students are far more observant of you than you can imagine. They want and need your guidance not just in academics, but in social skills, too. When you take the time to teach life-skills such as courtesy and when you take the time to model those skills yourself, you are really teaching your students how to be successful in your classroom and in life.

Strategies to Stop the Cycle of Rudeness

Rudeness is rarely a single act. Usually a rude remark or action is like a stone dropped in a still pond: there are plenty of ripples that seem to go on forever. These unpleasant ripples then build more momentum until finally a single small rude incident leads to a bigger conflict. There have been many news reports about violence that began with something as trivial as a careless student stepping on another's clean shoe.

You can prevent many problems associated with rudeness by teaching your students how they can respond to impolite behavior in a positive way. The following list of suggested responses to rudeness is not meant for those situations when a student's safety is at risk or for when a more serious response is required to stop more violence. Instead, these responses will help students deal with those smaller irritations caused by daily interactions with others.

- Ignore the person by walking away.
- Smile and say nothing.
- Count from one to ten five times.
- Return the rude remark with a kind one. Pay the offender a compliment.
- Tell a parent, a teacher, a friend, or a counselor.
- Take deep breaths. Exhale slowly.
- Cool off by going to the water fountain. Splash a little cool water on your face.
- Look at your watch and make a promise to yourself that you will allow two minutes to pass before you speak.
- Mentally picture the rude person as a small fluffy mouse wearing a silly hat.
- Think of the last nice thing that someone said to you.
- Ask yourself if this silly incident is really worth the stress.
- Open a book and read a page before you respond. Read two pages if you are very upset.
- Turn to a classmate and pay that person a compliment.
- Repeat "I am in control of my attitude" ten times.
- List ten things for which you can be thankful.

⬧ Make a conscious decision not to let the rude person upset you.

⬧ Make a list of your ten best personality traits.

⬧ Picture yourself walking across a field of freshly fallen snow.

Misplaced Behavior or Deliberate Rudeness?

When a student is rude, often the rudeness is not deliberate. How you handle rude remarks has a profound effect on the relationship you have with your students. When you see or hear something that you believe is rude, hesitate briefly to consider whether it is deliberate or not. How you will handle the misbehavior depends on this decision.

For instance, what should you do when you hear a student swear in your class? If the student was swearing at you or at another student knowing that you can hear the remark, then you can be certain that the remark was an act of deliberate rudeness. You would have to deal with this as an act of defiance. However, if you were to hear the same remark in a situation where it was obvious that it slipped out and that the student didn't mean for you to hear it, then you can see that this was not an act of deliberate rudeness. You would handle this offense with only a minor fuss—perhaps only a quick warning.

"Never give students an opportunity to waste time; they will."

—Barbara Knowles, 36 years experience

There are many misbehaviors that you will have to judge individually. That does not mean that you should tolerate misbehavior or rudeness; instead, it means that you should take into account that your students either don't know better or just make mistakes in judgment.

Some of the behaviors that you need to consider before determining that they are deliberate acts of rudeness can include the following.

• Not looking at you when you talk

• Talking too loudly

• Not following procedures for simple class routines

• Forgetting books and materials on a daily basis

• Talking back

• Hitting another student (especially if the hitter is used to horseplay at home)

• Saying rude things such as "shut up" or calling names

• Being late to class

• Putting head down on the desk

• Copying another student's work

Cultivate Grace Under Pressure

One of the worst mistakes that you can make is to lose your temper when you are upset in front of your students. Not only will giving in to the emotion of the moment cause you stress and sway your good judgment, but it can cause irreparable harm to your relationship with your students.

Learning to successfully control your emotions is not an easy task. If you have had a terrible time with one class, you often just do not have enough time to recover from the experience before the next class begins. However, taking out your anger or frustrations on innocent students is absolutely wrong.

While your students need to see your human side, they do not need to be subjected to your ill-temper. When you are tempted to lose your cool in front of your students, restrain yourself.

Students whose teacher loses control react in various ways, none of which are positive. Your outbursts can frighten some students, anger others, intimidate still others, and end months of trust-building efforts. Still other students will react to your loss of control by losing their own control. If you should ever raise your voice at a student, you can be certain that the student will then shout at you in return.

7 Strategies for Keeping Your Cool Under Pressure

There are many things that you can do to cultivate grace under pressure. Here are seven strategies that other teachers have found useful.

1. Keep in mind that losing control will only make the situation worse.

2. Count to ten before you speak. While you are counting, make your face appear as calm as possible.

3. Instead of shouting, lower your voice to just a whisper.

4. If there is a great deal of noise and commotion without a threat of violence, stand quietly and wait for it to subside. Shouting at your students to settle down will only add to the noise.

5. Use your journal to vent your frustration and plan ways to manage the situation differently.

6. Keep in mind that *you* determine what happens in your class. If you lose control, then you are not working to solve the problem. Channel your energies towards managing the situation.

7. Ask your students to help you when you are getting upset. This will redirect their attention towards making a positive contribution instead of adding to the problem.

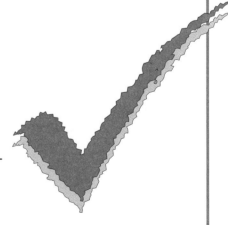

Journal Entries to Help You Connect with Your Students

▶ List the students who had an impact on your day. What can you learn from them? How have you affected them?

▶ Complete this statement: "I can tell when my students are _____ because . . ."

▶ What is your primary relationship with your students? Do you want to change anything about it? If so, how?

▶ Complete this statement: "I wish I had done _____ with my students today." How can you do this in the future?

▶ What did you do to help your students be successful today? What was their reaction?

▶ What would the ideal student be like? What parts of your own personality are reflected in your ideal?

▶ If you could find out the truth about _____ what would you like to know?

▶ Complete this statement: "When I have a problem with a student, I . . ."

▶ What does this statement reveal about how you can improve your relationship with your students?

▶ What emotions surfaced at school today? What effect did these emotions have on your class, your students, you?

▶ If you could choose your own students, whom would you select? Why?

Design Effective Instruction

Beep! Beep! Beeep! She grabbed her briefcase as she rushed out the door. The people in her car pool were so considerate that she didn't want to keep them waiting. Besides, she needed some advice.

"What should I do now?" she asked. "My whole class just failed a big test on the Middle Ages."

"The entire class? Didn't anybody pass?" one of the other teachers asked.

"Well, not very many. I just don't know what went wrong.

Her back seat partner said, "Why don't you let me check over your plans and your test for you? Maybe your test didn't match what you taught. That happens sometimes. It's not always easy to cover all of the material on your unit plans."

"My unit plans? You know, with the Valentine's Day assembly coming up I have been so busy after school that I just didn't have time to write them down."

"How long has it been since you last wrote out lesson plans?"

She thought for a few seconds, "Let's see. I had to show them the second week of school for my observation. I guess I haven't really written any since then. Look, I know the material and what I want my students to do every day. That's not the problem."

"Tell us again, how many kids failed that test?"

*L*esson planning is one of the most important tasks that you face as a first-year teacher, as a second-year teacher, and as a third-year teacher, and it will be just as important when you are a thirty-year teacher. Planning effective lessons is simply the blueprint for the success in your classroom and, ultimately, the success of your career.

Perhaps the most common mistake that veteran and novice teachers share is not spending enough time writing out lesson plans. This mistake results in hours and hours of wasted instruction time as well as frustration for teachers and students.

If the purpose of education is to effect a positive change in each student, then the importance of careful thinking about the design of instruction is undeniable.

Successful teachers think very carefully about what they are going to do. There can be no substitute for this process. Successful teachers plan every lesson every day.

> *"Don't compromise what your students need to know in your discipline. Don't pass students who are not competent in your subject area, but also don't put obstacles in the way of their learning. Your job is to set and enforce the standard and to assist all of your students in trying to reach that standard."*
>
> —Ken Pfeifer, 28 years experience

Common Planning Problems First-Year Teachers Face

While it is true that all teachers may have problems with planning effective lessons at some time, there are some problems that seem to be especially prevalent during the first few years of teaching.

As a novice teacher the biggest disadvantage that you face in creating lesson plans is that you don't have a wealth of tried and true lesson plans and materials to draw on. Every lesson plan you write your first year is an experiment. No matter how hard you work or how much effort you put into your plans, a lesson can fail simply because it has drawbacks that you are not yet aware of. But you can reduce the likelihood of an unsuccessful lesson by paying attention to some of the incorrect ideas that you might have about writing your plans. Here are just a few of the problems concerning lesson plans that many first-year teachers share.

- Rushing to cover material instead of teaching your students.
- Spending a disproportionate amount of time on a certain unit.
- Failing to connect current learning to previous learning.
- Focusing instruction on the *knowledge* level of thinking skills instead of the *critical thinking* levels.
- Not allowing for differences in learning styles.
- Failing to assess students' prior knowledge before starting new instruction.
- Failing to successfully motivate students to want to learn new material.
- Pacing a unit of study incorrectly.
- Neglecting to provide an anticipatory set for each day's lesson.

▶ Neglecting to provide closure for each day's lesson.

▶ Testing students on material that they have not adequately mastered.

▶ Failing to provide the correct amount of practice.

▶ Failing to provide enough "checkpoint" assessments before a final test.

▶ Mistaking a list of activities for a lesson plan.

▶ Not planning for the year, the semester, the unit, and each day.

Some Internet Solutions to Lesson-Planning Problems

Fortunately for first-year and experienced teachers alike, there are thousands of Internet sites offering lesson plans at all grade levels and for all subjects. Some of these sites have even been designed by teachers and contain a wealth of practical information.

A really good place to start working on lesson plans is your state's department of education Web page. By spending a minimum of effort you should be able to download the curriculum standards for your subject and grade level. Your school district should also have a Web page that could provide curriculum guidelines.

After you have researched the official state and district sites available to you, then you should begin to research other sites for helpful information. Try some of the following sites for fresh ideas and helpful solutions to planning problems that you may be experiencing. All of these sites contain general lesson plan information with links to specific topics, subjects, and grade levels.

www.iloveteaching.com

www.lessonplanspage.com

www.learningpage.com

www.lessonplans4teachers.com

www.theeducatorsnetwork.com

www.searchedu.com

www.ericir.syr.edu

www.bced.gov.bc.ca/irp/irp.html

www.funbrain.com

www.atozteacherstuff.com

www.teachervision.com

www.boston.k12.ma.us/teach

www.indiana.edu/~eric_rec/bks

Figure 6.1

Place a check in the box beside each of these successful planning strategies that applies to you at this point in your career. The more strategies you can check off, the more professional you should feel! And for all those strategies that you have not checked, set a goal to incorporate them into your teaching style.

- ☐ I follow my district's guidelines for planning lessons.
- ☐ I create a year's overview of the material I need to teach.
- ☐ I create semester guidelines.
- ☐ I create unit plans.
- ☐ I create weekly plans.
- ☐ I write detailed daily plans.
- ☐ I write daily plans two weeks in advance.
- ☐ I include motivational strategies in each lesson.
- ☐ I design assessments before I design the lesson.
- ☐ I use a variety of assessments in each unit.
- ☐ I include activities for different learning styles.
- ☐ I assess students' prior knowledge before planning a unit of study.
- ☐ I can correctly pace lessons.
- ☐ I include an anticipatory set in each day's lesson.
- ☐ I allow time for guided and independent practice.
- ☐ I plan the material that I will use as my input into the lesson.
- ☐ I plan the activities that students will complete.
- ☐ I provide critical thinking opportunities.
- ☐ I include appropriate homework assignments.
- ☐ I use a variety of materials and resources in each unit.
- ☐ I allow for differences in student abilities.
- ☐ I provide a syllabus to help students stay on track.
- ☐ I include authentic learning opportunities.
- ☐ I plan lessons that appeal to my students' interests and needs.
- ☐ I set aside a block of time each week to write my lesson plans.

"Teachers should never assume that students are experts at a particular skill just because it seems easy to others."

—Sabrina Smith, 2 years experience

10 Tips to Make Lesson Planning Easier

1. Begin the planning process by creating an overview of the year, of each semester, and of each unit. Try to do this before school begins so that you will have a clear picture of what you want your students to achieve.

2. Schedule a block of uninterrupted time each week to write out daily plans.

3. Create a lesson plan format that is easy to use for writing your daily plans.

4. If you don't use a computer to write your plans, use a pencil so that you can quickly make adjustments.

5. Use the school calendar that your district supplies at the start of the term to schedule your lessons around holidays or other events that may affect how your students will perform.

6. Keep your lesson plans in a binder with your other important school materials so that you can quickly check them each day.

7. Plan your lessons around the objectives that your state and district have determined for your grade level or subject. Objectives reflect the outcomes that you want for your students. Teach to those objectives.

8. Always plan more work than you believe your students will be able to finish. You can always use the extra plans for remediation or enrichment.

9. Write the final assessment for each unit of study before you begin planning lessons. If you do this, you will know what material your students will need to learn as you begin to teach the unit.

10. Never allow yourself to get behind in your lesson planning. It is almost impossible to catch up once you fall behind.

Three Planning Errors You Can Avoid

There are three very common errors that are easy traps for new teachers, but with a bit of effort and persistence, you can easily avoid them.

The first error is *planning lessons without objectives*. Objectives indicate the end result of the lesson—that is, what students will be able to do once you have taught a lesson. If you try to teach without a clear end result to meet, then you and your students will be frustrated. Use the curriculum guidelines available to you and create objectives before you plan instructional activities.

Another common planning error that you can avoid is to *focus too much on what you will be doing and saying rather than what your students will be doing to master the material*. If you look at the wide range of lesson plan formats available to you in textbooks and on the Internet, you will see that they are designed to engage the student in work from the beginning of the period until the end. Many novice teachers make the mistake of thinking that they have to be "on" all class long instead of coaching and directing their students as they learn. Remember to keep the focus in your plans on what your students will accomplish each day.

A final planning problem that you can easily avoid with some careful thinking involves *assigning work that does not contribute to successful learning*. It is easy to fall into this planning trap. If you spend too much time on a review of material that students should already know, for example, or plan a major test without checkpoint assessments to see if students are ready, then you have assigned work that does not contribute to successful learning. Another way to fall into this trap is to unsuccessfully adapt a lesson plan that worked for another teacher's students without carefully considering how it would benefit your students.

Just as there are many helpful Internet sites on lesson planning, there are also plenty of books. One author who has done more than any other to improve the way in which teachers design lessons is Dr. Madeline C. Hunter. Her book entitled *Improved Instruction* (Corwin Press, 1997) is one you will find particularly helpful in perfecting your lesson planning.

What to Include in Your Plans

The following list can help you as you begin to write your daily lesson plans. While there may be other items that you find useful to include, these will give you a basis for beginning.

- **Objectives:** Objectives indicate what the end result of a lesson will be, not what activities the students will do. The objectives for a lesson should be clearly stated in specific terms.

- **Necessary materials and equipment:** You need to determine what resources you and your students will need to learn as much material as quickly as possible.

- **Motivation/anticipatory set:** This should be an integral part of the opening exercise in your class each day. An anticipatory set allows students to mentally shift gears from what they were doing before class began and encourages students to become interested in and excited about the lesson they are going to begin. You must motivate your students to succeed if you want them to learn. This does not happen by chance. Plan the methods of motivation that you will use to engage every student.

- **Prior knowledge assessment:** You must assess your students' prior knowledge before you begin teaching a lesson to determine exactly what you have to review or introduce.

- **Explanation or teacher input:** Your input is necessary for a lesson to be successful. Carefully plan what it is that you are going to do or say to make your points.

- **Student activities:** These can include a wide rage of activities that involve independent and guided practice. You should plan them out in sequential order.

- **Alternative activities:** Allow for differences in student ability and speed of mastery with alternative activities that allow for enrichment or remediation.

- **Closure:** There are many successful ways to provide closure to a class. Make sure that you close each class with an activity designed to reinforce learning. Allowing students to drift from one class to another without a formal closure fails to make use of the tendency that students have to recall the opening and ending of a lesson with clarity.

Homework: Homework assignments should arise naturally from the lesson. They are part of what you teach and should be recorded in your plans.

Assessments: You should include a variety of assessments in each unit of study. Plan for several smaller ones before a major test or final grade so that you do not have to deal with a roomful of students who are not prepared to take a test.

Notes: Allow space on your daily plans to record your successes and failures and any other information that will allow you to teach this lesson more successfully in the future.

Capture the Big Picture

Before you can write a successful daily plan, you must have a clear idea of what your students will have to learn by the end of the school term. You must plan for the entire year before you plan for each day.

You should begin with a review of your state's standards. Because all states now have published their standards, you can easily find this information at your state's department of education Web site. Next, review your local curriculum guidelines, which will probably be closely aligned to the state curriculum. This has been a fortunate by-product of the push for national standards and improved student achievement.

After you have copies of the curriculum guides that you need to plan for the year, turn to your textbook and other teaching materials to see how you can use these resources to meet the standards set by your district and by your state. Carefully read this material. Although this will take you some time, it will save you the time and stress of dealing with unhappy and unsuccessful students later.

"Putting off your paperwork is what your students will try to do. How can you model what they are supposed to do if you neglect your 'homework'? How can you really expect them to turn in their work on time if you are turning in your lesson plans late? How can you expect neatness from their work if your work is a mess?"

—Ken Pfeifer, 28 years experience

The supplementary resource material that accompanies textbooks is also designed to be in alignment with your state's curriculum. Study it carefully. You should be able to find a wide variety of teaching strategies and a suggested planning sequence for each unit.

Finally, don't neglect one of your most important resources: your colleagues. Because as a first-year teacher you don't have a wealth of handouts and lesson plans already on hand, ask other teachers what resources they have that they would be willing to share with you. However, if you borrow materials, return them promptly and in the same condition that you received them, and be sure to write notes thanking the generous people who may have shared their personal materials with you.

Figure 6.2
A "To Do" List for Planning Lessons

I. Curriculum

- ☐ Checked state guidelines
- ☐ Checked district guidelines
- ☐ Created yearly plan or overview
- ☐ Created semester plan
- ☐ Created unit plans
- ☐ Created daily plans

II. Calendar

- ☐ Checked for holidays and upcoming events
- ☐ Determined length of unit
- ☐ Scheduled outside resources
- ☐ Scheduled assessments
- ☐ Given students a syllabus

III. Motivational Activities

- ☐ Anticipatory set
- ☐ Closure
- ☐ Others

IV. Student Activities

- ☐ Independent work
- ☐ Group work
- ☐ Guided practice
- ☐ Independent practice
- ☐ Enrichment
- ☐ Remediation

- ☐ Critical thinking activities
- ☐ Homework
- ☐ Projects
- ☐ Review
- ☐ Activities based on different learning styles
- ☐ Others: _____

V. Assessments

- ☐ Review of prior knowledge
- ☐ Frequent checkups
- ☐ Final assessment
- ☐ Others:

VI. Materials and Resources

- ☐ Textbook pages
- ☐ Media
- ☐ Hands on/manipulatives
- ☐ Outside resources
- ☐ Others: _____

After you have a general idea of what you are responsible for teaching each year, you need to decide on the scope and sequence of your instruction. In some districts, this may already be structured for you or you may have the opportunity to work on a horizontal or vertical planning team. However, you will typically need to determine the following.

- What you will teach
- When you will teach it
- To what extent you will teach it
- How long it will take

This task will be easier if you create an overview of your course to guide you and your students all year.

Create an Overview of Your Course

Step 1: Obtain the following resources: state curriculum guidelines, district curriculum guidelines, your textbook, and any supplemental resource materials that accompany the text.

Step 2: Make a list of the units that you will have to cover in order to meet state and district guidelines and objectives.

Step 3: Prioritize your list into three tiers of importance: 1) the units that you absolutely must cover, 2) the material that you would like to cover if you have time, and 3) the units that you plan to offer to students as enrichment or remedial work.

Step 4: Go through the text and select the material that you will use to create and teach each unit.

Here is a brief sample of an overview of the three tiers (step 3) for a course in world history.

State and district guideline: Students will be able to understand the cultural impact of unsanitary living conditions during the Late Middle Ages.

I. <u>Essential Units:</u> walled cities, rise of the Church, Black Death

II. <u>Time-Permitting Units:</u> medical superstitions, the sewers of London and Paris

III. <u>Enrichment Units:</u> medical cures from the period still used today, "London Bridges Falling Down" as a description of the Black Death, the lost rivers of London

IV. <u>Remediation Unit:</u> design and build a model of a walled city in the Late Middle Ages

Plan the Semester's Work

Now that you have a general idea of the material that you plan to teach over the course of the year, take time to organize it into a sequence that builds skill upon skill and knowledge base upon knowledge base.

Once again the place to begin with this type of planning is your course overview. You should now take the units that you have decided to teach and place them in a logical order with designated time frames for each so that you have a balanced curriculum and are not trying to cram in material during the last few days of school.

The keys to a successful semester plan lie in the importance that you give to building on your students' prior knowledge and on creating a successful continuum of instruction. If you begin the year with material that students find appealing because it is at least somewhat familiar, you encourage your students to become confident learners. Always build on your students' strengths. Further, there should be logical connections among the various units that you cover. This is much easier in some classes than others. For example, in a math class students have to know how to add before they can multiply. Pay attention to building connections in the units that you teach so your students not only progress throughout the semester, but so they are also aware of their progress. This awareness will build students' confidence and help you as you add a day's learning to the one before it and the one before that until the total adds to students' successful mastery of material.

How to Create Unit Plans

To create plans for a unit of study, you must first decide how long the unit will take from the first objective to the final assessment. Some units are much more detailed and difficult to teach than others. The length of time that you plan to spend on a unit will determine the activities that you plan. Another crucial step that you must take in preparing unit plans is to determine what your students already know about the topic. This, too, will determine the activities that you will include.

With a timeline and prior knowledge firmly established, you can find the materials you need to present the material to your students. While there are many places for you to find interesting materials, it is best to use what you have close at hand. Begin with your textbook and the supplementary materials that accompany it. Then, turn your attention to the resources in your building. Are there movies or other resources there for you to use? How about your colleagues? Do they have materials that they could share? Finally, turn to other sources such as the Internet and local libraries.

Using the state and district guidelines you have as well as your text and other materials, list the essential knowledge that students must learn in order to successfully achieve mastery of the material in this unit. Then take time to brainstorm some activities that will interest your students as you cover the material in the unit. Think of a wide range of activities that will appeal to students, meet their learning styles, and provide opportunities for them to engage in critical thinking. Let your imagination rove as you brainstorm ideas that you would like to use.

List the activities that you believe would be most useful to your students in the sequence that you want to present each one. Make sure that you plan around the calendar events that you noted as you planned your semester and year overviews.

Now, work out the assessments that you want to use. It may seem strange to create the assessments for a unit of study before you write your daily plans, but if you do this, then your daily plans will be in alignment with what you plan to assess.

Finally, create your daily plans. It is better to write out your plans for an entire unit of study rather than just a week at a time so that the logical sequence or flow of instruction is easier for you to see at a glance. You will also find it much easier to adjust the instructional pace if you have the entire unit prepared.

Sample Lesson Plan Flowchart

Here's a quick flowchart of the steps you can take in creating a unit plan.

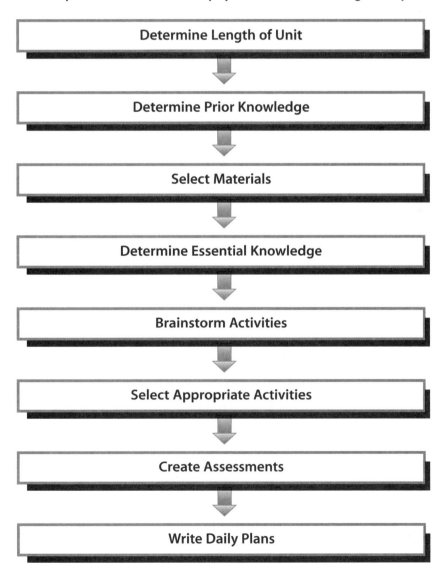

Determine Length of Unit

Determine Prior Knowledge

Select Materials

Determine Essential Knowledge

Brainstorm Activities

Select Appropriate Activities

Create Assessments

Write Daily Plans

Figure 6.3
SAMPLE FORMAT FOR A UNIT PLAN

Unit Title: _____

Dates: _____

Objectives:

1. _____

2. _____

3. _____

4. _____

5. _____

Materials:

_____

_____

Essential knowledge for mastery:

_____

_____

_____

_____

Activities:

_____

_____

_____

_____

Assessment types and dates:

_____

_____

_____

_____

How to Make Sure of Your Plans' Sequence Instruction

On Thursday I'm giving a quiz; on Friday we're watching a movie. Now, let's see, how can I fit in those oral presentations? Oh, and we've got a trip to the computer lab on . . . what day was that? I think I signed up for Thursday. But that's my quiz day . . .

This scenario presents itself every day in classrooms everywhere when teachers try to "fit in" all of the activities that they have planned for their students. Sometimes, what teachers plan for their students, for a variety of reasons, doesn't really follow the instructional flow. The result is instruction without a logical sequence.

The preceding scenario is common because it can so easily happen to a teacher—especially one who doesn't spend enough time planning lessons. With the following simple tips, you can be sure to avoid this common problem.

1. Awareness is important. Check your plans for a logical sequence. Make sure that the activities that you have planned arise naturally from the material and from the previous day's learning.

2. Teach to your objectives! Too often poor planning results in a list of neat activities that have little relationship to the serious business of mastering the information and skills in your objectives. Let objectives guide your planning.

3. Pay attention to your course year overview, semester plan, and the unit plans that you have created. If you have these in place, then you should find it easier to avoid hodgepodge instructional practices.

4. Use the anticipatory sets and closure activities that you design to help students see the connections among the activities that you assign.

5. If you plan and write your assessments before you write your daily plans, then you will have a clear idea of not just the essential knowledge that your students must have in order to master the material, but the order in which you must present it.

6. As soon as you finish plans for a unit of study, or even as soon as you complete a semester plan, arrange resources that must be scheduled ahead of time, such as computer lab, library, field trips, videos, guest speakers, etc. If you plan these far in advance, you will have a better opportunity of scheduling them on a date that fits in with your plans. Remember that you are competing with experienced teachers for these resources, and experienced teachers often schedule the resources at the beginning of the semester.

7. There are thousands of creative activities for you to choose from. When you look over your brainstormed list of instructional activities for each unit of study, don't just select the ones that you and your students would enjoy. First ask yourself how the activity will fit into your plans.

Daily Plans That Work for You and Your Students

Good classes don't just happen. If you want to have a good day at school, then you must plan it. While year, semester, and unit plans are the backbones of your curriculum planning, your daily plans are what will make the lesson come to life for your students.

Your daily plans should follow a standard format. Your school district may have a format that you will be expected to use. If not, then you should create a format that you can use easily. You will find one on page 167 that you can adapt for your classes. Many teachers design their own planning templates and photocopy them so that they just have to pencil in activities for each section. If you have daily access to a computer, then you can also create a template and adjust it as you need to. However, you will still need to print out a copy to refer to during the day.

You will also have to decide on how you want to organize your plans. Some teachers keep them in binders according to classes; other keep plans for all their classes in one large binder; and still others store their plans in color-coded folders so that they can quickly access them.

With your format and organization decisions under control, keep these pointers in mind to make sure that the lesson plans you write are not just effective, but easy for you to manage.

1. Make each day's lesson a gem. Your goal is not to just make it though a class, but to make sure that every student leaves your classroom having learned something new.

2. While you should vary your lessons, routines will keep students on track. Establish some routines so students can predict their days. For example, your routine can include a quiz every Thursday, a list of spelling words every Monday, or no homework on Tuesday nights.

3. You should not expect to cover every element of your lesson plan every day. Different activities take different times and it is impossible to fit them all in.

4. No matter what you have planned to do each day, there are two lesson elements that you must include. First, you must have an exciting anticipatory set that will encourage your students to recall what they did in your class during the last meeting and to look ahead to the current lesson. Second, you must also include a satisfying closure to your lesson. This will help your students recall what they learned in class so that they can leave the room secure that they have learned something new and worthwhile.

5. Your lesson plans should be written for your own use. Even though your supervisors will probably want to see your plans from time to time, you are really planning what you and your students are going to do each day for your own and your students' benefit. Your plans should have enough details so that you never have to fumble to find page numbers or handouts, but not so detailed that you actually write out every word that you are going to say. You will have to learn to strike a balance in preparing your plans. This will take time. At the beginning of your career, taking the time to write out detailed plans may give you a needed boost of confidence and feeling of authority.

Figure 6.4
AN EASY-TO-USE FORMAT FOR DAILY PLANS

Teacher _____ Date _____

Lesson Topic _____

Objectives:

_____

_____

_____

_____

Materials/Equipment/Textbook Pages:

_____

Prior Knowledge Assessment:

_____

Anticipatory Set:

_____

_____

Teacher Input:

_____

_____

Student Activities:

_____

_____

_____

Guided Practice:

_____

_____

Independent Practice:

_____

_____

Alternative Assignments:

_____

Closure:

_____

_____

Assessment:

_____

_____

Homework:

_____

_____

Notes:

_____

_____

10 Important Questions to Consider

Your daily lesson plans for the week are finished. You have created activities that you think will help your students learn. But how can you really be sure? Consider some of these questions as you look over your plans.

1. Do my lesson plans meet state and local guidelines?
2. Have I included activities that will open and close my class successfully?
3. Will the activities I have planned help my students master the material?
4. Will the assessments accurately and fairly evaluate my students' learning?
5. Is there a logical sequence to all of the activities I have planned? Does each activity build on a previous one?
6. Are the materials that I have selected the most appropriate ones I could choose for my students' age, interests, and readiness?
7. Have I included a variety of activities to appeal to my students' different learning styles?
8. Are there critical thinking opportunities throughout the lesson?
9. Have I planned activities for enrichment and remediation?
10. Have I made the best use of my students' time that I can?

How to Meet and Exceed Your State's Standards

Now that you are a teacher, you have joined, willingly or not, the national debate on standards and high-stakes testing. The standards themselves and the way that students' mastery is measured make headlines each week in news reports in every state across the nation.

Before the initiative for each state to create its own standards and testing instruments, school districts had few benchmarks or indicators of success. A "C" in one teacher's class could earn that same student an "F" in another teacher's class.

Nationally normed tests helped create more uniform standards, but the purpose of those tests was not to effect change in school and teacher performance, but rather to measure student aptitude and achievement. The new push for higher standards not only measures student mastery, but the effectiveness of school programs and individual teachers.

Of course, one result of high-stakes testing is high-stakes anxiety for everyone involved. But you can avoid much unnecessary anxiety if you teach so that your students meet or exceed your state's standards. Just in case you are tempted to blame your students, their unsupportive home lives, their lack of readiness, or their poor motivation . . . Stop. Such thinking is only self-defeating. Instead, you must face the task of educating your students with the belief that *you determine the success or failure of your students.*

Your students will only do as well as you think they can on any standardized measurement of their progress. Your students will succeed if you plan lessons that will help them master the standards that your state and district have established. If your lessons do not meet the guidelines, then your students can't succeed.

In case you still have doubts about your students' ability to succeed, keep in mind that teachers all across America, all across your state, all across your school district, and even in your own school work with students who are doing well on standardized tests—often to the surprise of other teachers who work with those students. If those students can succeed, then yours can, too.

Follow these suggestions to help your students meet and even exceed your state's standards.

- Become thoroughly familiar with your district's, state's, and national standards for your grade level or subject.

- Make your students aware of the standards. Post them in a conspicuous place so students can see them. Write them on tests. Put them in your grade book.

- Teach the curriculum and not to the test. If you teach the curriculum well, then the test will take care of itself.

- When you create your unit plans, semester plans, and year overview, make sure that you design curriculum that meets the objectives of the state standards before you include any special units just because they are appealing.

- Educate yourself and your students about any standardized tests that they will have to take. Find samples from old tests that have been released for teacher use or use other review material. Make sure your students have the test-taking skills that they will need to master the mechanics of taking the test itself.

Tap Your Students' Prior Knowledge

Experienced teachers know that their students' prior knowledge is a gift that students bring to class with them every day. Before you decide what you are going to teach, you first need to determine what it is that your students already know.

Determining your students' prior knowledge is crucial because it decides the approach that you will take with a unit of study. For example, if most of your students understand a math concept, then you may only review it briefly as a springboard to studying the next concept. Conversely, if most of your students are puzzled by information that you assume they know, you can take a more in-depth approach.

You can use what you learn about your students' prior knowledge in many different ways. For instance, if you discover that one student understands a math concept and can explain it to the rest of the class, that student can model success for your other students and motivate them to succeed. Using even incorrect prior knowledge is a trick that a savvy teacher can use to good advantage. For example, ask students to brainstorm what they know about a topic as you write their ideas on the board, including the incorrect ones. Then arouse your students' curiosity by asking them to predict which ones may be incorrect. They will want to learn more about the topic as they attempt to disprove their ideas with further study.

Determining previous learning is not difficult and need not take lots of time. There are many techniques you can use to do this, depending on the age and skill level of your students. You should be on the lookout in your own studies and in conversations with other teachers for techniques that will help you quickly and accurately determine just what your students know about a subject before you begin to teach it.

If you want to enjoy the benefits of tapping into your students' previous learning and avoid duplicating lessons they have already mastered, there are many strategies that you could use. Try adapting some of these techniques for your own students.

1. Ask students to write out a quick list of three facts that they already know or think that they know about a topic. After they have passed their responses to you, read some of them aloud (without revealing the authors) and ask the entire class to judge their veracity.

2. Ask students to write out a brief description of what they have already been taught about the topic you are about to study. You could even ask them to tell you when they were taught it, who did the teaching, and how the material was presented to them.

3. Create a brief sampling of some of the questions that you plan to include on a test or quiz later in the unit. Ask students to predict the correct answers.

4. Put your students into small groups and ask them to share everything they know about the topic. Set a two-minute time limit. After the time limit is up, have a representative from each group share what they discovered that they know with the rest of the class.

5. List the main points of the unit you are about to teach and ask students to write what they already know about each one.

6. List the key terms that students will be expected to learn. Have students write what they believe each term means based on what they already know about the topic. This assessment will also serve as an excellent motivator as students recognize the words when you teach them.

7. Put students in pairs and hand each pair a transparency or sheet of poster paper. Have each pair brainstorm a list of everything that they know about the topic. Share the lists with the class or display them.

8. Offer a puzzling scenario and ask students to solve it based on what they already know about the topic. For example, before beginning a unit on protective coloration in a science class you could present a problem involving birds and the various insects on which they feed. Have students keep their responses and ask them to verify their knowledge as they progress in their study.

9. Show students a photograph, cartoon, diagram, quotation, or brief article related to the topic that you are about to study. Ask them to share their reactions.

10. Create a Know/Want to Know/Learned (KWL) chart for your students. The assessment of prior knowledge, will, of course, occur when you have students complete the first two sections of the chart. You chart should look like this.

What Do You Know?

Today we are going to begin a study of _____. Complete the first part of the chart (Know) by telling me what you know already about the topic. After you have finished this section, open your text and quickly scan the chapter. Use the information you learned from the chapter to complete the second section (Want to Know). You will complete the third section at the end of the unit.

Know	Want to Know	Learned
1.	1.	1.
2.	2.	2.
3.	3.	3.
4.	4.	4.
5.	5.	5.

Perfect Your Pacing

Pacing a lesson means that you teach just what needs to be taught in the best way possible so that you can find the right mixture of activities to encourage your students to learn at the optimum rate for mastery.

Correctly pacing a lesson takes practice. It usually takes a few weeks of getting to know your students, a few months of designing instruction, and a few years of general teaching experience before you can feel that you have mastered the art of pacing.

Even though it takes time to really get control of the finer points of correctly pacing a lesson, there are several things that you can do in your first year of teaching to get on the right track with this teaching skill. Start with the following suggestions.

1. Like experienced teachers, the biggest problem you will experience with pacing is that *the work takes longer than you expect*. You might have planned an interesting week-long unit on prime numbers only to find that you need to cover missing background information. You also maybe surprised at how long it takes your students to complete assignments. Be as flexible with your schedule as you can. In addition, focus on what needs to be taught and add in the enrichment material later. This is the point where your careful attention to state and district guidelines will pay off.

2. Plan too much work for your students. If your students finish a day's work early, you should always have just one more activity that you can offer to keep them learning. But don't make this busywork. Design purposeful work that will truly help your students learn.

3. Make sure that the homework assignments that you plan are ones that will add to your students' learning. Used correctly, homework time is a valuable commodity that can increase the rate at which your students learn.

Another facet of perfecting your pacing skills involves using class time for its maximum value. Be sure to include a variety of activities in each class to keep students focused and working quickly.

If you divide your class into ten-minute blocks of time, you will find success with almost every student at any grade level, whether you teach on a traditional schedule or a variation of a block schedule. Breaking long blocks of time into smaller units will help you keep students' interests from flagging. After allowing ten minutes for the opening of class and another ten minutes for the closure to a lesson, you still have a fairly long block of time available for learning.

Remember that even though pacing takes lots of experience and practice, you can master the rudiments quickly in your first few weeks as a teacher.

Include Opportunities for Critical Thinking

One of the most welcomed educational movements recently is the emphasis on the development of critical-thinking skills for students of all ages. Critical-thinking activities enhance learning because, while students find them enjoyable, they also increase retention and lesson mastery.

When you plan lessons that involve critical thinking, you should be aware that students must first have some awareness of the material so that they have information to draw on. If you plan carefully, the activities that involve critical thinking will arise from the lesson itself and thereby enhance the opportunities for mastery of the objectives you are trying to teach.

In order to develop their critical-thinking skills, students need to practice these skills often. One of the best rewards you will receive as a result is watching your students as they become absorbed in their work. There are many different ways to include opportunities for critical-thinking skills into any lesson, including the following.

1. If your students are old enough, raise their awareness of what critical thinking is by teaching them about Bloom's Taxonomy. You will need a common vocabulary if you are to teach them to think.

2. Strive to build a community of trust in your classroom so students will be tolerant of the opinions of their peers as they learn to work well together.

3. Master the art of collaborative learning. When your students work well together, critical thinking is a dynamic way to learn. (You will find lots of information about collaborative learning in Section Nine.)

4. Teach students to look beyond the obvious. One simple way to do this is to hand everyone a simple object, such as a lemon or a small rock, and ask them to study it exhaustively. Then ask students to share with their classmates what they have discovered. Students are often shocked when they find out what their classmates have discovered that they overlooked.

5. Offer your students games, puzzles, riddles, and other lively exercises to get their thinking stimulated.

6. Encourage your students to deal with real-world issues as often as you can. Students who can connect their textbook learning to their real lives are already on the road to thinking critically.

As you can see, higher-level thinking skills are enjoyable aspects of designing and delivering instruction. You can amplify even mundane drill exercises by tweaking your approach just a little. To incorporate critical thinking in every exercise, you can ask students to:

- Give reasons for their answers
- Generate their own problems
- Generate multiple solutions
- Give extended answers
- Relate the lesson to their own lives
- Relate the lesson to other classes
- Trace the origins of their thinking
- Collaborate on responses
- Combine ideas from widely differing sources
- Evaluate each other's work

Give Directions That Encourage Critical Thinking

Another way to include critical-thinking opportunities in class is to carefully choose the language that you use to ask students to work. Instead of using broad terms such as "understand' or "appreciate," give students work instructions that will require them to delve beneath the surface. For example, you can tell students to state why they agree or disagree with a statement or develop criteria to assess the status of a situation. When you change the language that you use to ask students to work, you incorporate critical thinking in your class. For example, if you ask students to *retell* a story that they have read, you are only asking them to demonstrate that they have comprehended the events in the story. If you were to ask students to *classify* those same events according to whether they are causes or effects, then you are requiring students to not just comprehend the story, but to analyze it.

Here is a small group of words that you should avoid using when planning lessons, as they are too general or vague to lead to critical thinking: *understand, appreciate, know, enjoy,* and *believe.*

The following are lists of verbs or verb phrases that you may use in planning. Each list applies to an area of Bloom's Taxonomy and will involve your students in meaningful activities.

KNOWLEDGE LEVEL

This level involves the identification and recall of information.
These verbs will lead students to respond, recall, and recognize.

Choose	List	Enumerate	Recite	Label
Select	Outline	Name	Quote	Diagram
Recall	Recognize	Cite	Match	Omit
Identify	Define	Draw	Index	
Describe	Record	Read	Count	

COMPREHENSION LEVEL

This level involves the organization and selection of facts and ideas.
These verbs will lead students to interpret, explain, and demonstrate.

Estimate	Clarify	Add	Graph	Elaborate
Judge	Associate	Show	Represent	Express
Infer	Retell	Explain	Discuss	Extend
Characterize	Classify	Approximate	Distinguish	Determine
Articulate	Demonstrate	Select	Compare	

APPLICATION LEVEL

This level involves the use of facts and principles in new situations.
These verbs will lead students to demonstrate, construct, and solve problems.

Use	Translate	Change	Model	Judge
Acquire	Produce	Classify	Alphabetize	Solve
Explain	Compute	Tabulate	Allocate	Sequence
Predict	Customize	Sketch	Apply	Round off
Adapt	Project	Construct	Transcribe	

ANALYSIS LEVEL

This level involves the separation of a whole into component parts.
These verbs will lead students to dissect, uncover, and list.

Analyze	Break down	Inventory	Optimize	Separate
Dissect	Simplify	Infer	Order	Maximize
Audit	Categorize	Experiment	Outline	Minimize
Uncover	Translate	Characterize	Prioritize	Divide
Blueprint	Classify	Proofread	Compare	Summarize

SYNTHESIS LEVEL

This level involves the combination of new ideas to form a new whole.
These verbs will lead students to discuss, relate, and generalize.

Write	Budget	Form	Compose	Produce
Specify	Blend	Join	Lecture	Rearrange
Combine	Arrange	Construct	Propose	Portray
Reorganize	Revise	Integrate	Organize	Create
Animate	Modify	Invent	Generalize	Relate

EVALUATION LEVEL

This level involves the development of opinions or judgments.
These verbs will lead students to debate, judge, and form opinions.

Appraise	Conclude	Reject	Judge	Decide
Value	Rank	Select	Recommend	Critique
Assess	Contrast	Rate	Estimate	Evaluate
Compare	Recommend	Justify	Measure	Debate
Editorialize	Grade	Choose	Test	Verify

175

Figure 6.5
CRITICAL-THINKING QUESTIONS FOR STUDENTS

One of the easiest ways to incorporate critical thinking into a lesson is by asking open-ended questions designed to stimulate and direct thought. In the list below you will find some general questions grouped according to Bloom's Taxonomy. While there are thousands more questions for you to ask, these should help you focus on the higher-level thinking skills necessary for student success.

Comprehension

What are some things that we can learn from this experience?
Write a brief summary of today's class.

Application

What steps did you take to arrive at that answer?
How can you apply what you learned in class today to your life?

Analysis

What are the reasons for the behavior that we studied today?
What is the quickest way to learn the facts of today's lesson?

Synthesis

Group the items on the board according to a criteria that you devise.
List as many ways as you can that you are like a character we studied today.

Evaluation

What qualities caused the people in today's lesson to succeed?
How do you know that you have done a job to the best of your ability?

Give Your Students a Syllabus

A syllabus is a published lesson plan. You can probably recall the advantages of using a syllabus from the classes you have taken to prepare for a teaching career. Your students will also appreciate a syllabus. It can help them stay organized while it promotes self-discipline. Students who know what they are supposed to do and when they are supposed to do it are much more likely to succeed than those students who report to class every day waiting to hear what you have planned. Those students miss out on the big picture of what they are learning. Of course, not every student is old enough to handle the independence of a syllabus. You will have to determine the readiness of your students.

While there are many things that you can add to a syllabus to make it useful for your classes, some items that every syllabus should include are:

- Dates (of quizzes, tests, etc.)
- Spaces for students to record their grades
- Classroom assignments
- Homework assignments
- Due dates for projects
- Class objectives

You will have to make a syllabus part of the culture of your class. But first, you will have to teach your students how to use a syllabus, particularly if they are very young, and you'll have to be patient and persistent with their attempts to learn to check their syllabus for homework assignments instead of just asking you.

Don't be afraid to change your syllabus if you find that you've scheduled more work than your students can complete because of an unexpected event such as a snow day. When you show students that you are willing to work with them to adjust schedules, you are modeling responsible time management skills as well as good planning.

Figure 6.6
SAMPLE SYLLABUS FORMAT

		Syllabus		
Class: English 8		**Period:** 4	**Teacher:** Mrs. Thompson	
Date	**Objective**	**Classroom Activity**	**Homework**	**Grade**
10-1	Students will identify short story plot elements.	Discussion of the plot of "The Tell-Tale Heart"	Worksheet on story elements	
10-2	Students will identify short story plot elements.	Homework check/Group diagrams/Discussions	Review for quiz	97%
10-3	Students will identify short story plot elements.	Quiz on plot elements	Read "Charles"	98%

Offer Your Students Options

If you always make your students' success your first concern when planning lessons, then you will find that offering options is a reasonable thing to do. In fact, offering your students some options or alternative assignments is the hallmark of effective teaching. When you offer alternative assignments, you are not offering students a choice of whether to do the work or not. This is certainly not justifiable. Instead, you are giving each student the opportunity to engage more fully in the assignment.

If you have ever purchased an automobile from a successful salesperson, you have probably experienced the high art of offering options. For example, instead of asking you if you were interested in a car, the salesperson probably asked which car you liked. And instead of asking how you intended to scrape up the money on your teacher's salary, the salesperson probably asked if you wanted to finance the car with a bank or with your own company.

In both of these situations, you were offered attractive options that had the same objective: to encourage you to purchase a car. When you offer students options, you can make a lesson attractive by giving students a choice of activities.

Although not every lesson lends itself to options, there are many times when offering alternative lessons just makes sense. Consider offering alternative assignments when you and your students experience any of these situations.

1. The assignment for the day turns out to be too much work for students to accomplish at one time.

2. Students are successfully completing the day's work much faster than you had planned for them to do.

3. The work proves to be too difficult for many students.

4. You realize that students would benefit more from working together instead of working independently.

5. Students are increasingly restless and off task.

6. You discover that the material you are using is just not appropriate for lesson mastery.

7. Many of your students lack the background preparation to successfully master the material without more support from you.

Offering alternative assignments adds intrinsic motivation. However, offering alternative assignments is not something that you can do without thinking the situation through and without careful planning. Don't be tempted into making a snap decision as soon as you find your students becoming restless. Instead, if you have not prepared alternative assignment choices when you planned the unit, take time overnight to create the assignments so that they will have meaning and will assist your students in mastering the material. The assignments that you have created for enrichment and remediation are a good starting point.

Review the following suggestions when you want to offer students attractive and effective options. Not all of them will be appropriate for your students, but you can adapt them and add ideas of your own. There are spaces at the end of the list for you to add your own optional strategies.

1. Allow students to choose between the even and the odd questions when they have a long practice assignment.

2. List the day's tasks on the board and allow students to decide on the order in which they will complete them.

3. Allow students to choose the type of test they would like at the end of a unit of study: a traditional test with a mixture of question types or an essay test.

4. When assigning reading for class discussion, allow students to choose from a variety of articles that you have selected.

5. Let students select the role that they will assume in group work.

6. Allow students to skip directly to enrichment assignments as soon as they can demonstrate mastery of the lesson objective.

7. Give students a choice of assignments intended to appeal to different learning styles.

8. Allow students leeway in the length of writing assignments. Instead of saying, "Write a one-half page response," tell your students to write a response that is "at least one-half page long and may be as long as three pages."

9. Allow students a wide range of activities when they have completed their work. You can do this efficiently if you establish this early in the year as one of your class procedures.

Your ideas for alternative assignments:

_____

_____

_____

_____

> *"Have a Plan B in case Plan A fails."*
>
> —Barbara Knowles, 36 years experience

Double the Effectiveness of Your Lessons

There are many things that you can do to make sure that your lessons are effective. Some are easier to achieve than others. Unfortunately, there is no magic bullet that will turn any unexciting lesson into an effective one with just a single act. Instead, if you want to double the effectiveness of your lessons, you will have to use as many of the techniques in the list below as you can. If you have planned your lessons carefully, then you should have little difficulty tweaking them for maximum effectiveness.

Review and adapt these suggestions when you want to make sure that your lessons are as successful as possible.

1. Teach to the objective and not to a test.
2. Stop frequently for review and reteaching.
3. Make sure to gear your opening and closing exercises for mastery.
4. Design lessons that appeal to your students' learning styles.
5. Plan activities in ten- or fifteen-minute blocks.
6. Offer alternative assignments when appropriate.
7. Write assessments in advance of daily plans.
8. Incorporate a variety of materials and resources.
9. Use your state and district standards as guidelines.
10. Never stop looking for new lesson plan ideas.
11. Stay as far ahead in your plans as you can.
12. Plan the year and each semester before you make unit and daily plans.
13. Build upon your students' prior learning.
14. Make sure your lessons follow each other in a logical sequence.
15. Keep your students motivated by offering a wide variety of activities.
16. Allow plenty of checkpoint assessments before you give a final assessment.
17. Teach students to use their critical-thinking skills.
18. Keep your students on track with a syllabus.
19. Allow time for your students to reflect on their learning.
20. Spend time reflecting on your plans and the effectiveness of your techniques.

How to Adjust a Lesson That Isn't Working

It is not uncommon for students to feel frustrated by not grasping a concept or to have trouble staying on task. But when such behavior seems to become the norm rather than a temporary situation, you must be prepared to adjust your lesson plans so that they once again meet your students' needs.

While the methods of adjusting your plan will vary from problem to problem and from class to class, there are certain actions that you can take to correct most situations quickly. The following tips will help you turn a frustrating lesson into a successful one as quickly as possible.

1. Don't be tempted to give in to your own frustration and reprimand your students. Think about why they are off task and solve that problem instead.
2. Often just switching to another learning modality will engage students enough that they will work harder to overcome any small frustrations.

3. Reduce either the amount of drill and practice that you have assigned or make it more palatable by allowing students to tackle it in pairs or small groups.

4. Call a stop to the lesson. Assess the situation and determine what your students already know so as to avoid needlessly repeating what they know or leaving them behind by moving on to subject matter they are not ready to process.

5. If the lesson isn't working well because of interference from an exciting event such as field day, a holiday, or a snow day, consider allowing students to chat for a minute or two—set your timer—before settling down to work.

6. Another way to adjust a lesson that isn't working well because of interference from an exciting event is to incorporate the event into the lesson. For example, on a snow day, your students can write snow poems, determine the probability of missing the next few days, determine the mass of a flake, or even discuss the effect of snowstorms throughout history.

Evaluate Your Lesson Plans

Here is a list of questions that experienced teachers ask about their lessons as they write their plans. Answering these questions should lead you to a successful sequence of interesting lessons designed to meet or exceed your state's standards for student mastery of the material required for a grade level or subject.

1. How do these plans satisfy the state and district guidelines?

2. What are the objectives that will create successful mastery?

3. Are the resources and materials appropriate for my students?

4. How can I assess my students' previous learning?

5. What motivation strategies will work best with this lesson?

6. Do my daily plans help my students use their time effectively?

7. Does each day's lesson begin and end with activities that promote retention?

8. What areas are most likely to be confusing for my student?

9. What higher-level thinking activities can I include?

10. What progress checks should I use before the final assessment?

11. How long will it take my students to master this material?

12. What alternative assignments can I offer my students?

13. What preliminary work such as reading, researching, photocopying must I do in order to teach this material well?

14. What strategies can I use to ensure that my students retain this information?

15. When this unit of study is completed, what should I do to change how I present this information next term?

Journal Entries to Help You Examine Your Planning Skills

▶ What can you do to make your lessons exciting this week?

▶ What signs can you look for to determine if your lesson is successful?

▶ Describe when you have been most dynamic as a teacher.

▶ Describe the concept of learning. How would your students describe this concept?

▶ Describe a time when your students learned an unexpected lesson.

▶ What did you most enjoy about today's lessons? What did *you* learn?

▶ What do you know about lesson plans? What lesson planning skills do you need to improve?

▶ How can you incorporate critical thinking into every lesson?

▶ How can you include real-life experiences in every lesson?

Deliver Effective Instruction

It's the first student assembly of the year. She watches the band director in awe. The very same students who can't sit up straight and take notes in her class intently play a complicated piece of music with delightful harmony. The band director obviously knows the music and can inspire his band students into a peak performance.

When she had been a music student herself, the delivery of the music was not always quite up to this standard. At one performance, the band director had missed notes and entire sections of the band had been confused into a discord that was still embarrassing to recall.

Was this what she was doing with her students? Was she missing the notes?

A discordant performance can happen in any classroom to even the best-prepared teachers. A teacher may have the most detailed lesson plans in the entire school, but if he or she doesn't deliver the instruction effectively, then students just can't learn.

On the other hand, when a lesson is skillfully delivered, a cycle of success gains momentum. Confident teachers inspire their students. Successful students, in turn, create confident teachers. This cycle is one of the most satisfying reasons to teach.

What is an effective delivery and how does it give a teacher control? Many teachers believe that an effective delivery of instruction is speaking well in front of students. Although a teacher does need outstanding speaking skills, this is not the only part of delivering instruction well. Other components of a good lesson include discovery techniques, class discussions, questioning sessions, frequent reviews, practice, pairing, innovative student activities, and students working well together, just to name a few.

Best of all, when teachers know that students have made a complete transfer of knowledge through the various aspects of the lesson that they have delivered, then teachers can feel in control of a class period, the lesson, and the success of the students in their care.

> *"Ask questions—as many as possible."*
>
> —Denise Boyer, 12 years experience

Guidelines for Improving Your Classroom Charisma

If you look back on your own days as a student, you can recall with ease teachers who made learning fun. You wanted to be in their classes. Best of all, you were certain that those teachers liked you and missed you on those days when you had to be absent. Teachers hand students a gift when they make each child feel that he or she is necessary to the proper functioning of the class, because having the acceptance of the significant adults in their lives helps children grow into strong and capable adults.

Those gifted teachers in your past were probably one of the reasons that you wanted to be a teacher. If you succeed at nothing else in your new career, you should aim to create the same effect on your students that those teachers had on you.

What makes certain teachers gifted? Charisma. According to a standard definition, charisma is "a unique personal power belonging to those individuals who secure the allegiance of large numbers of people." Shouldn't this be the job description of every educator?

Fortunately for many of us, classroom charisma is a learned trait. It is something that you should begin to work on the very first day that you step to the front of a class, and you will still be working on it the very last day that you teach.

Here are some general guidelines to help you become a charismatic teacher. Begin by selecting the steps that you know you can manage with ease and then move on to the ones that need a more concerted effort on your part.

- The class should be about the students and their work. Make them the focus of your attention. Some less experienced teachers make the mistake of talking about their own lives too much or completing paperwork while ignoring students who are quietly not working. Stay focused on what's really important: your students and their work.

- Smile at your students. No one likes a grouch. A teacher with a pleasant demeanor has half of the charisma battle won. What if you don't feel like smiling? Do it anyway. You owe it to your students. And remember that your difficult students are the very ones who most need your smiling support.

- Stand at the door to meet and greet your students as they come into the classroom. If for no other reason, you should meet and greet your students to help make sure that discipline problems are kept to a minimum. At the same time, this will make your students feel valued.

- Overlook what you can. Although it is okay to be strict with your students, there is a very fine distinction between a strict teacher and a too-strict teacher. If you spend your days nit-picking over minor problems with your students, then you will not have enough time to get around to the larger issues. The atmosphere in your class should be one of relaxed but focused and purposeful activity.

- Early in the term establish the procedures and routines that you want your students to follow, and stick to them as much as reasonably possible. Students who know what they are supposed to do and how they are supposed to do it are much more comfortable and happy than those who are uncertain about what is expected of them. If you establish routines and procedures early, then you will be able to spend

Figure 7.1

IS YOUR DELIVERY EFFECTIVE?

Part One: Rate Yourself on the Standards for These Skills

Rate yourself on this part of the test by assigning yourself a letter grade for each area.

D = Needs work   C = Satisfactory   B = Good   A = Excellent

1. _____ My voice is loud enough for all of my students to hear me.

2. _____ I vary the expression in my voice.

3. _____ I always use standard English.

4. _____ I sound respectful and serious when I speak to my students.

5. _____ I have eliminated fill-in expressions such as "like" and "you know."

6. _____ I use a vocabulary that is appropriate for my students' age.

7. _____ I dress professionally.

8. _____ My posture projects enthusiasm and confidence.

9. _____ My gestures are inviting and not distracting.

10. _____ My body language invites my students to listen and learn.

11. _____ I use appropriate visual aids when I teach.

12. _____ I move around during the class period.

13. _____ I use questioning techniques that engage all students.

14. _____ I politely wait until I have everyone's attention before I begin.

15. _____ I use eye contact effectively.

16. _____ Every lesson is packed with a variety of interesting activities.

17. _____ I review key points often during the course of instruction.

18. _____ Class discussions in my room include every student.

19. _____ I use techniques that will appeal to all of my students' learning styles.

20. _____ I don't mumble or allow my sentences to just trail away.

185

Part Two: Pay Attention to Your Audience

Good speakers pay attention to non-verbal cues from their audience. You'll need to add some pizzazz to your delivery if you notice that your students are doing any of the following.

- Watching the clock
- Looking confused
- Flipping through their notebooks
- Staring off into space
- Talking to someone sitting nearby
- Refusing to look at you
- Putting their heads down on their desks to sleep
- Doing homework for another class
- Asking to go to their lockers, the restroom, the nurse, the phone
- Tying and retying their shoes
- Sighing loudly and rolling their eyes

Part Three: Rank Your Strengths

Think about what you can feel confident about when you deliver instruction. Rank your strengths from 1 to 10, with 1 being the skill you feel is your strongest and 10 being the one you feel is your weakest.

_____ I use appropriate body language and eye contact.

_____ I use a varied and enthusiastic speaking voice.

_____ I maintain an appropriate tone when speaking to students.

_____ I often use exciting and appealing visual aids.

_____ I design lessons that include interesting activities.

_____ I appeal to my students' different learning styles.

_____ I use engaging questioning techniques.

_____ I wait and command my students' attention before speaking.

_____ I stress practice and review techniques.

_____ I project a confident, knowledgeable, and professional attitude.

time with your students doing pleasant and interesting activities, because you will not have to repeatedly explain the day-to-day rules students are supposed to follow.

▶ Laugh at yourself. While you should not be the focus of the class—your students and their work should be—you should let your students know that you have enough confidence in yourself to not take yourself too seriously.

▶ Establish an atmosphere of mutual respect. This is a day-to-day process that involves thoughtful work with every student in your class. Begin by being careful that your body language and tone of voice convey that you enjoy and respect your students. When you establish a positive climate, you and your students will exhibit respect for each other.

> *"Keep smiling, no matter what. Everyone feels better when they see a smile."*
>
> —Denise Boyer, 12 years experience

▶ Make sure to eliminate distracting personal habits that can annoy many students. Some of the most obvious ones that can interfere with your classroom charisma are a monotone voice, poor eye contact, sloppy speech patterns, bad posture, a very messy classroom, an unprofessional appearance, and distracting gestures.

▶ Use multiple modes of learning to make sure your lessons are as dynamic and exciting as possible. Include visual aids, jokes, music, and other active learning strategies to involve every student in every lesson every day. Students should want to come to your class to see what you have in store for them to do and to learn.

▶ Convey your belief in your students. Every child should feel that he or she is capable of learning the material that you are presenting. Proceed with confidence in students as well as in yourself.

▶ Teachers with charisma talk much less than the students in their classes. Ask questions that will encourage students to share their ideas with you.

Figure 7.2

STUDENT FEEDBACK

Although there are many ways for a teacher to determine just how effective his or her delivery has been, too many of them neglect the obvious: asking students to evaluate the lesson. Use this mini-worksheet to elicit valuable feedback on just how you're doing from the most valuable source you have: your audience.

Evaluate Today's Lesson

Please write your reaction to today's lesson by completing these statements. Be sure to give enough information so that your feedback will be helpful.

Name: _____ Date: _____

(Note: *It is not necessary to write your name here. Please fill in the date.*)

1. The purpose of today's lesson was to _____

   _____

2. Three important facts or key points that I can recite are _____

   _____

3. I used listening skills to _____

   _____

4. I used reading skills to _____

   _____

5. I used writing skills to _____

   _____

6. The most interesting part of the lesson was _____

   _____

7. I felt challenged when _____

   _____

8. I need more information about _____

   _____

9. I can use the information I learned today to _____

   _____

10. I did not understand _____

    _____

Pitfalls That Plague Too Many Teachers

Many factors can interfere with a teacher's delivery of instruction. Teachers who are under a lot of stress, too tired to plan appealing lessons, or not quite in tune with the needs and interests of their students are likely to have a class lacking a smooth flow of instruction. Happily, most of the pitfalls in a teacher's day can very easily be avoided with just a bit of awareness, common sense, and planning. Here is a list of some of the mistakes you can easily avoid when you are planning how you will deliver instruction.

Whose voice is heard?

Don't talk more than your students.

Do design activities that encourage your students to talk to each other and to you.

Who does the work?

Don't create lessons that allow your students to be passive.

Do skip the fill-in-the-blanks worksheets you can spend hours creating and ask students to outline, take notes, highlight, or engage in other open-ended thinking activities.

What are you teaching?

Don't just teach the subject spelled out on your state's curriculum guides.

Do consider your students' interests, learning styles, needs, and prior learning when you decide what and how to teach.

Why deliver uninspiring lessons?

Don't stick to the same unvarying methods of instruction.

Do dare to be creative. Have fun designing games, competitions, and other ways to help your students enjoy learning.

Why let teaching opportunities go by?

Don't let the national push for higher standards and teacher/student accountability intimidate you into neglecting opportunities to use those serendipitous moments that occur every so often in any classroom.

Do seize every opportunity to turn any occasion into a learning event in your classroom. Capitalize on current events and student interests whenever you can.

How much material can you teach in one class?

Don't allow yourself to drift when it comes to finding the correct pace for the delivery of instruction. This takes practice, organization, and planning.

Do make sure to plan alternate lessons in case the pace you originally set for a lesson needs adjustment.

Who's in charge of your class?

Don't allow misbehavior to interfere with the instruction in your class.

Do establish consistent routines, procedures, rules, and consequences to keep the focus in your class on learning and not on misbehavior.

Which modes of instruction should you use?

Don't rely too much on your own favorite learning style.

189

Do be careful to include at least two modes of instruction and to vary the activities in your class so the diverse learning styles of all your students can be met.

How much time do you really need to teach the material?

Don't allow your students to sit around with nothing important to do while they wait for class to begin or end or for you to do housekeeping chores.

Do follow this practical advice from veteran teachers: plan at least twice as much work as you think your students will have time for in each class.

How will your students know what to do?

Don't confuse your students by giving hurried or unclear directions.

Do be extra careful to deliver a combination of written and oral directions and to check for students' understanding.

Why speak if no one will listen?

Don't forget your audience when you are speaking to groups of students.

Do command their attention and wait for them to listen to you before you begin.

What is the purpose of the lesson?

Don't neglect to deliver purposeful instruction.

Do make sure that every lesson is designed to meet a specific objective and that your students know what that objective is.

How to Make a Point Students Will Remember

Although there is an endless assortment of creative techniques that will help your students remember a point that you make during a lesson, you will have to plan and prepare in advance to make each technique successful. Successful teachers are those who are willing to experiment with all sorts of new approaches to help their students find success.

The following are some techniques you can use to help your students be alert and interested in a lesson. Don't be afraid to modify, adapt, and combine these ideas to shake up your own thinking about a subject so that you can get your points across to every student.

1. Help your students make a personal connection to the lesson. They should be able to identify with the people in the material under study. One way to do this is to use their names when creating worksheets or questions.

2. Incorporate the interests, hobbies, concerns, experiences, dreams, and cultures of your students as often as you can into each lesson.

3. Provide opportunities for students to display their work and to be recognized for their accomplishments. Students whose excellent math papers are displayed, for example, will feel proud and confident and knowledgeable about a unit of study. Be sure to get to know your students first to determine which students would be pleased by a public display of their success.

4. Use a banner, a poster, a computer display, or a "thought of the day" message to reinforce your point. You could quickly call your students' attention to this or you could let students discover the message and make the connection for themselves.

5. Invite guest speakers to speak to your students as part of a unit of study. Hearing a community leader talk about the importance of a local government, for example, will reinforce any point that you are trying to make about this topic.

6. Use plenty of models, pictures, examples and a variety of media when you demonstrate how to do something. Try these: newspapers, advertisements, T-shirt slogans, cartoons, movies, art, computers, television, magazines, videos, and music.

7. Give your students samples of food that pertain to the day's lesson.

8. Supply your students with a list of key words and phrases to pay attention to and recall as they study a particular unit.

9. Place items related to the unit under study in a large box. Wrap it with gaudy paper and a large bow. Ask students to guess what's in it. As they open the box, have them explain the significance of each item.

10. Play music that fits the lesson of the day. As you play bits and pieces of songs, ask students to write the significance of each to the lesson.

11. Hand out blindfolds and have your students put them on. Give them objects related to the message that you want them to recall and have them identify them without peeking.

12. Put a statement on the board that you want your students to recall. Guarantee that they will do so by immediately playing a videotape that supports it.

13. Give your students a checklist of the key items in the material that you are going to cover together. Ask them to focus on learning these first. You'll be surprised at how well your students can recall information that they learn in this way.

14. Hand out a newspaper or magazine with words cut out and have students supply missing information based on what they have just learned from your lesson.

15. Have students stand to tell the answer to a question. This will help them recall that point better than if you expect passive listeners. While this is an effective technique for most students, many shy students may not be comfortable with this technique. Know your students well before asking them to stand to answer.

16. Be enthusiastic about the topic and project that enthusiasm to your students. Pique their interest by allowing your own to show.

17. Present a slide show. Using this as a model, have your students prepare and present a slide show of their own.

18. Surprise students with a bit of theater. This will make your lesson fun, as well as one that students will recall far past the test. Try some of these to get started with developing your dramatic flair.

   ◗ Say something outrageously startling and interesting.

   ◗ Stage a reenactment.

   ◗ Videotape your students as they work out the points you want them to learn.

   ◗ Have them discover a message hidden in the room.

   ◗ Wear a costume or have your students wear costumes.

Figure 7.3

SET YOUR GOALS FOR GETTING YOUR POINTS ACROSS

Goal: I will deliver information so well that my students can easily recall key points. Some of the methods I can use include the following.

Music	Models
Costumes or props	Frequent reviews
Panel discussions	Puzzles
Class discussions	Humor
Debates	Visual aids
Role playing	Real life examples
Videotaping	Multiple modes of presentation
Audiotapes	Discovery techniques
Inspirational sayings	Provocative questions
Posters	Games
Graphic organizers	Other: _____

I will use at least _____ different technique per _____ (day/week/month).

What steps should I take to reach my goal?

1. _____

2. _____

3. _____

4. _____

5. _____

Who can help me reach this goal? _____

_____

What problems will I have to manage to reach my goal? _____

_____

How will I monitor my progress? _____

_____

How can I modify my goal if I have trouble reaching it? _____

_____

Brief Exercises That Will Improve Your Oral Presentations

One of the most important things to remember about improving how you speak to a large and possibly bored group of students is that you need to practice what you are going to say and how you are going to say it. Rehearse, rehearse, and rehearse some more! Maybe in a few years you will be comfortable enough to teach without rehearsals, but for now, consider rehearsing an important part of your lesson preparation.

In addition to lots and lots of practice, there are several other activities that you could use to improve the way you speak in front of a class. Try these exercises to make your oral presentations as interesting as possible.

Exercise 1: Videotape Yourself

One of the most effective ways to evaluate your delivery of instruction is to videotape yourself several times during the term. If you tape yourself several times, you will see how you have improved and where your weaknesses still exist. Of course, it is not enough to just videotape and then watch yourself unless you do so with the clear purpose of making an accurate assessment. As you watch your classroom presentation, consider the following questions to accurately assess yourself.

1. What annoying verbal tics do I have?
2. What annoying non-verbal tics do I have?
3. Is my voice loud enough and clear enough that all students can hear me?
4. Do I include all of my students by calling on them?
5. Do I project enthusiasm, authority, and confidence?
6. Do I vary activities enough so that all students can succeed?
7. When I speak, do I command my students' attention?

Exercise 2: A Well-Trained Voice

One of a teacher's most effective tools is an authoritative voice; therefore, you should be sure yours is well trained. If you have ever had a public speaking class, you have probably had to do this useful exercise. Choose a quiet time when you can be in a room by yourself. Find a fairly long sentence and practice saying it with various emotions, at various volumes, and while standing in different parts of the room. Use these oral presentation variations in presenting lessons to your students.

Exercise 3: The Art of the "Pause"

This is an exercise you will need to do in your classroom and with students present. Practice the art of the pause. Learn to restrain yourself from enthusiastically "walking all over" a student's response. When a student speaks, mentally count to three before speaking or before allowing others to jump in. Similarly, when students are slow to respond to a question or have a more in-depth response than others, don't rush in to "save" them from an awkward silence. Pause long enough to allow your students to think.

Exercise 4: A Pleasant Expression

Even though it sounds like a statement of the obvious, this is a vital skill for any person who stands in front of a class. Practice having a pleasant expression on your face. As a teacher you need to be aware that you are always on stage. If you habitually appear irritated, confused, bored, or worst of all, look like you dislike being in the classroom, those emotions will be reflected in the way your students treat each other and you. So, smile!

> *"Remember that communication is the key to success, and always look for the happy side of a situation. It takes less energy to smile than to frown."*
>
> —Joyce P. Kennedy, 11 years experience

Exercise 5: Eye Contact

Another important skill that teachers must quickly master is eye contact. As you speak with your students, refrain from looking at a wall, at the clock, or even at the floor. Focus your attention on every student in the room by making a point to keep your eyes focused on two or three for a few seconds and then move to another group. It is especially difficult to maintain eye contact while you write on the board. The real trick to this is to not face the board at all, but to almost face the class by turning to the side, writing, and continuing to talk. Consider, too, using an overhead projector so that you are facing the class as you present material. If you maintain eye contact throughout class, all students will feel that you have spoken directly to them.

Conduct Class Discussions That Engage Every Student

If, like many teachers, you have fond memories of classes where everyone seemed to be completely involved in discussing a topic of burning importance, you probably want to help your students have that experience, too. Whether it was the theme for the prom, the causes of the Revolutionary War, or the best way to conduct an experiment in science class, opinions flew back and forth as your classmates debated the topic. You probably left the room exhilarated, still debating your point, and in full possession of strong opinions that you did not hold when class began.

Class discussions are an excellent way to deliver instruction that students will remember long after the period is over. Discussions are exciting for students as well as for teachers. Best of all, class discussions create active learners who are in the process of perfecting their thinking skills while expanding their knowledge of a topic.

What role should you take in a class discussion? First of all, envision yourself as the facilitator of the discussion. Your job is to plan the discussion, keep things running smoothly, and wrap up at the end. It is not your job to give your opinion about the topic under discussion. Think about your role in making this a successful and stimulating method of delivering instruction in three steps: what you have to do to prepare for the discussion, what you have to do during the discussion, and what you have to do after the discussion is over.

Before the Discussion:

▶ To make a class discussion a successful experience for every student, not just the more outgoing ones, determine the procedures that you want your students to follow *before* the discussion begins. Post these procedures in a prominent place in the classroom. You should consider how you want your students to relate to each other and to you. Here are some student guidelines you might want to establish.

> • Wait until you are recognized by the moderator before you speak.
>
> • You may not speak after you have reached your limit of speaking opportunities.
>
> • Treat other people's opinions with tolerance and respect.
>
> • Listen more than you speak.

▶ Determine the purpose of the discussion. What outcome do you want? Do you want students to analyze an issue? Predict an event? Combine information in a new way? Brainstorm new ideas? Gather facts? Expand current knowledge? It is best if you could communicate the purpose to your students so that you can be sure that the discussion is focused and purposeful.

▶ Create the questions that you will ask during the discussion. The questions that are most successful for class discussions are ones that are not only clearly expressed, but those that require higher-level thinking skills. Move beyond the comprehension level to application, analysis, synthesis, and evaluation to create successful discussion questions. Most importantly, give your students advance copies of the questions so that they will be familiar with the topics and so that they can prepare.

▶ How many questions should you prepare? Of course this will depend on your class, the topic, and the amount of time that you have, but it is always better to have too many questions than too few. For the first discussion, prepare ten serious questions and use the reactions of your students to gauge how many to create for future sessions.

▶ To further enhance the classroom environment for the discussion, set up chairs so students can see each other's faces. If you take the time to do this the way you want it done the first time, you establish how you want them arranged thereafter. In subsequent class discussions, all you will need to do is ask students to move their chairs for a discussion and then wait for them to accomplish this.

During the Discussion:

▶ As the discussion gets underway, remind students of the importance of the conduct procedures that you have taught them for class discussions. Be steadfast in enforcing them. It may be difficult for your students to adjust to them at first, but with persistence, you will succeed in having productive class discussions.

▶ Introduce the topics of discussion by displaying the questions with an overhead projector, writing them on the board, or by asking students to review their advance copies.

▶ Teach your students the importance of supporting their opinions. When someone makes a point, keep probing by asking questions until ample evidence for support has been presented. Students need to realize that it's not enough to just express their opinion; they must also be able to defend and support their beliefs.

▶ Elicit more thoughtful responses by trying these techniques after a response: invite comment, ask for elaboration, ask someone to refute, or ask for a restatement.

▶ Keep outgoing students who want to express themselves at the expense of everyone else in check. One easy way to do this is to give all students the same number of slips of paper. Every time someone speaks, he or she has to give up one of the slips. When a student is out of slips, that person is out of opportunities to speak.

▶ To determine who gets to speak, have an unbreakable object such as a book or a stuffed toy for students to hand to each other as they take turns speaking.

▶ Make it as easy and non-threatening as you can for all students to risk answering. Encourage and validate answers when you can.

Refrain from dominating the discussion. A class discussion works best when all students are prepared and when all students do the talking.

After the Discussion:

▶ Ask students to give you written or oral feedback on what went well and what could be improved.

▶ Ask for a recap until all of the most important points are covered once more.

▶ Consider asking for a written summary of the discussion.

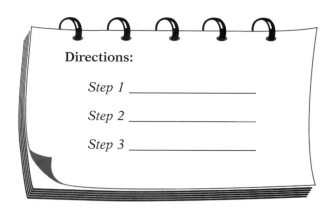

Directions:

Step 1 _____

Step 2 _____

Step 3 _____

Meet the Needs of Students with Diverse Learning Styles

Imagine this scene in a typical classroom: An enthusiastic teacher steps to the front of the class and carefully explains the material in that day's lesson to a room full of attentive and motivated students. When students ask questions, the teacher carefully reexplains. When test time comes, some students do well, some show partial mastery of the material, and some fail. The students who didn't do well are frustrated because they tried their best and still failed. Their discouraged teacher tells a colleague, "I told them over and over how to do it. Why didn't they learn?"

Unfortunately it is true that even the best-intentioned teachers and students won't succeed if students' learning needs are not met. Fortunately for the classroom teacher, much scholarly attention has been focused on this issue in recent decades. Educators now have a much better idea of how different students learn and what they need to do to reach every child. In fact, there is so much conflicting information now available, that it can be overwhelming to try to decide which learning needs to address first. A good way to begin is to start with the most basic needs of the pupils in your class. Your students can usually be grouped according to these three learning preferences:

1. **Visual learners.** These students prefer to take in material through a variety of activities based around reading, writing, and reorganizing material visually.

2. **Auditory learners.** Students who learn this way prefer activities that involve listening and speaking to others, and reorganizing material orally.

3. **Kinesthetic/tactile learners.** These students prefer activities that allow them to physically interact with the material by touch or actions. They need to reorganize material though movement and touch.

There are many inventories you can use to determine which learning preference applies to each of your students. You can start by having your students fill out the simple learning style inventory in Figure 7.4.

It is tempting to believe that all people can be conveniently grouped into one of these three categories; however, that is obviously a simplistic view. Although many individuals have a single preferred learning style, a good many seem to operate best with a combination of learning preferences. With this in mind, it is prudent for teachers to pack all three modes of instruction into as many assignments as possible.

What is the most efficient way to do this? Here are a few tips to get you started.

- Begin by examining the material you need to cover.
- Decide on the activities that you want your students to perform to master the material.

▶ Analyze the modality in each activity.

▶ Add alternative activities to each assignment until at least two learning styles are addressed in each one.

Here's an example of an assignment that has been revamped to include activities that meet all three learning preferences.

Original assignment: *Finish reading pages 17–21 of Chapter 1 and answer the questions at the end. You will be tested on the material in pages 13–21.*

Now here's the same assignment presented in a manner that incorporates the learning preferences of all students in the class. Note that although there are many more steps for students to follow, each one is brief. Students should be able to complete this work in roughly the same amount of time as the original assignment.
Instead of *"Finish reading pages 17–21 of Chapter 1 . . ."*

▶ Look at the illustrations on pages 14 and 16 and jot down two unusual things you notice in each one. *(Visual)*

▶ Read the chapter subsection titles and key ideas. List them in your notes. *(Visual)*

▶ Take turns reading pages 17–20 aloud with your study partner. Write the key words from each subsection in your notes. *(Auditory/Visual)*

▶ Create an idea map of the information on page 19. *(Kinesthetic/Tactile)*

▶ Share your map with your partner and combine ideas. *(Auditory/Visual)*

Instead of *"and answer the questions at the end."*

▶ When you and your partner are finished, move to the computer monitor to record your answers to the questions on page 21. One of you should read your answers aloud as the other types. *(Auditory/Kinesthetic/Tactile)*

▶ Correct your answers by checking the video display on the television monitor in the back of the classroom. *(Visual)*

> *"Some students learn better by reading the text from cover to cover, others by watching a video about the material, still others listen well and absorb every word from your mouth, and then there are those that will 'create' a poster, diorama, shoe box display, or needle craft rendition of the material. Include all or most of these different venues in your teaching style."*
>
> —Marlene M. Stanton, 23 years experience

Figure 7.4

LEARNING STYLE INVENTORY

Name _____ Date _____

I. Place a check in the blank in front of each activity that you enjoy.

I learn best when I:

1. _____ read on my own.

2. _____ repeat aloud.

3. _____ rewrite my notes.

4. _____ look at maps and charts.

5. _____ make charts and graphs.

6. _____ participate in a class discussion.

7. _____ debate an issue.

8. _____ watch a movie.

9. _____ tape record my teacher.

10. _____ finger-spell words.

11. _____ describe something to someone else.

12. _____ check off the key points in a list.

13. _____ solve word puzzles.

14. _____ role play.

15. _____ survey the reading material first.

II. Circle the number of each activity that you checked. For example, if you put a check next to number 5, "make charts and graphs," circle the number "5" here in the *kinesthetic/tactile* category.

Visual: 1, 4, 8, 13, 15

Auditory: 2, 6, 7, 9, 11

Kinesthetic/Tactile: 3, 5, 12, 16, 18

III. Determine what type of learner you are by counting the number of responses in each category. The category you chose most often is the learning style with which you are most comfortable.

Visual _____   Auditory _____   Kinesthetic/Tactile _____

Activities That Meet Diverse Learning Styles

Many teachers find it difficult to try to translate activities into more than one learning modality. Most teachers have no trouble helping students with a visual learning style; the difficulty comes in meeting the needs of auditory or kinesthetic learners.

Below you will find brief lists of suggested activities for each modality. Use them to get started designing activities that will meet the learning needs of each of your students. Some of these activities can be interchangeable because they depend on whether you ask students to do them verbally (auditory mode), by moving (kinesthetic/tactile mode), or by sight (visual mode).

Visual learners are comfortable when you ask them to:

- Read
- List
- Make a flow chart
- Create quiz questions
- Scan
- Make a timeline
- Outline
- Keep a journal
- Survey
- Diagram
- Illustrate ideas
- Find photographs
- Graph
- Recognize
- Read and compare
- Look at maps
- Chart
- Look at illustrations
- Examine
- View a video
- Watch
- Inspect
- Make a graphic representation
- Design a game board
- Solve word puzzles
- Write
- Check off

Auditory learners are comfortable when you ask them to:

- Tell
- Explain
- Prepare a monologue
- Interview
- Repeat
- Tape record
- Interpret orally
- Read aloud
- Listen
- Retell
- Listen to a recording
- Hold panel discussions
- State
- Listen to music
- Talk over a process
- Tell a partner
- Restate
- Recite
- Debate
- Describe
- Express
- Discuss
- Listen to music
- Call out
- Fill in the blanks while listening

Kinesthetic learners are comfortable when you ask them to:

- Write
- Draw
- Make a graph
- Design a costume
- Point out
- Map
- Role play
- Dramatize
- Trace
- Alter
- Create
- Build
- Underline
- Finger spell
- Play a board game
- Create a diorama
- Illustrate
- Construct
- Make a bookmark
- Teach the lesson
- Circle
- Check off
- Build
- Make a video
- Employ
- Complete
- Sketch
- Demonstrate
- Jot down
- Dissect
- Touch
- Smell
- Inventory
- Take apart
- Assemble
- Experiment
- Form
- Reorganize
- Separate
- Make a model

Changing a Dull Delivery into a Dynamic One

Although teachers long to deliver lessons that are so interesting that students hate to leave at the end of class, sometimes it is not easy. Teachers know that they need to challenge students with lessons that are designed around dynamic, effective, and innovative activities. They know that they should be careful to deliver material in such a way that students have the opportunity to discover and not sit passively as adults drone on and on. The problem for many teachers is knowing where to begin to change a dull delivery into a dynamic one. It's not always easy to think of fresh activities that will engage students. Here is a list of activities that will help you get started in your quest to provide interesting lessons. As your students take part in thinking and discovering for themselves, you can enjoy the satisfaction of a classroom full of interested, cheerful, and engaged students.

Kinesthetic learners will enjoy these:

Construct a diorama.

Hold a treasure hunt.

Make a model.

Make a collage.

Plant a garden.

Bury a time capsule.

Send a greeting card.

Give expert advice.

Share a snack.

Put together a quilt.

Visual learners will enjoy these:

Write a graffiti wall.

Create a timeline.

Make a message board.

Make a Venn Diagram.

Draw a poster.

Diagram the action.

Create a scale model.

Design a banner.

Take photographs.

Write an obituary.

Make up a questionnaire.

Illustrate a book.

Use a suggestion box.

Make a bulletin board.

Research a topic.

Make a chart.

Make a flip book.

Paint a picture.

Write a memo.

Graph something.

Create a class scrapbook.

Set up your own art gallery.

Design a computer game.

Create a computer slide show.

Use graphic organizers.

Use an overhead projector.

Bring in a news item.

Make a booklet.

Record data.

Auditory learners will enjoy these:

Prepare an oral report.

Perform an original song.

Ask a riddle.

Listen to an old radio show.

Make a tape recording.

Sing a mnemonic song.

Tell a joke.

Read aloud.

Voice an opinion.

Listen to a guest speaker.

These activities offer a combination of learning styles:

Make a sketchbook.

Stage a talk show.

Write a letter.

Draw a comic strip.

Teach a class.

Demonstrate a skill.

Create a tabloid.

Be a critic.

View a movie.

Plan a party.

Make a 3-D scene.

Volunteer your skills.

Make a brochure.

Create a wall of fame.

Stage a mock trial.

Tutor a younger student.

Make a bookmark.

Interview someone.

Celebrate an unusual holiday.

Make a flag.

Invent a dialogue.

Conduct a survey.

Plan a field trip.

Hold a fair.

Quiz your neighbors.

Create a sculpture.

Stage a play.

Fake a crime scene.

Reenact an event.

Go to the state fair.

Take a sample test.

Invent something new.

Form an investigative panel.

Critique each other's work.

Vote on an issue.

Form a study group.

Share a favorite book.

Brainstorm ideas.

Edit a paper.

Submit sample quiz questions.

Set a goal for the class.

Share a famous quotation.

Evaluate the day's lesson.

Practice taking rapid notes.

Strategies for Asking Engaging Questions

Asking engaging questions is a skill that will take you some time to perfect, but one that can guarantee a lesson that will excite and benefit your students. Regardless of a teacher's experience or the age and ability of students, all teachers can learn to ask just the right question in just the right way at just the right time. The following steps will help you develop the skill of asking questions that will draw your students into a lesson and make them eager to participate.

Step 1: Plan Questions

The first step that you must take in learning to ask engaging questions is to plan questions that will generate the types of answers that you want from your students. There are two types of questions you can choose from. *Recall questions* require a response based on facts your students have learned prior to the questioning session. *Thought questions* require a more in-depth response and are often open-ended. The latter are excellent ways to engage your students in higher-level thinking activities.

Step 2: Establish a Routine

The next step is to teach your students the routine that you want them to follow during class questioning sessions. Even if you have created the most interesting questions possible, they will be useless if students shout out answers at random, refuse to listen to each other, or are not respectful of each other's answers. Teaching students these routines and the importance of following them will take you more than just one or two attempts, but will be worth the effort. Before establishing the guidelines for question and answer sessions, visualize how you want your students to behave during these sessions and plan how you will teach and encourage that behavior. Some simple rules you should consider include the following.

- Don't talk while others are talking.
- Don't speak without raising your hand.
- Treat other students' answers with respect.
- Listen to the questions without interrupting.

Step 3: Ensure That All Students Benefit from Question and Answer Sessions

With practice and planning you can make sure that question and answer sessions in your class are ones that benefit every student. Try to incorporate as many of the following strategies as you can to involve every student in productive learning.

1. Have students write responses first. The one strategy that will absolutely guarantee success in a questioning session is to have students write out responses to your

questions as you ask them. The easiest way to do this is to have students use scrap paper and write numbers in a column to set up a place to write their answers. As you ask questions, wait for students to write answers. You could hold all oral responses until you have asked all questions, or you could check after you have asked a few questions to see if students are on the right track.

2. Wait for a response. The most common mistake that teachers make in asking questions is not giving their students enough time to respond. You must learn to allow your students enough time to think through a question and formulate a response before you call for an answer. This technique will also require that you teach your students not to blurt out answers, but to wait for you to call on them instead.

3. Ask the question before you call on students by name. It is important to ask the question first and then wait for a response. If you call out a student's name before posing the question ("John, can you solve the next problem?"), you immediately send a message to the rest of the class that only John has to think about the question.

4. Hold students accountable for answering all questions. If a student refuses to answer a question that you have asked of the entire group, there are probably many reasons for this refusal. One way to hold this student accountable for participating in the session and still save face is to say, "I'll come back to you." With these words you are pleasant but firm in your expectation that students will participate.

5. Avoid large group shouting matches. It is impossible to hear all of your students if they all shout out responses at once. When some of your less-interested students see that you aren't listening, they will grab the opportunity to tune out. Refuse to allow this by teaching your students to raise their hands and be recognized by you before they speak.

6. Don't follow a pattern. When students see that you follow a pattern to decide whom to call on, they will again tune out or will count to see what questions they will be asked and work to answer only those. There are several ways to avoid following a pattern. One is to create a spreadsheet of your roster or to photocopy your grade book. Use these lists to mark off your students' names as you call on them. Another method that works for many teachers is to make a note card for each student at the beginning of the term. When you are questioning, flip through your note cards and place a mark on each student's card as you call on him or her.

7. Establish simple signals. If you are reviewing questions that simply require a yes-or-no response, there are many signals that you could invent to let your students express their thoughts. For example, you could make up response cards in advance with "yes" on one side and "no" on the other. If you are asking students to classify information, you could give them cards with a category heading on each side. You could also use physical signals such as thumbs up or thumbs down. The possibilities are endless. Often a simple little trick like using response cards will be just the thing your class needs to become involved.

8. Provide a safe environment. Your students must be allowed to risk mistakes. Never be sarcastic with a student who has risked an incorrect answer. Don't allow students to laugh at each other's responses. Instead, encourage teamwork by saying, " Who can help with this answer?"

9. Emphasize listening and speaking skills. Try to avoid either repeating your question or a student's response. Your students should listen to you and to each other. They should also speak loudly enough for all to hear. If someone hasn't understood your question, then ask another student to rephrase it for the class. If a student is so soft spoken that most of the class can't hear, ask that student to repeat instead of restating the response for the class yourself. Once students are in the habit of listening well and speaking clearly, question and answer sessions will go smoothly.

10. Respond to every question. It is easy to be caught up in the classroom dynamics and in anticipating the next question, but you must take time to respond to a student's answer. Don't just nod or grimace. If a response is correct, affirm it. When it's not, say so but keep your reaction neutral. If part of a response is correct, acknowledge that part and continue probing until you have an answer that is entirely correct.

11. Move around the room. It is almost impossible to hold exciting questioning sessions from behind your desk or podium; conversely, it is really easy to keep everyone on task by moving around. If you see students' attention beginning to wander, often just standing nearby will draw those students back into the session.

12. Find the correct pace. Finding the best pace to question your students in any given class is a challenge. Pay attention to the reactions of all students throughout the questioning session. If your pace is too slow, many will be bored and will tune out. If your pace is too quick, then just as many others will tune out because they will stop trying to keep up. Be sensitive to the pace of your questions and work to keep as many students engaged as possible. Pacing is a skill that comes with practice and experience.

13. Ask only one question at a time. If you bombard your students with several questions, they will not be able to keep up.

14. Go beyond simple answers. After you have become reasonably confident that you can successfully manage simple question-and-answer sessions, then move on to questions that require more thoughtful responses from your students. If you can move beyond recall questions, you will encourage students to think, to take risks in their answering, and to become more involved.

15. Promote student interaction. One way to involve every student more effectively is to set up "crossfire" situations where you ask students to comment on each other's responses. This will guarantee that your lesson will be a lively event for your students.

16. Ask for a recap or a poll. There are two excellent ways to end a questioning session. The first is to ask students to recap the session. You could either do this orally with students taking turns stating information, or you can ask students to write three, five, or more facts that they recall from the session. Another way to end a question and answer session is to poll your students. Force them to take a stand on an issue you have just discussed. Giving students the opportunity to express their opinion will involve them much more fully than if they are allowed to passively absorb information from others.

Provocative Questions You Can Adapt

The questions you can ask your students are as varied as the subject matter you're teaching and the interests of the students in your class. Here are a few to get you started.

Comprehension-Level Questions

- What are some things you can learn from this?
- What are some of the things that you already know about this topic that we could use here?

Application-Level Questions

- How could you modify this outline so that all of the key points are easier to remember?
- What steps did you take to arrive at that answer?

Analysis-Level Questions

- What are the underlying principles that caused you to arrive at this conclusion?
- What is a more efficient way to learn these facts?

Synthesis-Level Questions

- What are the relationships among these four items?
- How would you group these facts if you had to divide them into three categories?

Evaluation-Level Questions

- How do you know when you have done your very best work?
- What mistakes do you think the people we studied this week made?

Helpful Responses in Question-and-Answer Sessions

The following are some helpful responses that you may want to use during question-and-answer sessions.

"I'll come back to you."

"Hold up your card to show me your response."

"Now remember, I won't repeat the question so you'll have to listen carefully."

"Raise your hands so I can call on you to speak."

"Remember not to interrupt."

"That's correct. How did you arrive at that answer?"

"Mike, can you help Joseph with that answer?"

"Jessica, do you agree with Rachel's answer?"

"What are the three most important things you've learned today?"

"Thumbs up if the answer is 'yes' and thumbs down if the answer is 'no.'"

"Would you repeat that so we can all hear?"

"What do you think about that?"

"Would you please restate the question?"

"Decide on your answer first and then I'll call on as many people as I can."

"Number your papers 1 to 10 and quickly jot down the answers to these questions."

"Nice try. Part of your answer is correct. Would you like to try again?"

"That's exactly right! Great job!"

Teach, Don't Tell

When you recall your own school days, what were the learning experiences that you enjoyed most? Were you sitting quietly in your neatly aligned desk taking outline lecture notes or were you conducting an experiment, studying with a friend, planning a skit, or just sharing notes?

Even the most fascinating lecturer can't compete with the buzz of excitement in a classroom when students set out to discover information. Many teachers have found success by assuming the persona of a friendly, knowledgeable coach who shares information, resources, and expertise. How? The answer is simple: Don't lecture. Spend less time talking *at* your students and more time talking *with* them. Ask questions. Then ask more questions until your students have gained the insights that you want them to have.

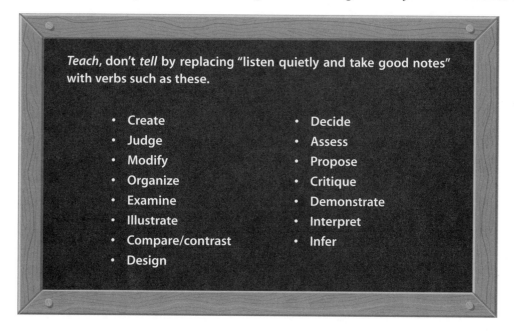

Teach, don't *tell* by replacing "listen quietly and take good notes" with verbs such as these.

- Create
- Judge
- Modify
- Organize
- Examine
- Illustrate
- Compare/contrast
- Design
- Decide
- Assess
- Propose
- Critique
- Demonstrate
- Interpret
- Infer

Tips for Including Discovery Techniques in a Lesson

Keep students motivated by giving the opportunity to *discover* interesting facts and concepts, instead of just spoon feeding information to them. Try the following strategies:

Instead of closed-end tasks such as:
"Locate these places on your map."

Try questions that allow students to draw inferences, such as:
"Why do you think towns are located beside water?
Why don't trees grow tall in the desert? Why is the Mississippi called "Big Muddy"?

Instead of rote assignments that don't allow for any creative thinking, such as:

"Answer the questions at the end of the chapter."

Try giving students the opportunity to anticipate what they will learn by giving them instructions such as:

"Follow these steps as you read: 1) survey; 2) scan; 3) predict what the chapter will be about; 4) use a graphic organizer as you read to help comprehend relationships; and 5) check your predictions.

Instead of relying too often on tasks that don't offer new information such as:

"Outline your notes."

Try engaging students by drawing on their previous knowledge with activities such as:

Hand students a flowchart with some items missing. Ask them to fill in the missing steps by predicting. At the end of the day's lesson, discuss the accuracy and techniques of guessing logically by checking and revising the flowcharts to reflect new learning.

Instead of vague activities that appeal to only one learning style such as:

"Listen to my explanation."

Try offering students the opportunity to use research techniques and work together frequently. For example:

Hand out note cards with partial bits of the day's information on each. Give students a few minutes to look over their material and do research to find information to complete the missing parts. Have students share what they have learned and combine their information into a whole.

Pairing Students for Maximum Learning

Many teachers who have trouble tackling the problems of group work can find success with another method of collaborative learning: putting students in pairs. When you put students in pairs to work together, they are not as easily distracted by other students and tend to stay focused on their work. Further, a student who is having difficulty with an assignment can often get help from a partner. Working in partners allows students to quickly work out problems while they are still minor, and gives less able students confidence because their problems remain manageable.

In order to ensure the successful pairing of students, be sure to select the pairs yourself; otherwise, students are likely to choose their friends. Although this is a pleasant choice, it does not always make for optimal working partnerships. Get to know your students well and then spend time working out pairs of students whose strengths and weaknesses complement each other.

After you have selected the pairs and announced them, have students move to sit near each other. Then, be sure to have a structured activity for the pairs in your class. If you just tell students to "study together," they will not be as efficient and focused as they would if they were given a specific assignment. Finally, the pairs you establish should not outlive their purpose. Once you see that a particular partnership is no longer positive and productive, switch pairs. You may also consider switching pairs at established time intervals.

Partner Activities for Your Classroom

The following are just a few of the tasks that work well as partner activities.

1. Check each other's homework.

2. Read the other's notes and fill in any missing information.

3. Make sure that the partner understands how to do the assignment correctly.

4. Check over an assignment before turning it in.

5. Ask for help from a partner before turning to the teacher.

6. Call out review questions to each other.

7. Listen as the partner explains information.

8. Share the workload when there are lots of questions or problems to do.

9. Share resources on a project.

10. Combine ideas on a paper, project, or other assignment.

11. Take turns reading the assignment aloud to each other.

12. Brainstorm facts to determine prior knowledge.

13. Preview a reading assignment.

14. Take a pre-test together.

15. Generate lists of study questions for a test.

Teach Your Students to Follow Directions

Unfortunately for many students, teachers expect them to follow even the most complicated directions with ease. Many students fail to properly follow written or oral directions simply because they have never been taught how to do so.

Part of the problem lies in our students' impatience with reading long directions (more than three steps) or listening to what they perceive to be a long explanation (more than three seconds). However, another part of the problem lies with teachers who often have so much information to cover that they optimistically assume that students already know how to follow simple directions because someone else has taught them this skill.

Following directions well is an important skill that is neither hard nor time-consuming to learn. If you are willing to take the time to teach your students this skill early in the school year, your efforts will be rewarded daily once they have mastered the skill.

Here are some tips to get you started.

▶ Make following directions well a part of the culture of your classroom. Talk about it every day. Work on it with everyone until your students see that following directions is not just something that their teacher thinks is important, but a necessary life skill.

▶ When you are ready to go over written or oral directions, expect your students to stop what they are doing and pay attention to you from the beginning of your explanation to the end. Expect and command attention.

▶ Ask students to rephrase directions until you are sure that everyone knows what to do. If you make this a part of each assignment, your students will soon come to see that it is important.

▶ Raise your students' awareness of the importance of following directions in a certain order by giving them a paragraph-style jumble of directions and asking them to sort them into manageable steps.

▶ To practice following oral directions, try a modified game of Simon Says. Ask your students to do such silly things as placing both hands over their ears, standing by their desks, nodding three times, and holding up one thumb and three fingers.

▶ Teach your students origami. Following even the most basic origami instructions will not only be fun for your students, it will also increase their ability to follow written directions. You can find directions for quick and simple figures in library books as well as on the Internet at www.learnorigami.com/.

▶ When you're giving a test, teach students to read through the directions on the test with you. They should not be trying to complete the first page as you explain how to answer the questions on the last page.

▶ Don't be fooled by students who impatiently inform you that they know what to do. Chances are good that these impatient students don't really have a clear understanding of the assignment and just want to get started.

How to Give Written Directions All Students Can Follow

It is puzzling to many teachers that the same students who can effortlessly tape their favorite television shows by deciphering the complicated directions that come with video-recorders can't follow simple directions for written assignments. One of the problems, of course, is that students don't always see the importance of following school directions. Sensible teachers take care to build relevance into every assignment. The other problems associated with your students' inability to follow written directions are just as easy to solve. Here are some ideas to help your students succeed in following the directions that you write for every assignment.

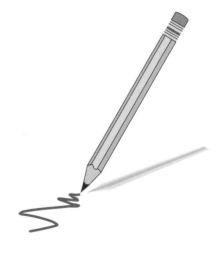

1. Make sure your directions satisfy the objectives of your lesson. This will help students understand the "big picture" behind the assignment.

2. Divide large tasks into manageable smaller ones.

3. Think of the steps that students should accomplish to complete the assignment. Express directions in the form of logical steps that your students can follow.

4. List and number the steps in the order that you want your students to complete them.

5. Don't arrange directions in a paragraph style. Instead, use space to separate each one in a list.

6. Pay attention to the verbs that you use. Be as clear and as specific as possible. For example, "Look over page 17" is not a clear direction, whereas telling students to "Read to the bottom of the first column" is more specific:

7. Keep each statement brief. For example, try "Write your answers on your test paper" instead of "Be sure to put all that notebook paper on your desk away because I want you to just write on the test. Don't forget those books, too."

8. Provide concrete examples that will help your students understand what to do. It is better to give too many examples of how to do a task than too few.

9. One of the most successful ways to give directions for a long assignment is to use a numbered checklist that students can use to stay on target.

10. If the various parts of an assignment are worth different points, be sure to include the point values.

11. Make it a habit to use the same key words to signal to your students what you want them to do. For example, if you expect your students to show their work when they complete any math assignment, make sure you've given that instruction and clarified what it means many times before ever directing students to show their work on a math test.

12. Take the time to go over the directions orally with students. This is especially important on tests where there may be several different sections with different directions for each one.

13. If you want to call attention to a difficult or important step, call attention to it by underlining, using a bold font, drawing arrows, using all capital letters, or any other eye-catching device.

14. Check for understanding by asking students to restate or clarify the directions and by monitoring students' work after they begin the assignment.

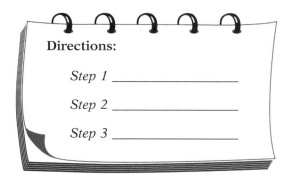

Directions:

Step 1 _____

Step 2 _____

Step 3 _____

Figure 7.5

WRITTEN DIRECTIONS THAT WILL KEEP STUDENTS ON TASK

Examine these two versions of directions for the same assignment. You'll soon see how to write directions so that all students know what's expected.

The Most Confusing (and Most Common) Version

Answer questions 1–10 on page 17 using pages 10–16 to find the answers.

Here are the problems with these directions:

1. Students don't know if they are to read this section or just find answers.

2. Students will have to decipher the sentence to figure out what to do.

3. Students don't know the format for correctly answering these questions.

4. Students don't know the point values of each question.

5. Students don't know how long they have to complete this work.

6. Students don't know what to do with it once they are finished.

The Improved Version

- *Read pages 10–16.*

- *Turn to page 17.*

- *Use complete sentences to answer questions 1–10. You do not have to copy the question.*

- *You should refer to pages 10–16 to look up your answers.*

- *Questions 1–5 are worth 15 points each. Questions 6–10 are worth 5 points each.*

- *You have 30 minutes to complete this work.*

- *When you are finished place your completed assignment in the tray by the door.*

What's the Improvement?

In the improved version students know exactly what to do, how to do it, the order to use to accomplish each step, and how the assignment will be graded.

How to Give Oral Directions to an Entire Class

Giving clear oral directions is a key element in delivering effective instruction. Your students have to know what you want them to do and how you want them to do it. Imagine students' frustration at hearing a teacher say, "Turn to page 167 in your books and begin reading all of Section 18. Then answer questions 1 to 9 and 11 to 17 at the end. You have 45 minutes to complete this. If you finish early, begin on Section 19. Put your work on my desk when you're finished."

While this teacher is presenting the assignment, two students slip in tardy, another puts finishing touches on her makeup, three rummage in their book bags, two realize that their books are in their lockers, and no one really knows what to do.

How could you avoid the mistakes that this teacher made? It's not hard if you remember these simple guidelines.

1. Don't rely just on your voice to convey your message.
2. Don't present your students with a maze of steps to follow.
3. Don't begin to give directions until you have everyone's attention.

Here are some strategies that will guarantee that every student in your class understands your oral instructions.

Before class:

- Write the instructions in a place where students can read them as you go over them orally. Where? Try: on the board, on slips of paper for each student, on a transparency for the overhead projector, on a computer display, or on a large sheet of bulletin board paper. You could even write the instructions on a poster.

- Divide the instructions into small, achievable, numbered steps so that students know the sequence they need to follow in order to succeed. Try something like the following.

    Step 1: Open your books to page 167.
    Step 2: Begin reading at Section 18. Read all of this section.
    Step 3: Answer questions 1–9 and 11–17 on page 169. Each one is worth 10 points.
    Step 4: You have until 9:45 to finish. Put your work in the tray on my desk when you have completed the answers.

- Word each step simply and positively. For example, "Turn to page 117" is a well-expressed direction. "Turn to page 117 and begin about halfway down the page—you don't need to read the top of the page" is not as easy to follow.

- One strategy that many teachers have found useful in eliminating distractions is to have students clear everything from their desks before beginning to give them the instructions.

During your presentation:

- Find a spot in the room where every student can see you and where you can establish eye contact with every student. Use this spot every time you give oral directions.

- Call for your students' attention by using the same signal every time. Something as simple as, "May I have your attention!" is enough to let your students know that they need to listen to you.

- Wait until all students have stopped what they are doing and can look at you. Take as long as you need to allow students to focus their attention on you and are no longer opening their books, rummaging in their book bags, or trying to borrow a pen.

- Speak clearly, loudly, and seriously. This is not the time to joke around with your students.

- Use the written instructions you prepared in advance to reinforce what you say.

- Check for understanding by asking a student to restate the directions.

- If necessary, ask students to clarify and explain until everyone is clear about what to do.

- If you're giving oral directions, recommend that your students jot them down. Some teachers find that students who listen and then jot the instructions down before beginning work do a better job than those who have to constantly refer to the board.

After you have given instructions:

- Stay on your feet and monitor students to see that they are starting the work correctly. Circulate and answer questions or provide encouragement.

- If you see that more than one or two students are having trouble with one of the steps, don't hesitate to stop class and clarify it for everyone.

Guidelines for Ensuring Your Directions Are Clear

If you want to make sure that your techniques for delivering oral and written directions are clear, refer to this checklist.

Written Presentation

- Directions must satisfy the objective of the lesson.
- Don't use a paragraph style.
- Divide large tasks into manageable smaller ones.
- Give directions in numbered steps.
- Make each step brief.
- Include point values for the various parts of an assignment.
- Include plenty of examples.
- Go over the directions verbally with students. Ask students to clarify or restate.
- Use the same key words whenever possible.
- For longer assignments use a checklist to help students stay on task.
- Use devices such as underlining to emphasize key words.
- Check for understanding by carefully monitoring as students begin the assignment.

Oral Presentation

- Post written directions where students can refer to them as you explain.
- Stand in the same spot every time you give oral directions.
- Teach your students to pay attention to you.
- Use the same signal every time to set a serious tone.
- Command attention by speaking clearly, loudly, and forcefully.
- Establish eye contact with as many students as possible when you speak.
- State instructions in simple, positive, numbered steps.
- Include point values for various parts of an assignment.
- Directions must satisfy the objective of the lesson.
- Involve students by having them clarify or restate.
- Check for understanding by carefully monitoring as students begin the assignment.
- Consider having students clear their desks to listen or take notes after you speak.

Practice: The Neglected Success Strategy

"An 'F'? How could I have an 'F'? I did my work?" Too many teachers hear this plaintive cry when students receive graded papers. Somehow students have ignored their teacher's sensible advice to "study hard" and "review your notes" and have paid for this with failing grades. Students are sincere when they say they don't understand why they failed. They equate the effort that they expend in doing the work their teacher requires of them in class and for homework with success. In addition, many students don't understand that mindlessly completing an assignment is not the same as learning. For example, many students can look up complicated definitions for a long list of vocabulary words while watching television and, at the end of this task, be unable to recall even one of the definitions they copied. Ineffective study techniques combined with a lack of review and practice are frequently to blame for a student's failing grade. All too often a practice session or two is all that students receive after the introduction of a new topic. This is seldom enough review for many students.

A teacher's task is to help students make the mental and emotional connections that will help them understand that they must work with *attention to learning* in order to succeed in mastering their work and that completing assignments is not enough. One of the most effective ways to make this connection is through practice.

Practice is the systematic review and recitation of knowledge until students thoroughly know the material. This practice must be an ongoing part of the teaching of a particular lesson or subject area. One of the worst choices that teachers can make is to delay reviewing until right before a test. By then there is so much material that a quick once-over is all that time permits, and this is never sufficient for ensuring that students have truly grasped the key information they are expected to learn.

When students practice, their confidence rises with each successful review of the material. They begin to see the connection between their efforts and what they have learned. It is a study skill that can be incorporated into any lesson and it should be. It does not require large amounts of time, but it does require frequent application in order to be successful.

How can you begin to incorporate practice techniques into your lessons?

Start by taking a two-minute break from an assignment to quickly review material that students have just learned or that was part of the preceding day's lesson or homework assignment. Stop and ask students quick questions about their work. If you do this several times in a class period, your students will have a better chance of knowing the material than if you expect them to comprehend it through their own efforts. The keys to successful practice are to make it *brief*, *repetitious*, and *frequent*.

---

15 Practice Activities

Here are fifteen practice activities your students can use for increased comprehension.

1. Write a fact from the lesson on a scrap of paper and share it with the rest of the class.
2. List every important fact from a section of the reading.
3. Make a quick outline of their notes.
4. Summarize the reasons why an event happened.
5. Rewrite three definitions into their own words.
6. Create a mnemonic device.
7. Match five terms to their definitions.
8. Share a fact from the lesson with a classmate who then writes it into his or her notes.
9. Write a key word on a scrap of paper and pass it to a classmate who then has one minute to tell five things about it.
10. List five things that happened in class last week.
11. Get out flash cards and practice with a partner for three minutes.
12. Scan the material in yesterday's material to find . . .
13. Participate in a quick review bee.
14. Supply five missing words in a cloze assignment.
15. Participate in a rapid-fire drill over the facts in a lesson.

Using Class Time to Review

"But I read them the test! How could they all fail? I wish my teachers had told me the test and the answers when I was in school."

At first glance this review strategy would seem to be very effective. After all, the guesswork has been taken out of the process. So, what can go wrong? Because students are passive receivers of the material, they tune out.

If you want to improve the way you deliver instruction, you should consider review time as an integral aspect of the success of your students. Reviewing is not something you should force your students to do right before a test. It should be part of the daily fabric of the lessons in your classroom. If you think of lessons as layers of information that your students need to know instead of one huge unit, it will be easier for you to find the ways and means to incorporate review into each day's work. Students should thoroughly learn the information that you teach each day before going on to the next day's information. A key component of students' learning process is reviewing. When you assume the responsibility for creating daily review opportunities, then your students should be able to build on their knowledge.

When is the best time for reviewing instructional material with your students? A five-, ten-, or fifteen-minute review mini-session is effective. Each day offers time to review. Research and common sense identify the beginning and end of a class as the times when students are more likely to recall information. These are the times when you are traditionally either gearing students up for the day's lesson or making a final push for mastery before they leave the room.

If you use the small moments of time that are available to you and your students each day instead of waiting until right before a test, you will not overwhelm your students with too much information. Instead you will use review time to reinforce what they have recently learned, making it easier for them to retain what they have already learned and to build on it.

7 Effective Review Techniques

Don't be tempted to read the test to your students and call that an effective review; instead, use the following seven techniques to make review an integral part of your instructional style.

1. Have students go through their notes for the day's lesson and highlight the important facts or other key items.

2. Conduct oral drills where you quiz students over and over until everyone knows the material.

3. Give a short pre-test each day. Let students know that these could be the questions that they would see on a longer test.

4. Use flash cards to help students recall information. You could make them up in advance or you could have students create them. However, it's not enough to just create them; students need to get into the habit of practicing their knowledge by using them.

5. Ask students to retell—either orally or in writing—the facts or other pertinent information in the day's lesson.

6. Have students go through their notes and list the key words. This will be much easier for students to do if you have them take notes in the double-column style.

7. If you create a study guide for the test as soon as you plan an entire unit, you can review effectively by having students complete various parts of it each day.

20 Review Activities to Enliven Your Class

1. Have students predict five possible quiz questions. Ask each student to share one with the class and discuss the answer. To extend this lesson, ask students to share the criteria they used to predict that you would use that question. This technique will not just review facts, but encourage important test preparation skills.

2. Use a few minutes to teach just one quick and interesting word, fact, or concept about the lesson your students have just learned. Relate it to the earlier lesson in such a way that students will leave your class with something new and interesting to think about.

3. Hold a rapid-fire drill covering some of the facts that you've taught recently. You could do this daily, keeping a running tally of the scores for your students or classes in a "tournament of knowledge."

4. Students of all ages love to play board games. You can design a giant one for the chalkboard or the wall. Divide your class into teams and have them roll dice to move along the board if they can answer drill questions correctly.

5. You could read a brief passage related to the day's topic to your students and ask for their reactions. An interesting twist on this idea is to read a passage that does not seem to be related to the topic and ask your students to explain how the two might be connected.

6. Divide students into review teams of three or four. Hand each team a clear transparency and transparency marker. Allow three minutes for students to write as many review facts that they can on the transparency. The real review occurs when students share their facts with the class.

7. Use an overhead projector to show a cartoon or illustration that is related to the day's lesson. Students will soon be eager to bring these in to share with the class when you encourage them. Another way to use this technique is to blot out the caption and have students create a caption using a concept from the day's lesson.

8. Hand students a small slip of scratch paper and ask them to write two facts that they could share with a person who is not in the class. Ask each student to reveal the name of the person they selected to tell these facts to when they share them with the rest of the class.

9. Use the last ten minutes of class to review just one more time the underlying principles of the material that you have covered in the day's lesson or in the last few classes. If you can do this regularly, you will help students focus not just on detailed facts, but on the big concepts in a lesson.

10. Have students write three difficult questions and their answers from the lesson. Have them select one to read aloud to stump their classmates.

11. Use a computer, an overhead projector, or a wall chart to reveal a graphic organizer that will help your students study the material in a new way. If you have been using an outline format for key information, a Venn diagram or cluster web could be an effective way to reorganize and reinforce your students' learning.

12. True or false tests are an interesting way to review. Put a short true or false test on the board or the overhead and ask students to take it.

13. An interesting variation on the true or false quiz as a review technique is to play a modified version of the popular game of Tic Tac Toe. You could set up a grid on the board and divide your students into teams and taking turns answering true or false questions. The team that can first blank out the grid in a horizontal, vertical, or diagonal row wins.

14. Divide the class into teams and play a trivia game based on the material you want to reinforce.

15. Be sure to show students the cause-and-effect relationships in the material that you have just taught. For example, as a wrap-up to a lesson on propaganda techniques in wartime, first hand students a mock propaganda flyer from World War II. Then ask students "If . . . then . . ." questions such as "If you were a German citizen and read this flyer dropped from an American plane, what would you believe about . . ." You will be surprised at the depth of the responses that this type of open-ended question can bring to your class.

> " 'Hook' them with props, music, action, photos, speakers, novels, readings, puzzles, word games, challenges, quotations."
>
> —Barbara Knowles,
> 36 years experience

16. Have students link ideas and facts in a "knowledge chain." Begin by asking one student to state a fact from the lesson and select another student to repeat it and add a fact to it. This person, in turn, repeats both facts and adds a third. The chain can go on until you run out of facts, students, or class time.

17. To avoid ever having to answer the question, "Why do we have to learn this stuff anyway?" ask students to list two new ways that they can use the day's lesson in another class or in real life. Ask them to share one of their answers with the class.

18. Give students a crossword or word search puzzle to complete with just a few hidden major words or concepts.

19. Teach students to review their notes by underlining, starring, circling, or highlighting the most important terms using colored pencils.

20. Review important information by making flash cards for your students. You could even make this easier for yourself and involve students more thoroughly by having students create their own flash cards or ones to share with the rest of the class.

Journal Entries to Help You Deliver Effective Instruction

▶ When I worked to make my lessons as dynamic as possible, what did I do right? What do I need to improve?

▶ My worst fault when asking questions of a large group is _____ . I know I can remedy this if I . . .

▶ What can I do to make sure that discussions in my class are not just learning experiences, but memorable for the way that my students enjoy them?

▶ When I give oral directions to a class I tend to _____ . To improve my students' comprehension of directions I need to . . .

▶ I know that all students don't learn in the same way. To make my instructional style more effective for all my students I need to . . .

▶ How can I make sure that I emphasize the most important points in each lesson so that my syudents can retain them?

▶ What are my strengths as a public speaker? How can I use these to my students' advantage?

Evaluate Your Students' Progress

As the last student handed in a test, he added it to the stack of papers from his morning class and headed to the lounge. He planned to grade every test before his next class so he could get them back to his students tomorrow and still have dinner with friends tonight.

Twenty minutes later, he finished grading the fourth test. He glanced at his watch, counted the papers, and did some rapid calculations. At five minutes a test, it would take five hours to grade all sixty test papers. He groaned. There went dinner.

Just then another teacher came into the lounge and noticed his distress. As he explained, she looked through one of the tests.

"I think I can help you," she said as she flipped each of the remaining tests to the second page. "Grade all of these pages at the same time before you move on to the third page, and write the points that each student misses for that page at the bottom so you can add them quickly when you've finished all of the pages."

As he watched in disbelief, she sat down and picked up a pen. "I'll help you do these now and tomorrow I'll give you a copy of one of my old tests so that you can figure out how to give a reliable test that doesn't take five hours to grade."

Learning how to give tests that are not time-consuming to grade is just one facet of assessment that you will have to master as a first-year teacher. You will have to determine how to give tests that are reliable evaluations of your students' progress, and you will learn to use other testing instruments to achieve a balanced and valid assessment of what your students have learned.

You will have to learn to do this in the midst of one of the most widely publicized debates in the history of education: the controversy over high-stakes testing—the standardized tests that are now given in every state to determine student achievement.

There is no doubt that the stakes are very high. Students and school districts have much to lose when students do not perform well on state-mandated standardized tests. In some localities, students who fail standardized tests are not promoted to the next grade or allowed to graduate. Scores are not only published school district by school district, but often by school, and sometimes, even by teacher's names. Thus, the pressure to have students who do well on these tests is no small matter.

No matter what the final resolution of the high-stakes debate will be in your school district, tests, quizzes, and other assessments will still serve three important functions in your classroom.

Function 1: Assessments help you determine what your students know and what they don't know. For example, if several of your students fail a quiz on key facts from a chapter, you know those students don't understand that material and the students who passed the quiz do.

Function 2: Assessments also allow students to determine their own progress. When students of any age hand in a completed test paper, they frequently will go back to their desks and look up the answers they did not know. After you hand back graded papers, students have an idea of what they still need to learn before the next test.

Function 3: Classroom assessments also let you know how you are doing as a teacher. They allow you to know what material you did not get across to your students, what material you taught successfully, and how to adjust your teaching strategies so that you can reach everyone.

Creating Effective Assessments

Whether it's a third-grade quiz on multiplication tables or a senior final exam, your students need teacher-made assessments that are fair and accurate. Fair and accurate assessments can motivate students to direct their own studies so that they master the material that you want them to learn.

To be sure your assessments are fair and accurate, avoid using assessment instruments that:

- Are too long to complete in the allotted time
- Don't assess what you have taught
- Use a format that is hard to follow
- Don't list point values
- Ignore higher-level thinking skills
- Contain poorly worded directions
- Don't match your objectives
- Don't meet the needs of all learners
- Contain trick questions
- Don't match the test-taking skills of your students

Figure 8.1

WHAT DO YOU KNOW ABOUT ASSESSING STUDENT PROGRESS?

Use this true or false assessment to determine what you already know about assessing student progress.

✔ Write *true* in the blank before each statement that you believe is true and *false* in the blank before each statement that you believe is false.

✔ At the end you'll find a scoring key to check your answers. You'll also learn more about the advantages and disadvantages of using a true or false assessment such as this one.

1. _____ Three important issues you must pay attention to in evaluating your students' progress are planning, constructing, and administrating effective assessment instruments.

2. _____ An assessment is valid if it is accurate and consistent in how it evaluates student performance.

3. _____ Multiple-choice tests assess student comprehension and ability to apply information.

4. _____ Because students often feel intense pressure to do well on tests, you should take precautions against cheating.

5. _____ Short answer questions can require answers that range from one word to a paragraph in length.

6. _____ You should teach a unit first and then use that information to create a test.

7. _____ You should include hints, advice, and encouragement on tests.

8. _____ All point values should be listed at the top of the test right under the directions.

9. _____ You should put the easy questions at the beginning of a test or quiz.

10. _____ Traditional teacher-created tests tend to place a strong emphasis on higher-level thinking skills.

11. _____ Standardized tests in general have more of an impact on student learning than teacher-created tests.

12. _____ You should allow students to choose at least some of the questions that they will have to answer.

13. _____ The format of a test is a crucial element in how quickly you can grade it.

14. _____ Portfolio assessments should only be used when students have studied more than one unit of content.

15. _____ You should include a variety of question types on your tests.

© 2002 by John Wiley & Sons, Inc.

16. _____ One of the disadvantages of open-book tests is that students do not study carefully for them.

17. _____ Your students should use a rubric at the end of the assignment that you are evaluating.

18. _____ On average, quizzes should last about twenty-five minutes.

19. _____ Standardized tests focus on a variety of learning styles.

20. _____ You should allow students an opportunity to express their concerns when they want to challenge a grade.

Answer Key

1. **True**

2. **False.** A test is *reliable* if it is accurate and consistent in how it evaluates student performance. A *valid* test is one that is useful in making predictions about student achievement.

3. **False.** Essay tests measure comprehension and application. Multiple-choice tests measure mastery of detail and specific knowledge.

4. **True**

5. **True**

6. **False.** You should create a test when you plan a unit of study. It will help you stay focused on your objectives.

7. **True**

8. **False.** Point values should be listed beside each section throughout a test.

9. **True**

10. **False.** Teacher-made tests too often focus exclusively on recall of information and not on higher-level thinking skills.

11. **False.** Despite the attention that standardized tests receive, teacher-created tests have a much greater impact on student performance. Teacher-created tests have a significant impact on what, how, and when students learn.

12. **True**

13. **True**

14. **False.** A portfolio assessment can be used for any group of assignments. It is appropriate for evaluating student mastery of a single unit of study.

15. **True**

16. **True**

17. **False.** Students benefit most when you give them a rubric at the time that you make the assignment so that it can serve as a guide.

18. **False.** Your students should not spend longer than fifteen minutes on a quiz.

19. **False.** Standardized tests are usually designed to appeal only to those students with verbal/linguistic strengths or who are visual learners.

20. **True**

True or False Tests

There are two significant advantages and two significant disadvantages to using true or false tests.

Advantages

1. You can assess a wide variety of information very quickly.
2. You can grade test papers very quickly.

Disadvantages

1. Because students can guess the answers, these tests are not reliable.
2. It is difficult to construct statements that don't give away the answers with clues such as *never* or *always*.

"I have found that in all aspects of teaching, you will have the most success if you are fair and consistent with what you do."

—Ken Pfeifer, 28 years experience

Design Effective Tests and Quizzes

Tests and quizzes are the chief tool many teachers use to assess their students' progress. While tests and quizzes offer many advantages, there are a few disadvantages to using these instruments. Too often tests and quizzes focus on lower-level thinking skills and offer question formats that do not appeal to the learning styles of all students.

You can successfully handle these problems and learn to design effective tests and quizzes that can help you determine how well your students have mastered the material that you want them to learn. The following strategies offer ways for you to design tests and quizzes that will be fair, reliable, and valid measurements.

- Plan tests and quizzes carefully. It takes time to create an accurate assessment.
- Aim for content validity by making sure that the test or quiz covers the content that you want to assess. One way to do this is to create the test when you plan each unit of study. Focus first on the objectives for your course and then on the smaller objectives for each unit of study.
- Include a variety of question types on each test or quiz. Objective questions do not give you an accurate assessment of your students' thinking. Striking a balance

between objective questions and essay questions will provide a better assessment of your students than either type will by itself. Vary the types of objective questions that you ask to provide more success opportunities for students who may not excel at one particular type.

▶ Write questions that require students to go beyond the recall level of learning. You can still do this in an objective format if you model your questions after the format used by many standardized tests. These tests often offer students a reading passage followed by questions that require that they apply their knowledge, judge the validity of a statement in the passage, or use another higher-level thinking skill.

▶ You will prevent many problems with cheating if you present different versions of the same test to your students. You can do this by giving different tests within the same class or by giving each class a different test. You should also plan to give students next year different versions of this year's tests.

▶ Share tests with your colleagues. If you and another teacher cover the same material, then you will save time if you can use some of the best questions from each other's assessments.

▶ Tests that are cumulative often reinforce what students have learned previously and encourage students to study as they synthesize their learning.

▶ Begin any test or quiz with simple questions that your students will find easy. This will help them over the initial anxiety when they begin. As they work through a test or quiz, your students should find that the questions become more complex and difficult.

▶ Make sure that you give clear directions that are easy to follow. When you change question types, you must give new directions even when the procedure seems obvious to you.

▶ Humanize your tests and quizzes with encouragement, hints, and advice. You can give suggestions on how long a section should take to complete, underline key words, and even wish students good luck.

▶ Avoid questions that are vaguely worded or too lengthy for students to comprehend easily.

▶ Make your tests and quizzes easy for your students to follow by grouping similar question types together.

▶ Place the point value for each section beside the directions for that section so that your students can judge their own progress.

▶ Don't give assessments that are so lengthy that your students will not be able to finish them. To judge this, take the test yourself and allow four times that amount of time for your students to complete it.

Quizzes are similar to tests in that they require the same careful attention to fairness, reliability, and validity. You should follow the same guidelines for designing quizzes that you do for tests with few exceptions. Here are some suggestions for making sure the quizzes you design will be accurate assessments of your students' progress.

▶ Design quizzes to last fifteen minutes or less. Because they are less comprehensive than tests, quizzes should be much briefer.

▶ Use quizzes to lead up to a longer assessment. If you give your students several quizzes before you give them a test, you will have a more accurate measurement of their test readiness than if you only offer one quiz.

▶ It is fair to warn your students that you plan a quiz. Students tend to regard pop quizzes as vengeful. If you want your students to prepare, then warn them that you intend to also test them on the material.

▶ Give students quizzes on paper instead of using the overhead projector or a television monitor. Oral quizzes are also very difficult for students who have trouble processing auditory information.

▶ One of the chief benefits of using a quiz as an assessment is that it can offer immediate feedback to your students. Grade and return them promptly—ideally, the next day.

Create Useful Objective Questions

Objective questions have many advantages for teachers and students. While it can take a very long time to construct valid and reliable objective questions, they are very easy to grade. Objective questions are also not subject to the same bias of subjectivity as essay questions. Use the following tips to write useful objective questions that can help you accurately assess your students' knowledge and understanding of the material that you want them to learn.

True or False Statements

▶ This type of question is less reliable than many others because students can often correctly guess answers.

▶ Don't have a pattern to your answers.

▶ Avoid ambiguous statements.

▶ Avoid giving away the answers with words or phrases such as *not, none, at no time, never, all of the time,* or *always*.

▶ If you would like to increase the thinking skill level of a true or false statement, ask students to explain or rewrite the answers they find false.

Matching Questions

▶ You can involve higher level-thinking skills by asking students to do more than recall information. For example, instead of asking students to just match a character to a short story, ask them to match a character to a conflict type that the character may have experienced.

▶ Don't have a pattern to your answers.

- Be sure to work out the answers before you give the test so that you can find any words that may inadvertently be spelled with your answers.

- Allow students to cross out answer choices as they use them.

- Offer more answer choices than you have questions.

- It is better to give several short lists of ten to fifteen items rather than a longer list that students will find difficult to follow.

- Arrange matching questions to fit on the same page so students won't be confused by flipping back and forth.

Short Answer Questions

- It does not take long to create these questions, but it does take longer to grade them.

- The advantage of short answer questions is that they allow you to see how your students write and how they think.

- Because some answers will not be predetermined, short answer questions are useful for higher-level thinking opportunities.

- Design short answer questions to yield responses that are anywhere in length from a word or a brief phrase to a paragraph in length.

- Avoid giving clues such as "a" or "an" to indicate the answer. Instead use "a/an" to let your students make their own choice of answers. For example, An idiom is a/an
  _____.

- When you are asking questions that require brief answers, make all of the blanks the same length, otherwise many students will interpret the length of the line as a clue to the answer.

Multiple-Choice Questions

- This type of question can measure your students' mastery of both simple and complex concepts.

- Don't have a pattern to your answers.

- Avoid overusing one letter. You can do this by making up the answer pattern in advance and arranging the questions so that the answers conform to that pattern.

- Make sure that the main idea that you are testing is in the stem of the question.

- Provide answer choices that are about the same length to avoid giving away the answer.

- Make every answer choice a possibility by not including outlandish options that students can immediately eliminate as possible answers. For example, if your science test includes a question about who discovered DNA, don't give George Washington as one of the answer choices.

Essay Tests Aren't Just for English Class

Essay tests are frequently a source of anxiety for students. And they are not alone. Educators who teach disciplines other than English can also be intimidated by the prospect of administering and grading an essay test. However, such tests offer many advantages, and when you overcome your own apprehension about them and help students overcome theirs, you and your students will reap several benefits.

Benefit 1: Essay tests allow you to judge many of your students' higher-level thinking skills because they enable students to use their own words to integrate and interpret knowledge from a variety of sources.

Benefit 2: Essay tests focus on bigger issues and not merely on details; therefore, students have to study more extensively for them. This extra preparation will usually result in better performance.

Benefit 3: The personal nature of an essay test requires that you relate to your students in a more human way. You will be able to comment and give positive feedback on their thinking, on the way they write, and their grasp of the material.

Despite these benefits, two reasonable concerns can keep teachers from using essay tests: the difficulty in asking the right questions and the length of time that it takes to grade the tests. Both of these intimidating concerns can be successfully managed with attention to test construction. You will find more information about grading essay questions efficiently on pages 230–231.

The difficulty in asking the right essay question is a genuine concern. If you ask the right questions, you will have a very clear assessment of what your students do and don't know. If your questions are too vague to yield the information that you want to assess, then you and your students will be frustrated. Here are three suggestions to help you write useful essay questions.

1. Focus first on the large objectives for the subject that you teach. Use these as a springboard for asking questions about the larger issues that the material covers.

2. If you allow your students to choose from a limited number of essay questions, they will be more successful.

3. Use Bloom's Taxonomy of thinking skills to ask students to write answers that go beyond the knowledge level of thinking. Here are three of the many verbs that you could use to create questions at each level of thinking.

Comprehension level: Ask students to write answers that require them to *summarize*, *explain*, or *predict*.

> Example: Summarize the three most important events that lead to the discovery of the Grand Canyon.

Application level: Ask students to write answers that require them to *modify*, *solve*, or *demonstrate*.

> Example: If two trees of the same species grew side by side, why would one tree flourish and the other one not grow as tall?

Analysis level: Ask students to write answers that require them to *infer, illustrate,* or *differentiate.*

> Example: What are the underlying causes for the conflicts between the two main characters?

Synthesis level: Ask students to write answers that require them to *rearrange, combine,* or *compile.*

> Example: Describe how you can rearrange the elements in this painting to change the effect on the people who see it.

Evaluation level: Ask students to write answers that require them to *compare, justify,* or *support.*

> Example: Compare the way that state and local governments regulate water use by small businesses.

How to Grade Assessments Quickly

Many teachers do not like to grade papers because the task can be time-consuming and tedious. It can be even more onerous if students aren't successful.

You don't have to find grading papers an unpleasant chore. Grading student assessments can be done more efficiently and quickly with just a bit of attention to the construction of the test and to planning how you want to respond to your students. How you teach your students to take the test and how you mark the papers will also help. The following techniques will help you grade both types of questions quickly.

GRADING ESSAY QUESTIONS

- Decide on the basic information that you want from your students for each question and list it on a note card or sheet of paper to refer to as you grade an entire set of papers.

- Assign a point value for each topic that you want your students to include in an answer. This will make grading less subjective.

- Teach your students to use the first sentence of an essay response to list the main points of the answer in the order that they will appear. You can check this sentence first to see if any of the basic points that you expect are missing. Then you can check the answer to see how thoroughly the student explained each point.

- Be sure to prepare your students by showing them models of good essay answers and by pointing out how they can write answers similar to the models.

- Don't try to write correct answers for your students. Instead, give them enough information that they can revise their own answers.

- Find a balance between negative and positive comments. Your students need to know what they do well as well as what they don't know.

- Teach your students that neat handwriting in an essay answer is important. Refuse to accept papers that are too sloppy to read.

- Separate essay papers into several stacks so that you can take a break between stacks.

GRADING OBJECTIVE QUESTIONS

- Group similar items together. For example, place all true or false questions together and all short answer questions together.

- Place questions with the same point value together so that you don't have to keep checking the value of each question.

- In general, you should put the questions with lower point values at the beginning of a test.

- Keep the number of total points on a test at 100 so you can quickly add a student's missed points and subtract them from 100 to determine the percentage.

- Number each page of a test to make it easy to follow.

- If you ask students to write short answers, provide lines for them to write answers. They will find it easier to write and you won't have to decipher answers that slant off the page.

- If you have a long test, create a blank answer key on a separate sheet for students to use to record their answers.

- You can grade true or false questions very quickly if you teach students to use a plus sign for a true answer and a minus sign for a false answer. It is not always easy to distinguish students' answers if they use a "T" or an "F."

- If a student leaves an answer blank, draw a straight line through where the answer would have been instead of an "X" to prevent students from adding answers when you go over the graded papers together.

- Insist that your students use dark ink to take a test. It will be much easier for you to read.

- Grade all of the same pages at once rather than grade each test separately. For example, grade every first page, then, go back and grade every second page. This will make it easier to stay alert as you work through the answers.

- Put a space in the lower right-hand corner of each page to record the number of points that the student missed on that page.

> *"I always put papers to be graded in a special bag and carry it with me so whenever I am sitting or waiting, I can pull out a few and work on them."*
>
> —Verna Jones, 27 years experience

Write Useful Comments on Student Papers

You should think of grading papers not just as an exercise in finding incorrect answers, but as an opportunity to help your students focus on what they did well and how they can continue with that success. Every assessment that you grade should reflect a balance of positive and negative comments about the work. Plan ahead to allow a bit of extra time while grading papers, so you will be able to write comments and give advice that will help your students learn. Giving useful advice is crucial if you want students to improve. But how much advice should you give? When you write comments on your students' papers, focus on one or two items that need to be corrected and one or two other items that are done well. The key is to balance negative and positive comments, regardless of the student's grade. If you use a checklist or a rubric for grading, your students will find it easy to separate the grade expectations you have for their work from your comments.

40 Ways to Let Your Students Know They Are on the Right Track

It is not always easy to find a fresh way to tell students that their work is good and that they are on the right track. Use these quick short-cuts to let your students know when they are on the right track with their papers.

1. First-rate work!
2. Good thinking!
3. Very well done!
4. Commendable work!
5. Your best work yet!
6. A world-class product of your effort!
7. Keep up the good work!
8. This shows your brain at work!
9. Good work!
10. You deserve kudos!
11. A superior accomplishment!
12. Remarkably well done!
13. This shows a great deal of work!
14. Great job!
15. An interesting point!
16. Superb insights!
17. I am proud of you!
18. Outstanding effort!
19. You're doing better!
20. You're improving!
21. Distinguished effort!
22. This is the correct way to do this!
23. Impressive thinking!
24. A powerful masterpiece!
25. Clear thinking!
26. A first-rate accomplishment!
27. I commend your outstanding work!
28. You catch on quickly!
29. Good point!
30. Remarkable work!
31. A superior piece of work!
32. Nice wording!
33. Laudable effort!
34. A superlative achievement!
35. Meritorious attention to detail!
36. This shows your diligent effort!
37. Show this to your parents!
38. Insightful points!
39. You are on the right track!
40. Your determination has paid off

Conduct Rules for Quizzes and Tests

When your students take quizzes and tests, they should not cheat and they should not disturb others who may be struggling with an answer. You can prevent both of these from invalidating an assessment by teaching and enforcing rules for your students to follow when taking a quiz or test.

The following rules will make it easier for you to give quizzes and tests in your classroom.

1. Set a serious tone for a test by settling students to work quickly on a written warm up assignment at the start of class.

2. Don't allow students a few minutes to study before a test. Ill-prepared students may take advantage of this opportunity to write cheat notes.

3. Use scrap paper to provide students with a cover sheet. Encourage them to use it to cover answers during a quiz or test. Have students turn in their cover sheets with their papers.

4. Limit the materials on their desks to only the minimum of necessary paper and one or two writing utensils. Students with extra paper can hide cheat notes in it. If students want to pad their paper to make writing easier, allow them to fold papers in half.

5. Before giving an assessment, have students neatly stow away their belongings under their desks and not beside them. All notes and loose papers should be inside a binder. Check to make sure that materials are ready before you begin.

6. Require that students sit facing the front with their knees and feet under the front of their desks. Allowing students to sit sideways during a quiz or test will dramatically increase the chance that cheating will occur in your classroom.

7. If students need extra paper, pens, or pencils while they still have a test paper, require them to ask permission first.

8. Stay on your feet and monitor carefully until all papers are in. If students have a question, teach them to raise their hands and wait for you to come to them. Do not allow them to walk to you.

9. Don't allow any talking at all until all test papers are turned in. Not only will other students be disturbed, but you will find it impossible to control cheating.

10. Once students turn in their papers, don't allow them to go back and get their papers to add answers.

11. Set a reasonable, but firm time limit. Students who take much longer than others to take a test not only have more opportunities to cheat, but cause the rest of the class to become restless waiting for them to finish.

12. Take time to routinely check for cheat notes written on your students' hands, desks, and shoes. Students who know that you will check them will be less apt to attempt cheating.

13. Make sure that you don't leave an answer key where students can see it. Be sure to erase the board cleanly to remove any information that will be on the test.

WHAT TO DO WHEN YOU SUSPECT A STUDENT OF CHEATING

When you suspect a student of cheating, be certain that you have enough clear evidence of cheating before you speak to the student. Then, begin by speaking privately with the student. Don't be confrontational; instead, remain calm as you present your point of view.

If, after talking with the student, you are still certain that cheating has taken place, you must follow your school's guidelines for handling cheating incidents. These will almost certainly involve contacting the child's parents, informing an administrator, and a loss of points for the assignment.

If you have an incident where you suspect several students are involved in a single incident of cheating, you still need to speak to students individually and to handle the problem one student at a time. It is important to involve an administrator early in the process, because you will need support to deal with all the students involved.

What You Should Do if Many Students Fail a Test

Few things are as discouraging to a teacher than having a great number of students fail a test. When this happens, there are three possible causes: 1) the test itself could be flawed, 2) students did not prepare for the test, and 3) you did not sufficiently help students master the material before giving the assessment. Here are some suggestions to handle each problem.

A flawed test: Look at the test itself. Is the format easy for students to follow? Are the point values logical? Do the questions match the way that you taught the material? You can correct this situation by designing another test and using the one that students failed as a pretest and a study guide.

Students did not prepare for the test: Determine the reasons that your students did not prepare for the test. One way to do this is to ask them to describe how they studied and why they did not study more. Teach students the way that you want them to review. Give them opportunities to practice. You can also correct this problem by designing a new test and using the one that students failed as a pretest and a study guide.

You did not sufficiently help students master the material: Sometimes it is easy to underestimate students' readiness to take a test. If you determine that this is what happened, learn from your mistake and work to make sure that students master material better before the next test. You can correct this problem by using the failed test as a review guide to help students determine what they don't know. Remediate by providing additional instruction and retest.

> *"If the students bomb a test, obviously I didn't teach the material very well. I think when this happens the teacher needs to go over the test, review the material again by trying to come up with a different way to teach it if possible, give many examples and practices, and then retest."*
>
> —Donna Nelms, 26 years experience

Teach Your Students Successful Test-Taking Strategies

Many students have never been taught even rudimentary information about how to take a test. Without this skill, even good students will fail the tests you construct for them. Even if you design tests that are fair, reliable, and valid, if your students don't know how to take a test intelligently, the picture you have of their progress will not be accurate.

You can overcome this problem by teaching students some of the basic strategies that they will need to be successful at taking tests. In recent years a large amount of research on how to teach testing strategies has become available to you online. Here are three Internet sites that can help you learn more about how to incorporate test-taking skills into your lessons:

> www.eop.mu.edu.study/
> www.csbsju.edu/academicadvising/help
> www.ed.gov/pubs/parents/TestTaking

10 Test-Taking Strategies Your Students Should Learn

Teach your students the following test-taking strategies and post them where your students can frequently review them.

1. Read all of the way through a test *before* you begin answering questions. Use what you learn as you read to plan your strategy for taking the test.

2. You should first estimate how long each section should take. Watch the clock as you work through a test.

3. You do not have to answer questions in the order that they appear on the test. Do the questions that you are sure of first.

4. Pay attention to point values. Spend more time on questions with higher point values.

5. Make sure that you have your teacher's permission to mark on a test first, but when you can, circle the questions that you are unsure of so that you can return to them if you have time. You should also underline key words to make sure that you focus on them. As you work your way through a matching section, neatly mark off the choices you have used.

6. Neatness counts. If your teacher can't read an answer, it will probably be counted as incorrect. If you need to erase, make sure that your erasures are clean.

7. When you have an essay question, read it all of the way through and answer every part.

8. As you take a test, even if you have read it though when you began, carefully reread the directions for each section before you begin those questions.

9. If you don't know the answer to an objective question, make an educated guess. If you leave a question blank, you have no chance for a correct answer.

10. Double check your work right before you turn it in. You can catch many careless errors this way.

Alternative Assessments

Alternative assessments are evaluation instruments you can use in addition to traditional "pencil and paper" tests and quizzes to measure student achievement. Alternative assessments have become popular in the last few years as educators realize that traditional methods do not meet the needs of all learners.

Students who do not read or write well struggle with tests and quizzes even though they may know the material as well as students with stronger verbal skills. Recognizing the need for a variety of assessments, educators have developed a wide variety of evaluation instruments that can more accurately measure what their students know.

As you begin to use alternative assessments in your classroom, you will find that the best way is to begin slowly with assessments that are easy to manage. As you grow in your confidence and as you get to know your students' strengths and weaknesses, you can then incorporate more extensive assessments.

How can you determine if an alternative assessment will be successful with your students? Follow these suggestions.

- Make sure that the assessment is very closely aligned with the material. For example, in an English class, asking students to demonstrate how to do something is an appropriate task after you have taught them about exposition in writing and the qualities of a successful oral presentation.

- Give the scoring information to students when you make the initial assignment. Whether you use a rubric, a checklist, or a holistic scoring sheet, your students need to know the criteria for success as they begin their work.

- Ask students to reflect on their work as they progress through a task and as they complete it. Students should become skilled at self-evaluation with practice.

Later in this section you can learn more extensive information about holistic assessments, rubrics, and portfolio assessments. Here, however, is a brief list of some of the other alternative assessments that you should find particularly easy to incorporate into your lessons.

ASSESSMENT 1: OPEN-ENDED QUESTIONS

The advantage of open-ended questions is that students can reveal what they know about a topic without the artificial restraints of fixed-answer responses. Skillfully worded questions can elicit a great deal more information about a topic than objective questions. If you use open-ended questions based on real-world situations or ask students to solve authentic problems, you will elicit meaningful responses that require students to use higher-level thinking skills. Here's an example of an open-ended question: How are the hardships experienced by pioneer settlers in 1825 similar to the hardships experienced by you and your classmates?

ASSESSMENT 2: OPEN BOOK/OPEN NOTEBOOK TESTS

By allowing students to use their books and/or their notes on a test, you will remove a great deal of test anxiety. However, a drawback of these assessments is that students don't always study for them adequately. You can make open book and open notebook tests accurate measurements of what your students know by designing questions that require students to synthesize information from a unit of study.

ASSESSMENT 3: OTHER VARIATIONS ON TRADITIONAL TESTS

There are many variations on traditional tests that can meet the needs of your students while helping you assess their knowledge. You could use one or more of the following.

- Group tests: Students work as a group to answer questions.
- Take-home tests: Students take the test home to work out the answers.
- Pairs tests: Students work in pairs to answer questions.

ASSESSMENT 4: PERFORMANCE ASSESSMENTS

Instead of asking students to write their answers, you can give them a task to perform to elicit the information that you need to measure. Some examples of activities suitable for this type of assessment include:

- Science experiments
- Oral reports
- Skits
- Demonstrations
- Book talks
- Projects

ASSESSMENT 5: JOURNALS AND LEARNING LOGS

Journals and learning logs are particularly useful as alternative assessments because they allow students to reflect on their learning. Journals and learning logs are different from traditional journal assignments because they do not focus on diary-style entries. Instead, students write about what and how they learn material. Both of these assessments are particularly easy to adapt to students of all ages and abilities.

In addition to the information here, there are thousands of Web sites you will find useful in learning more about alternative assessments. The following sites are a good place to start.

www.uvm.edu

www.essentialschools.org

20 Alternative Assessment Opportunities

Veteran teachers know that it is important to offer frequent and varied assessments to meet the needs of every learner. In addition to using tests and quizzes to assess your students' knowledge, consider incorporating some of these techniques in addition to traditional measurements when you make up your next assessment.

1. Oral reports	11. Work contracts
2. Research projects	12. Problem solving
3. Project progress reports	13. Self-evaluation
4. Graphic organizers	14. Peer evaluation
5. Posters	15. Comparing and contrasting
6. Projects	16. Completing experiments
7. Models	17. Debates
8. Booklets	18. Putting items in order of importance
9. Analogies	19. Putting items into chronological order
10. Puzzles	20. Class newsletters

Holistic Grading Techniques

Holistic grading is a method of assessing student work based on established criteria. What is unique about holistic grading is that it is usually done by a team of teachers, and that their assessment focuses only on the established criteria. When you assess a paper for only a few very specific errors, you will help students correct those particular errors.

An example of holistic grading would be a group of teachers who all teach civics and who have all assigned the same project to their students. All teachers would agree on the criteria for successful projects and would grade the projects together.

Holistic grading techniques are successful because they reduce the amount of time that teachers spend grading, and because they reduce the subjectivity of the grading process. Holistic grading techniques are very similar to rubrics in that they deal with two issues: criteria and quality. The chief difference is that holistic grading techniques are often used by *groups* of evaluators looking at the same assignments.

Here's how to begin to use holistic grading techniques.

Step 1: Talk with other teachers. You and other teachers who teach the same course should first make sure that your standards on a shared assignment are the same.

Step 2: Develop criteria. Decide what you want to evaluate in an assignment. Select several qualities that are particularly important as focus points.

Step 3: Develop the scale. Align the criteria that you have developed to a grading scale. Although there are as many versions as there are teachers, you will find it easy to grade assignments if you use a scale that corresponds to the traditional A–F scale. Here is an example of a scale useful for grading an expository paragraph written by a middle school student.

A This paragraph is well organized around a central idea expressed in a topic sentence. There are three well-developed points of proof supported with specific details. There are only minor grammatical errors.

B This paragraph is well organized around a central idea expressed in a topic sentence. There are three points of proof offered to support the topic. There are fewer than four grammatical errors.

C This paragraph is well organized around a central idea expressed in a topic sentence. There are two or more points of proof offered to support the topic. There are fewer than six grammatical errors.

D/F This paragraph is not well organized. The topic sentence is either flawed in logic or inaccurate. The writer does not offer sufficient proof and there are numerous grammatical errors.

Step 4: Grade the work. Work together to grade the work. If more than two people assess the same piece of work according to the same criteria and using the same grading methods, when their individual scores are averaged, an accurate assessment is the result.

You will find that holistic grading techniques are most successful when students are aware of the criteria and the scale in advance. Consider these tips for ensuring this for your students.

- Teachers should make sure that students have criteria and scale information when they first introduce an assignment.

- Providing models or examples of assignments that fit each level on your scale is important for students to see exactly what they are supposed to do to be successful.

- Some teachers have found that their students are capable of contributing information to develop the criteria and the scale. This is an excellent technique if your students are mature enough to contribute meaningfully because it promotes student ownership of the assignment.

- Some teachers have found that allowing students to use holistic grading techniques to evaluate rough drafts of other students' assignments enables students to have a focused approach to helping each other improve their work before turning in a final product.

Rubrics

A rubric is a sophisticated assessment tool that more and more teachers are using to evaluate what their students understand. Like other good ideas, rubrics began simply and have grown in usefulness as more teachers learned to adapt them.

A rubric is a scoring chart that students and teachers can both use. (See Figure 8.2 for a sample rubric.) Teachers use them to assess student performance, and although rubrics do save teachers time grading student work, their success lies mainly in the clarity they give to assignments.

Goals are very clear when students receive a rubric before they begin an assignment. Because students know what to do, teachers find that the work is usually of higher quality than with traditional assessments. An added benefit of rubrics is that they force students to become self-critical as they reflect on their work. Rubrics will help students find and solve problems before their teachers have to subtract points for errors.

How can you use rubrics in your class? While it takes practice and patience to learn to develop clearly expressed rubrics, you should begin with these steps:

Step 1: Determine the criteria by which you will grade an assignment.

Step 2: Decide on the levels of quality or mastery that you want in an assignment. Begin by determining the best and the worst levels and then determine the levels in between. Although you can use a scale with only three or four levels of quality, it will be easier for you to assign a final grade if you use a scale that matches a traditional A–F scale.

Step 3: Use a chart format similar to the one in the sample rubric in Figure 8.2 to create your own rubric.

Step 4: Show students models of acceptable and unacceptable assignments. Demonstrate how you would evaluate each assignment using a rubric.

Step 5: Encourage students to practice using a rubric with model assignments before you move them to assessing their own work.

Figure 8.2

SAMPLE RUBRIC

Here is a sample rubric that students would use with an assignment requiring them to create a map of the United States of America.

Criteria	Qualities			
	Excellent/A	**Above Average/B**	**Average/C**	**Needs Work/D–F**
Neatness	Pencil lines are erased. Lettering very neat. States colored.	Pencil lines are erased. Lettering neat. States colored.	Most lines are erased. States colored.	Lines are not erased. Sloppy lettering. States not colored.
Accuracy	All states, capitals, features correct.	Almost all elements correct.	More than 75% of the elements correct.	Less than 75% of the elements correct.
Details	States, capitals, cities, towns, all major features	States, capitals, cities, towns, some major features	States, capitals cities, few major features	States, capitals cities, no major features

To learn more about rubrics, check out the following Web sites devoted to this topic.

www.intranet.cps.k12.il.us

www.esc20.net

www.school.discovery.com/schrockguide/assess.html

> *"Don't be afraid to admit that you don't know an answer. Ask for their help in finding the correct answer."*
>
> —Edward Gardner, 36 years experience

Incorporate Portfolio Assessments into Your Instruction

At their most basic level, portfolio assessments are collections of student work over a period of time. However, portfolios can play a much more complex and useful role in your class as you learn to guide your students in developing their portfolios. When you begin to use this type of assessment, you'll see there are several advantages.

Advantage 1: Portfolio assessments allow students to see a relationship among the various assignments that they have to complete in a given period of time or about a specific topic.

Advantage 2: Students present a full picture of their work and their progress at one time so that you can see the development of skills and knowledge. More important, students will see their own growth. Older students will even be able to assess their growth as they compare their finished products to the goals that they have established at the start of the portfolio process.

Advantage 3: The portfolio process, by nature, requires students to engage in higher-level thinking skills. Students will have to reflect on the quality of their work as they decide what to include in a portfolio.

Advantage 4: The flexibility of portfolio assessments allows you to accommodate the different learning styles of your students. When students are comfortable in how they present material, their self-confidence can boost the quality of their work.

Because portfolios are so flexible, there are many different types. You can select the type that suits your needs or you can develop the kind of portfolio that you want for your students. Here are three commonly used types:

1. **A collection of a student's best work over a period of time,** such as a portfolio of the student's best work over a marking period or semester.
2. **A collection of work relating to a unit of study,** such as a portfolio of assignments relating to writing essays or to a certain period of history.

3. **A collection of work relating to the steps in a process,** such as a portfolio of all of the material students would create to complete the steps in a researched writing project or to conduct a scientific experiment.

To begin to integrate portfolio assessments in your class, follow these steps:

Step 1: Ask students to collect their assignments into a working portfolio. There are many ways to collect this material, depending on the type of assignments they will need to save. Students can use boxes, folders, or other ways to store their work products.

Step 2: Select certain work products for students to include in the portfolio. With guidance, your students can also select some of the products that they would like to include.

Step 3: Ask students to evaluate each item in their portfolio. You can use a wide assortment of criteria for this self-evaluation: quality, relationship to the other items, suitability, or others.

Step 4: Assess the portfolio according to the criteria that you established for your students when you gave the initial assignment.

To help you learn more about portfolio assessments, check out these and other Web sites.

www.ed.gov/pubs/OR/ConsumerGuides/classuse.html

www.luc.org

www.sdcoe.k12.ca.us

Keeping Track of Grades

Although you hope that it won't happen to you, many teachers have had to produce their grade books as evidence in court. Because your grade book is considered a legal document, you must meticulously maintain it throughout the year. Your school district will have very strict policies about how you are to keep student grade records, and you should follow them to the letter.

Because of the increasing popularity of electronic grade books, there are currently three different ways that you can record student grades: 1) you can keep all grades electronically, 2) you can keep all grades on paper, or 3) you can use a combination of paper and electronic record keeping.

The combination approach is currently the most common way teachers maintain grade records. This is a good idea for the following reasons.

- Electronic programs can fail.
- You can lose a paper grade book.
- A paper grade book is portable and electronic grades are not usually so.
- One method can serve as a back up for the other.

To successfully manage both types of grade books, you will have to plan ahead and be very organized. Here are some tips to help you be successful with three very important aspects of managing student grade records: general information about grade management, paper grade books, and electronic grade books.

GENERAL INFORMATION ABOUT GRADE MANAGEMENT

1. Allow for a wide variety of different assessments during the course of a marking period so that you have a balance in the types of grades that your students earn.

2. You should have several grades for each student each week, so that you can have an accurate idea of your students' progress.

3. You should determine how you will weight your grades before school begins. In general, you should allow for a heavier percentage of objective measurements than subjective ones. For example, because most teachers are subjective in how they grade essays and book reports, these assignments should not have as great a weight in the final average as objective tests and quizzes.

4. You must inform your students of how you will weight their grades. Many teachers post this in a conspicuous place as well as send it home in a letter to parents and guardians at the start of the term.

5. You should plan the assessments that you are going to give during a marking period before it begins. While you don't have to know what every small assignment will be, you should know basic information such as that you plan to use a portfolio at the end, or that you plan on ten quizzes and four tests.

6. When you plan your grades, you also must plan how you are going to handle missing work, make-up work, and homebound assignments.

7. Students' grades are not only confidential, they are protected by privacy laws. You should *never*:

    • announce grades.

    • post grades (even if you use student numbers or false names).

    • tell a student's grades to a classmate.

    • allow students to look in your grade book.

PAPER GRADE BOOKS

1. Never leave your grade book on top of your desk where a student could take it. Keep track of your grade book by keeping it in the same place during class. You should either lock it away securely at night or take it home with you.

2. Use black ink in your grade book whenever you can. Be very neat.

3. Record your students' names in alphabetical order. You should also include student identification numbers if you will be required to use them for various reasons.

4. You should record the dates that your class will meet on the top of the vertical columns. You will especially need to do this if your grade book is also a place where you maintain attendance records.

5. At the bottom of the vertical columns, you should record the specific names of assignments. For example, use "Quiz on Chapter 1," "Fractions Test," or "Homework—page 17" rather than "quiz," "test," or "homework" so that you can quickly identify the assignment later in the year.

6. When you record grades, place a line under the box where a student's grade will go if the student is absent and needs to make up the assignment or assessment. Convert this line to a circle when the student makes up the work. This will be very useful when you need to transfer your paper grades to an electronic program or when you have to average grades by hand because you can add it in quickly.

ELECTRONIC GRADE BOOKS

1. Schedule a set amount of time each week to update your electronic grade book. Trying to record hundreds of grades the night before you are supposed to give report cards to students is almost impossible.

2. Back up your grades to a disk or zip drive as well as to your hard drive. Be very careful to keep all backup copies secure.

3. Be aware that students can read the screen when you record grades while they are present. Place your computer in a spot where you can maintain confidentiality.

4. One good reason to print out grades and give them to students often is so that your students can help you correct errors. To maintain students' privacy, keep the printouts of your students' grades in a secure place just as you would a grade book.

5. If your school district does require you to keep electronic grades, you should use a password to protect them.

6. If your school district doesn't provide an electronic grade program for you, there are several good ones that you can try. Here is a list of some of the ones that other teachers have found easy to use.

- Making the Grade
- Eagle Gradebook
- Teacher's Aid

- Gradekeeper
- Jackson Gradebook
- Gradebook Plus

Figure 8.3

SAMPLE GRADE BOOK PAGE

#	Name	M 3/1	T 3/2	W 3/3	TH 3/4	F 3/5	M 3/8	T 3/9	W 3/10	TH 3/11	F 3/12
1	Atkins, Joe	100	98	89	96	90	96	94	89	93	85
2	Cushman, Bob	90	78	91	89	89	92	90	83	89	92
3	Russo, Melissa	98	100	93	97	90	88	95	100	89	95
		Quiz 1, page 17	Fractions worksheet	Quiz 2, page 23	Decimals worksheet 1	Decimals worksheet 2	Questions 1–9, page 29	Quiz 3, page 36	Homework, page 40	Review homework	Test, Chapter 1

Teaching Students to Track Their Grades

Many students are surprised when they receive their report cards and their average does not match their expectations. This is usually because they do not know how to estimate their final average. Often students seem to believe that the negative impact of several failing grades will be erased with a single good grade or that low grades at the beginning of the term won't matter at the end. While much of their confusion is the result of wishful thinking, much of it occurs because teachers do not always explain the criteria for success in their class.

You can eliminate your students' confusion by teaching them to keep a running progress check on their grades. The Student Grade Tracking Sheet in Figure 8.4 is an easy way for you and your students to work together all term to help them keep track of their progress because it helps students see the connection between each assignment and their report cards. Follow these four steps to manage this form successfully.

Step 1: Have students complete the top portion of their form and then clip the forms into their notebooks.

Step 2: Whenever you return a graded paper, ask students to first circle the grade on their paper. This will force them to pay attention to it.

Step 3: Ask students to record the grade on the Student Grade Tracking Sheet, being careful to fill in every space.

Step 4: You will raise your students' awareness of each grade's effect on the final average if you have students complete the "impact" column. Students should use a plus sign to indicate that the new grade has raised the average, a minus sign to indicate that it has lowered the average, and a zero to indicate that there is not a significant improvement or loss because of the new grade.

Figure 8.4
STUDENT GRADE TRACKING SHEET

Name _____Class _____Goal Grade _____

The grading scale for this class is:

_____

_____

_____

_____

_____

_____

Date	Assignment	Grade	Impact

What You Should Do When Students Challenge Grades

It is only natural that your students will challenge their grades throughout the term. If you do not handle their challenges well, the problems that will result can cause long-term resentment. Here are four suggestions for dealing with student challenges so that everyone benefits.

1. **Take a proactive attitude.** You can anticipate that for almost every assignment that you assess as well as the final averages, at least some of your students will challenge their grades. With this in mind, prevent as many problems as you can by being proactive. Here's how.

    ◗ Make sure that your assessments and the weights for each one are in keeping with your district's policies.

    ◗ Publish the grading scale for your class so students know just how much weight a particular assignment will have.

    ◗ Use a tracking sheet such as the one in Figure 8.4 so students are aware of the impact of individual grades on the final average.

    ◗ Be careful to have many assessments for your students and to vary the types of assessments that you use.

    ◗ Don't take the challenge personally. Focus on the complaint and not on the fact that a student is questioning your judgment.

    ◗ Listen to students. Their complaints, even if not legitimate, are the result of confusion. Take what they have to say seriously.

2. **Challenges to daily or weekly assignments.** When you go over a graded assignment with students, tell them that you could have made mistakes in how you marked their papers. Ask them to let you know about mistakes that you have made by putting a large question mark beside any item that they would like you to look at again. They should also write a note on the paper to let you know why they challenge the grade. Collect these papers and look at them again. By doing this, you are letting your students know that you will address their concerns and you will not have to deal with a group of students shouting at you.

3. **Challenges to progress reports or report cards.** You can preempt many of these challenges by letting students know their averages more often than when progress reports and report cards are distributed. If you use an electronic grading program, print out copies of averages every two or three weeks or even more frequently. If you average by hand, try to do so every two or three weeks also. Another advantage of this practice is that students can catch errors that you may have made while recording grades and you can correct them before the final printout.

4. **When a student is mistaken in a challenge.** If a student challenges a grade and is mistaken, take care to explain the error completely. Thank the student for checking with you and encourage him or her to continue to be concerned about the work.

Success with Standardized Tests

It is highly likely that your students may have to take at least one standardized test this year. More and more school districts rely on them to assess not only the performance of individual students, but also how well teachers achieve the goals of the school district. High-stakes standardized tests have serious implications for everyone.

Because of what's involved, you will receive a great deal of information from the administrators responsible for testing in your district about the standardized tests that your students will have to take. *When you receive this information, take it seriously.*

Teachers who offer the wrong kinds of assistance on standardized tests have been fired for this offense. Often you will be asked to sign an acknowledgment that you have received information about the particular test that your students will be taking. When you sign this, you indicate that you understand the kind of help that you may offer your students before and during the testing time.

In addition to taking a professional approach to administering standardized tests, you can help your students by teaching them some useful test-taking skills that can be used for almost every standardized test. The following tips can help you teach these important test-taking skills.

1. Students often get bogged down in a difficult reading passage and just skim the questions. Teach them to read the questions carefully first and then skim the passages looking for the answers.

2. When students have passages to read, teach them to underline the parts of the passage that are covered in the questions. They can also circle key words or write notes to themselves in the margins.

3. Show your students how to mark their answer choices in the test booklet before they write them on their answer sheets.

4. Add another step to the traditional process step of asking students to narrow the choices to two and then guess. At this point, students should not guess, but continue reasoning to determine the better of the two answers.

5. Students must learn to go back and check their work. If the test is a very long one or if it is timed so that completing it in a set amount of time is necessary, teach students to check the questions that they are uncertain of first, and then check the ones that they are more confident of as time permits. When students have math problems to check, teach them to use another method to solve the problem as they check the accuracy of their answers. For example, instead of adding numbers again in an addition problem, students can check the answer by subtracting.

Journal Entries to Help You Evaluate Student Progress

- What problems can you anticipate that your students will have with traditional assessments? How can you resolve these problems?

- What are some organizational strategies that you can adopt to successfully manage every aspect of the record keeping that you have to do with your students' grades?

- Have you given an assessment that was very successful? What qualities made it successful? How can you duplicate those qualities in other assessments?

- How can you incorporate new assessment techniques into the next unit that you plan to teach?

- Which of your students causes you the most trouble when it comes to assessments? How can you design an effective and meaningful assessment to meet that student's particular needs?

- What can you learn from your students' reactions as they take a test? How can you use this knowledge to help your students?

- Which assessment types are you most comfortable with? How can you expand this to meet the needs of your students?

- Think back on the tests and quizzes that you have taken as a student yourself. How could you improve these particular traditional assessments? What lessons can you learn from them?

- What benefits do you want assessments to create for your students? Brainstorm ways that you can guarantee these benefits.

- When have you personally failed? How did you react to this failure? How can use this experience to be a better teacher?

Motivate Your Students to Succeed

His principal stood in the doorway, watching the controlled pandemonium. He and his students were too intent on what they were doing to notice their visitor.

Students were all over the room. Two of them were rummaging through the supply closet to find construction paper. Another group was engaged in a heated debate over something they were composing at the computer. Still others were setting up a video camera to film the six actors who were rehearsing their lines.

Two girls were on their way to the media center to check facts for the next day's presentation, and two others were signing up on the board for a conference with their teacher. The poster group was calling out words to a trio of students checking defintions in dictionaries.

A group with a coffee can full of magic markers bustled past as the administrator motioned for the teacher to step into the hall. "I couldn't help but notice the noise," she began.

She continued before he could defend what he was doing, "When a class is this noisy because every child is completely engaged in the lesson, this noise level is more than acceptable. It's what school should be. Show me how you accomplished this."

*I*f your students are so busy and engaged in their work that they groan when the bell rings to end class, then you know you have been successful in motivating them to work. If you are not successful in motivating them, even beautifully planned lessons and a flawless presentation will be in vain, because your students will not be interested.

Motivate Your Students

In order to successfully motivate your students, you should include the following ten practices in your repertoire of teaching skills.

1. **Call on every student every day.** Students who know that they will not be held accountable for answering a homework question or responding in a class discussion are not going to try as hard as students who know that you are going to call on them sometime during class.

2. **Ask students to evaluate themselves.** If students know in advance that they will have an opportunity to reflect on their own work and to assess how well they accomplished their goals, they will work harder to meet those goals. Evaluating work as a group or with a partner has a similar effect of encouraging students to have a serious attitude about their work.

3. **Employ cooperative assignments.** Students usually enjoy the process and excitement of being in a group. Working in groups not only forces responsibility on members, but also makes the workload easier to manage with a division of labor.

4. **Provide audiences for student work.** If you are the only audience that your students will have all year, they are missing many opportunities. When students know that their work will be on display, published, read aloud, or shared over the school public address system, they take it more seriously than if you are the only person who will see it.

5. **Ask open-ended questions.** This will give students the opportunity to employ higher-level thinking skills and creative approaches to problems. In addition, it reduces the risk of failure. Many students who hesitate to answer objective questions will welcome the challenge of open-ended questions.

6. **Make sure your expectations are high.** If students perceive that you do not think them capable of hard work, they will not deliver it. Students are often more capable than their teachers believe them to be. Motivate your students to do their best and they will strive to live up to your expectations.

"The students' assignment was to do research reports on inventors and their inventions. Rather than just assign the inventors, I put names into a bowl, and the students made their selection. I then provided poster board, magic markers, and other materials for these projects to be done in the classroom. Their posters were displayed for all to enjoy. It was fun, they learned, and they did the work."

—Marlene M. Stanton,
23 years experience

7. **Arouse their curiosity.** If you ask students provocative questions, give them a quotation to mull over, show an odd painting or even hold up a large box and ask them to tell you what it inside, you get their attention and make them want to learn more.

8. **Allow student input whenever you can.** Your students should be involved in planning some of the assignments they have to do. Students who have choices will be more involved than if they are just passive receptors of information. Allow them to adjust deadlines, suggest projects, and offer other suggestions whenever possible.

9. **Let your own enthusiasm show.** If you are interested in a subject you are teaching, you should let that enthusiasm show. Students may not always be interested in a topic that you teach, but they will never be interested in a topic that you do not teach with enthusiasm.

10. **Offer in-depth assignments.** It is better to cover less material well than to try to cover everything in the textbook as fast as you can. While you do need to meet your district's objectives, you do not have to assign every problem or question at the end of a chapter. Spend enough time with some units of study so that your students can do independent research and other challenging assignments that will stretch their imaginations.

30 Quick Motivation Techniques

Fortunately for busy teachers, there are many techniques available for motivating students to be interested in their work. Try these techniques to find the ones that will appeal to your students.

1. Surprise students at the start and end of class.
2. Help students set goals for themselves so that they can work with a purpose.
3. Use hands-on activities when you can.
4. Include higher-level thinking skills in every lesson.
5. Be positive and upbeat with your students.
6. Give sincere praise.
7. Encourage students to collaborate on their work.
8. Use non-verbal language to convey your interest in your students.
9. Use student's names in practice exercises.
10. Design activities so that your students do more talking than you do.
11. Allow students to have a voice in class decisions.
12. Use tangible rewards such as treats or stickers.
13. Show students how they can use their learning in other classes.
14. Incorporate students' interests into lessons.
15. Use a variety of media such as music or art.

16. Ask, "How can I help you?"

17. Send home positive notes.

18. Show your students that you believe in their ability to succeed.

19. Display or publish student work.

20. Encourage peer tutoring.

21. Display inspirational banners, posters, and quotations.

22. Ask students to write out a response to a question instead of just yelling out their first thought.

23. Pace your lessons so they don't drag.

24. Teach students how to correct their answers on a paper instead of just looking over the work to see what grade they earned.

25. Reward effort.

26. Give students real-life problems to solve.

27. Make sure your expectations are high.

28. Use various modalities and learning styles.

29. Write more positive comments than negative ones on papers.

30. Use lots of learning games

"Why Do We Have to Learn This?"

If your students ask you this question, then you have failed in one of your most important tasks: making students aware of the benefits of their instruction.

Students often don't automatically understand the connection between a long homework assignment or sitting for hours at an uncomfortable desk and the successful life they envision for themselves when they are adults. You must make these connections for them. You can do this and preempt their questions at the same time by making sure that you teach your students why they need to know what you are teaching them. Here's how you can do this.

WHEN YOU INTRODUCE A UNIT OF STUDY:

▶ Put the benefits on the board so students will know them right away. Tell students how their lives will be better for knowing the material that you intend to teach.

▶ Begin a unit by connecting it to previous learning so students can see a progression of knowledge and skills in their schooling.

▶ Be very specific. Say, "At the end of class today you will be able to _____ . You will need to know this because _____ ."

THROUGHOUT A UNIT OF STUDY:

- Take time every now and then to ask students to tell you why they need to know the information you are presenting. Make a list of their ideas and post it in a conspicuous spot.

- Make a checklist of the benefits of the information and check them off as students master various parts of the information.

- Focus on why students need to know the information right now and why they will need it in the future.

- Draw connections between what students do in your class and what they do in other classes. Teach them how they can apply the knowledge or skills in your class to another one.

- Draw connections between what your students are doing now in your class and what they will be doing later in the term in your class.

The following are some answers you should *not* give when students ask "Why do we have to learn this?"

- You need it for your test next week.

- Your teachers next year will expect you to know it.

- You will need it for college.

- Because I told you so.

Use Body Language to Keep Your Students Working

Just by glancing around the room and reading students' body language, you can tell which students are interested, restless, or tired. At the same time, students can read non-verbal signals from you, too. Even young students are able to correctly gauge their teachers' feelings with astonishing accuracy.

Your students can tell right away when they have your full attention. They can also tell when you like them, when you find a lesson interesting, and when you are reaching the limits of your patience.

The non-verbal language you use in your classroom can be a powerful way to motivate your students. First, you must learn to use it effectively.

CONFUSING OR NEGATIVE BODY LANGUAGE

You have to make sure that the body language signals that you send match the verbal ones. For example, if you try not to laugh when you are trying to scold a student who has misbehaved in a way that you find funny, no one will take you seriously. Or, if you are praising your class, and you are unconsciously frowning, you will confuse your students. To avoid sending mixed signals such as these, review these confusing or negative body language cues.

- Pointing at your students
- Standing with your hands on your hips
- Putting your hands too close to a student's face
- Speaking too loudly or in a monotone
- Jabbing a finger at a student's chest to make a point
- Tapping fingers to show impatience
- Leaning away from students
- Snapping your fingers at students
- Laughing while delivering a serious message
- Rolling your eyes as if in disgust
- Ignoring a student who is upset
- Slamming doors or books

EFFECTIVE BODY LANGUAGE

You can also use non-verbal language to let your students know what you expect from them. These signals are effective because they convey your message without interrupting other students. One of the most productive ways to use this technique is to stop students from misbehaving and redirect their attention to their work. The following are some of the non-verbal signals that you can use to help your students stay focused on their work.

- Making eye contact
- Lightly touching a student on the hand or the arm
- Putting your hand on an object near a student
- Glancing pointedly at the clock when students are dawdling
- Giving a "thumbs up" or a "thumbs down" signal
- Shrugging your shoulders
- Nodding your head and raising your eyebrows
- Shaking your head
- Holding up your hand with the palm facing students
- Leaning forward to indicate that you are interested
- Raising your eyebrows in surprise
- Pointing to an object you want them to focus on

10 Tips for Using Visual Aids Effectively

If you are like many teachers, you already use visual aids in your class. You post information on the bulletin board, write on the overheard, make computer presentations, use maps, and draw diagrams on the chalkboard. You can expand how you use visual aids to motivate your students to work. Follow these guidelines for making sure that your visual presentations are effective.

1. Use visual aids as often as you can. While many of your students will be visual learners, the ones who are not will also appreciate them.

2. Make sure that your visual aids are eye catching and colorful, but not cluttered with too many graphics and too many different fonts.

3. When you hold up objects for students to see, hold them high enough that everyone can see them clearly. If necessary, pass them around after you have finished talking about all of the objects you have to show.

4. When you demonstrate how to do something in front of your class, be sure that everyone can see you work. If you have a handout that students can follow as they watch the demonstration, then they will find it easier to learn what you are teaching them to do.

5. When you write or draw on the board, write large enough and neatly enough so students sitting in the back can read what you have written. Erase cleanly. Be sure to allow space between columns or groups of words so students will not be overwhelmed with a completely covered board. If you have a white board instead of a chalkboard, use the brighter markers to draw attention to certain points. If you use a chalkboard, use colored chalk for the same purpose.

6. Students like to watch movies. They especially like to see movies that they have created. Student-made movies have a powerful motivating effect.

7. If you want your students to see photos or other smaller illustrations, don't try holding them over your head. Use a scanner to reproduce them to a transparency and project the image with an overhead projector.

8. If you are making a computer presentation on a continuous loop, adjust the rate so that even your poor readers can take in all of the material before the screen changes.

9. When you use an overhead projector, you should project on a wall or screen that all students can see easily. Use a large, plain font. If you have a column of items, don't try to fit them all into one transparency if doing so makes it hard to read. Create a transparency that all students, including those sitting at the back of the room, will be able to read comfortably.

10. Use graphic organizers to help students interpret text. A graphic organizer quickly enables students to understand the most important points and how they relate to one another.

8 Tips for Using Models Effectively

When you use a model—or a "blueprint"—to show your students how to do a task, you will eliminate the confusion that many students feel when faced with new material or a new skill to learn. You can and should use models at the beginning of an assignment to show what the end product should be.

Follow these guidelines for making sure that the models you use are effective.

1. When you use models at the beginning of an assignment, be sure that you leave them out where students can refer to them throughout the time that they are working on the assignment.

2. Models are effective motivational tools because they show students how to do their work well. Make sure that you select models that serve this purpose.

3. Use several different models if you can to prevent students from slavishly copying from one instead of adapting the information in a model for their own work.

4. Spend plenty of time going over a model to really explain its strengths and weaknesses so students can grasp the concepts that you are promoting.

5. If you have models from students, be sure to ask their permission before you use their work.

6. Never embarrass a student by using his or her model as an example of poor work.

7. When you use a model with your students, you can increase its effectiveness by pairing it with a checklist so that students can see the key features of the model as you demonstrate it and as they begin using it for their own work.

8. If you display a model a week or two before you actually teach the material, you will stimulate curiosity and increase motivation.

Add Interest to Assignments

Many educators complain that they find it difficult to compete with the fast-paced entertainment that consumes so much of their students' time. And although your role is not to entertain your students, but to teach them, your lessons should still be lively and interesting.

If students enjoy an assignment, they will take it much more seriously. Listening to a lecture for one hour is not intrinsically interesting to many students. Working in a group solving a problem or playing a simulation game is a much more effective way to reach your students.

Making assignments enjoyable is an important part of your teaching duties. You do not have to entertain your students, but you do have to make the material as appealing as possible to your students. One way to do this is to add creative touches to each unit of study. Here is an example that will help you modify assignments to increase their motivational potential.

Topic: A seventh grade history unit of study on the 1920s

Original assignment: In one week, students will read the chapter, take notes, listen to a class discussion, and answer the questions at the end of the chapter.

Modified assignment: In one week, students will read the chapter on the 1920s and prepare a four-minute researched report accompanied by a project. All students are expected to take notes on each other's projects and to review the content of the chapter.

Modified assignment timeline:

Monday:	Students read the chapter aloud in class. They receive a list of the project topics for their reports on Friday. Each student will choose a topic to research. Students review the chapter for homework with a worksheet.
Tuesday:	Students check homework and begin their projects and reports.
Wednesday:	Students work on projects and reports.
Thursday:	Students continue to work on projects and reports.
Friday:	Students present reports to the class. Each report is a four-minute oral presentation. The students in the audience take notes. Each report must be accompanied by a project.

Report Topics for Students to Select for Independent Research:

- The life of one of the presidents during this time
- The life of one of the First Ladies during this time
- Reasons for the stock market crash
- The relationship among races in different areas of the United States
- Popular fashions
- Sports teams
- Medical discoveries
- Newsworthy events in the town where their school is located
- Songs and popular music
- What schools were like in the 1920s
- Leisure activities of children
- Fads
- Nobel prize winners
- Transportation
- Notable crimes

Project Suggestions:

Students are to create one of these projects to accompany their four-minute report.

- Postage stamp
- Poster
- Overhead transparency
- Computer presentation
- Comic strip
- Diorama

- Sketch
- Map
- Photo collage
- Flip chart
- Banner
- Scrapbook

Points to Note:

- Each student has to master the major concepts of the chapter.
- Students have a choice of topics.
- Each report is very brief.
- Students are expected to take notes on each other's reports.
- The projects are not time-consuming.
- The time frames of both assignments are the same.
- The modified assignment will involve students fully because:
  - Students have choices.
  - The topics are engaging.
  - The topics will enhance the general knowledge students gained by reading the chapter.
  - Students have an audience other than the teacher.
  - The projects are hands-on.

Peer Tutoring

Peer tutoring is motivational not only because it is high-interest, but also because it encourages successful learning. When students work together to help each other learn, both the person learning the material and the tutor benefit.

There are two types of peer tutoring that you can use with your students: informal sessions and formal sessions. Informal sessions are generally spur-of-the-moment, and formal sessions can be planned to occur after school. The following pointers can make both types effective motivational tools for your class.

- Carefully monitor two or more students studying together to ensure that they stay on task. It's easy for students' conversation to stray to topics other than the one they're studying, so you must be careful to let them know that you are aware of what they are doing when they work together.

- Peer tutoring will be most efficient when students have specific information to cover in a session. For example, instead of reviewing material for a unit test, students should focus on particular areas of weakness within that material.

- Before you encourage students to work together, discuss with them what peer tutoring is and the behaviors you want from them while they are working together. You should encourage them to stay on task, keep their voices down, and be respectful of each other.

- Limit the time that students work together to sessions of fifteen minutes or less during class and less than thirty minutes after school. If you allow longer sessions than this, students will find it easy to wander off task and the tutor will not be using his or her own time as efficiently as possible.

- Be careful not to allow students in your class who are quick to understand the work spend too much time tutoring their classmates. Although it is acceptable to ask your more able students to help their classmates on occasion, it is not the best use of student time if it's used too often. If you have several students who often complete assignments significantly more rapidly than the rest of the class, you should involve them in more challenging work and in enrichment activities.

- One of the most successful uses of peer tutoring happens when you can involve students who are less able than others as tutors. Students who have to work hard to learn the material can grow more self-confident by teaching what they know to others.

Student Study Teams

When you allow your students to work together to learn, you enrich the learning climate in your classroom by giving students the opportunity to tap into their shared resources. You will also save instructional time that is lost when students don't know what to do or aren't successful at grasping material quickly.

Student study teams differ from other collaborative groups in that they exist only for students to help each other throughout the term. The objective is not for students to work together to complete assignments, but rather to support each other academically.

When these small groups within the larger group work well together, students find that they have built-in support when they are absent and when they don't know how to complete an assignment. If you are contemplating setting up permanent study teams in your classroom, consider these points.

- Observe how your students relate to each other for a few weeks before you assign teams. If you pay careful attention to how you create the initial teams, you will avoid having students ask to switch teams later in order to work with more compatible people.

- Study teams usually work best if they are larger than most other collaborative groups so responsibilities are shared evenly. A study team can comfortably hold four to six members.

- Make study teams permanent unless you see that there are irreconcilable differences among students. If that happens, move students who aren't working well together.

- Be clear with your students that their study teams are different from teams that they may work with on occasion because they are permanent and oriented to the goal of helping team members stay focused and be successful in school. You do not have to seat these students together as you would other groups.

- When you assign teams, you must teach students how you expect them to function. Make it clear to students that their function is to provide academic support for each other. Study team members' responsibilities include helping each other when one student is out or when some members are struggling to learn a concept or skill, taking notes for each other, collecting handouts when someone is absent, and reminding each other of due dates and other important class information.

- One of the greatest benefits of study teams results when students share study techniques with each other. When students with different learning styles and different abilities are assigned to work together, they will be able to learn new study skills from each other.

- Allow students to not only exchange contact information, but to get to know each other as members of a special team. Encourage them to plan how they could benefit from a permanent group devoted to academic support. Ask them to share their ideas with the class so that other groups can benefit.

- At first, you will have to take an active role in encouraging students to work together and in suggesting activities, but as students become more familiar with the group they will find themselves finding new ways to help each other.

Students Working in Groups

Group work is usually one of the most enjoyable activities that you can assign your students. Because of its popularity and because it allows students to share ideas, group work is a motivational tool well worth the effort it requires. Teachers who have carefully planned group work activities will see that it can eliminate many of the problems that some of their students may be having. Conversely, teachers who allow group work but take little time to carefully plan group work activities are likely to experience many problems: high noise levels, off-task students, confusion, and misbehaviors.

Using group work to advantage in your classroom requires that you spend time planning what your role will be, creating groups, designing general strategies that you will want to incorporate, fostering a team spirit, managing noise levels, and evaluating groups fairly.

YOUR ROLE IN GROUP WORK

- You should create the assignments for each group. Make sure that your students have clear and measurable objectives for each activity so that they will stay on task and benefit from working together.

- Group work often requires special resources or adaptations of existing materials. For example, students will need different handouts if they are to complete an activity where each student is responsible for a separate section of an assignment that they will later combine into a whole.

- You will have to show students how to work well together. If they are to work as an effective team, they should learn how to relate politely to each other, how to divide tasks, how to remind each other to stay on task, and how to signal for assistance.

- Plan to spend time coaching and actively monitoring your students throughout the time that they will work together so you can help them stay on track.

- You will have to be available to your students when they work together to solve problems and to help them solve their own problems.

- You will have to quickly resolve problems that group members cannot resolve for themselves. One of the most common problems requiring your intervention will be students who are reluctant to assume responsibility for their part of the work. Here are some suggestions for how you can handle this successfully.

  - Offer support and affirmation that you know he or she can do the work well.
  - Break large tasks into manageable activities.
  - Assist students in resolving their differences.
  - Contact parents.
  - Remove the offending students and allow the rest of the group to work without distraction.
  - Don't lower the grade of other group members for the misbehavior of one member.

CREATING GROUPS

- Although students will insist that they are the best judges of how they should be grouped, you should take an active role in selecting the students who should work together. Taking time to explain that you want them to be teammates and not playmates will help students accept your grouping decisions.

- Some teachers use random selection to create groups that will work together for only a brief time. Some ways of randomly grouping students include students' birthday months, counting off by seat assignments, pulling numbered slips of paper from a hat, or by rows.

- While random selection is acceptable for very brief activities, when grouping students for long-term assignments, you should spend time planning more successful group configurations based on factors such as compatibility, learning styles, work ethic, and ability.

- You will find that a group that includes a mixture of ability levels and interpersonal skills is the most productive combination for maximum learning. It is usually best to start with teams of pairs and triads so that you can closely monitor their activities and so that they can learn to work together well. After you gain confidence in your students' ability to work together, you can create larger groups. The task, group interpersonal skills, the age and maturity of students, and the length of time involved are all important factors to consider in determining the ideal size for a group.

- Avoid allowing friends to work together when you can. While students are often comfortable working with friends, they are not always as productive as they will be when working with other students.

GENERAL STRATEGIES

- You will have to plan solutions to any concerns you have about group work before your students work together. Some areas that you may want to consider include ways to increase student responsibility, how to control noise levels, how to increase time on task, and group evaluation.

- Teach your students the interpersonal skills that they will need to work together well, including the following.
  - Listening to each other
  - Asking questions
  - Staying on task
  - Remaining open-minded
  - Assuming responsibility for group success

- A brief successful activity once or twice a week is preferable to a long-term unsuccessful group collaboration. Make sure that the activity you assign is one that is ideal for group work.

- Have a clear objective for group activities and take time to ensure that your students are clear about how they are to achieve their objectives. One way to make sure every group member understands the objective is to have students explain it to one another after you have presented it to the group.

- Design activities that will encourage your students to collaborate and not just divide the workload.

- Encourage students to share ideas as they answer questions or brainstorm lists of possible responses.

- Establish a few ground rules for group work. The following are some rules that other teachers have found effective.
  - Stay seated.
  - Listen to each other.

- Face each other.
- Don't talk to other groups.
- Ask questions of each other before requesting outside help.

▶ Teach students how you want them to manage their questions or concerns in the best way possible so that they do not lose valuable time. One technique that you can use is to have students write their questions or concerns on the board for you to address later.

▶ Avoid assignments that require too much of the work to be done outside of class. This often results in an uneven division of labor. If students are working in class, you can take an active role in supervising them and making sure that all students are making a valuable contribution.

▶ After students have worked together on an assignment, have them reflect how well they worked together as a group. They should assess their strengths and weaknesses and how they could work together more efficiently in the future.

▶ One of the negative consequences of using group work in your class is that students can be confused about when it is acceptable to work together on other assignments and when it is not. Clearly explain the differences to your students.

WAYS TO FOSTER TEAM SPIRIT

▶ Take photographs of students working in groups and display the photos.

▶ Allow students to name their groups.

▶ Celebrate small achievements and successes.

▶ At the end of a group session, ask students to share what they learned from each other during the session.

▶ Provide each group with stickers to award to each other for categories such as best communicator, most on-task team member, hardest worker, or best contributor.

▶ Assign specific roles to each person in the group so that every person has an important task.

▶ Have a team reporter write a brief report on team successes to share with the entire class at the end of the assignment.

MANAGING NOISE LEVELS

▶ Managing noise must be everyone's responsibility, not just yours. Select a team member to monitor the noise from a group and alert teammates when the group is too loud.

▶ Spread groups out in your class whenever you can to discourage them from talking with students in other groups.

▶ Be consistent about enforcing acceptable noise levels.

- Before you begin an activity, explain the acceptable noise levels and ask students to share suggestions for controlling noise.

- Establish signals to let your students know that they are too noisy. You will have to devise signals that won't require shouting to be heard.

- Have students move their chairs close together so that they don't have to talk loudly.

- Teach students to listen carefully to members of their group to avoid needless repetition and raised voices.

EVALUATING GROUPS FAIRLY

- Assign individual grades, not one grade to the whole group.

- Keep a record of students' work as you observe them working on long-term group projects. You should then be able to assign grades based on participation as well as on their products.

- Do not penalize an entire group for one student's poor contribution.

- If you use rubrics to structure and assess assignments, make sure that students are aware of how you intend to grade their contributions to the group.

- Try to design activities that allow for measurable objectives as well as individual contributions.

> *"Find a way to let students know that what they like is important to you. For me, music has been successful. Playing a CD that my students would normally listen to sends a powerful message. This lets them know that I care about what they like."*
>
> —Rick Shelton, 3 years experience

Use Positive Reinforcement to Motivate Students

Positive reinforcement is a much more powerful motivational tool than punishment. Even though it may seem as if you should take a firm stand and punish students for misbehaving, you will have more success in getting students to behave by encouraging and praising their good behavior instead. If you want students to act in a certain way, you should reinforce that action.

One of the reasons that positive reinforcement works with students is that many of them are so used to negative reinforcement that it no longer motivates them successfully. Positive reinforcement, on the other hand, sets a supportive tone that allows students to see the connection between their efforts and the results. Positive reinforcement is also effective because it can move students away from failure and towards the intrinsic motivation that is necessary for self-discipline.

There are two important ways to use positive reinforcement in your classroom: praise and rewards. Using each effectively will help you motivate your students to succeed and to behave well. The following guidelines will help you make both practices a part of your teaching style.

USING PRAISE EFFECTIVELY

Regardless of their age, all students like to be recognized for doing well, and all respond positively to praise when it is given in a sincere manner. Help your students behave by using praise in the following ways.

- Communicate your high expectations to your students. Students whose teachers expect a great deal from them will soon be students who are confident that they can accomplish a great deal. Don't over-praise students for behavior that is only minimally acceptable, because this communicates to them that you do not believe that they are able to accomplish much.

- Make it very clear to your students when you praise them that you are commenting on their work or their behavior and not on their worth as a person. For example, you should replace, "You are such a neat kid!" with "Your work is very neat!" This will place emphasis on the activity and will encourage them to continue their good work.

- When you praise a student, be careful not to overdo it. If you are over dramatic your students will find your praise insincere, and you also risk embarrassing sensitive students.

- Be aware of the connection between your body language and the praise that you give your students. Let your expression and the tone of your voice express approval along with your words.

- Praise individual students whenever possible, and vary what you say to each one so that they will know that you see them as individuals. Also, occasionally follow up your praise with a positive note or phone call home.

- Be careful to reach every student. Some teachers may unconsciously favor some students. Be positive with every student at least once during every class.

- Identify specific actions when you praise students. For example, instead of "Good work," say "Thorough and insightful analysis," and instead of "You behaved well today," say "I was proud of the way you continued to work quietly while I spoke with our visitor." Knowing exactly what they did well will enable and encourage students to repeat the action.

- Be sensitive to whether students prefer public recognition or private praise. Some of your students prefer not to be in the limelight for any reason. Be careful to consider their preferences if you want your encouragement to be effective.

- Encourage effort. If you have students who are struggling, encourage them to persevere by praising their efforts. Also, boost their confidence by praising their successes along the way.

REWARDING STUDENTS FOR APPROPRIATE BEHAVIOR

Tangible rewards have become increasingly controversial since research shows that students who work for rewards instead of the intrinsic motivation in assignments are less likely to sustain effort. Use tangible rewards judiciously, according to the following guidelines.

➧ Be prompt in giving rewards for good behavior so students will be able to identify the action for which they are being rewarded.

➧ Be careful to combine rewards with praise. If you don't make this connection for your students, they may not understand that they earn rewards through their own efforts.

➧ You do not have to spend a fortune on rewards for your students. The most effective rewards are activities that students enjoy. Try playing a game such as a history trivia game or a geography bee to reward students with enjoyable activities.

20 Ways to Reward Your Students

Instead of going shopping for stickers or other treats to use as rewards for your students, give students some of these free rewards.

1. Using the library during free time
2. Extra time on the computer
3. An educational classroom game
4. Being team captain
5. Time to work on a puzzle
6. Extra credit points
7. A bulletin board featuring their work
8. Having their names displayed in a wall of fame
9. Having their work displayed
10. Watching a film
11. Time to do homework for another class
12. Being on a class honor roll
13. Being "Student of the Week"
14. Earning extra time to complete an assignment
15. Borrowing a book from the classroom library
16. Time for independent reading
17. Encouraging notes on their work
18. Having you write a positive note home
19. Having you call home with a positive message
20. Having their photographs in the class newsletter

Adopt a Positive Attitude

It isn't always easy to be positive about a class or a student or even about a certain time of the school year. If you find yourself beginning to lose your joy in what you and your students are doing, you can correct the situation by consciously adopting a positive attitude. Even though this is an excellent way to deal with your own stress, it is also important to promote a positive class atmosphere for your students. When you see that your students and you can use a boost, try some of these strategies.

- Set aside bulletin board space to maintain a running list of the good things that you see your students doing. You can list good deeds by class or by individual students.

- Ask your students to tell you what they have done well during the course of the week or even during a class period.

- Hand students a scrap of paper and ask them to write out a positive statement about a classmate. Share these with the class after you have reviewed them.

- Teach students to be thankful for the small kindnesses that they offer each other. Take notice when a student lends another a pen or when students offer to share books.

- Use stickers and stamps to let them know that you appreciate their work. In focusing on students' successes, you will also give yourself a boost by noting the progress your students have made.

- Ask students to assess their own progress when they are working on a long-term project. Ask them to tell you what they have learned so far instead of focusing on what they still have to do.

Intrinsic Motivation

Intrinsic motivation is the incentive to work that is built into an assignment as an essential part of the lesson itself. Although praise and tangible rewards can be effective in boosting students' self-confidence and their desire to do well, intrinsic motivation is the most effective way to promote a fundamental change in student effort and achievement, because its effects last much longer.

There are many ways to include intrinsic motivation into every assignment. Many effective teachers do this automatically when they offer a variety of activities, arouse curiosity, and play games with their students. You can increase the intrinsic motivation in each lesson that you teach by including one or more of these ten techniques into each lesson.

1. Help students make a personal connection to the material that they are studying. There are many ways to show students how the material is relevant to their concerns. Try one of these.
   - Use their names in examples and questions.
   - Ask students to write a response before giving them the opportunity to engage in a discussion. This will automatically involve all students in thinking about a response instead of just listening to their classmates.

- Ask students to draw comparisons between what they are studying and their own lives.
- Have students explain material in their own words.

2. Incorporate your students' interests, backgrounds, and concerns into lessons as often as you can.

3. Challenge your students to beat their personal best on a test or other assignment. Or tell them that you are going to time them and then start watching the clock.

4. Open class with an anticipatory set that will help students recall their previous knowledge about a subject. This will add interest to the new information that you are about to present.

5. Show students how to work to achieve their goals by accomplishing a series of smaller goals.

6. Make an assignment dependent on the successful completion of an earlier one. Make sure students recognize that in order to understand the next topic you are going to study they have to know the current material.

7. Involve parents and guardians in class activities. Keep them informed of due dates and other information that will help them encourage students to stay on task.

8. Combat students' piecemeal approach to their education by using a course outline or a syllabus. Too often students are not aware of the "big picture" and don't understand how one assignment will lead to another one.

9. Include opportunities for discussion in your class. Encourage students to debate topics of interest and share their mastery of a lesson. In a math class, for example, you can have teams of students solve the same problem and then explain to the class how they derived their answer.

10. Encourage your students to be open-minded and tolerant of ambiguities so they won't be afraid to take intellectual risks. Often students are not motivated to attempt their work because they are afraid of failure.

The Thought of the Day

Many teachers have adopted the practice of motivating their students by putting a thought of the day on the board. Students from elementary grades on find these inspirational messages a pleasant part of their school experience.

Although you can incorporate the daily message into different activities such as a writing exercise or a history lesson, a daily inspirational message can just be a gentle reminder to students that they can be successful.

Create a folder where you can keep a list of quotes that your students find particularly interesting so you can easily update your daily inspirational message to students. There are many places that you can find inspirational messages for your students. If you do not have ready access to books of quotations in your class, you can search the Internet. These sites are helpful places to begin your search.

www.quoteland.com

www.bartleby.com

www.geocities.com/Hollywood/Hills/2844/QP7.htm

Students themselves are also good sources for inspiring quotations. They will enjoy bringing in quotations to share with the class if you make it an assignment or even if you just ask for contributions. If students bring in quotations to share with the class, make sure that you read them first for suitability. Song lyrics, in particular, can contain messages that are not appropriate for school.

Games in Your Classroom

Your students love to play games. You can capitalize on this natural interest by playing games in your classroom. Consider arranging team games to help them review, to teach each other information, or just to work together in a planned fashion.

Before your students engage in a classroom game, you must establish ground rules so that the activity is a successful one for everyone. Here are some suggestions for managing the games in your classroom.

- Teach good sportsmanship in advance of the game day. Be very clear with your students about the behaviors that you expect from them and the behavior that is not acceptable.

- Make sure there is a sound educational purpose for each game and that you are not simply using it as a pleasant way to pass time.

- Pay attention to safety. If you see that students are so excited that the competition is too intense or they are becoming unsafe, stop play at once.

- You should select the team members, so that no one will be left out. The more decisions students make about scoring procedures and rules of sportsmanship, the better. Allow them to discuss these issues before they begin playing.

- Keep a container of numbers or other markers on hand so students can draw from it to determine who goes first or makes other decisions.

- While you don't really need prizes in class games, you could offer ribbons, stickers, trinkets, or bookmarks.

- Your students will find it easier to get into the spirit of the game if you add realistic touches like music or other props.

- Have students assume the role of score keeper, time keeper, and master of ceremonies so you can monitor activities.

- Prepare to move a class to a location where they won't disturb other students if the game gets noisy.

GAMES YOUR STUDENTS WILL ENJOY

There are many ways to incorporate games into your lessons. Here are some suggestions that other teachers have found successful.

Talk Show: Have your students stage a talk show to interview characters in fiction or history or in any other discipline. Choose the most outgoing and reliable student to be the host and let that student interview others who pose as guests.

Storytellers: Have students sit in a circle. To play, one student begins a story, stops after a few sentences, and points to another student to continue. You can adapt this activity to teach vocabulary, order of events, facts, or other information.

Quiz Bowl: Set up a tournament of quick questions and answers involving as many of your students as possible. You can have various levels of difficulty, rules of play, ways of scoring, and incentives.

Board Games: Design your own board game to fit your topic. You can either make small boards and photocopy them for students to play in a group, or you can make a large one for the entire class to play. The tasks you assign your students in a board game range from simply answering questions to solving problems. Students also enjoy creating and playing their own board games.

Twenty Questions: Write an answer on a slip of paper and have students take turns asking a question each until they guess the answer. Keep track of the number of questions that they have to ask in order to guess correctly. In this game, the lowest number of questions wins.

Name That Person, Battle, etc.: This game is similar to Twenty Questions in that students try to guess answers with as few clues as possible. You should make up the clues in advance. On game day, you'll call them out one at a time until someone can name the targeted person, battle, and so on.

Ball Toss: Line up your students into two teams facing each other. As soon as a student correctly answers a question you ask, that student tosses a soft foam ball to a student on the other team. That student has to answer the next question.

Chain Making: This is an educational version of the old alphabet game that small children play. One player begins thinking of an object relating to the unit of study and beginning with the letter "A." The next student has to repeat that clue and add an object with the letter "B." The game continues until students are stumped or until they reach the end of the alphabet.

Sporting Events: Divide your students into teams and use the chalkboard to play games of football, soccer, or whatever sport is currently of interest to your students. Students advance by correctly answering questions or completing assigned tasks.

Journal Entries to Help You Motivate Your Students to Succeed

▶ How can you effectively use praise with students who need it most? How can you identify those students?

▶ Which motivation techniques have been ones that you enjoyed in the past? How can you use them in your classroom?

▶ Which motivation techniques do you already use with ease? Which ones do your students respond to?

▶ What compliments have you paid your students this week? What opportunities to compliment them did you overlook?

▶ What compliments have your students paid one another? What compliments have they paid you?

▶ How can you make every lesson relevant to the needs of your students? How can you determine those needs?

▶ How can you make your students understand that the material in your class prepares them for the future? Which students already understand this concept?

▶ What benefits do your students gain from working together? What are some mistakes that you have made in making group work assignments? What successes have you had?

▶ What motivates you to be the best teacher that you can be? How can you use this knowledge to maintain a positive outlook with your students?

Help Your Students Become Successful Learners

"But I did my work! How could I have an "F" on this test when I did the work? I did my work in class every day and I did my homework every night!"

He watched in frustration as his students reacted to their low test grades. He knew the test had been a fair one and that it matched what he had taught. His students had done their work.

Why hadn't they learned the material? There had to be a good reason.

That night he made up a questionnaire about the test. He asked questions about everything that could have caused the low grades.

When he reviewed his students' completed questionnaires, the reason for the low grades was painfully clear: His students didn't know how to study.

How could this happen? Surely someone had taught them how to study.

The next day he told his class what he had discovered. And he told them something else: He was going to teach them how to attack their work so that there would be no more low grades. He was going to teach them how to study.

Many teachers, no matter how young their students are, make the mistake of assuming that someone else has taught them how to study. The fact is students are rarely taught this important skill, even in schools that offer a course in study skills. All of the students in your class need your help in learning how to do their work successfully.

The rewards for teachers who teach their students how to learn are satisfying; confident pupils are a pleasure to teach. Conversely, failing students are a constant drain on the emotional and physical energy of every person in the class. Teaching students how to study efficiently can prevent years of frustration and failure for students.

Teaching students how to be successful in their learning is the job of every teacher at every level of instruction. If you want to create a roomful of confident learners, teach them the tools they need to unlock their learning. Complete Figure 10.1 to find out what you know about how students learn.

Figure 10.1
WHAT DO YOU KNOW ABOUT HOW STUDENTS LEARN?

On the line preceding each statement, write whether you believe the statement to be true or false. Then check your answers against the scoring guide at the end.

1. _____ Students should start their homework just as soon as they arrive at home.

2. _____ Students who take a break every twenty minutes do better than students who take breaks every hour.

3. _____ Every student needs a quiet place to study at home.

4. _____ Students who get along well with their teachers tend to make higher grades.

5. _____ Test-taking skills can't be taught to very young students because their attention spans are too short.

6. _____ Recopying notes each night is a valuable way to study.

7. _____ Teachers should not expect students to memorize facts.

8. _____ Students should be encouraged to correct their mistakes on tests.

9. _____ Writing notes in paragraph form is an excellent way to record lecture information.

10. _____ There is some truth to the old tip that students can learn while they sleep by listening to a tape.

Key

1. **False.** While some students work well right after school, others work more efficiently after taking a break.

2. **True.** Students learn best in short bursts of concentrated effort. Breaking up a long study session is a good idea.

3. **True.** Even though students assure their teachers and parents that they can study while watching television or talking on the phone, this isn't true. While a study area doesn't have to be silent, it does have to be free of distractions.

4. **True.** Students who get along well with their teachers are more likely to be cooperative, and cooperative students tend to be focused more on their work.

5. **False.** Very young children should learn test-taking skills every year. There is no age limit on learning how to be a good student.

6. **False.** Simply recopying notes is not a good way to study. Students who put their notes into their own words or into another format such as a graphic organizer learn the information more efficiently.

7. **False.** With the push for an increase in critical-thinking exercises, memorization has developed an undeserved poor reputation. Memorizing information can be a very useful tool when used appropriately. For example, students need to memorize their multiplication facts or the letters of the alphabet.

8. **True.** Students who correct their tests learn what to do to avoid errors in the future. Students who just look at their grade and put away their papers do not.

9. **False.** Although this is the most common way that inexperienced students take notes, it is the hardest to read. Encourage your students to use graphic organizers, two-column notes, key words and facts, or outlines instead.

10. **False.** Listening to a tape of information while a student is awake works. Sleeping through a tape does not. If it did, why would we ask students to remain awake in class?

25 Study Skills to Teach Your Students

Here is a list of twenty-five study skills that you can share with your students as you show them how to attack their work intelligently and efficiently. Each one is written as a student tip that you can quickly post on the board.

1. Attend class. Students who are in class do better than those who are absent.

2. Prioritize your time. You'll have to make choices about all of your activities if you want to do well in school.

3. Focus your attention in class and while you are studying. Concentration is an acquired skill. Make it yours.

4. Plan your work as far in advance as you can. Learn to use a calendar or a planner and allow plenty of time for projects that may take longer than you think they should.

5. Be an active learner when you study your notes. Don't just look them over; underline or circle key points.

> *"Teachers should remember how long it took them to learn some things and not overly idealize their own intellectual maturation."*
>
> —Ken Pfiefer, 28 years experience

6. Pack your book bag at night and leave it by the door so that all you have to do in the morning is grab it on your way out.

7. Make sure that you write down all of your homework assignments. Trying to remember page numbers and question numbers can be confusing after several classes have gone by.

8. As class is coming to an end, don't just sit and watch the clock; instead, tune in to the closing or, if you're working independently, try to fit in one more problem or read one more page.

9. Allow enough time to study. For example, if you have homework in three subjects on the same night, you will need to spend more time doing homework than on nights when you only have homework in one subject.

10. Homework isn't something you should do if you have the time. It's something you must do.

11. Set up a comfortable study area at home where you can store your supplies and work without interruptions.

12. Limit the amount of phone calls you have on school nights. Make arrangements with your friends so that you can still keep up with them and get your work done, too.

13. Find a friend with whom you can study. You'll both benefit from the encouragement that you give each other.

14. Don't give in to the temptation to stay up too late on school nights. You need to have enough rest so that you won't be sleepy in class.

15. Take a break from your homework about every fifteen or twenty minutes. Make it a short break, but get up and move around.

5 Ways to Incorporate Study Skills into Every Lesson

Instead of taking the approach that students need a separate course in study skills, you should incorporate study skills into every lesson. Here are four easy ways to make learning study skills part of your daily classroom routines.

1. Incorporating study skills into your class is not difficult if you first think in terms of what your students will be doing, not what you will be doing in class. Then, choose one or two useful skills as a focus in each lesson. For example, if you are going to lecture, begin by teaching students how to take notes while listening.

2. Be a good role model for your students by taking a serious approach to your own work. When you pass out handouts, explain how you had to proofread your paper, plan times to use the copier, and make sure the handouts were neatly done before you handed them out. By talking about your own work habits and through consistent modeling, you will raise your students' awareness of the quality of work that you expect and how to achieve it.

3. Provide lots of examples, practical suggestions, and models for your students. If you model the skill and then show them how other students have accomplished it, you are off to a good start. If you then follow these actions with another example or model, your students will certainly have an advantage over those students whose teachers ignore their need for instruction in study habits.

4. Put a study skill on the board each day for students to record and discuss. You can hand over the task of researching good study habits to your students by having them contribute a new study skill each day.

5. Check out a few of the more than 23,000 Web sites dedicated to study skills! Here are a few of the most popular ones for you and your students to investigate.

    www.how-to-study.com
    www.smc.maricopa.edu
    www.csbsju.edu/academicadvising
    www.angelfire.com
    www.elearnaid.com/elearnaid/index
    www.student-tips.com

16. Take notes in pencil or erasable pen so that they will remain neat.

17. Develop a few abbreviations for some of the words you use most often in your notes.

18. Always label your work and your notes with the date, subject, and page numbers so that you can find it again quickly when you need to review.

19. When you find that your locker, book bag, and notebooks are getting messy, take a few minutes and clean them out. Staying organized is an important part of being an efficient student.

20. Be an active listener when your teacher is lecturing. Take notes and try to understand all of the points in the lecture.

21. If you have to miss class, have a study buddy take notes for you. Make sure that you pick someone who takes thorough notes that are easy to read.

22. Learn your learning style and use it when you review on your own for tests.

23. Study your most difficult or boring subjects first. You will find it easier to do them well when you are not tired.

24. Try to study at a time of day when you are most alert. Most people are more alert during daylight hours.

25. Make a list of your goals and the reasons you want to do well in school. This will help you stay on track when you are tempted not to give school your best effort.

Help your students determine the strengths and weaknesses of their study techniques by having them complete the self-assessment in Figure 10.2. This should give them an idea of what they do well and what they need to improve.

Setting and Achieving Goals

Students need many powerful messages from the adults in their lives if they are going to succeed in school. One of the most powerful messages that we can send our students is that they can achieve their dreams. We send this message to students when we give them a solid reason to study: to achieve a dream by setting worthwhile goals and working consistently towards them.

Use the worksheet in Figure 10.3 to help your students set goals for themselves and determine how they will achieve them. Students who work with a goal in mind are far more likely to succeed than students who just drift through school.

Teach Your Students to Manage Their Time

A high school teacher once asked a first-grader whose homework assignment was to write three sentences how long it would take to write the sentences. The child sighed and answered, "Forever." Much like this first-grader, many of our older students really do not have a clear concept of how long it takes to complete their assignments.

Figure 10.2

STUDENT ASSESSMENT: HOW WELL DO YOU STUDY?

Rank each statement as it applies to you by putting the appropriate number in the blank beside each of these excellent study strategies. If you can't mark "Always" beside a strategy, it is one you can improve!

4 = Always   **3 = Sometimes**   **2 = Seldom**   **1 = Never**

I use these study strategies:

1. _____ Take planned study breaks

2. _____ Have a quiet place to study at home

3. _____ Tape record my notes

4. _____ Focus my attention in class

5. _____ Take time to proofread

6. _____ Rewrite notes into my own words

7. _____ Make up missing work on time

8. _____ Spend enough time studying for tests

9. _____ Study with a friend or group

10. _____ Plan what I need to study

11. _____ Finish my homework

12. _____ Write neatly

13. _____ Create my own study guides

14. _____ Have someone quiz me

15. _____ Have enough supplies

16. _____ Use a planner to schedule my work

17. _____ Do difficult homework first

18. _____ Ask for help

19. _____ Use colored pens to review notes

20. _____ Take good notes during lectures

21. _____ Take good notes while reading

22. _____ Have a plan for taking tests

23. _____ Skim material before reading

24. _____ Work towards a goal

25. _____ Keep an organized notebook

Figure 10.3

STUDENT WORKSHEET: SETTING AND ACHIEVING GOALS

Goal 1: _____

The date when I expect to achieve this goal is:_____

Steps I will have to take to achieve my goal are:

1. _____

2. _____

3. _____

A problem I will have to solve to achieve my goal is:

_____

_____

Goal 2: _____

The date when I expect to achieve this goal is: _____

Steps I will have to take to achieve my goal are:

1. _____

2. _____

3. _____

A problem I will have to solve to achieve my goal is:

_____

_____

From a first-grader's ten-minute homework assignment to the ninety minutes in a block-schedule class for a senior, many students have difficulty planning how use their time to accomplish what they need to do to succeed in school. Because there is so much that teachers need to teach, it is easy to overlook opportunities to teach time management strategies. The loss to pupils when teachers do this is a grave one. Many students become so overwhelmed at what they are expected to do that they simply give up on school. Teachers can stop this downwards spiral by teaching students to manage their time well. There are many ways to do this so that it is part of the daily conversation in a classroom. The following guidelines will help you as you develop your plans for teaching time management techniques.

1. When you assign work, ask students to make an estimate of how long it should take them to complete it. With practice, your students will become proficient at estimating the length of any assignment.

2. Use a kitchen timer to teach your students to pay attention to time. When you want them to finish an activity within a certain amount of time, set the timer to keep them on task. This will help students work purposefully to complete an assignment within a set amount of time.

3. Show your students how to survey a test before taking it. They should then plan the strategies they need to correctly answer as many questions as they can in the time allotted for the test.

4. Use a checklist for daily assignments so students can prioritize their work. When you go over the checklist with students, discuss how long each assignment should take.

5. Raise your students' awareness of time management by asking them to list the ways that they waste time in various situations such as the end of class, while waiting for class to begin, after finishing an assignment, during lectures, and while doing homework.

6. Have your students set goals for themselves and work towards those goals.

7. Consider asking successful older students to talk to your students about how to manage their time well. Older students can offer practical, first-hand advice that younger students will pay more attention to than they will to a lecture from a teacher.

Even very young students can be taught to make the most of the time that they have to study. Have your students complete the assessment in Figure 10.4 to help them determine which time management skills they need to improve.

"Be flexible. The classroom is a constantly changing environment."

—Denise Boyer, 12 years experience

Figure 10.4

STUDENT ASSESSMENT: HOW GOOD ARE YOUR TIME MANAGEMENT SKILLS?

Here is a short list of some of the problems that many students have when they don't manage their time well. Which of these have happened to you?

1. _____ I have turned in assignments late.

2. _____ I have crammed for tests.

3. _____ I have stayed home pretending to be sick on the day a project is due.

4. _____ I have completed homework for one class during another.

5. _____ I have missed lunch to get caught up on homework.

6. _____ I have hoped my teachers would not call on me because I was not prepared.

7. _____ I have volunteered to be last during oral presentations because I was not prepared.

8. _____ I have not done my homework, but told my teachers that I did and left it somewhere else.

9. _____ I have turned in messy work because I had to rush through it.

10. _____ I have received a bad grade because I did not finish my homework.

15 Time Management Tips for Students

Here is a list of fifteen time management tips that you can share with your students as you show them how to do their work intelligently and efficiently.

1. When you have to read a selection and then answer questions about it, read the questions first so that you will read the rest of the selection with a purpose.

2. Make sure you have the supplies you need for class and for projects. This will save you trips to the store the night before a project is due or having to borrow pens and paper.

3. When you pack up at the end of a class, don't just shove papers into your book bag or notebook. Spend thirty seconds stowing away your work in an organized way so that you can find it quickly.

4. Write down your homework assignments so that you won't have to waste time phoning around to find out what they are or worrying if you did the right ones.

5. Use your class time wisely. It will save you time at home if you learn the material in class.

6. Work with a purpose in mind. If you do this instead of daydreaming, you will cut down on the time that it will take you to do your homework.

7. Reward yourself for staying on task for a week or for even a day if you had to struggle to do it.

8. When you take breaks from your homework, get back to work as quickly as you can. Stay away from the television and the phone during breaks.

9. When you have a test, read it over first, paying attention to the point values of each question so that you can plan a sensible strategy for taking it. If you don't think that you will finish all of the questions, do the ones with the higher point values first.

10. Review your class notes before your start your homework. This will refresh your memory and make doing homework much easier.

11. Take the time to do each assignment correctly the first time so that you don't have to redo it.

12. When you have facts to look up and learn, concentrate on learning them as you look them up. It will take you at least twice as long to master the material if you have to memorize them afterwards.

13. Set aside the same amount of time each night to study. If you don't have any written assignments, get ahead on reading or review your notes for an upcoming test.

14. At the end of a homework assignment, ask yourself what you could do to learn just one more fact in the assigned work.

15. While you want your work to be accurate and neat, don't be a perfectionist. It's not sensible to waste time picking over mistakes that only you can notice.

Teach Your Students to Think on Paper

In today's society, written information is a fact of life. From Congressional vetoes to fishing licenses to birth and marriage certificates, people have important information on paper. Further, a builder wouldn't think of starting a house without a written plan. A state trooper would have a very difficult time enforcing driving laws without the ability to document offenses. Not only do people have the important events of their lives written down, but many people get out a pen and paper when they start to plan out their day, make a shopping list, or leave the baby-sitter an important phone number.

Somewhere in their education, people learned to do this. A teacher showed them how to plan, how to organize information—how to think on paper.

If you would like for this important skill to be part of the culture of your classroom, there are several ways for you to make it happen. Try some of these techniques when you want to teach your students how to think on paper.

1. Whenever you ask a question in a class discussion, instead of having a few students blurt out answers, ask your students to jot down their answers. Wait until you see that everyone has had a chance to finish writing before you ask them to share answers.

2. Teach your students how to take notes. When you take the time to show students how to outline a chapter or take notes from a lecture, you are really teaching them how to reorganize their thoughts on paper.

3. Ask students to predict information in a lesson at the start of a unit of study by writing out what they already know or what they would like to know.

4. Ask students to write out a plan for accomplishing an assignment or completing a project proposal.

5. Ask students to analyze a subject by writing out their thoughts in a quick response. For example, you can ask students to write out how they solved a math problem, tracing the steps of the procedure.

6. When you have a question for a large-group discussion, ask students to write out notes for their responses the night before so that they won't waste class time thinking of something to say instead of adding well-thought out comments.

Graphic Organizers Help Students Reach Mastery

Can you imagine how hard it would be to make up a seating chart without the chart? You would have to laboriously write sentence after sentence explaining who would sit where. Instead of this, you save time when you plan where your students are going to sit by using a learning tool called a graphic organizer.

Graphic organizers are no more than visual representations of material. They are composed of elements of both diagrams and words. Students like them for their non-linguistic appeal. Teachers like them simply because they work.

Graphic organizers not only help students decode, process, and understand material, but they do so in such a way that helps students retain information. They can also help students solve problems and comprehend material quickly. When students create graphic organizers, they can quickly see the relationship between the important elements in the assignment and their parts. Moreover, students of all ages and ability levels can use them successfully for a variety of purposes, including the following.

- To take notes on lectures and on reading
- To describe people, places, events, ideas, or objects
- To compare and contrast
- To determine the validity of assumptions
- To classify and categorize information
- To determine effective details
- To see how parts make up a whole
- To solve problems
- To predict outcomes
- To plan reading and writing activities
- To understand cause and effect
- To support arguments
- To organize concepts into key components
- To analyze vocabulary words
- To organize text material

You will find that there are several common patterns for graphic organizers. Below is a very brief list of some of these patterns, a brief description of what they can be used for, and the names of some of the graphic organizers that could be associated with each one.

Pattern 1: Concept Maps. These allow students to understand the attributes of a concept. Some examples include:

- Herringbone maps
- Venn diagrams
- Spider maps
- Network trees
- Outlines
- Novel/story matrices
- Hierarchy maps

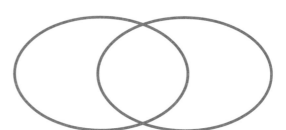

Pattern 2: Description Maps. These allow students to select the facts that describe a person, place, thing, idea, or event. Some examples include:

- Characterization maps
- Family trees
- Clustering
- Webbing
- Episode maps

Pattern 3: Time Sequence Maps. These allow students to put items in chronological order. Some examples include:

- Timelines
- Continuum maps
- Circle story cycles
- Story boards
- Story maps
- Chain of events maps
- Cycle diagrams
- Linear strings

Pattern 4: Cause-and-Effect Maps. These allow students to see the relationships that result when one event causes another. Some examples include:

- Flow charts
- Step ladder charts
- Problem/solution charts

If you would like to read more about graphic organizers, two useful books are *Visual Tools for Constructing Knowledge* (1996) and *A Field Guide to Using Visual Tools* (2000). Both are by David Hyerle and were published by the Association for Supervision and Curriculum Development in Alexandria, Virginia.

To find up-to-date Internet information on how to use graphic organizers, try these Web sites.

www.graphic.org
www.thinkwizard.com
www.nuatc.org
www.thinkingmaps.com
www.mapthemind.com
www.strategictransitions.com

To illustrate the universal practicality of graphic organizers for any student in any grade, three graphic organizers for vocabulary word mastery are shown in Figures 10.5, 10.6, and 10.7. Because all students are exposed to new words as part of their learning, graphic organizers can be a very helpful replacement to the traditional exercise of having students look up words in a glossary or dictionary.

Figure 10.5
GRAPHIC ORGANIZER 1

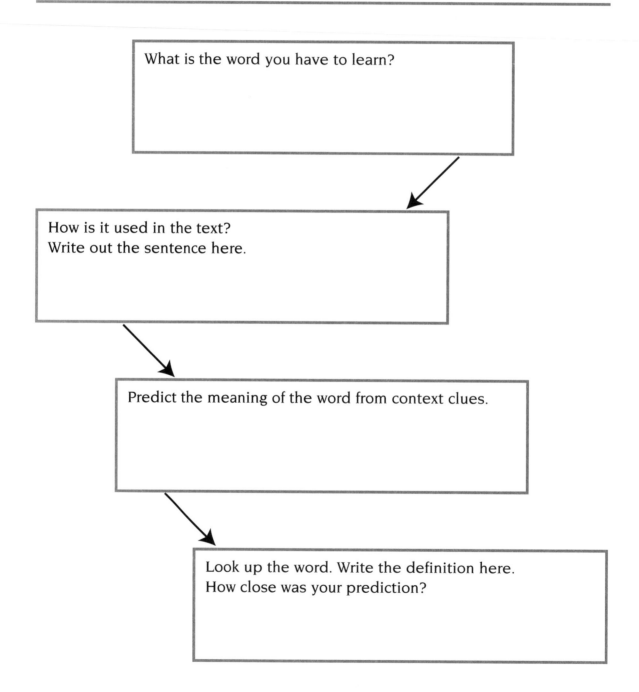

Figure 10.6
GRAPHIC ORGANIZER 2

Complete this Venn Diagram for any two of your vocabulary words.

What You Know About Word 1	What They Share	What You Know About Word 2
Word 1: _____		Word 2: _____

Figure 10.7
GRAPHIC ORGANIZER 3

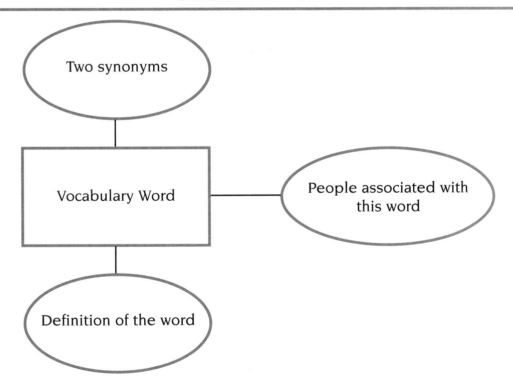

Stop the Futile Cycle of Delayed Learning

Perhaps you can recall from your own school days the satisfying feeling that you had when you successfully completed writing definitions for a list of vocabulary words. That feeling may have vanished the next day when you realized that you had only defined the words, but your teacher expected you to have learned them.

This happens daily in schools everywhere. Students do their work without thinking about what they are doing. They just do what they are told to do. Older students often realize that they should be learning the material, and will tell their teachers that they plan to study the night before the test. They seem convinced that the pressure of a test deadline will focus their attention. Their convictions fade when test day arrives and they still have not learned the material.

The futility of this cycle of delayed learning has serious consequences for student success. Students who just go through the motions of doing their work never learn enough to do well on tests. Their delay in learning is simply too great to be overcome.

There is a great deal that you can do to prevent your students from delaying their learning. First, you can make your students aware of the importance of learning their work when it is assigned. Teach them the difference between completing an assignment and learning the information that the assignment is supposed to teach. Stress the importance of learning information the first time it is presented.

Another strategy you can use to engage students in continuous learning is to extend assignments until your students learn the material. Instead of just asking that students read a chapter, ask them to complete such activities as taking notes, completing graphic organizers, outlining, selecting key terms, making flash cards, or designing a quiz. All of these activities will force students to become more fully engaged in the material.

You can also prevent the delay in studying until just before a test by including frequent reviews and knowledge checks early in the unit. If students are prepared for a daily quiz three days in a row, then being prepared for a test at the end of the week should be easy for them. Hold students accountable for their learning every day, not just on test days.

A final way to stop delayed learning is to increase student awareness of the importance of concentrating while working. Many students can daydream in class and still appear on task because they are not disturbing others. Still others regularly do their homework while watching television. Help them break both of these bad habits—make learning efficiently an open topic of conversation in your class. Create posters and banners to remind them to concentrate and learn.

Your students can succeed if you teach them the importance of taking an active role in their learning. Just "doing the work" should not be enough to get by in any classroom.

Extra Credit Solutions

Extra credit is often a controversial topic for teachers. Some teachers are adamant about its usefulness while others believe that offering extra credit encourages poor study habits. Either way, extra credit can be a trap for the unwary first-year teacher. When you are trying to decide on a workable extra credit policy for your students, follow these guidelines to avoid problems.

- Before you give in to student pressure for extra credit, think through what you really expect from your students. Don't give in on the spur of the moment when students want extra points.

- Make sure that the plan you have for extra credit is in line with your school's policy. If the policy is not in your faculty manual, check with a colleague or your grade level chairperson or department head.

- Be aware of just how easy it is to skew grades with extra credit points. If you assign extra work without considering the impact it will have on grades, you will devalue the importance of the other work that you have assigned all grading period.

- If you do offer extra credit, it should be offered at the beginning of a marking period with a clear due date and point value attached. If you don't do this, you will find yourself grading too many papers at the end of a marking period.

- Extra credit assignments should have rubrics just as other assignments do and you should grade them on the quality of the work and not just on effort.

- Extra credit should also be offered to every student in your class and not just to students who request it. If you don't offer it to everyone, then you can be accused of favoritism.

- Make sure that the extra credit you assign is related to class topics and not just for enjoyment. For example, assigning a researched report on a famous person connected to a unit of study is related to a class topic. Assigning a report on students' favorite sports teams is not.

- Don't offer extra credit for activities that require that your students spend money. For example, don't give students the extra credit assignment of going to see a local play. Some students will not have the admission fee, no matter how small it might be.

- If you offer bonus questions on a test, make sure that they are not worth as much as the other questions. The purpose of such questions should be for students to stretch their minds, not earn easy points to make up for what they did not know.

Help Your Students Meet Deadlines

Prepare yourself! Terrible things can happen to homework assignments after students complete them. Here are some of the homework crises you can expect to hear about this year.

"I left it at home."
"I left it in the car."
"I left it in my locker."
"Another teacher took it by mistake."
"Our printer is out of ink."
"My baby brother hid it."
"The power was out."

Students never seem to fully understand that their teachers are not so gullible as to believe all of these excuses, yet it can be hard for teachers to know what to do when an earnest student offers a plausible excuse for missing work. It's hard to draw the line between being inflexible and being a pushover.

You can avoid many of these problems if you help your students meet their deadlines. Some strategies that you can use to help your students become responsible include the following.

- Use a planning calendar for the week or for long-term projects. This will help students be aware of what they have to do each day.

- Write assignments in a conspicuous spot and expect your students to write them down, also.

- Create a policy for late work and make sure your students are aware of it. In fairness to the students who did their work on time, you should take off points for work that is late. The exception to this penalty would be the students who speak to you about problems that they are having well in advance of the due date or who bring in notes from home asking for your assistance.

- Break up large projects into smaller, manageable units of work so that all students can stay on target. Make sure each smaller unit has a reasonable due date.

- Encourage older students to set due dates for themselves earlier than the ones that you establish. This is an excellent way to promote self-discipline.

- Post a countdown of days on the board. For example, if a researched project is due in ten days, students will be aware of the passage of time if you tell them when there are nine days before it is due, and then eight . . . down to one.

- Call home if you believe that a student has a problem with making deadlines on time. Enlist the help of family members to keep this from becoming a problem. It will also alert them to any grade penalties for missed work.

- Use a computer and some small labels to print out reminders for students of their due dates. They can use these little reminders in their planning calendars.

- Make sure you clearly post the due dates for projects, tests, and other assignments on the board, near the clock, by the door, and in other obvious places so that students can see them as they move around the room.

Create a Homework Partnership

The practice of assigning homework is once again under fire. For decades the issue of homework and its impact on home life has been a concern for families and schools. The pendulum of debate seems to swing with the social climate; however, homework has remained a staple of education in our country despite the problems associated with it. The tension created between students and teachers, teachers and parents, and parents and students over homework has grown in recent years into a national debate.

The debate is particularly heated over two issues: 1) assigning homework to young students, and 2) the view of many parents that homework is an infringement on their family time. Many homework advocates find this ironic when surveys show that American school children spend many more hours watching television every day than they spend doing homework.

Teachers of all levels of experience are judged by their homework assignments. If you assign too much, you are too difficult. If you assign too little, then you are perceived as too easy. The problem with both of these judgments is that teachers can't please everyone. You will have both extremes in your classes: parents who take an active role in homework and parents who resent the demands of homework assignments.

You can overcome many of the hassles that homework can bring by creating a strong partnership with students and families. You should be the first to reach out, of course. The best way to do this is by communicating your expectations in a letter and by being consistent in adhering to your plan. (You can find a sample letter that you can adapt in Figure 10.8.)

If you teach young students, consider a homework folder. Many teachers have found that this is a convenient way to contact parents. These teachers laminate a folder for each child to take home each night with returned papers and the day's homework assignment tucked safely inside.

Many school districts now provide better communication opportunities for teachers and parents by using homework hotlines or voice mail for homework questions. Many teachers also have school e-mail accounts that parents can use to clarify any homework questions. Families have found that using both of these electronic tools can reduce confusion about homework assignments.

You can also help students and their families with homework by going online for support. There are more than 20,000 sites on the Internet dedicated to homework! Research some of them for your students and offer the addresses to those students who may need the extra help. Although many sites are limited to a specific content area or grade level, many are not. Here are a few addresses to help you begin your investigation.

www.mathgoodies.com/homework

www.chatterbeeshomework.com

www.framingham.com

www.homeworktips.about.com

Another recent online resource for teachers and students involves online posting services. At these sites, you can create a Web page for your class. Then you can give the address to your students and their parents and guardians for the times when they need help with homework. The sites listed below are not only very easy to set up and use, but are free. They are worth the extra time that it takes to set up a page and update it. Try setting up a homework Web page at the following sites.

www.schoolnotes.com

www.myclass.net

www.teacherweb.com

Remember, you will avoid many of the problems associated with homework if you involve parents and guardians early in the year, communicate with them frequently, alert them quickly if a problem arises, and are very structured and organized about homework. (See Figure 10.8.)

Develop a Homework Policy

Experienced teachers know that homework success doesn't just happen. Homework has to be approached with the same degree of planning and preparation as other assignments. One way to help your students do this is by developing a homework policy for your class.

Begin this process by finding out if there is a formal policy for your school district or your school. If there is no formal policy, then you should find out how the other teachers in your school handle homework.

Next, you will have to answer some tough questions. Use the space beside each of the following questions to write out how you want to handle each one of these concerns.

What is the purpose of homework in your class?

_____

_____

When will you assign it? When will your students not have homework?

_____

_____

How will you grade homework?

_____

_____

How much weight will you assign to homework grades?

_____

_____

Figure 10.8

SAMPLE HOMEWORK POLICY LETTER

Dear Parent or Guardian of _____:

I am writing to let you know about the homework policy for your child's class. Homework is a powerful tool for learning and a necessary part of any student's successful mastery of skills and knowledge. You can expect that your child will have homework on Monday through Thursday nights. These assignments will usually take no longer than thirty minutes to complete. On weekends, I will make no formal assignments, but students can take this time to read, research, and work on projects.

Homework due dates will be given on the day it is assigned. I expect work to be turned in on time. If there is a problem, please send in a note to let me know so that I can help your child. The first time an assignment is not completed, I will speak with your child to see if I can help. After that, I will contact you when assignments are not turned in on time.

I will make sure that my students write their assignments down each day. I will also record the assignment on my voice mail, which you can reach at

_____.

You can help your child do well on homework assignments by helping him or her set aside a study time each night, encouraging good work habits, and contacting me if there is a problem that we can solve together.

Please discuss this with your child. Please sign below and return it to school with your child. Keep the part above the dotted line for your reference.

Sincerely,

Julia G. Thompson

- -

I have read this homework policy and discussed it with my child.

_____   _____
Parent or Guardian's Signature   Student's Signature

What will the consequences for not doing homework be? How will you handle late assignments?

_____

_____

How long should each homework assignment take?

_____

_____

What types of homework will you assign?

_____

_____

Now that you have established a homework policy for your class, you need to make sure that you take the next two steps: 1) communicate it to students and their families, and 2) be consistent in how you enforce your policy all year long.

10 Tips for Successful Homework Assignments

When students don't do their homework, it becomes more than just an assignment; it becomes a headache—for parents, students, and teachers. Here are ten homework preparation strategies you can use to avoid almost all homework headaches and help your students find success.

1. Ask your students their opinion about homework assignments. Go beyond the initial complaints to discover the types of assignments students feel they can learn from and still find enjoyable.

2. Allow your students as many choices as you can. For example, students could choose either the even or the odd problems or one of several essay questions.

3. Consider designating some nights as homework-free nights. This is a good way to dispel some of the complaints that busy families make about too much homework. If you leave weekends free of new homework assignments, your students could use that time to get caught up on long-term projects or other work.

4. Be careful to balance the amount of homework that you assign with other work students have to do and with their individual needs. Typically, you should assign more homework to older students than to younger ones.

5. Students need to have a clear idea of what the final product will be. Show plenty of examples and models.

6. Make the work as interesting as possible. Use real-life examples, television shows, actual student names, sports, and other eye-catching details to engage students.

7. Assign work for which the audience is someone besides you. For example, have students write letters to the editor or give oral reports.

8. Expect that your students will help each other on homework assignments, even ones that you want them to do independently. Allow them to consult with each other when they all have the same assignment.

9. Never assign homework as punishment. This is not only unfair, but it encourages the perception that homework is a burdensome task.

10. Have a clear purpose for each assignment that you make and make sure your students understand it. Acceptable purposes for homework include reviewing material, applying learning, practicing, and previewing new material. Here are *some* examples of each of these assignment purposes.

Reviewing material:
- Making flashcards
- Outlining material

Applying learning:
- Creating real-life examples
- Solving problems

Practicing:
- Creating test questions
- Completing new problems

Previewing new material:
- Brainstorming
- Reading ahead

Figure 10.9
Steps to Follow Before, During, and After Making Homework Assignments

One way to make sure that homework is a success in your class is to see it as a three-step process. Use the following information to help you make assigning homework a successful experience for you and your students.

Before the assignment:

☐ Follow your district's homework policy or be sure that your own is in line with that of other teachers in your school.

☐ Aim for assignments that are reasonable in length, based on objectives, and can be done independently.

☐ Teach study skills and time management skills so your students will complete their work with little or no anxiety.

☐ Have a well-structured schedule for homework so students can anticipate assignments.

While presenting the assignment:

☐ Make sure students know why they have to do each assignment and how they will benefit from the work.

☐ Spend enough time going over the assignment and checking for understanding so students know that you are serious about it.

☐ Don't wait until the last few minutes of class to assign homework. It should not be a last-minute concern if you want students to take it seriously.

☐ Write the assignment in the same spot on the board each day. Do this even if you also give your students a syllabus, post it online, and record it on your voice mail.

☐ Avoid confusion by making sure that all students understand exactly what they have to do.

☐ Show models and examples of successful assignments.

☐ Ask students to estimate how long it will take them to do the assignment so they can set aside the time to do it.

After the assignment:

☐ A note or phone call home when a student does not complete an assignment will often correct the problem of missing work. If nothing else, it alerts the parent or guardian to be more vigilant about checking their child's homework.

☐ Offer help to students who may need extra assistance in doing their work. A bit of extra time with you after school will often clear up a problem a student has and give him or her an added boost of confidence.

☐ Be reasonable if a student brings in a note from home requesting an extension. Sometimes unforeseen events can cause even the most conscientious child to not be able to complete homework on time.

☐ If a student does not submit homework on time, have that student write out the reason for not doing the work and a phone number where parents or guardians can be reached so that you can easily contact them.

☐ Check homework at the start of class on the day it is due. If you do not take homework assignments seriously enough to provide feedback, then your students won't either.

☐ Grading homework can be overwhelming! Follow these tips to make giving prompt feedback a manageable task:

- Collect and grade only some assignments yourself.
- Go over the work together as a class. Give a grade for completion.
- Go over the work together as a class, but have students check each other's work.
- Go over the work together and then give a quiz on it.
- Check the work every day. Have students slip their assignments into a weekly portfolio. Have them then select their best work for you to assess.
- Have students work in small groups discussing their answers.

"You can really learn when you teach someone else something. Have your students work together. When students jump in and help each other, I just stand back and watch in amazement at what they can learn that way."

—Carole Platt, 35 years experience

25 Creative Homework Assignments

Try some of these assignments or adapt them to the interests and needs of your students. Your students will appreciate the higher-interest level of the work and you will appreciate their enthusiasm for the work.

INSTEAD OF:	TRY:
1. Read the assignment.	Read a magazine article.
2. Find the cause.	Find the cause of a crime in the news.
3. Write about a character.	How is this character like you?
4. Study the parts of a letter.	Write a letter of complaint.
5. Read about a social problem.	Brainstorm solutions to a social problem.
6. Read the chapter about weather.	Watch the weather report and take notes.
7. Rewrite your notes.	Draw a cartoon about part of your notes.
8. Retell a process.	Write out directions to your house.
9. Read the chapter.	Research two new facts on the Internet.
10. Read about this era.	Name a discovery that changed history.
11. What is your opinion of . . .	Survey five friends on their opinions concerning . . .
12. Read about this time period.	Interview an older person about it.
13. Retell the ending.	Rewrite the ending using other characters.
14. Learn these facts.	Write a rap to help you recall these facts.
15. Write a review of this book.	Write a review of a television show.
16. Answer these questions.	Sketch a scene from the chapter.
17. Use these terms in sentences.	Tell how famous people would use these terms.
18. Take notes.	Make a cluster map of the main ideas.
19. Read about an experiment.	Conduct an experiment.
20. Complete a puzzle.	Make your own puzzle.
21. Do these math problems.	Comparison shop in advertisements.
22. Read about these people.	Invent a dialogue between these two people.
23. Read about an event.	Write a first-hand report.
24. Review your notes.	Create a board game about the facts.
25. Write a paragraph.	Explain how this instrument works.

Teach Your Students How to Organize a Notebook

Students who have notes to study from to prepare for a test or who can find their homework papers on the day they are due find school easier than students whose work is less orderly. Teaching students how to organize their notebooks is the responsibility of all teachers. Don't assume that your students know how to take notes or keep their papers organized. No matter what age children you teach, there is a good chance that they have never been taught how to keep their notes and papers in order. The following strategies can help you teach your students how to organize their notebooks so that they have ready access to their work.

- Teach your students to organize their papers by date. This will make it easier for them to find the work they need when reviewing for a test.

- Tell your students how keeping an organized binder or notebook will benefit them in all their classes.

- Take time at the beginning of the term to make sure students are getting off to a good start with organizing their notebooks. After this initial organization, spend a few minutes each week to make sure your students know how to keep their papers in order.

- Encourage your students to use three-ring binders instead of paper folders. They are worth the extra money because they can be used for years. Have a three-hole punch available for students' use. This will make it much easier for them to file the papers you want them to keep.

- Require students to neatly label the front of their notebooks with their names and homeroom so their notebooks can be returned to them if misplaced.

- Show students how reinforcing and protecting the edges of a notebook with sturdy tape will extend its life.

Additional tips for orderly notebooks include the following.

- Have older students use pens instead of pencils so their notes will remain easy to read.

- Students with more than one notebook should color-code them by subject.

- Encourage your students to keep a recloseable pouch for pens and other small objects.

- Have students label every assignment so that they can quickly find their work.

Strategies for Teaching Students How to Take Notes

There are many strategies you can use to help your students learn to take good notes, regardless of their age or the subject you are teaching. To get an idea of where to begin in instructing your students in the art of note-taking, ask them to tell you what they already know about note-taking.

Teach students to come to class or to approach their homework prepared to take notes. At a minimum, they will need paper and pens. Students who are prepared for class will take much better notes than those who are not. Also, teach students that although there is a difference between the way that they will take notes as they read and how they will take notes as they listen, both types of notes involve three steps: 1) paying attention, 2) writing, and 3) reviewing the information.

1. PAYING ATTENTION

- If you really want to have a successful class, never lecture on cold material. Have students preview the material in their texts or in a preliminary handout before you begin the day's lecture.

- If you have an outline or an agenda for the notes you want your students to take, they should have access to it.

- List the key terms or other parts of the material that you want them to make sure to include on a handout. You can also use an overheard projector or the board to help students focus and concentrate.

- Before you begin a lecture, have a brief review session to help students focus on the key points that you want them to learn from the day's class.

2. WRITING

- Teach students how to use outlines and other methods of organization instead of taking notes in paragraph form.

- Work with your students to develop a bank of common abbreviations and symbols that will reduce the amount of time they spend writing, but will still enable them to read and understand their notes.

- Students also need lots of cues from a teacher as they take notes in class or on a reading assignment. Spend time showing them how to use text information such as boldface type or captions. When you give notes, put an outline on the board or give them the key points in advance so that they can capture the essence of the material.

- Teach students the rule of the Five Ws and H: *who, what, when, where, why,* and *how.*

- Teach students the Cornell system of double-column note-taking. Although there are many different versions of this technique, the basics are simple. Students divide their page into two parts by drawing a vertical line all the way down the page, dividing it into a one-third segment and a two-thirds segment. In the larger section, students should record information that they hear or read—that is, they take notes. After students finish taking notes, they should record the key points of the material in the smaller segment.

▶ Have students take notes as they listen to you read a very brief human interest article from the newspaper. Spending just a brief amount of time on this each day for a few days will boost your students' confidence in their note-taking ability.

3. REVIEWING

▶ Work with your students to help them understand that just taking the notes is not enough. Students need to learn the material in their notes in order to be successful. Many students, especially younger ones, fail to realize this.

▶ Teach your students that just "looking over" their notes is a waste of time, and that studying with a pencil is a better way to learn. Teach them to highlight key words, underline or circle important points, and use other symbols to call attention to the points that they must learn.

▶ Students should review notes within twenty-four hours if they are to learn the material. Don't assume that your students will do this on their own until you have taught them the importance of this practice and gotten them into the habit.

There are many Internet sites that will assist you in the specific skills your students need to know to develop their note-taking skills. A good place to start your research is www.infoplease.com/homework/studyskills2.html.

Help Students Improve Their Reading Skills

No one can doubt the link between good reading skills and academic success. Students who read well do their work quickly and accurately. They quickly become independent learners and enjoy school. The opposite is true for poor readers. The link between poor reading skills and the dropout rate is a solid one. The daily misery of students who are poor readers affects classroom after classroom. It is a situation that affects all teachers regardless of experience. Teachers with decades of experience have to struggle with this just as diligently as first-year teachers.

As a new teacher, there is much that you can do to help your students read better. Your school district will probably offer workshops or classes about teaching reading to all students. You should take advantage of such opportunities. The time that you will spend outside of class will be more than repaid when your students are able to work independently and well because they are competent readers.

You can also research some of the 13,000 Internet sites that offer reading assistance to teachers and students. Two excellent sites to begin this research are:

- www.smc.maricopa.edu
- http://cars.uth.tmc.edu

Another good strategy that you can use is to offer reading assistance on every assignment to every student. Even advanced secondary students can benefit from skills instruction appropriate for their level of work. One of the easiest ways to offer general assistance is to make sure that students know how to use the SQ3R method for reading material. This method has been a staple of education for decades and is just as valid today as it was in your own school days. SQ3R is a good technique for students to use to attack material in their textbooks because it is geared to help them use all of the print and non-print clues in the text to help them read and learn quickly.

When students use the SQ3R reading method, they take a five-step approach to reading an assignment, no matter what the length of the assignment. The steps are as follows.

1. **S = Survey.** Students preview the selection from beginning to end. They determine what it is about in general and familiarize themselves with the content in general. You can practice this with your students as a group using a homework reading assignment.

2. **Q = Question.** Students generate a list of questions that they want answered while reading the material. These questions will help to focus students' reading around a specific purpose.

3. **R = Read.** Students read the material carefully. They should find answers to the questions that they generated in the last step and take other notes as needed.

4. **R = Recite.** Students study the material that they have just learned by saying it out loud as they go over the selection again.

5. **R = Review.** Students make sure that they have learned the material by reviewing it several more times. The first review should take place within twenty-four hours for maximum retention.

Help Students Improve Their Writing Skills

In the last two decades, many research studies have traced the effectiveness of writing as a learning tool in all subjects and in all grade levels. The end result was clear: Every teacher teaches English. This is only common sense. All teachers teach English by modeling the language that professionals use when speaking with their students, when writing for students, and when asking them to write.

Along with modeling good language skills, you should teach students writing skills and hold them accountable for their writing. You don't have to be an English teacher, a grammar expert, or even a veteran teacher to teach your students to write well. The following are some ways in which you can help your students become effective writers.

- Keep a dictionary on your desk and let students catch you using it often.
- Encourage your students to use a dictionary and a thesaurus. If your school doesn't provide a class set of these books for each teacher, then borrow a few from other teachers.

▶ When students ask, "Does spelling count?" say "Yes. How can I help you spell a word?"

▶ Encourage students to use the writing process whenever possible. When you ask students to write even brief essays for you, encourage them to plan or pre-write their answers, write a rough draft, edit and revise that draft, and create a final copy to turn in to you.

▶ Encourage students to catch your errors. When you make a mistake, acknowledge it and correct it so that you show students that correctness is not something that ends when English class ends.

▶ Don't be sarcastic when correcting student papers. Sometimes students will make ridiculous or very funny errors. Be kind and save your frustration and amusement for later. The purpose of marking a paper is to have students learn.

▶ Circle obvious errors on papers. You don't need to circle every one or use elaborate editing marks. You should not correct the mistake yourself; instead, just make students aware of a mistake by circling it and asking them to make a correction.

▶ Make a deliberate error or two when you are writing on the board and ask students to find them. When students see that you are not afraid to risk errors and to take correction gracefully, their confidence will grow.

▶ Before assigning essay questions on tests, teach your students how you want them to answer them. (See Section Eight.)

▶ Encourage your students to think by writing out their answers before sharing.

▶ Point out unusual words or spellings when you introduce material. For example, tell your students where words such as "piano," "canyon," and "groovy" originated. You can help students learn the unusual spelling of words such as "colonel" or "Arkansas."

▶ Because students tend to write like they talk, speak Standard English around your students and expect them to speak it, too.

▶ Model good writing for your students. Proofread your own work.

▶ Offer lots of writing opportunities for your students. You can do this on tests and quizzes as well as in daily informal assignments and projects such as reports.

Neatness and Accuracy Count

Although some teachers have been known to ask students to recopy papers with only one misspelled word, other teachers happily accept crumpled or ripped papers. Although neatness and accuracy are very important, you need to strike a balance. Having requirements that are too strict will discourage students, yet allowing students to turn in papers that are obviously of poor quality sends the message that you do not expect much from them.

What should you do when a student turns in a paper that is obviously not acceptable? Speak privately to the student and ask, "Do you want me to grade this paper you have handed in?" If the students says yes, simply say, "I'll be glad to grade this paper, but you must rewrite it so that it is neat and accurate. Would you like some help so that you know just what to do for it to be acceptable?" With such a fair and reasonable approach, students will be more willing to redo their work. If you have a student who seems reluctant to redo a paper, consider speaking with the child's parent or guardian about the problem.

Although there will be times when you will have to ask students to redo their work, some preventive measures will go a long way to reducing such occasions. Start by making sure that all your students know exactly what to do and how to do it well. Then make neatness and accuracy a strong component of the culture of excellence in your class by applying the following guidelines.

- Teach your students how to proofread or check their work for accuracy before turning it in to you. Many students simply do not know how to do this. You can even give students time in class to proofread their papers or have them switch papers with a partner and review each other's writing.

- Make it easier for students to have neat and accurate papers by posting a handwriting chart in your room and by providing dictionaries or thesauruses.

- Encourage your students to use a computer for their work. Teach them how to check their spelling and grammar using computer programs. Be sure to explain the limits as well as the advantages of using computer grammar- and spell-checking programs.

- Model what you want from your students. Use the enlarging feature of a photocopier to create a poster-sized example of an excellent paper and post this paper for your students to use to check their own.

- Talk with your students about the importance of accuracy, not just on papers for school, but in other parts of life as well. One way to open this discussion would be to ask them how their lives would be different if doctors, architects, pharmacists, and automobile drivers were not concerned with accuracy or how they would react if you consistently miscalculated their grades?

- When you give written work, include a brief reminder to follow the class format. Making papers neat and accurate should become a habit for your students.

- When you correct papers, make sure that your marginal comments are helpful. (See Section Eight.)

- Some students' work is sloppy because they lack the supplies to do neat work. You can solve this by creating a bank of shared supplies for your students to use. (See Section Five.)

- Your school probably has a standard manuscript format for students. This is a standard way of heading papers, creating margins, and other preparation concerns. If such guidelines are not available, ask other teachers how they handle this issue or create your own. Guidelines should address the following areas.

  - Where should student names go?
  - Where should the date go?
  - How should students label or title their papers?

- Should students write on the front only?
- Can students use a pen or pencil?
- What kind of margins do you prefer?
- How many misspelled words are acceptable?

Student Checklist: Review That Paper Before You Hand It In!

Some teachers find it helpful to give their students an assignment review checklist that students can keep in their notebooks to refer to at home or when completing work in another class.

You can use the following checklist or adapt it to meet the needs of your students and the requirements you have established for them.

Assignment Review Checklist

☐ Is your name on your paper in the right place?
☐ Is the date on the paper in the right place, also?
☐ Have you put a title or label on your paper so that you know what it is about?
☐ Is your work legible?
☐ Have you proofread your work?
☐ Did you check to see that you have answered all of the assigned questions or completely solved all problems?
☐ Did you complete the assignment?

Help Students Become Good Listeners

Listening is the primary way that humans communicate with each other and a key tool in learning about the world around them. Good listening skills are crucial for academic success. Students who don't just hear their teacher, but who actively listen are far more successful than students who tune out as soon as they hear, "May I have your attention?"

Listening well is a skill that anyone can learn. You can help your students become good listeners by presenting information in a way that optimizes their chances of listening success and by helping them actually work on specific listening skills.

PRESENT INFORMATION FOR OPTIMAL COMPREHENSION

The first way you can improve how you present information is to make yourself easy to listen to. Tape record yourself as you speak to a class and listen to the tape when you have time to really think about your performance. Judge the quality of your speaking by paying attention to the following factors.

Rate of speech: Do you lose students by speaking too rapidly? Do you speak so slowly that students lose interest before the end of a sentence?

Volume: Can all students hear you clearly no matter where they sit?

Enunciation: Do your words trail off at the end of sentences? Do you slur your words?

Mannerisms: Do you have distracting mannerisms in your speech? Do your sentences end on a questioning rise at the end? Do you find yourself repeating words such as "okay" or "like"?

You can also improve how you present information by considering your audience. Try these quick tips.

- Don't just speak to one or two students in the front of the room. Make eye contact with everyone.

- Plan what you are going to say before you say it so your presentation is organized rather than rambling.

- Make sure that you know what you are talking about. Many unpleasant speech mannerisms can be traced to an uncertain speaker.

- Enliven your lecture with interesting examples and highlights.

- When lecturing, follow an agenda that you have written on the board or displayed on an overhead projector so students can have a better context for the information you present.

- Make sure your body language conveys confidence. Stand straight, make eye contact, and don't hide behind your desk.

- Pay attention to the signals your students give you. If half your students have their heads down while you're lecturing, you need to do a better job of considering the needs of your audience.

HELP YOUR STUDENTS IMPROVE THEIR LISTENING SKILLS

You can help students become better listeners by teaching them how to be active listeners. Here are some tips to help you with this.

- Teach students what it means to be an active listener who pays attention to what is being said.

- Talk with your students about the importance of maintaining an open mind when someone is speaking. They should listen closely to their teachers and not quit listening when they disagree with what they hear.

- Teach students to learn to listen carefully to pick out the key topics under discussion. This is important when you are teaching students to take an active role in their learning.

◗ Teach your students to generate questions as they listen to you, but to hold their questions until you call for them.

◗ If students are not sure if they have caught the main points of a lecture presentation teach them to ask themselves if they can summarize it. If they can summarize what they've heard, then they are competent at active listening.

> *"Have a sense of humor. This goes a long way toward making a comfortable classroom. I think humor helps students see that you are comfortable with yourself, comfortable with them, and comfortable with life in general."*
>
> —Ken Pfeifer, 28 years experience

The Process of Long-term Projects

In recent years teachers have begun assigning more long-term projects to students at all grade levels. Even very young students have been assigned a wide range of projects: oral reports, dramatic presentations, science fair experiments, and researched or creative booklets and reports.

Few teachers have been able to avoid the sinking feeling that occurs when a project looks terrific in the lesson plan stage, but fails miserably in practice. The problem is compounded by the length of these projects and by their importance to students' grade averages. If nightly homework projects can cause teachers, students, and parents stress, the potential for trouble in long-term projects is even greater.

Long-term projects can be successful for everyone involved when you teach your students how to successfully plan and carry out each stage. With a bit of planning and by teaching the skills your students will need, these projects can become the enjoyable and productive learning processes that you want them to be.

PROJECT PLANNING

To increase your students' success in completing long-term projects, follow these guidelines.

◗ Choose a topic and a format that your students will enjoy. Remember that real-life situations have intrinsic appeal and that students who can choose their own topics tend to be more motivated and successful than those who have no choices.

◗ Think of a long-term project as a series of smaller steps. Each step should have a separate due date and grade. This can help alert students and their parents to any early concerns that you have with their work. Your students will also need plenty of models and examples of each step in the process, not just the final project. You should also include checklists, flow charts, or other visual aids so your students know just when each part is due and how it fits into the entire project.

⬧ Be careful to plan enough time for students to complete their work successfully. If you miscalculate, you will have to either deal with frustrated students or extend the due date.

⬧ Be sensitive to the fact that not all students can afford resources such as art supplies or make several trips to the public library.

⬧ Schedule times for your students to work together to review each other's work and to meet with you to make sure that they are on the right track.

TEACHING PROJECT SKILLS

Although your students may have had to complete projects before, don't assume that they have also been taught the skills needed for successful completion of the projects. Apply the following steps in teaching your students the skills for completing long-term projects.

⬧ Before you assign a project, brainstorm a list of the skills that your students will need to complete it satisfactorily. Plan how you will teach each one.

⬧ Teach students how to plan their projects themselves. Have students write proposals telling you about the materials they will need, the time they will have to spend on each part, and what they want to accomplish. You can help students solve problems before they become serious.

⬧ It is never too early to teach your students about plagiarism and how to avoid it.

⬧ Teach students any shortcuts that will make the work easier for them. If they can work together or use a computer and still learn the essential skills involved in that part of the project, encourage them to do so.

⬧ Stress the importance of good work habits when students work on projects. Have high standards for each step of the project process and help your students turn in excellent work.

⬧ Ask students to assess their projects and reflect on how well they completed each step. This type of closure provides meaning and insight for your students and for you.

Help Students Improve Their Retention

There are several steps that you and your students can take to improve their retention of material. Of course, you know that skillful teaching is crucial to having students understand the material and then retain that understanding. In addition, consider using the following strategies when you want your students to focus on remembering information.

⬧ Provide opportunities for plenty of practice. Many teachers underestimate the amount of practice that it takes for students to learn material and then retain it.

⬧ Connect new knowledge to previous learning. Students who build skills on skills or who can add something that they just learned to something that they already knew will retain both new and old knowledge to a greater degree than if information is taught in isolation.

◗ Take time for frequent reviewing. If you stop class once or twice to ask students to summarize what they have just learned or to go over the notes they have already taken, they will retain that information much better than if you wait until the end of a unit of study to review.

◗ Teach students to write information down. Students who have complete notes or who are actively engaged in writing what they are supposed to learn not only have a record of the information, they are also actively engaged with learning.

◗ After students have taken notes or completed other written work, teach them to go back and review their notes frequently so they can transfer the knowledge on the page to their brains.

"Never apologize for high expectations."

—Barbara Knowles, 36 years experience

◗ Use real-life situations. For example, if you are trying to teach students to identify the subject of a sentence, the process will be more logical for them if you use classmates' names as subjects.

◗ Students of all ages should be encouraged to assume the responsibility for making the concentrated effort that it takes to learn anything new.

Teach Students How to Memorize

Memorization has earned an undeservedly bad reputation. Memorizing facts just for the sake of memorizing them is not a practical use of instructional time, but learning information is.

Even though critical-thinking skills have been the topic of many workshops in recent years, there is also much to be said for teaching students to memorize information. Much of what we ask our students to do involves memorizing material. For example, when students learn the definitions of key terms or their multiplication tables, that involves memorizing.

There are many ways that you can help your students learn to memorize material quickly and retain it. If you make developing and strengthening their memories a part of your classroom business, then you are helping your students learn. Follow these guidelines when you want to help your students use their memories to learn material quickly.

◗ Provide students with frequent review opportunities. Students who review frequently and at short intervals tend to do better than those students who try to learn too much information at one sitting.

◗ Make memory practice meaningful. Just learning something for the sake of learning is not something that your students will enjoy. They will enjoy real-life applications, competitions, games, and intrinsic rewards for the memory practice that they do.

◗ Allow students enough time to memorize material when you ask them to. No one can memorize material well when stressed, tired, or rushed to get an assignment done on time.

- Structure the assignment so students can learn a small part first and then piggyback another part to that one and another and another until the entire assignment is completely learned.

- Teach your students to use visual organizers to help them memorize material. They should use diagrams, charts, or even silly sketches to help them recall the important parts of an assignment.

- Show your students how to use more than one modality to learn. For example, if they make flash cards and tape record the same material, they are not only using sight and sound, but are far more likely to retain the information.

- Remember how you used mnemonic devices such as *HOMES* to recall the names of the Great Lakes, or a rhyming verse to recall the number of days in each month? Teach your students to make and use their own mnemonic devices for the information you want them to learn.

- Show students how easy it is to learn something when they can make a rhyme out of it. This is the reason that most of us find it easier to recall songs or bits of poetry than prose. Your students can make rhymes out of almost any subject if you give them a chance to do so.

- Teach your students the importance of actively listening in class. They should hear you say "focus" and "concentrate" often as you help them memorize new material.

- Learning anything new takes repeated efforts. Discuss the importance of repetition at various intervals with your students and build in opportunities for them to review by repetition. Encourage them to enlist each other's help in this.

- One of the surest ways to memorize anything is to write it over and over. Encourage your students to engage their pens as well as their minds.

- Teach your students to study in intense brief bursts of time. Students who actively work at memorizing information for fifteen minutes will be more successful than those who contrive to look busy for thirty but daydream through most of that time.

Help Students Make Up Missed Work

"Did we do anything when I was out?" When a student asks you this, do not give into temptation to be sarcastic. Your student is only asking for a chance to make up work.

Attendance problems are part of every grade level of school. Very few students have perfect attendance for even one year of school. Because of this, helping students make up missed work is a responsibility that you will undertake almost every day.

Helping students make up missed work will not be difficult if you establish a policy, make sure your students understand it, and enforce the policy consistently. Here are some guidelines that will help you with all of these areas.

ESTABLISH A POLICY

▶ Find out your school's policy on making up missing work. Your policy should be aligned with this one. If there is no formal policy for your school, ask if there is one for your department or grade level.

▶ A workable policy for making up work should include the due date of the assignment, how much and what kind of help a student may receive from others, when you are available to help students make up work, the point at which you will contact parents or guardians, and the penalty for late work.

▶ Be sure to inform parents and guardians of this policy in the letter introducing yourself that you send home at the beginning of the term.

▶ Make a point of encouraging students to make up work quickly. Consider offering incentives to students who make up work ahead of schedule.

▶ If you use a syllabus, encourage students to follow it as closely as they can while they are absent so that they will find it easy to catch up after an absence.

MAKE SURE STUDENTS UNDERSTAND WHAT TO DO

▶ Spend time at the beginning of the term and at intervals later discussing the issue of making up missing work with your students. Make sure that making up missing work is not a hidden policy in your classroom.

▶ Divide your students into study teams early in the term. In each team, students can help each other make up missing assignments by calling absent members, sharing notes, collecting handouts, and reviewing the difficult parts of the assignment. Even very young children can help each other on a study team.

▶ Consider having students rotate the task of recording class events and work to be done on a large calendar, on a bulletin board space, or even in a folder each day. When students return from absences, they can then check the class record or log book to see what they missed and what work they need to do.

▶ Set aside board space to keep a running list of make-up work reminders. In this space you could post a list of the students who owe work, their missing assignments, and the final date that you will accept the assignments.

▶ Use a reminder notice like the one in Figure 10.10 to help students stay on track. (See page 314.)

▶ Keep all papers to be returned and new handouts in a special folder so that students can check there to pick up missing papers when they return.

▶ Set aside a generous amount of time before or after school each week to meet with students and help them make up work. Post your hours and make sure that parents and guardians also are aware of them.

▶ If a parent asks you to send work home, be prompt and very specific. Give details that will enable the child to complete the work at home. Write a note offering extra help. This is not only professional, but also courteous.

6 Tips to Help You Enforce Your Policy Consistently

1. Although allowing students to make up missed work during class time is certainly convenient for your students and for you, it causes the student to miss yet more work. It is better to have students make up missing work before or after school rather than miss more class.

2. Make time to speak with each student who has been absent about missing work. Make sure the child knows what is due and when it is due. Be very specific and detailed. Document that you have had this conversation with the child.

3. If a due date is approaching and the child has made no effort to make up the missing work, call home. This is time consuming, but sends a clear message that you are serious about students making up their work.

4. Don't allow students to turn in missing work past their due date just to raise their grade. This will only encourage students to be irresponsible.

5. If you have several students out at the same time, adjust your expectations and offer extra help.

6. Be flexible. There will always be situations where you will have to use your best judgment. For example, if a student is absent because of a serious illness or because of a death in the family, you will need to react with compassion. You will need to adjust the make-up work and the amount of support you offer the child in this situation.

Figure 10.10

MAKE-UP WORK REMINDER NOTICE

I, _____, understand that because of my absence from class

on _____, I owe the following assignments:

_____

_____

_____

I agree to turn in this missing work on or before it is due: _____

Student signature: _____

Teacher signature: _____

Journal Entries to Help Your Students
Become Successful Learners

▶ What is a successful student? How can you help your students become successful?

▶ Who really listened to you today? What did you do to cause this response?

▶ Complete this statement: "I know a lot about _____. I want my students to learn more about . . ."

▶ Complete this statement, "My students know more about _____ than I ever will because _____. I can benefit from this by . . ."

▶ Complete this statement: "I can avoid some common homework problems by . . ."

▶ What did you observe about how your students tackled their work today?

▶ What situations will you face where you will have to remain self-possessed? How can you teach your students to maintain control of themselves?

▶ What experiences in your past have given you insight into the difficulties that students have with their study habits?

Make the Most of Your Instructional Time

"Psst, Ms. Jackson, come here. Check this out."

The young man lounging in the doorway of his classroom held out an origami frog made from an old quiz paper.

"That's a really nice frog, Nathan. I didn't know you knew origami. Is this art class?"

"Art class? No way, this is math. He always lets us have a break at the end of class. Why don't you ever do that?"

She peeked in the door. Some students had their heads down on their desks; others were engaged in animated conversation. The sounds of chatter and books slamming against the desks filled the air. She spotted one student checking her watch against the clock, counting the minutes until class was over.

"Good bye, Nathan, I'll see you in just a few minutes when our class begins."

She hurried back to her classroom, thinking about Nathan's class. Now she could understand why that group of students was sometimes hard to settle down and why they clamored for free time.

In the classroom right next to her own, she paused. There was even more noise coming from this room than from Nathan's class. Every student was energetically competing in an intense review game.

How your students will spend their school days is an issue that will affect your career for years to come. There are many people who believe that the traditional school year calendar with its long summer vacation is no longer useful. While students value their time off from school, long vacations mean the loss of valuable instructional time each fall as teachers try to assimilate students back into a school routine.

Whether you teach in a district with a traditional school calendar or one of the many variations of the extended school year, how your students spend their time while in school is of great importance to everyone concerned. And though you will probably have very little

317

input into the debate over school calendars at this point in your career, how your students spend their school time is something that you do control.

You Control the Time Your Students Have with You

There are very few teachers whose classes are not interrupted routinely by intercom announcements, commotion in the halls, or by unruly students. You will have to find ways to successfully cope with these obvious disturbances as well as with many of the other disruptions to your class routine.

You may be tempted to believe that your day is so consumed by interruptions that other circumstances regulate what happens in your class, but this is not true. While there are certainly many things that you can't change about your school situation, you do have control over the way that your students spend their time while they are with you.

How much control do you have? If you waste only two minutes of your students' day—a few seconds at the opening of class, a distraction or two, a lost handout, maybe even a minute of free time at the end of class—over the course of a typical school year, these two minutes a day could add up to the loss of more than six hours of instruction. That's an entire school day. Although this may seem like a tolerable loss, some studies have shown that in many classes only about half of class time is devoted to instruction.

The results of this misuse of instructional time are pretty grim. Teachers who do not use class time wisely experience far more discipline problems than teachers who make use of every minute, and have to cope with the problems of students who are unable to succeed academically. Discipline problems and academic failures not only make a teacher's workday unpleasant, they can eventually lead to burnout.

What can you do to avoid this time-waste pitfall? Start by making a commitment to yourself and to your students that you will teach them every minute that they are with you. Resolve to make good use of the time that your students are in your class.

Figure 11.1
How Much Do You Know About Using Class Time Well?

Test your knowledge of effective class time with this scenario of the first seven minutes of class. Read each time frame and decide how much time was actually used productively. At the end you will find a key to see how you scored.

8:01–8:02: Mr. Martinez met his students at the door with a pleasant greeting for each one. As each student entered the class, he handed out the day's assignment.

8:02–8:04: After all the students were settled in their seats, he called roll and asked for a volunteer to take the attendance information for the day to the office.

8:04–8:05: Almost as soon as the volunteer had left the room, Mr. Martinez noticed a tardy student trying to slip into class unnoticed. After a brief discussion about why the student was late, Mr. Martinez asked for another volunteer to take the corrected attendance information to the office.

8:05–8:08: Standing in front of the room, Mr. Martinez called his students to order. He waited patiently for students to get our their books and find the right page. He gently reminded two students to stop talking and helped the two volunteers find the right page. Just as he was ready to begin, he noticed one student still trying to borrow a pen.

Decide how many minutes Mr. Martinez used productively in each time frame.

	Total instruction time:	**Time used productively:**
8:01–8:02:	1 minute possible	_____
8:02–8:04:	2 minutes possible	_____
8:04–8:05:	1 minute possible	_____
8:05–8:08:	3 minutes possible	_____

Now, see what you know about the efficient use of class time by checking your answers against this scoring guide.

8:01–8:02: Mr. Martinez used all of this time efficiently. He saved valuable time by greeting students and passing out papers as they entered the room.

8:02–8:04: Mr. Martinez used none of this time efficiently. He could have saved time by waiting until later in the class to take attendance by using his seating chart and by pre-arranging for a student to take the information to the office instead of distracting the entire class by calling for volunteers.

8:04–8:05: Mr. Martinez did not use this time productively. Asking a student about the cause for tardiness in front of the class disturbs everyone. Having to ask for volunteers again also involves the entire group as well as the second student who has to leave the room.

8:05–8:08: Mr. Martinez did not use any of this time productively. Students had to wait while their classmates settled down before they could get started on their class work. Reminding students to stop talking and having to assist the volunteer students also wasted the other students' time. Finally, students without materials can't do their work.

Here is a better way for Mr. Martinez to manage the first seven minutes of his class.

8:01–8:08: Mr. Martinez met his students at the door with a pleasant greeting for each one. As each student entered the class, he handed out the day's assignment. Students went quickly to their assigned seats, checking the board for their warm-up activity page numbers and the handout with the day's assignment. Mr. Martinez walks around the room monitoring students quietly, giving help and encouragement. As he walks around, he makes mental notes of which students are absent. He will record this information right before independent work time ends and the student who is in charge of running this errand for the week will take it to the office. When a tardy student enters, Mr. Martinez moves to the student's desk with the day's assignment. He will discuss the student's tardiness later, in the hall, to maintain the student's privacy and to keep everyone else on task. Two students make use of the bank of shared supplies that Mr. Martinez maintains for those students who may have forgotten a pen or paper. As the timer to end the warm-up activity sounds at 8:08, students check the board again for the next part of their day's assignment.

25 Common Time Wasters

One of the best ways to make sure that you are using the time in your class to the best advantage is to be aware of how easy it is to waste this time. The following are some of the most obvious ways in which many teachers misuse class time.

1. Teaching lessons that are not relevant or interesting to students
2. Not using the first few minutes of class effectively
3. Allowing students to goof off for the last few minutes of class
4. Not intervening quickly enough to keep problems manageable
5. Confusing "teachable moments" with straying from the topic
6. Not establishing routines for daily classroom procedures
7. Allowing students to sleep as long as they don't cause trouble
8. Not starting a new unit because a weekend or holiday is near
9. Calling roll instead of checking attendance by a seating chart
10. Not enforcing a reasonable policy for leaving the classroom
11. Misjudging how long it takes to teach a lesson
12. Not returning papers promptly
13. Interrogating tardy students in front of other students
14. Not providing assistance for those students without materials
15. Allowing students to decide when class is over

16. Not determining students' prior knowledge of new material
17. Giving an inappropriate amount of work
18. Not giving feedback designed to help students learn
19. Giving confusing directions
20. Not teaching students how to work collaboratively in groups
21. Having poor transitions between activities
22. Not teaching students study skills
23. Spending too much time sitting behind a desk instead of monitoring
24. Not teaching students to be self-disciplined
25. Giving homework that is only busy work

10 Principles of Effective Classroom Time Management

Learning to use class time wisely is a skill that will take time, patience, and practice. However, the rewards are well worth the effort. You and your students will benefit every day from classes that run smoothly.

Although there are many tips that you will learn from listening to your colleagues and from your own classroom experiences, the following general principles can guide your attempts to use class time wisely.

1. **Reduce distractions.** The old image of restless students staring dreamily out of the window has much truth to it. Students of all ages are perfectly able to entertain themselves by paying attention to the distractions in your classroom instead of to you. Although a well-decorated classroom can enhance student learning, one with too many distractions can impede it. Look around your classroom for some of the things that might distract your students and move students away from them. Some of the most obvious distractions in a classroom may be windows, desks too close together, doorways, pencil sharpeners, trash cans, screen savers, too many posters or banners, graffiti, and—the most enticing one of all—other students.

2. **Raise student awareness.** While no one likes to be rushed all class long, your students need to learn that time is important in your class. Discuss the importance of using class time well as often as necessary to make sure that your students understand that you expect them to work productively while they are in your class.

3. **Establish routines.** If you have routines in your class for the daily activities that can take up too much time if students don't know what to do, you will save minutes each day and hours each week.

4. **Monitor constantly.** Monitoring your students is of primary importance for the smooth running of your class for a variety of reasons, not just for efficient time use. Staying on your feet instead of sitting at your desk will allow you to help students

when their problems are still small and will encourage students who may be tempted to misbehave or to be off task to work instead.

5. **Be very organized.** If your students have to wait while you find your keys or a handout, that is not a good use of their time. Although lapses in organization can occur to anyone, make a point to be so organized that you will be able to keep yourself and your students on task.

6. **Have a back-up plan.** If a lesson isn't working, a guest speaker cancels, or if the equipment you need to use for class isn't working, you will certainly need to be ready to provide an alternative way to teach the material you planned for your students to cover. There are always other ways to teach a lesson. Keep them in mind and have a back-up plan in place so that you can quickly shift gears if your first plan doesn't work out.

7. **Take a door-to-door approach.** Think about the activities that your students will be doing in class with the idea that you will engage them in learning from the time that they enter your classroom until the time that they leave. Many teachers make the mistake of thinking that students need a few minutes of free time at the start of class and at the end of class to relax. Although students do need time at both ends of class to make effective transitions, they do not need free time to do this. Instead, give them interesting activities that will direct their attention to the day's lesson.

8. **Use small blocks of time.** Just as you can accomplish many of your own tasks with brief bits of concentrated efforts, so can your students. If you only have five minutes until dismissal, don't allow students to do nothing because it will take too long to get working on a new assignment. Instead, use this time, and the other small blocks of time in a class, to review or teach a new fact.

9. **Teach to an objective.** If you teach a subject that you enjoy personally and that you know that your students will enjoy too, it is tempting to spend more time on it than the curriculum dictates. Also, if you don't have a clear purpose in mind for the work that you ask of your students or if you don't communicate the purpose to them, you will have trouble keeping them motivated and on-task.

10. **Give enough work.** There are few ways to waste time that are as blatant as not giving your students enough meaningful work to do. If students finish a task, there should be another waiting for them. For example, students who sit around after a test waiting for others to finish before going on to the next activity are obviously wasting time. Always make sure your students know what they are supposed to do after they finish their current assignment.

> *"Don't ever give students enough time to misbehave. Keep them engaged every minute of class with interesting and fun activities that go along with your curriculum."*
>
> —Kristin Sanderlin, 5 years experience

Raise Your Students' Awareness of Time

You are not the only person in your class who is concerned about how your students spend their time. Your students are, too. They want to spend their days successfully doing the work that you ask them to do.

When you have to deal with a series of petty misbehaviors, it is easy to forget that your students want to do well in school. They want to spend their time doing interesting and useful work. You can take this natural interest and use it to help your students learn to become efficient at their classroom tasks. Because you cannot manage this feat by yourself, it only makes sense to enlist the support of the people you are trying to help.

A good way to make your students more aware of how they spend their time is to discuss it with them. When students see that you are not just nagging or rushing them through their work, they will be more willing to work well with you. Discuss with your students the intangible rewards that they receive when they use class time well. You may even choose to discuss the problems that result from misusing class time.

Teach them key word signals such as "Focus" or "Concentrate" so that they know exactly what to do when they hear you say these words. Make concentration an expected behavior in your classroom so students will be aware of when they are not as attentive to their work as they should be. Offer to teach your students time management tips and show them how to achieve good grades without having to spend hours on their work. (See Section Ten.) Your students will appreciate this.

Keep constant reminders of the importance of using time well around your class by displaying banners and posters that address the issue. You can use some of the time management tips from Section Ten, create your own and ask students to share their own, or even find quotations about time in books or on the Internet. A good place to begin your search for inspirational quotations about time is the following Web site: www.bartleby.com/100.

Another technique that will help students be aware of how they spend class time is to have them complete a questionnaire such as the one in Figure 11.2 on page 324. This exercise will allow students to think honestly about how they misuse time and how they can improve the way they use time in your class.

Figure 11.2
STUDENT ASSESSMENT: TRACK HOW YOU USE TIME

Name _____ Date _____

Think back over class today and answer these questions as accurately as you can. The more thorough your answers, the easier it will be for you to improve how you use time in class.

1. Class is _____ minutes long.

2. Of the _____ available minutes in class today, I estimate that I did NOT use

    _____ of them wisely.

3. Put a check in the box next to the item that applies to you.

I was off task during the . . .

☐ first five minutes
☐ first ten minutes
☐ last ten minutes
☐ written assignment
☐ reading selection
☐ class discussion
☐ listening section

4. I know that I used class time well today when I _____

    _____

5. I am easily distracted when _____

    _____

6. The most productive part of class was _____

    _____

7. A suggestion I have for my teacher is _____

    _____

8. I can improve the way I use class time by _____

    _____

How to Handle Interruptions

One of most stressful parts of any teacher's school day involves class interruptions. Many teachers are frustrated when their carefully planned lessons are interrupted by a fire drill, a class visitor, or even too many students who need to sharpen their pencils.

Interruptions destroy instructional time not just because they distract you, but because they tend to also distract every child in your class as well. The best defense you have against losing instructional time because of the negative effects of interruptions is an interesting lesson. Students who are fully engaged in meaningful and interesting work hate to leave the class at the end of the period, much less pay attention to a visitor or another student sharpening a pencil.

If you want to minimize the negative effects of interruptions, you can handle them successfully by meeting three goals.

Goal 1: You should prevent as many interruptions as you can. Some teachers have found that putting signs such as "Learning in Progress. Please Do Not Disturb" on the door serves as a gentle reminder to those whose business may not be urgent. Others have worked with colleagues whose classrooms are nearby so that one teacher will not schedule a noisy class activity on the same day that another has planned a test or other quiet activity. Still others have talked with the principal about poorly timed intercom announcements. There are many steps you can take to prevent many of the distractions that interfere with your class.

Goal 2: You should minimize the disruption caused by an interruption. While you can prevent many interruptions during your school day, there are some that are just unavoidable. For example, you cannot prevent the interruption caused by a message from the office requesting that a student be released from class for an early dismissal. In such situations, your goal must be to minimize the disruption. Find ways to handle the matter with the least possible commotion and with minimal disruption of the rest of your students. When you have interruptions, if you remind yourself that your goal is to minimize the disturbance, then you will be likely to teach a successful class.

Goal 3: You can plan ahead and prepare for predictable interruptions. There are some unavoidable interruptions that you can prepare for so that you have a plan in place when they happen. This will not only give you confidence, but your students will behave better because you know what to do in almost any situation. When you make your plans for these predictable interruptions, keep your solutions simple so that you and your students will be able to respond appropriately when they happen. Make sure that you teach these procedures to your students so that they know what to do when the situation arises. Here is a quick list of some of the predictable interruptions that many teachers have to handle successfully. Think about how you want your students to deal with each one and write out a plan for each.

- A student has no paper, pencil, or pen
- Students request to leave the class to use the restroom, see the nurse, or go to their lockers
- Students need to listen to broadcast announcements
- Students will miss class because of a pep rally, assembly, or inclement weather
- Students engage in several small misbehaviors (inattentiveness, talking, etc.)
- A student disrupts class in a serious incident of misbehavior
- A visitor asks to speak with you
- A student from another class asks to speak with one of your students
- Students need to sharpen pencils or dispose of trash
- Students leave class early or arrive to class late
- There is a commotion from the hallway or from another classroom
- The grass is being mowed outside, there is an insect buzzing around the room, someone dropped a book noisily . . . The possibilities are endless.

Save Time by Establishing Class Routines

A well-run class is one in which students know what to do and go about their business with confident efficiency. These classes don't just happen. They are created by teachers who develop a few simple routines or procedures for some of the daily tasks that students have to do.

Teachers who show their students what is expected of them in various situations empower those students to do their best without nagging or scolding. These well-prepared teachers experience fewer misbehavior problems than teachers whose students are not sure about what they are supposed to do. Students in a well-run class are well behaved, confident, and successful.

At the beginning of the term, get your students off to a good start by establishing a few simple procedures for routine classroom activities and then spending a sufficient amount of time teaching these procedures. (See Figure 11.3 on page 327.) Doing this will result in saved class time every day.

Sequencing Instruction

Your students are working quietly on an assignment that should take about ten more minutes for them all to finish. One student finishes early and asks to be excused to the restroom. Because the student has finished, you allow him to go. Another student finishes and asks to leave, and then a third. There's still a little time left till the rest of the class will be done, so you let them go.

Some other students who have finished early are doing homework for other classes, while still others are just sitting quietly staring off into space. The less able students are working frantically to finish their work before you call for it.

Figure 11.3

YOUR CLASS ROUTINES

There are many activities that you must manage efficiently in each class, and teaching your students your expectations for many of the routine ones will save valuable instruction time. Your students must know the procedures for the following routine activities.

- Beginning class
- Ending class
- Sharing materials
- Turning in homework
- Turning in class work
- Turning in make-up work
- Finding out about missed work
- Paying attention to you
- Leaving the classroom
- Asking for assistance
- Heading papers

- Storing supplies
- Moving desks for group work
- Finding out about homework
- Handling visitors or other interruptions
- Cleaning their work area
- Switching from one activity to another
- Requesting a conference with you
- Turning in attendance notes
- Stapling papers, sharpening pencils, etc.

Both types of students lose in this situation—the ones who finished quickly and had nothing to do and the ones who struggled to complete the work on time. The problem with such a lesson plan is that it supposes that all students will work at the same speed. This simply does not happen.

One of the best ways to avoid this loss of instructional time is to design lessons that flow from one part to the next without you having to stop and start the entire class at the same moment several times in a class period. Following are two versions of the same class period—one in which class time was used efficiently, one in which it was not.

AN INEFFICIENTLY PLANNED LESSON

Objective: Students will master a math concept

Lesson Plan

Minutes 1–20:	Opening exercise followed by the teacher's explanation of the concept.
Minutes 21–50:	Students are to complete problems 1 to 30 as practice.
Minute 36:	The first student finishes the assignment and turns it in.
Minutes 38–49:	Soon others follow and look around for something to do. They wait patiently for the others to finish. Some misbehavior occurs. Three students are excused to the restroom.
Minute 49:	Several students ask for more time to finish the problems. Their teacher agrees and tells the others to start on their homework.

AN EFFICIENTLY PLANNED LESSON

Objective: Students will master a math concept

Lesson Plan

Minutes 1–20:	Opening exercise followed by the teacher's explanation of the concept.
Minutes 21–30:	The entire class does problems 1 to 5 together to make sure that everyone is clear about the concept. They discuss their answers.
Minutes 31–35:	*All students* complete problems 6 to 10 while working with a study buddy, talking over their answers. They check their answers against a key to make sure they are on the right track.
Minutes 36–45:	*Students who are still not clear* ask for assistance from their teacher. After assistance, they begin working on problems 10 to 20. They check their work after finishing these problems.
	Students who understand the work complete problems 10 to 20 and check their work again.
	All students show their completed work to the teacher as they finish it to determine what they need to do next.
Minutes 46–55:	*Students who need extra practice* are directed to complete problems 21 to 25, check their work, and show these problems to the teacher.
	Students who have mastered the concept are given a choice of three enrichment activities and move on to complete the activity.
	Students who need the extra practice show their work to the teacher. After receiving additional help from the teacher they move on to complete the rest of the problems.

In the efficiently planned lesson, the teacher was an active member of the class, circulating, monitoring, offering support and assistance, and working with individuals who needed help and encouragement. Students moved from activity to activity with only a glance at the directions on the board and a consultation with their teacher to see what they needed to do next. No student was left with nothing to do.

You can begin to use every minute of class time wisely by planning well-sequenced lessons. Keep these points in mind.

> *"I learned early in my first year that if I have several tasks for my students, I should do the things that we will complete together first so that I can control the length and speed of a lesson. I save the independent work for the last part of class because I don't want to interrupt students when they have settled down to work. They find it too frustrating."*
>
> —Yann Pirrone, 10 years experience

▶ When you design a lesson, pay attention to three levels of students in your class: those who will finish quickly; those who will finish their work in the time you have allotted for them (the majority of your students); and those who will take longer to grasp a concept or complete the work. You will have to meet the needs of all three groups if you are to have a time-efficient class.

▶ Plan plenty of enrichment activities that will benefit students and that are interesting enough so students will want to complete their work to do them. Enrichment should not be just more work for students to plow though; it should be intellectually stimulating.

▶ Stay on your feet and monitor your students' progress. You will need to devise a routine for students to use when asking for your help. (See Section Twelve for more information on successful monitoring techniques.)

▶ You will have to decide at what point all of the various groups of students in your classroom will be pulled together for a culminating exercise. It may be that your well-sequenced instruction could take more than one day. If so, make sure that all students have mastered the material before you attempt the exercise.

▶ Consider posting a list of activities that students who finish their work early can choose from. Activities can include: starting homework early, working on long-term projects, using the computer, reading library books, doing puzzles or other interesting worksheets, working with another student on an extra project, straightening and organizing notebooks, and studying for a test or quiz. Modify this list according to the age and ability of your students as well as the subjects that you teach.

▶ Post the instructions for the day's work on the board or on a handout for students. This is especially important if they are all to complete the same assignments (unlike the varied practice amounts in the example on page 328). If you use a checklist format, students will be able to check off items as they finish them and work at their own pace without having to wait for other students. See Figure 11.4 for a sample checklist to adapt for your class.

Figure 11.4
STUDENT CHECKLIST OF CLASS ACTIVITIES

Class Work for Friday, March 2

Place a check in the box beside each part of today's class work as you complete it.

☐ Brainstorm a list of five things that you already know about prime numbers.

☐ Share your list with your study partner until you have a list with seven items on it.

☐ Skim the review explanation of prime numbers on pages 16–19.

☐ Write two questions that you would like answered about prime numbers.

☐ Take careful notes on the explanation material. Put them in your notebook under today's date.

☐ Complete problems 1–15. Check your work against the class key as you go.

☐ Complete problems 16–25. Turn these in to be checked.

☐ Work on your report about famous mathematicians. It's due Monday.

> *"Reel them in before you think it's necessary . . .*
> *anticipate reactions and tell students what is acceptable*
> *and appropriate."*
>
> —Barbara Knowles, 36 years experience

The First 10 Minutes of Class

At the end of the first ten minutes of every class you want your students to be so fired up and ready to work that you can barely contain their enthusiasm. Wouldn't it be wonderful if this happened in every class? It can happen in *your* class.

Too often teachers overlook the power inherent in the opening minutes of class. They allow students to drift into class and visit with their classmates as they leisurely rummage around to find pens and paper and last night's homework. After they find their materials, students will often just sit and wait to be told what to do.

Often, if they are quiet enough and if there are too many pressing demands on a teacher's time at the moment, more than ten minutes can vanish before class starts. No wonder so many older students are tardy to class. They have little reason to be on time.

You can use the first ten minutes to get your class off to a great start or you can choose to waste it. Whether you realize it or not, during these first minutes you set the tone for the rest of the class. If you are prepared for class and have taught your students the opening routine you want them to follow, this brief time can be one where your students make the effective mental and emotional transitions from the last class or subject and prepare themselves to focus on learning new material.

You should establish a comfortable and predictable routine for the opening of class. Students who are focused on learning and achieving instead of trying to figure out what to do are far more likely to be successful than those students who have to wait to be told what to do each day.

Here is a simple opening routine that many teachers follow and that you can adapt to meet the needs of your class.

The teacher greets each child as he or she enters the class. You can hand out any papers that need to be distributed at this time. You can also use this time to answer questions, collect attendance notes, and check the emotional states of your students. Your students will appreciate that you care enough to stand at the door and greet them.

Students go immediately to their seats and sit down. You will avoid many problems if you strictly enforce this part of the routine. Students who wander around the room while you are busy at the door can cause problems that last all class long. Further, students often carry over problems that happened earlier in the day or in another class to your room. By insisting that your students take a seat right away, you will help focus their energies on your class and on learning.

Students should check the board for a predictable organizing exercise. The organizing exercise should allow them enough time to settle down, organize their materials, and shift mental gears to what is going to happen in class. Your message on the board can include these directions for your students:

- Please get out a pen and paper. Head your paper for today's class work.

- Open your textbook to page _____ .

- Copy tonight's homework assignment into your notebook.

- Place last night's homework on your desk.

- Read the objectives for today's class work.

Students should complete an anticipatory set activity. The anticipatory set activity that you assign your students should be one that arouses curiosity and relates the day's new learning to previous knowledge. It should not just be interesting, but should be simple enough that students can complete it independently. This will boost their confidence so that they are even more interested in the lesson that lies just ahead of them.

Use your creativity to create activities that your students will enjoy as they look forward to the opening of the day's lesson. To get started, you will find twenty of them in the box on page 332.

20 Anticipatory Set Activities for the Opening of Class

You can ask students to do one of the following activities or modify them to suit your students' needs.

1. Complete or create a graphic organizer.

2. Use stick figures to illustrate a concept or event.

3. Write a rhyme to help recall _____ .

4. List what they already know about _____ .

5. Skim the day's lesson and predict what they will learn.

6. Create flash cards.

7. Complete brain-teaser problems.

8. List three reasons to study the day's topic.

9. Summarize the information in a news article.

10. Combine information with another student.

11. Listen to a tape-recorded message and take notes.

12. Watch a video clip and write about it.

13. Brainstorm ideas.

14. Complete a pre-writing exercise for an essay.

15. Label a map.

16. Write a response to a quotation.

17. Answer a provocative question.

18. Look at objects and predict how they will relate to the lesson.

19. Tell about the problems they may have had with homework.

20. Ask a question about yesterday's class.

Productive Transitions

Because your students are accustomed to the fast-paced action of modern life, they can lose interest very quickly in a lesson that seems to last too long. Teachers have learned to create a positive learning environment by designing lessons around several brief activities. While this is a sensible decision, it calls for transitions between activities that will encourage students to be productive.

Transitions are difficult to manage well because they require that students do three things in a very brief amount of time: 1) mentally close out one task, 2) prepare for the next one, and 3) refocus their mental energies on a new topic. Fortunately, there are several things that the wise first-year teacher can do to help students handle transitions effectively.

Start by designing activities that flow naturally from one to the next, requiring a minimum of large-group instruction from you. (See "Sequencing Instruction," page 326) Lessons that do this encourage students to manage their own learning.

Try using a kitchen timer to set a time limit for your students when it is time to change activities. When students know that they have only a minute or two to switch from one activity to another, they are much more likely to move quickly.

Finally, make transitions productive parts of your class by giving your students activities that will convert their useless waiting time into learning opportunities. These small blocks of time can be enjoyable for you and your students because they will be engaged in actively thinking and learning. These small activities, called "sponges," can add interest, new information, and motivation to a lesson.

20 "Sponge" Activities for Transition Times

"Sponge activities" are useful ways to "soak up" time that would otherwise be wasted in your classroom while students make the switch from one activity to another. Even though these activities are brief, their impact on the productivity in your classroom can be significant.

The sponges listed here are written in the form of directions for students to follow. Adapt, adjust, or add information to these to create other activities that will keep your students involved in productive learning all period long.

1. List ten words associated with the lesson that we are currently studying.

2. Open your book and read the first three paragraphs from yesterday's lesson. What is something new that you learned today that you had not learned yesterday?

3. How can the information that you have just finished learning be applied to the lesson that you are about to begin?

4. Write out three study skills that you have found particularly useful this week.

5. Find a word from today's lesson. Copy it into your notes, define it using a glossary or a dictionary, and then use it in an original sentence.

6. What is the most important character trait for a good student to have? Why do you feel this way?

7. Time a classmate who is reciting the main facts of the day's lesson. Switch roles and have that person time you.

8. Make flash cards to help you recall the definitions of the terms you have studied today.

9. List three ways that you are like someone in today's lesson.

10. Create a fair question for a test on this material. What is the answer?

11. Using what you now know about this topic, explain why . . .

12. How can you connect what you learned today with another subject?

13. What did you change your mind about during the lesson?

14. Justify the rule for . . .

15. Make a quick outline of your notes so far in class today.

16. Write a fact about what you have just learned on the board.

17. Unscramble these vocabulary words.

18. Use two of the key terms from this unit in the same sentence.

19. There are seven errors in the passage you have been given to read. Can you find all of them?

20. Group these items according to a criteria that you devise based on the information you have learned so far in this lesson.

Requests to Leave the Room

"Can I go to the restroom?" "Can I go to my locker?" "Can I go use the phone?" "Can I take this lunch money to my brother?" Sometimes it can seem as if you are the only person who doesn't ask to leave the room.

Learning how to manage student requests wisely can save you and your students lots of time and trouble. The time that you spend planning how you will cope successfully with student requests will be amply rewarded when students develop the self-discipline to manage such requests themselves.

In handling student requests to leave class, you also need to determine whether students are truthful in the reason they give you for why they need to leave class. If your hall pass has places for signatures of other professionals, such as the nurse or media specialist, then check those signatures to ensure that students went where they told they needed to go. Be alert to the direction in which your students head as they leave your class. By establishing a fair policy for handling requests to leave class, you can eliminate many of the temptations that could cause students to be dishonest.

Where do your students want to go when they leave your class? Here is a list of some of the places students at all levels of schooling ask to go to when they leave class, along with quick suggestions for how to handle each one successfully.

Library. You can allow students go to here because there is another adult present to supervise them. If you are sending more than one or two students, you should check with the librarian first. Make sure that your students have a specific task to perform there and know when you expect them to return.

Nurse. You can also send students to see the school nurse without worry, because there is another adult there to supervise them. If a student asks to go to the clinic too often, just check with the nurse to see if the requests are genuine. If a student is gone too long, make sure that you check to see if there is a problem. Also, if a student is obviously ill, consider sending another student along to assist the ill child.

Another classroom. Sometimes a student will ask to go to another teacher's class. For example, cheerleaders may want to make posters for the big game or drama students may want to rehearse. These requests should not come from students. If another teacher asks that you release students from your class, then that teacher should contact you about it. You have no other way of knowing if the requests are legitimate ones. Speak to the other teacher before you send students to another class. You should also refuse to be pressured into letting students leave if you do not believe that they can make up the work that they will miss in your class.

Locker. If you have a bank of shared materials for students to use and if you allow students to turn in any assignments that they may have left in their lockers immediately after class without a penalty, then you have eliminated some of these requests. Then you can determine the validity of other requests on a one-to-one basis. Although you can allow students to go to their lockers if it's a legitimate request, you must also avoid giving the impression that students can use such requests when they feel like taking a little break from class.

Parking lot or car. Never send a student out of the building without checking with an administrator first. If a student has left something that needs to be turned in during class, offer to accept it after school instead with no penalty rather than send a student to the parking lot.

Phone. Your school probably has a policy about student use of pay phones or office phones during class time. Check your faculty manual or with your mentor to find out what it is. Unless it is an emergency, tell your students to use the phone between classes or at other times when they are not supposed to be in class.

Guidance office. Before you send a student to the guidance office, make sure that a counselor will be there and able to see the student. Students have been known to wait for hours in the guidance office waiting patiently for a counselor rather than attend class.

Office. If a student requests to see an administrator, make sure that the administrator is available and willing to see the student before you honor the request.

To see another student. Sometimes, in the middle of your class, students will remember that they have the lunch money for their siblings or a note excusing a younger family member's tardiness to school. Do not allow students to leave your class to attend to this non-emergency business. Instead, allow students to take care of it between classes or during a break.

Water fountain. Unless a student is coughing or obviously in need of a drink of water, say no. Students use this as a way to stretch their legs and break up a monotonous class. Make sure that you design your class so that you break up the monotony caused by sitting too long and that you encourage students to stretch their legs at appropriate intervals.

Restroom. You should never refuse a student's request to use the restroom. If you do and the student is ill or telling you the truth about a dire need, then you have created a much bigger problem than one caused by a simple request to leave the room. Instead of saying "no" outright, you could say "Have you finished your work? Can you please wait a few minutes?" If the student insists, then honor the request.

GUIDELINES FOR HANDLING STUDENT REQUESTS TO LEAVE CLASS

Making good decisions about whether or not to allow a student to leave the classroom is never easy, no matter how much teaching experience you have. Consider the following guidelines as you begin to make decisions about the policy for leaving class that you want your students to follow.

- Do not allow more than one or two students to leave at one time. When you have several students out of the room at the same time, you should rethink the lesson that you have planned for the day so that the needs of your students can be served.

- Do not refuse to allow students to go to the restroom or to the clinic. Use your best judgment about other requests.

- If you have students who may be making too many requests to leave the classroom, privately speak with them about the problem. If this does not work, call a parent or guardian. This will help because if there is a problem, then the parent or guardian can apprise you of it. If there is not a problem, then enlist their help in keeping the student focused and in class. Often, just knowing that you are serious enough to call home will convince the student to make fewer requests.

- You can prevent too many requests to leave the room by designing fast-paced and interesting lessons that will keep your students so engaged that they will not want to miss anything exciting.

- When you send students out of the room, make sure that they will be supervised by an adult whenever possible. You are responsible for your students until that responsibility is taken over by another adult.

- Never allow students to leave the building without contacting an administrator first. Older students will request to go back to the parking lot to retrieve items that they may have left in their cars. Studies show that school parking lots can provide opportunities for violence and other misbehaviors.

- Make sure that you keep all used hall passes if you do not use a generic one. File them in the folder you maintain for each student. You may need to show these later in the term. You will also be able to keep up better with how many times a student has left the class.

- If you intend to keep track of how often a student may leave the class, you will need to devise a workable system. Some teachers use a sign out sheet, others make notes on a class roster, and others still issue a certain number of personalized hall passes each marking period and reward students who do not use all of them.

- There are many ways to refuse a request in a polite, but firm manner. Instead of brusquely refusing, try saying one of these instead.
  - "Can you wait a few minutes?"
  - "Have you finished your work?"
  - "Let me check to see if _____ is in the _____ office."
  - "Our school policy prohibits students from _____ during class."
  - "Can you do that right after class?"

HOW TO ESTABLISH A FAIR POLICY

You will need to establish and enforce a fair policy about leaving the classroom. Ask your mentor or a colleague if there is a school policy or how other teachers handle this matter. If there is no formal school policy, then consider these issues when creating your policy.

- How often is it acceptable for a student to leave your class during a grading period?
- Where will you allow students to go without first consulting another adult?
- How will students ask permission so that the interruption is minimal?
- How will you maintain records of which students have left your class?
- Where will students sign out?
- When students return to class, where will they put their hall passes for you to keep?
- How will you enforce your policy? What consequences will your students face if they do not comply?

KEEPING TRACK OF STUDENTS WHO LEAVE THE ROOM

Because you will have to keep track of who is out of your class, you should have a sign out sheet as well as hall passes. A sign out sheet can take many forms. You can post a sheet for students to fill out as they leave or have them sign out on a computer, or you could maintain a class logbook. If you are fortunate enough to teach in a peaceful or very small school, a generic hall pass may be acceptable. If you don't use a generic hall pass, then your school probably has a hall pass form for you to use. You will need to keep plenty of these forms on hand.

The Last 10 Minutes of Class

You have two goals at the end of class: to have students who are not only reluctant to leave, but who retain the information that you have just taught them. The last ten minutes of class is the ideal time to accomplish both of these goals.

The routine that you create for the end of class should be predictable, but also one that students can anticipate with enjoyment. Here is a simple two-step plan for the ending of class that you should follow to make sure that the last few minutes of class are as productive as the earlier ones.

STEP 1: 8-MINUTE CLOSING EXERCISE

Use this brief amount of time to help students retain information by reviewing what you have just taught and by helping students look ahead to what they will be learning next. Here are ten activities that you can adapt to make sure your class ends on a positive note.

1. Have students list five things they have learned that day. Have them share this list with a classmate or with the entire group.
2. Ask students to predict what they will learn next.
3. Ask students to predict the meaning of the key terms for the next part of the unit.
4. Have students write a quick explanation of the most interesting aspect of the day's lesson.
5. As your students to write a question that they still have about the day's lesson.
6. Hold a quick review, vocabulary, or spelling bee.
7. Ask students to explain the directions for how to do the night's homework one more time. Be sure to ask them to estimate how long it should take them to complete the assignment successfully.
8. Unveil a final thought for the day that you have hidden under a sheet of paper taped to the board earlier in the day.
9. Give your students an additional brief reading passage and ask them to comment on it.
10. Show a cartoon or relevant illustration on the overhead projector.

STEP 2: THE 2-MINUTE DISMISSAL

After the closing exercise, you should have two minutes for your students to prepare to be dismissed at your signal. During this time, they should have a routine to follow. This should include the following.

- Disposing of trash
- Stowing away books and materials
- Checking to make sure that nothing is left behind

You should allow talking at this time if students stay in their seats and keep their voices down. You can teach this part of the routine by timing your students and rewarding the class for successfully completing it.

During the last two minutes of class, you should move to the door and speak to every student as the class leaves. This will prevent any last-minute misbehaviors and show your students that they have a teacher who cares about them. You should not allow students to congregate at the door or jump up and bolt when the bell rings. Insist that you will dismiss class and that they should wait for your signal. You should not detain students after the bell has rung.

Journal Entries to Help You Make Effective Use of Instructional Time

- What catches your attention about how your students use the time they have in your class?

- What is your worst habit about how you use time? What bad time-use habits do your students have that you can help them with?

- Explain how this statement applies to time in your class: "You reap what you sow."

- What are the qualities of a well-managed class? Do your classes have these qualities?

- Complete this statement: "I am not going to _____ again because . . ."

- What activities can you build in to make the opening of class a pleasant and productive time for your students?

- Complete this statement: "One of the biggest ways my time was wasted when I was a student was . . ."

- How will your students benefit from a class where every minute counts? How will you benefit?

- How can you go about designing lessons that will keep students engaged in productive activities all class?

Classroom Management Through Early Intervention

As she rushed down the hall, she could hear a deafening racket coming from her room. She stopped in the doorway, unable to believe the chaos before her. Every single one of her students was misbehaving! Some were shouting, a few were trying to tip over the file cabinet, and still others were chasing their classmates around the desks. Paper airplanes whizzed through the air.

She shouted for them to stop. No one listened. Maybe they couldn't hear her. She shouted again and waved her arms. Her students were ignoring her!

Two boys who were fighting rolled on the floor at her feet. The other students crowded around, cheering them on. She tried again to get them to stop. Nothing was working. The two boys suddenly stood up. The looks on their faces made them almost unrecognizable and filled her with fear. They began to chase her down the corridor.

Heart racing, she sat up in bed. What a nightmare.

She had been warned about the anxiety dreams that often plagued first-year teachers at the beginning of the school year. In fact, she had been told by a veteran teacher that even experienced teachers had these nightmares.

Even though she felt a little better knowing that she wasn't alone with her fears, she was still worried. Was this what it was going to be like? What if her students wouldn't do what she asked? How would she ever be able to control her classes?

The biggest fear that new teachers have may be that they won't be able to control their classes. Unfortunately, this fear is not as unfounded as it should be. In the last few years, more than half of the schools in America reported an incident of violence severe enough to require police involvement. Many educators leave teaching because they become discouraged by the lack of respect and even basic social skills among their students.

You do not have to be one of those teachers who give up on the profession. You can learn the classroom management skills that you will need to not just control your classes, but to enjoy your students.

Can you recall a teacher who was able to control a class effortlessly? The fact is, it's never effortless—skilled teachers only make it seem that way. Every teacher has discipline problems. These problems can involve simple issues such as the best way to organize the traffic flow in a classroom as well as serious concerns about what steps to take if a student becomes violent.

While classroom management can be a daunting concern, it is also one of the most important aspects of your new career. Successful classroom management means that you have the procedures in place to prevent or solve behavior problems.

Other aspects of successful classroom management include motivating your students to succeed, skillful teaching, and maintaining a caring relationship with your students. When all of these elements come together, you will experience very few serious discipline problems. Experienced teachers will tell you that it is far easier and more productive to prevent problems rather than deal with their aftermath.

Why Punishment Is Not the Answer

Punishment as a behavior management technique has been around for hundreds of years. In spite of what enlightened educators know about classroom management, punishment and fear of punishment are still the most often employed techniques to make children behave.

While negative consequences can deter students from making poor decisions for themselves, harsh punishments will not turn troublemakers into well-behaved students. There are several problems with using punishment as a means of crowd control.

First of all, punishment is a short-term solution to a long-term problem. Adults simply cannot bully students into good behavior. If you use punishment techniques often enough, you can expect a backlash. If you do succeed in making your students afraid of you, then you can expect to have students refuse to work, talk back to you, vandalize your personal belongings, or worse.

Punishment is also ineffective because it doesn't effect a permanent change in your students. A class that is controlled by a tyrant is one that quickly falls apart if there is a substitute teacher in the room. Students who are frequently punished do not grow into self-disciplined learners who take control of their own behavior because no one has shown them how.

Another reason not to use punishment is that, sadly, some of your students will probably be immune to cruelty and harsh behavior. It is highly likely that at least some of your students will have such chaotic and dysfunctional home lives that a cruel teacher is just another adult who is unkind to them. Wouldn't it be better to offer your students a safe haven from violence rather than inflict more misery?

Finally, it is important not to rely on punishment to motivate students because of the effect that it will have on you. Did you really become a teacher to play the part of a prison warden? Teachers who try to rule their classes with an iron fist will burn out as soon as they see that this strategy does far more harm than good.

Punishment is a behavioral management practice that has outlived its dubious usefulness. When you create a behavior management plan for your students, you are planning to minimize the role that punishment will play and maximize the importance of some of the positive strategies at your disposal.

15 Discipline Techniques to Avoid

There are many techniques that you may be tempted to employ to discipline your students. Some of these will just not work. The following fifteen ineffective discipline practices are ones that you should definitely avoid.

1. Commanding students to comply with your directives
2. Accepting excuses or being a pushover
3. Making bargains with students to coerce them into obedience
4. Making fun of students
5. Raising your voice
6. Telling students that you are in charge by using expressions such as "Because I said so," or "Because I am the teacher"
7. Bribing students
8. Throwing students out of class
9. Nagging
10. Being confrontational
11. Being sarcastic
12. Embarrassing students
13. Being a poor role model
14. Losing your temper
15. Compelling students' friends to take sides

"Don't sweat the small stuff! Choose your battles! The teacher's reaction to a problem sets the tone."

—Patty Muth, 9 years experience

Early Intervention Strategies

Preventing misbehavior is much easier and more productive than having to cope with discipline problems once they have already disrupted your class. Unfortunately, there is no single action that you can take to prevent problems from occurring. Preventing misbehavior relies instead on many factors that work together to create the harmonious classroom that you want for your students.

In addition to the intervention strategies you will learn about in this section, there are many others that teachers have found to be successful in preventing discipline problems. Some of these strategies are discussed in depth in other sections of this resource, as follows.

- **Engage students in meaningful work all class long (Section Eleven).** Although it is only common sense that students who are busy learning will not have time to misbehave, it is easy to underestimate the length of time that it can take students to finish an assignment. Plan to engage your students in meaningful work from the beginning of class until the end and you will prevent many of the problems that will occur when students do not have enough to do.

- **Create a sense of community in your class (Section Five).** Students who feel that they are a valuable part of the group will hesitate before letting their classmates down by misbehaving. When you and your students work in harmony, you will all benefit.

- **Reward your students when they are successful (Section Nine).** Rewarding good behavior successfully prevents bad behavior for two reasons: 1) it lets students know which behaviors are acceptable, and 2) it encourages them to choose those productive behaviors instead of misbehaving.

- **Use frequent non-verbal signals instead of interrupting the entire class (Section Nine).** There are many actions that you can take to let students know what to do without ever having to stop them from working. Depending on the age of your students, you can use signals such as flicking the lights, ringing a bell, or even just moving close to students who may be off task. Many teachers have found using interesting non-verbal cues to signal students an effective way to keep them working productively all class long.

- **Seek support from other adults in the child's life (Section Four).** Students who know that the significant adults in their lives are working together for their benefit are far less likely to misbehave than those students who feel that no one cares about them. From phoning home to talking with another teacher, you can tap into many sources of support.

- **Talk with students when you see a problem beginning to develop (Section Five).** You can forestall many behavior problems by talking directly with a child who is beginning to misbehave. When you know the reason for misbehavior and act on that knowledge, you can prevent problems from recurring or from involving other students.

Figure 12.1

HOW EFFECTIVE ARE YOU AT PREVENTING PROBLEMS?

Read each of these positive management practices and grade yourself on how well you do at each one. You will find that your school day is much more pleasant and productive if you have an "A" average. Use a traditional letter scale:

A = excellent   B = very good   C = average   D = needs improvement   F = failing

_____ I have a set of positively stated rules posted in my classroom.

_____ I use a friendly but firm voice when I ask students to do something.

_____ I make sure that I build relevance and interest into every lesson.

_____ I make sure that all of my students know that I care about them.

_____ I have taught my students the routines and rules that will make class run smoothly.

_____ I use non-verbal interventions to keep misbehavior manageable.

_____ I consistently enforce my classroom rules.

_____ I consistently enforce school rules.

_____ I design lessons that will engage my students all class period.

_____ I do contact my students' parents or guardians to keep problems manageable.

_____ I praise my students more than I criticize them.

_____ I monitor my students constantly.

_____ I refuse to nag or bribe students into good behavior.

_____ I respect the dignity of all of my students.

_____ I accept responsibility for what happens in my class.

Review your grades and congratulate yourself for all the As. Then make it your goal to master the skills that you currently manage at a lower than excellent level.

Some Internet Sites You Can Explore

Because teachers everywhere are eager to find painless ways to maintain classrooms free of misbehavior and mayhem, there are thousands of Web sites that address the subject. Here are a few you may want to explore to learn more about how to prevent problems through early intervention.

www.behavioradvisor.com

www.classroom-management.com

www.proteacher.com/

www.angelfire.com/ky2/socialskills

www.masterteacher.com

www.disciplinehelp.com

www.educators2000.com

www.edusmile.com

www.youthchg.com

www.inspiringteachers.com

Create a Safe Environment for Your Students

A safe environment is absolutely necessary for the well being of your students. Because school safety practices are not always written in faculty manuals, it's likely that you will have to learn about school safety by observing other teachers or by making mistakes.

By being attentive to the environment that you create for your students, you can prevent many discipline problems. Here are some the common-sense actions that you can take to prevent discipline problems caused by an unsafe school environment.

- Report suspected guns or weapons immediately.
- If you hear threats or rumors of a potential fight, contact an administrator promptly.
- Never allow one student to torment another one. Report bullies to an administrator.
- Keep your classroom locked when it is not in use.
- Never leave your students unsupervised.
- When you permit your students to leave your room with a hall pass, you are still responsible for them. Pay attention to where your students go and how long they are out of your room.
- Send students who say that they feel don't feel well to the school nurse as quickly as you can. Make sure that you pay attention to notes from a doctor or from home about potentially dangerous medical conditions.
- Return phone calls from parents as quickly as you can. This is not only professional, but the parent may have a concern that needs to be addressed at once.

▶ Keep matches, scissors, teacher's textbook editions, money you have collected, and your personal belongings in your desk or in another secure place. Make sure that you teach students not to take items from your desktop without your permission. Instead, provide materials for their use in another part of the room.

▶ If you suspect that a child has been abused, act quickly by sending the student to a counselor.

▶ Take suicide threats seriously. Contact a counselor at once.

▶ Teach with the door to your classroom closed to prevent interference from outside.

▶ Take a stand against drugs and alcohol. Your students need to hear adults speak against under-age drinking and drug use.

▶ Allow no tolerance for racial or other prejudices in your classroom.

▶ If you hold students after school, stay with them until their rides arrive. They need your supervision.

▶ Never give students rides home from school.

▶ Don't give the keys to your classroom or to your car to a student. If you ask students to retrieve something from your car or your room, accompany them.

Teach and Enforce School Rules

You will prevent many discipline problems and create a positive classroom environment if you take the time to teach and enforce the school rules that govern all students. Consistent enforcement is especially important, because many of the conflicts that you will have with your students will arise from teachers who inconsistently enforce school rules. The following guidelines will help you enforce school rules.

▶ **Know the rules thoroughly.** In order to successfully teach and enforce school rules, you need to become thoroughly familiar with them yourself. The time to do this is before school starts.

▶ **Follow the rules yourself.** Students are quick to point out what they believe to be hypocrisy. For example, if students are not allowed to have food in class, they will think that you are rude if you eat in front of them. A particularly sensitive area for many students is the dress code. You will find it very difficult to enforce the rules for student dress if you violate them yourself.

▶ **Take the time to teach school rules to your students.** One mistake many teachers make is to assume that someone else will teach students school rules. While there may be assemblies or other ways for students to learn school rules, you should go over the rules with your students to make sure that everyone knows what to do. A good time to do this is at the first meeting with them, or shortly after. You will have to repeat them from time to time to make sure that students have a clear understanding. One way to make school rules relevant is to ask students to share some of the rules that adults have to follow at work and the rationale for these rules. When you then draw a comparison between family or work-related rules and school rules for students, you will make it easier for students to accept them.

▶ **Enforce school rules consistently.** If you have a serious reservation about a particular rule, then you should speak with an administrator about its purpose and whether or not it should be changed. However, no matter what you personally think about a school rule, you should enforce it. Students are quick to take advantage when teachers are not consistent in enforcement.

Creating Classroom Rules

Rules will protect your right to teach and your students' right to learn not only because they set limits for student behavior, but also because they provide guidelines for what is acceptable and what is not. When you create a set of classroom rules for your students, you establish a common language for the expectations that you have for good behavior.

Rules also send the message that good behavior is important and that you expect students to work productively. Even though your students may earnestly try to convince you that rules are not necessary, they really do not want—nor do they need—total freedom. Students of all ages benefit from the guidance that classroom rules can provide in establishing a tone of mutual respect and cooperation.

In creating rules for your classroom, you can take the following step-by-step approach.

Step 1: Determine what areas your rules need to cover. Begin by asking yourself these questions.

- What are some behaviors that make it possible for students to succeed?
- What are some behaviors that make it difficult for students to succeed?
- What limits can I set to guarantee that all students have the right to learn?

Step 2: Draft a rough set of rules. After you have determined the areas that you want your rules to cover, write a rough draft. At this point, you may want to show your rules to a colleague to make sure that they are in line with the school rules and that they are appropriate for the age and ability of your students.

Step 3: State classroom rules positively. Take your rough draft and change the wording so that the rules are stated in positive terms, conveying a tone of mutual respect and consideration.

Step 4: State rules so that they are easy to remember. Can you combine any of your rules so that they cover a general range of student behavior? For example, you could combine "Bring your textbook every day" and "You will need paper and pens in this class" to read "Be sure to bring the materials you will need for class." Your students will also find it easier to recall your class rules if you only have a few. Many experienced teachers recommend having fewer than five.

Step 5: Determine if your rules will be successful. In order for class rules to be successful, they should be:

- Stated in positive terms
- General enough to cover a broad range of student activity
- Easy to remember

To determine if your rules are working for your class, ask yourself these two questions: 1) Do all students understand the rule or is it too vague? 2) Do students understand the rationale for and importance of this rule?

If you are still not sure that your classroom rules will work, here are some that experienced teachers have found successful. Adapt them to meet the needs of your students.

1. Use class time wisely.
2. Do your work well.
3. Treat other people with respect.
4. Follow school rules.
5. Bring your materials to class every day.

Teaching Classroom Rules

In the press of covering the academic material that your students need to learn, it is easy to overlook the importance of teaching classroom rules. A complete set of well-expressed rules is useless if your students don't know what they are.

You can help your students understand the importance of following rules by spending some time teaching your students how to behave correctly. Teaching appropriate behavior is not something that you can complete in one class period, rather it is a process that will last all term.

Students who know how to behave correctly will not lose time in bad behavior. Incorporate these strategies into your daily lessons, and you will find that the time you spend on teaching students the rules will save you instructional time.

1. Send home a letter with your classroom rules so that you can enlist the support of your students' parents and guardians. You can find a sample letter in Section Four.
2. Post a copy of your class rules in a prominent spot so that all of your students can easily be reminded of them.
3. Although teaching classroom rules is a process that will last all term, you should focus on teaching them during the first three weeks of the term to make sure that your students know that you are serious about a positive classroom climate.
4. When you are ready to talk about rules with your students, don't just try to bluff your way through a brief presentation. Instead, present them in a dynamic lesson. Try some of these activities.
   - Have students create a Venn diagram comparing the rules they have at school with the rules adults have at work.
   - Place students into groups and have them brainstorm the reasons why everyone should follow various rules. Ask other groups to list what could happen if no one followed a rule.

- Have students write their class rules in their notebooks. Ask them to see if they can improve the wording of a rule or if they can create examples to explain each one.

- Have students debate the positive and negative effects on the entire group when students follow or don't follow rules.

- Ask students to explain the rules to you in their own words.

- Divide students into groups and assign each group a rule to teach to the class in a skit.

Enforcing Classroom Rules

Classroom rules empower teachers who want their students to see that they are serious about good behavior. By vigilantly and consistently enforcing classroom rules, you will prevent many serious discipline problems. When a student breaks a rule and you care enough to spend the time enforcing that rule, then you send a powerful message not just to the rule-breaker, but to every student in the class. Thus, by enforcing a classroom rule, you prevent many other infractions.

When a student breaks a class rule, calmly and quietly enforce the rule. Don't threaten, nag, or lose your temper. Follow this five-step procedure.

Step 1: Ask, "What rule have you broken?"

Step 2: Help the student understand that the rule applies to this occasion.

Step 3: Ask the student to explain the reasons for the rule.

Step 4: Ask the student to tell you the consequences for breaking the rule.

Step 5: Carry out the consequences that you have for students who break rules.

One fact you can take comfort in is that frequently students will break a rule not from a desire to misbehave, but from a momentary lapse in good judgment. By calmly and firmly enforcing your rules, you acknowledge that lapse and remind students not to repeat the offense.

> *"You cannot hold grudges. You need to remember that your students have short memories and trust you to always do the right thing. If there is a problem, settle it, then just continue as if nothing happened."*
>
> —Sarah Walski, 25 years experience

5 Tips for Enforcing Class Rules

Here are a few more quick tips to help you successfully enforce your class rules:

1. When students break a rule the first time, talk privately with them to make sure that they understand the rule and the consequences.

2. Before you rush to judgment, determine why your students broke the rule. Do they need more attention from you? Did they run out of meaningful work to do? Does the rule need to be restated so that it is easier to understand?

3. Accept that enforcing rules is part of your job as a teacher. Be patient. Your students are going to misbehave from time to time.

4. Reward good behavior as often as you can. Rewarding students for behaving well will encourage them to continue.

5. Don't be a pushover. While it may be tempting to make an exception to a rule, think carefully before you do. You should balance the needs of all of your students with the needs of the student who broke the rule.

Consequences

When you create your classroom rules, you also need to decide the consequences that will follow if students break the rules. You must teach these consequences when you teach the rules, so your students will know what to expect.

The consequences that you create must meet several important criteria. First, they should arise logically from the infraction. For example, if students leave their work area messy, they should have to clean it up. Consequences should also fit the infraction. Asking students to clean their work area after leaving it untidy is a consequence that solves the problem. Asking students to clean their work area because they were late to class does not.

You should also create a hierarchy of consequences so students know that continued rule breaking will result in more serious consequences. For example, the first time a student forgets a textbook, a reminder or warning is sufficient. If a student habitually forgets his or her textbook, a referral to an administrator would be warranted.

While consequences will vary depending on the age and ability of your students, when you begin to plan your classroom consequences, consider creating a hierarchy such as this one.

First offense:	Reminder
Second offense:	Warning
Third offense:	Phone call home
Fourth offense:	Fifteen-minute detention

351

Other consequences that you could employ include:

- Loss of small privileges
- Time out
- Letter home
- Parent conference
- Referral to an administrator
- Longer detention

Writing should never be assigned as a consequence. Having students write sentences such as "I must be respectful" numerous times, or any other writing assignment, is not an acceptable consequence because it makes writing an unpleasant task and adversely affects the work of language arts teachers.

The Crucial Step: Monitoring

Almost everyone has had at least one teacher who was able to write notes on the board and tell students in the back of the room to stop making faces at each other at the same time. One of the most important skills that you can develop as a teacher is monitoring—actively overseeing your students from the moment that they enter the room until they leave.

Being acutely aware of what each one of your students is doing every minute of class is not relaxing. However, the reward of such vigilance is a peaceful and productive classroom. By paying careful attention to your students, you will help them stay on task and be successful. Further, any problems that might arise will stay small if you are actively working to facilitate instruction through monitoring.

Here are six more benefits that you and your students will receive when you know exactly what each one is doing at any given moment. When you successfully monitor your students, you:

1. Create a positive class atmosphere.
2. Keep problems small.
3. Reinforce good behavior.
4. Keep students on task.
5. Help students stay focused on learning.
6. Maintain a strong connection with every student.

BECOME AN EFFECTIVE MONITOR

Learning to be an effective classroom monitor is not difficult although it will require effort before it becomes a habit. The following suggestions will help you get started.

1. You cannot monitor effectively from your desk. Get up and move around. Your students will be far less likely to stray off task than if you just sit at your desk.

2. When you arrange your classroom, make sure that you place student desks so that you can easily move around the room. Avoid putting desks too close together or against walls where you can't get around them.

3. Make sure that you ask students to place their book bags and other belongings underneath their desks so you can move around the room without tripping. After a day or two of reminders, this should become a habit.

4. If you find that students are becoming distracted, it is often enough just to stand near them for a minute or two. If this doesn't work, then a quiet word, a glance, or a quick nod will usually suffice.

5. Practice the twenty-second survey. Stand in one spot and take about twenty seconds to look over the class to see who is on task and who is not before you act.

6. After your students settle down to work, wait about two minutes before you start walking around to see what they are doing. This will give them time to get started on an assignment and for problems to arise.

7. Work on maintaining good eye contact with your students. This will let students know that you are aware of them and discourage them from misbehaving.

8. Many teachers tend to focus on only a few students. To determine how evenly you spread out your attention, carry a copy of your class roster. When you speak with a student, place a mark next to the student's name. After doing this for a day or two, you will be aware of the unconscious patterns you follow in the way that you attend to your students and able to make any needed adjustments.

9. Don't spend too much time with some students and ignore others. For example, don't give a student ten minutes of your time while several others wait.

10. Try not to allow a large group of students to congregate around you while waiting for you to help them. Instead, try asking students to put their names on the board so that you can see them in order. Or have them actually take a number from a stack of note cards that you have numbered. You could also have students who may have a question that they think others will have write the question on the board so that you can address it for everyone.

11. If you create a checklist for your students to follow as they work, then you will be able to check their progress as you come by their desks. You can also ask students to show you each item on their checklist as they work through them.

12. Arrange signals so that your students can let you know quickly how they are doing. An approach that other teachers have found useful is to tape three note cards together to form a triangle or tent that can stand on a desk. On each side you could place a signal for students to use to let you know how they are doing. A question mark could indicate that the student has a question, a smiley face could mean that the student has no questions, and a frownie face could mean that there is a serious problem.

13. Ask students who have finished to write their names on the board. This not only lets you know who is finished, but it also lets other students know which classmate can help if you are busy.

14. Use one of these three very productive statements.

    • "At this moment, what are you doing that's right?"

    • "How may I help you?"

    • "When I come by your desk, please show me _____."

When You Should Act

Like many other teachers, you may sometimes have trouble knowing at just what point you should intervene to stop a problem from becoming serious. When you should act will depend on the type of problem you have to cope with. Behavior problems can be divided into two categories: non-disruptive and disruptive.

Non-disruptive behaviors are ones that involve only the student doing the action and no one else. Daydreaming, sleeping, and poor work habits are common examples. Try these interventions to end a non-disruptive behavior.

• Move close to the student.

• Remind the entire class to stay on task.

• Place your hand on the student's desk.

• Maintain positive eye contact.

• Praise the work the student has completed.

• Offer your help.

• Glance at or smile at the student.

• Offer to let the student briefly move around.

• Ask if another student could help.

• Consider moving the student's seat.

Disruptive behaviors involve other students and affect the learning climate. When students become disruptive, your goal must be to keep minimize the effect on your class. Begin by enforcing your class rules as calmly and quietly as you can. If this does not improve the situation, move the misbehaving student to the hall for a private conversation.

Most of the time, just talking quietly with a student will solve the problem. Listen to what the student has to say and offer your help. Remind students who misbehave that they do not have the right to interfere with the rights of all students to learn. If you find that you cannot prevent the student from misbehaving further, then you should enforce your class rules using the necessary consequences. (See Section Thirteen for more information about how to handle disruptions once they begin.)

"Catch 'em Being Good"

Take a positive approach to preventing discipline problems in your class. If your students all settle down quickly after a pep rally, for instance, be sure to praise their maturity. When all your students turn in a homework assignment on time, be sure to tell them how much you appreciate their efforts. When you "catch 'em being good" your students will not only understand what you expect of them, but they will also feel encouraged to continue their good behavior.

There are hundreds of opportunities for you to tell your students when they are successful. Don't hesitate to take advantage of them; you and your students will benefit from the positive learning environment that will result.

One of the easiest ways to increase positive behaviors and decrease negative ones is to chart your students' success. When your students see a chart of their positive behaviors, they will understand that good behavior is recognized and appreciated. You will find a sample chart of some of the behaviors that you should see in Figure 12.2.

"Do not try to be the students' friend. They have friends their own age; they need a teacher— you! Do your job: teach, assign homework, class work, projects, tests. . . . Discipline when needed, listen to those who want to discuss a problem they may be having, hold parent-teacher conferences. . . . Just don't become their 'buddy.'"

—Marlene M. Stanton,
23 years experience

Be a Consistent Teacher

As a teacher, you will have to make dozens of decisions every day. Many of these decisions will not only have to be made quickly, but in front of a crowd of students—all of whom have different needs. You will never have enough time to carefully think through many of the choices you will be called on to make; you will have to learn to think fast.

The number of quick decisions that you have to make will sometimes make it difficult to be consistent. But remember that consistency is one of the most important tools that you have in preventing problems because it gives your students a safe framework with well-defined boundaries for their behavior. Consistent classroom management provides a predictable environment with established rules and consequences.

Even though consistency is crucial to successful management, it is one of the most difficult skills to manage. You may find it difficult to be consistent in these circumstances.

▶ If school rules dictate consequences that you believe are too harsh for a particular infraction.

▶ If you believe that overlooking an infraction "just this once" will be acceptable.

▶ If the infraction occurs at an inconvenient time or place.

Figure 12.2
Behavior Modeling Chart

Number of Students Who Do This

Behavior	M	T	W	Th	F	M	T	W	Th	F

Additional Notes

_____

_____

_____

_____

_____

- If you have different expectations for students whom you perceive to be less able than others.

You will find it easier to be a consistent teacher when you follow these guidelines.

- Be well prepared and organized, as this will facilitate good decision making under pressure.
- Teach the rules and procedures that you have established for the smooth operation of your class.
- Be careful to enforce the rules for all students every day.
- Don't make idle threats. Mean what you say when you talk with your students about their behavior.

Figure 12.3

ANALYZE YOUR PREVENTION STRATEGIES

Ask yourself the following questions to analyze the effectiveness of your misbehavior prevention strategies. Jot down your answers in your teacher's binder or someplace else where you can easily review them.

What student behaviors would I like to change?

What strategies have I tried that did not work?

Why didn't they succeed?

What strategies have I tried that were at least partially successful?

Which strategies can I adjust so that they will succeed?

What are some other options that I could implement?

"Never threaten unless you can carry it out. If you can't carry out the consequence, your words will ring hollow and you've lost them."

—Marlene M. Stanton,
23 years experience

Strategies for Minimizing Routine Disruptions

In the rest of this section you will find fifteen situations that many educators routinely have to deal with. Each of these situations has the potential to interfere with the learning environment you want to maintain, but you can learn to manage them successfully so that the disruption is minimal.

SITUATION 1: FIRE DRILLS

You have just handed out quiz papers to your students when the bell signaling a fire drill rings.

1. You should expect a fire drill at least once a week during the first month of school. Before the first fire drill, you should teach your students the procedures that you want them to follow.

2. Make sure you have the evacuation route posted during the first week of school. Go over it with your students as soon as you can.

3. Select a responsible student to lead the others to a designated spot where you can meet with them and check to make sure that everyone is safe. Make sure that your students know to stay in this spot until you give them permission to leave.

4. When you teach your students the procedures that you want them to follow for a fire drill, adopt a serious tone so that they will also take the matter seriously.

5. Take your class roster outside with you so that you can call roll. Make sure that they know that you take this responsibility very seriously and will answer promptly when you call their names.

6. Make sure that you also teach your student the procedures that you want them to follow when they return to the room. Don't allow students to dawdle in the hallway because of a fire drill.

7. If your students are taking a test or a quiz during an evacuation, expect that the integrity of the test or quiz has been compromised. Either disregard the objective portions or allow students to use the assessment as a study guide for a retest on the next day.

SITUATION 2: STUDENTS COMPLETING WORK FOR ANOTHER CLASS IN YOUR ROOM

Your students have just settled down to work on the day's assignment when you discover that some of them are rushing to complete their homework for another class instead of doing the work you assigned.

1. You can prevent this from happening by assigning meaningful work that will engage your students from the start to the finish of your class. Hold your students accountable for their work and make sure that your expectations are high enough to keep them challenged and on task.

2. When students do work for another class in your room, simply ask them to put it away and redirect their attention to your assignment.

3. Do not make the mistake of taking the students' work or books from them. This is unnecessarily harsh to the student and will also have a negative effect on the other teacher's class.

SITUATION 3: DRESS CODE VIOLATIONS

When you are monitoring homework in first period, you notice that one of your students is wearing a T-shirt with a message that promotes alcohol. This is a violation of the dress code.

1. Make sure that you are familiar with the dress code rules before you try to explain them to your students.

2. Be careful not to violate the dress code yourself. It will be impossible for you to attempt to enforce it if you are in violation.

3. Make sure that your students understand the rules. If violations seem to be a problem with your students, post the dress code so that they can check it for themselves.

4. Ask other teachers how you are expected to handle violations. For example, if students are dressed inappropriately, are you supposed to send them to the office? If you are, when are you supposed to do this—at the start of class or at the end?

5. Always handle dress code issues privately. If a child refuses to comply with your requests, then enforce your school's policy or send the student to the administrator in charge of dress code issues.

6. Be extra careful to preserve the child's dignity. Sometimes a student may not have anything else clean to wear. If a child is wearing inappropriate clothes to be defiant, then you certainly do not want to give that person an audience by attempting to discuss the issue where others can overhear.

SITUATION 4: PASSING NOTES

You think that your students are busy working on an assignment when you notice that two students are passing notes to each other instead.

1. All you need to do is ask students to put the notes away. Most students are so concerned that others will read their notes that they will comply immediately. Stand nearby to make sure that the notes have been put away.

2. Because notes were not written for you to read, don't read them. When you do this you violate your students' privacy and embarrass them. Some teachers even humiliate students by reading their notes aloud to the class or by posting them on a bulletin board. This is not only unnecessary, but a cruel misuse of adult power.

3. If you really think that you should read student notes, are you prepared to deal with the information that you will encounter? What will you do with this information?

4. Consider why your students have time and opportunity to pass notes in your class. Perhaps you can improve your monitoring skills or lesson plans to forestall this problem.

> *"After a disruption, I always say, 'Where were we?' to let the kids know that no matter what happened, nothing is going to interfere with class."*
>
> —Carole Platt, 35 years experience

SITUATION 5: TALKING BACK

You tell a student who has not yet turned in a test paper that the time for the test is over and that you must have all papers. The student becomes belligerent and loudly tells you and the class that you don't know anything about teaching.

1. Although it is very natural that you would have something to say in your own defense, resist the temptation to argue, be sarcastic, or reprimand the child in front of the class.

2. Ask the student to step into the hall for a private conference when you are calm enough to manage the situation well. Talk with students who talk back about the effects of disrespect on you and on the rest of the class. Take a problem-solving approach to the situation instead of escalating the confrontation and ill will.

3. Make an agreement with students who feel the need to talk back that you want to hear what they have to say and are willing to listen, but that they should speak to you privately and respectfully. When you take this friendly approach, you offer students a chance to approach you in a positive manner, a way to deal with frustrations, and an opportunity to learn how to resolve conflicts in a positive and respectful manner.

4. Make time to encourage good behavior in all of your students by praising them when they do the right thing. When you do this, you call attention to the behaviors that you want to see from them.

SITUATION 6: CHRONIC ILLNESS

You receive a notice that one of your students will have homebound instruction for the next few weeks. You are to send work home as soon as possible.

1. Work with the homebound instructor to help the student successfully complete the work. Take an active role by contacting the student and the instructor and offering your help.

2. Be as flexible as you can about some of the picky requirements of an assignment. Adjust what you can, keeping in mind that your student does not have direct instruction from you and will find it hard to keep up.

3. Contact the student's parents or guardians and offer your assistance and encouragement. Stay in touch with the student, too, by visiting the hospital if appropriate, sending cards, and having classmates send cards.

4. When the student is able to return to class, be sensitive to the difficulty that he or she will have in catching up and getting back into a school routine again. Offer assistance and monitor your student's progress for the first few days.

SITUATION 7: COMPLAINTS

One of your students seems to find fault with everything you ask your students to do. You are losing patience with the constant complaints.

1. Don't become defensive or act annoyed. These actions will only alienate the student further.

2. Take the student's complaints seriously. Ask the complainer to meet with you in a private conference and listen sincerely to what he or she has to say. Allow plenty of time for the student to explain the problem and to work out a resolution.

3. If the complaint is a legitimate one, correct the situation and show your appreciation for bringing it to your attention. If the complaint is not legitimate, explain why. Be sure to indicate that you take the student and the complaint seriously.

"Don't back your students into a corner. Don't use your adult power in a negative way."

—Rebecca Mercer, 25 years experience

4. When you are meeting with the student, discuss the best ways to express constructive complaints so that you have a positive working relationship.

5. Be very attentive to two needs that students who complain have: for you to listen carefully and to succeed in your class. Allow opportunities for both of these on a daily basis.

SITUATION 8: STEALING

You've collected money for a class trip and left the money on your desk for just a few moments while you help a student in the front of the room. When you get back to your desk, you realize that the money has been stolen.

Prevention

1. Be aggressive in preventing theft. Don't leave your personal belongings in the open or on your desk. Many teachers do not carry very much cash at school and leave their credit cards at home.

2. Be very careful about how you handle money that you collect from your students. Deposit it as quickly as you can to avoid problems.

3. Remind your students that they can prevent theft by taking good care of items that are attractive to thieves: calculators, headphones, pens, money, jewelry, electronic devices, hats, tapes or CDs, books, notes, and yearbooks.

4. Leave your classroom locked and don't give your keys to students. Discourage students from taking items from your personal space at school.

Dealing with a Theft

1. If the stolen item belongs to you, don't threaten your students. Instead, offer a small reward for its safe return. Promise to "ask no questions" and honor that promise. What is important is that your belongings are returned.

2. If the stolen item belongs to a student, remain calm and follow these steps.

   Step One: Don't use the words "steal" or "theft."

   Step Two: In a matter-of-fact manner, ask that anyone who may have picked up the item by mistake return it. Don't expect students to tell on each other and don't expect a student to confess in front of the class.

   Step Three: If no one returns it, then notify an administrator. Your students may need to be detained and an administrator's help is necessary for this.

   Step Four: Don't accuse students or continue to talk about the situation unless an administrator is involved. Try to maintain as normal a class atmosphere as you can to minimize the disruption.

   Step Five: When you catch a student stealing, keep that information as private as possible. You will have to involve an administrator and the student's parents or guardians, but try to preserve that student's dignity.

   Step Six: Work with the student to help him or her learn from the mistake and move forward. Make sure to maintain a strong relationship with students who make mistakes so that you can help them improve their self-esteem enough to resist the temptation in the future.

SITUATION 9: EXCESSIVE TALKING

You have a couple of students who enter the door talking and would talk all class long if you allowed it. You find yourself reminding and reprimanding them often, but nothing seems to work.

1. Be very clear with your students about when it is appropriate for them to talk and when it is not. For example, they should not talk if you say "May I have your attention, please?" or "This assignment is one that you have to do without talking to other students."

2. Remind students who test your patience by talking when they are not supposed to talk that they are not being respectful to you or to their classmates.

3. Focus their attention and settle them at the start of class by giving them an opening exercise that requires writing. This will help your students make the transition from the last class to yours.

4. Make sure that you design a lesson so that there is not much time for students to talk instead of work on the assignment.

5. Transitions are often difficult for talkative students. Sequence your instruction so that they can move quickly from one assignment to the next independently.

6. If students are excited about a special event, allow them two minutes of time to talk before settling down to work. Time them and be very strict about the time limit.

7. Enlist your students' help with the problem. Use positive peer pressure to keep students working together on solving their talking problem.

8. If you have a very talkative group that is otherwise mature in their behavior, direct their talking. Some students learn best by interacting with others. Get them talking about their work in productive ways by staging activities such as debates and round robin discussions.

9. Separate classmates who like to talk to one another during class if their talking distracts them from their work.

10. Many teachers have found that they can send a friendly, but firm, message to their students about their talking by using signals. Some that you might try include the following.

   • Writing a reminder on the board
   • Saying a code word
   • Flicking the lights
   • Moving to a certain spot and waiting
   • Counting backwards from ten
   • Turning music on or off
   • Holding up a sign
   • Covering your ears
   • Writing a time-limit countdown on the board
   • Holding your hand up and counting by folding your fingers

SITUATION 10: LYING

Your students had a long-term project due today and three students told you they were in a morning rush and left their projects at home. Two others told you that their printers were broken and four more told you that they did the project, but left it in their lockers. You suspect that none of these students did their project.

1. Never call your students liars. Instead, discover the reason for their behaviors.

2. Make sure that you do not allow your personal distaste for a lie to color your relationship with the student. Make sure that your students know that you care for them and accept them even if you don't accept their lying behavior.

3. Speak in private with students whom you suspect of lying. Ask the student to tell you the lie again. Usually, a student will not care to repeat the lie if you give a knowing look or press further.

4. When you talk with a student about lying, take a problem-solving approach. Try to understand why the student needs to lie. Often lying reflects low self-esteem or a need to protect oneself. Pay attention to the needs that a lying student may be trying to cope with.

5. If a student lies often, there is a serious reason for such behavior. You should schedule an appointment with the child's parents or guardians and a guidance counselor or an administrator to discuss the situation.

SITUATION 11: DEFIANCE

One of your students has made a mess while working on a project in class. When you ask that it be cleaned up, your student refuses to clean the mess, saying, "Why should I?"

1. Absolutely refuse to reply to a defiant student in a rude way. Silence is better than a sarcastic retort or insisting on compliance. Do not argue or raise your voice.

2. A first approach to try is to look surprised and tell the student that you thought you heard wrong. This gives the student a chance to back down. If this happens, just carry on with class. Later on, you should meet quietly with the student and discuss the situation calmly.

3. Another approach that many teachers have found effective is to talk quietly and privately with the student. Begin by asking the student to tell you what is wrong and offering your help. You may not feel very patient, but this approach solves the problem and prevents a reoccurrence. A confrontation will only make things worse.

4. When you have a conference with this student, discuss the importance of mutual respect and the negative effect that defiant behavior has on the rest of the class. Listen carefully to what the student says. Reach an agreement on how to treat each other with respect.

5. If the situation persists, you must involve the student's parents or guardians and an administrator. Meet with them with the student present to work out a plan to solve the problem.

SITUATION 12: LOST PAPERS

You hand back a set of homework papers and notice that some of your students do not have their papers. You tell them that you never received their work. They, in turn, assure you that they did the work, turned it in on time, and you must have lost it.

1. Be very organized about how you manage student papers. By appearing very organized, you will prevent many false accusations because students will not think that they can take advantage of your disorganization. If students see sloppy stacks of papers on your desk, they will be quick to accuse you of losing their work.

2. Grade papers and hand them back as quickly as you can. The longer you delay in returning papers, the harder it is to keep track of them.

3. If you use an in-basket for students to hand in their work as they finish it, be sure to move their papers to a labeled folder before the next class can add theirs to the stack.

4. If you are unable to check a set of papers within a day or two, at least check to make sure that all students have turned in work. This will preclude any surprises for students who are expecting to receive graded papers.

5. Don't be absolute in denying your guilt. Instead, try to solve the problem by first asking students with missing papers to check their own notebooks or lockers to see if they could have taken them from the room accidentally. If the papers don't turn up, then offer the students more time to redo the work and turn it in.

6. When you check to see if the papers could be misplaced, look first in the folders you have for other classes. Students will sometimes slip their work into the middle of a stack of papers not checking to determine if the work belongs to their classmates.

SITUATION 13: ASSEMBLIES

Your students have been excited all week because of an eagerly awaited assembly; however, during the assembly they are rude, talking non-stop through the performance.

1. You should teach your students in advance of the assembly the behaviors that you expect to see from them. Make sure that this lesson includes the positive and negative consequences of their behavior.

2. When you teach students the good behavior that you expect from them, focus on the reasons for it: Everyone has the right to enjoy the performance without distractions and those performing deserve the respect of their audience.

3. Many students are used to loud interactions at concerts and movies. Discuss the difference in the behaviors that are appropriate for those events and those that are appropriate for a school assembly.

4. You will reduce distractions if you encourage students to leave their personal belongings such as combs, makeup, and book bags in the classroom.

5. If you are to sit with your students during the assembly, make sure that you create a seating chart for them. If possible, seat them in a block where you can speak to each one instead of across a long row. Having an assigned seat will send the message that you expect good behavior during the assembly.

6. Model the good behavior you expect from them. Don't take papers to grade. Instead, sit with your students and be attentive.

7. Reward students who behave well.

SITUATION 14: VIDEO VIEWING

You show a video that other teachers have recommended, but only a few of your students watch. Most are bored and restless.

1. Always preview a film you are going to show to make sure it fits the needs of your students. While you are watching, create a worksheet for students to complete as they watch. You can also plan the points where you will stop the movie for discussion.

2. Talk to your students in advance about the courteous and attentive behaviors that you expect from them while they watch a video.

3. Make sure that every student can see. Allow time for them to move their chairs if they need to.

4. Don't have the room too dark. You should avoid glare, but total darkness will make it impossible for your students to do their assignment.

5. Plan a closing activity for your students in which you hold them accountable for what they should have learned during the video and during any discussions. Make sure that you tell your students about this in advance so that they can be prepared.

SITUATION 15: GUEST SPEAKERS

Another teacher invites your class to attend a meeting with a guest speaker. You believe that your students would enjoy the experience but are not certain how you should prepare them.

1. Think of a guest speaker as part of a lesson plan. Design activities that will lead up to and prepare your students for the speaker, activities for them to do with the speaker, and activities that will provide closure afterwards.

2. Teach your students the behaviors that you would like from them while in the presence of a guest speaker. Be very specific about how you expect them to behave. Be especially careful to talk about the importance of positive body language. Some speakers may not appreciate it if your students sleep through their presentations, pass notes to friends, or otherwise convey their inattention.

3. Make sure that your students prepare thoughtful questions to ask the speaker, even if there is no time for them during the visit, as this will help focus their attention.

4. Take time after the visit to evaluate your students' behavior. Praise the things that they did well and what they need to improve before the next speaker.

5. Require that your students write thank-you notes mentioning specific points from the presentation. This is not just polite, it will reinforce the information that the speaker covered.

Journal Entries to Help You Make Use of Early Intervention

- What anxieties do you have about how you will control your classes? How can you cope successfully with these anxieties?

- What are some of the discipline techniques that you can recall from your own days as a student in the grade level you are teaching now? What was effective about these techniques and what was not?

- What would you do if a student became violent in your classroom?

- What are some monitoring strategies that you would like to try with your students? Brainstorm a list and decide how you can implement them.

- What difficulties will you likely face in trying to consistently enforce class rules? How can you overcome these problems?

- What classroom rules have you noticed other teachers in your school using? Can you adapt any of them to your class? Which classroom rule do you think is the most important one?

- Are there any school rules you are uncomfortable with? Why? Think of an incident when a teacher deliberately chose to ignore a school rule. What were the negative consequences? What were the positive consequences?

- What common behavioral problems can you prevent by using early intervention strategies?

- Which early intervention strategy are you most confident about using? Which makes you hesitate? Why?

- How can you "catch 'em being good" and what can you do to let your students know that they are doing just the right thing at that moment?

Handle Behavior Problems Effectively

Fifteen minutes after beginning the movie in his first period class, he notices that one of his students appears to be sleeping. When he moves close to awaken the sleeping girl, he almost chokes from the odor of marijuana that hangs around her like a smog.

He awakens her and sees at once that her eyes are glassy, too. What is he supposed to do now? If he accuses her of drug abuse and she isn't high, then he not only looks foolish, but that will destroy his relationship with her. Still, if she is high, then she's violating the district's zero tolerance policy—to say nothing of having a substance abuse problem. And if she's high and he pretends not to notice, will she do it again? Why does she think that he won't notice? What is he supposed to do?

He can distinctly recall the stern directive from the principal at the last faculty meeting. No teacher was ever supposed to send a student to the office without contacting the student's parents or guardians first. All teachers were supposed to follow the school's discipline policy to the letter. The principal was quite emphatic with them about the importance of calling home. But did that discipline policy apply to drugs? After all, smoking marijuana was against the law. Was he supposed to send her to the office when he just suspected drugs?

What about the other students? Did they think she'd been smoking marijuana? He looked around the room. No one was watching the movie anymore. All of his students were waiting expectantly to see what he would do.

The wide rage of discipline problems that confront teachers in recent years is more than disheartening. Research studies show that one of the primary causes of the national teacher shortage is the concern that teachers have about classroom behavior problems. Part of the problem lies in the different types of behavior issues that teachers are supposed to manage successfully. A forgotten pencil can disrupt learning; so can students who openly resist even reasonable requests from their teachers.

The variety of behavior issues that you will have to handle in your classroom is not the only quandary you will have to resolve. Many factors outside of your classroom will have a negative effect on what you and your students want to accomplish each term.

Just a quick glance at cartoons produced for children and teens shows how negative much of what students view can be. Your students are barraged with thousands of messages that tell them that opposition to authority is admirable and that teachers are nerdy people who exist mainly to interfere in the fun that students could be having.

Another negative influence on the discipline climate in your classroom may be a surprising one for you as a beginning teacher. You will learn that not every parent will be supportive of the orderly environment that you want for your students. When you call home to talk over a problem only to find that parents are indifferent or unable to help, you can understand why some of your students have problems behaving well in your class.

Your school's climate may also contribute to some of your behavior problems. If students are permitted to misbehave in common areas such as the halls or the cafeteria, it won't be easy for you to impose order in your classroom. Further, in such a chaotic climate, administrators and other teachers may be too overwhelmed to offer the support you need to manage your class effectively.

A final aspect of the discipline dilemma that you will have to successfully manage is your inexperience and the ways in which it may contribute to the mix of issues that you will have to handle. For instance, one mistake many new teachers make is to be overly lenient at first to win their students' trust, but this only compounds the behavior problems in their classrooms and undermines their authority. When your own policies are ineffective, you will find it even more difficult to overcome the other negative influences on your students' attitudes toward authority and discipline.

Control Your Anxieties with Proactive Attitudes

Despite your anxiety, you should feel confident that you will soon learn how to handle all of your students' discipline problems! Handling discipline dilemmas is complicated, and it is understandable that you may feel anxious, because you may not be able to manage all of them successfully at first. Most teachers report that worries about discipline problems are especially serious for the first-year teacher, but as you gain experience and confidence in your ability to cope with the daily events in your classroom, your anxieties will lessen.

One way to help yourself control your anxieties as you learn how to control your class is to adopt proactive attitudes to guarantee that you are on the right track. The five attitudes in the box on page 371 will keep your confidence level high as your daily experiences will help you learn how to handle the behavior problems that you will have to confront.

5 Attitudes That Will Boost Your Confidence

1. **Put school rules and classroom rules to work.**

   - If you consistently enforce school and classroom rules, your students will soon stop testing their limits.

   - Because both sets of rules already have consequences attached, you will be able to act quickly and without having to agonize over the right course of action to take.

2. **Motivate and encourage students.**

   - Be generous with your praise and appreciation and you will establish a strong bond with your students that will help them stay on the right track.

   - When you motivate and encourage students, you improve their self-esteem, which, in turn, will eliminate many behaviors that will arise when students do not feel valued by their teacher or their classmates.

3. **Deliver meaningful and interesting lessons.**

   - Students who are busily engaged in meaningful and interesting work will not have time to misbehave.

   - When lessons are well planned, students will find it easier to be successful. Success breeds more success and that will eliminate many problems.

4. **Every day will add to your knowledge.**

   - As you become familiar to your colleagues, you will find that you will have a large supportive network of people who are willing to help you.

   - Each successful day will make it easier for your students to trust you and for you to learn more about them.

5. **Have confidence in yourself.**

   - You will find it easier to control your emotions as you see that you really can teach and that you really can maintain control of a group of students.

   - Keep in mind that the most important factor in every successful discipline plan is the teacher. You and no one else can control the discipline climate for your students.

Classroom Management Techniques to Avoid

Following are fifteen ineffective classroom management practices. Put a check in the box before any statement that might apply to your class during the past week. Then carefully consider how you can eliminate ineffective management practices from your classroom.

In the last week, I . . . :

☐ Allowed students to be rude to each other
☐ Failed to contact a parent or guardian when I needed to
☐ Singled out students for punishment
☐ Assigned punishment work
☐ Spoke negatively about a student in front of others
☐ Threatened a student
☐ Allowed students to sleep in class
☐ Raised my voice
☐ Called students names, mostly in fun
☐ Accepted bad behavior from one student and not from another
☐ Lost my temper
☐ Talked over inappropriate student noise
☐ Used negative body language, such as pointing at students
☐ Nagged students
☐ Allowed students to ignore me

Behaviors You Should Not Accept

Almost every teacher has a clear understanding of what the ideal classroom atmosphere should be. Well-disciplined classes share three important characteristics.

1. Students and teachers know and understand the rules and procedures that guide the entire class.

2. The focus is on learning and cooperative behavior is valued.

3. There is a persistent tone of mutual respect and even affection among the students and between students and their teacher.

When you and your students work toward the goal of a well-disciplined class, you should avoid behaviors that can destroy the fragile positive atmosphere that you've established. Here are ten behaviors that teachers and school districts across the nation have determined are not acceptable in any classroom.

1. **Threats and intimidation.** Students are not allowed to threaten or harass each other or you. This includes bullying, teasing, sexual harassment, and threats of physical harm.

2. **Substance abuse.** Almost every school now has a "zero tolerance" policy regarding illegal substances or over-the-counter medications at school. All medications should be administered by the school nurse or a designee—even medications such as cough drops are covered in most zero tolerance polices. It is against the law for students to have alcohol, tobacco, or illegal drugs on school property.

3. **Interference with others' right to learn.** No student has the right to stop other students from learning. This policy is the rationale behind school dress codes that prohibit students from distracting other students. It also covers students who are loud enough to interfere with the normal routines of the school day as well as many other seriously disruptive actions.

4. **Disrespect for authority.** This behavior includes the refusal to comply with a reasonable request from a teacher, administrator, or other staff member. It also includes various forms of defiance, both overt and subtle: talking back, rolling eyes, sighing, sneering, and other rude behavior directed at an authority figure.

5. **Failure to complete work.** Teachers should monitor student progress closely enough so that all parent or guardians are aware of the situation if a child refuses to complete work. Students are expected to do their schoolwork.

6. **Unsafe behavior.** This can range from running with scissors, horseplay, or running in the halls to ignoring safe driving rules in a secondary school student parking lot. It also includes students with matches or other fire starters at school, leaving the school grounds without permission, and using school equipment in an unsafe manner.

7. **Dishonesty.** Students should not forge notes from home, cheat on their work, commit plagiarism, or lie to teachers or another school official. Almost all incidents of dishonesty will require that teachers report the behavior to parents as well as administrators.

8. **Tardiness.** Students are expected to be at school and in class on time. Tardiness to class is not acceptable and is part of the attendance policy in many states.

9. **Truancy.** Almost every state requires that local school districts enforce very strict attendance policies. It is the responsibility of the classroom teacher to maintain accurate attendance records.

10. **Violence.** School districts in all states take violence very seriously. Students are not allowed to fight or to "boost" a fight by cheering on the combatants. Regulations against violence include weapons and look-alike weapons at school.

What Do Your Supervisors Expect from You?

It is not always easy to determine just how permissive or how strict you should be. Many teachers take a long time and make many mistakes as they attempt to figure out what their supervisors expect from them as they learn to manage their classes.

Although the expectations for student behavior will vary from school to school and from grade level to grade level, there are some discipline expectations that your supervisors are likely to expect. Follow these ten suggestions as you create a safe and productive discipline climate.

1. Prevent as many behavior problems as you can by working to contain or minimize disruptions.

2. Establish, teach, and enforce reasonable class rules, and have reasonable consequences to accompany them.

3. Teach and enforce school rules, even those with which you disagree.

4. Make student safety a priority and never allow any activity that could endanger your students.

5. Help your students stay focused on learning and on productive behavior instead of misbehavior.

6. Take charge of your class to create and maintain and orderly environment that supports learning.

7. Handle most of your own discipline problems, but refer a student to an administrator when your school's guidelines require it.

8. Although you are not expected to know every statute of school law, you are expected to know the basic laws that govern schools and especially students' rights and responsibilities.

9. Never surprise supervisors with long-term, serious behavior problems.

10. Maintain accurate behavior documentation. Your supervisors expect that you will have an up-to-date file on each of your students.

You May Be the Troublemaker

There are all kinds of mistakes that you can inadvertently make as a teacher: misjudge the time it will take your students to complete an assignment, fail to correctly assess their needs, misread their reactions, and a host of others. Sometimes the mistakes that you make will create discipline problems. The upside is that once you make a mistake and recognize that you have done so, you can take steps to correct it and avoid repeating it.

Here is a list of ten mistakes that many teachers have found not only easy to make, but a source of discipline problems, as well. Along with each mistake listed, you will also find suggestions for effective actions you can take.

Mistake 1: The punishment you assign for an offense is inappropriate.

Example: Students receive only a warning for getting into a loud argument in front of the rest of the class.

Suggestion: Because this is a serious offense that could escalate into a more serious altercation, students should be removed from the class and an administrator notified. When you create your class rules, make sure that the consequences match the seriousness of the offense.

Mistake 2: You accuse the wrong student of misbehavior.

Example: While you are absent from school, the substitute teacher reports that one child has taken your teacher's edition. When you return, you see that student trying to put the book on your desk. You make an accusation only to find out from the rest of the class that the student had taken it away from the thief and was trying to return it.

Suggestion: Always determine guilt and innocence before you act. It will take you longer, but the time you spend will save you days of hurt feelings from the falsely accused students. When a substitute teacher leaves a negative note about your class, ask your students to write you an account of the event before you act. Finally, when you incorrectly accuse a student in front of the class, always apologize in front of the class.

Mistake 3: You are too permissive, too tentative, too easily sidetracked.

Example: You want your students to have ownership in the class and allow them to set the class rules in a democratic fashion. Now your class is disrupted by students who are not only breaking the class rules, but who are also not cooperative.

Suggestion: Take the time to think through what you want from your students academically and behaviorally. Force yourself to act in a decisive and take-charge manner when you are with your students. You are the adult in the room. When you allow your students a voice in class decisions, control their options. Never agree to rules or consequences that make you uncomfortable.

Mistake 4: You are unclear in the limits that you set for your students, resulting in constant testing of the boundaries and of your patience.

Example: You have allowed some mild swearing in your class by pretending that you did not hear it. Now students are not just swearing now and then, but using more offensive language.

Suggestion: Be very specific when you set the limits for acceptable and unacceptable behavior for your students. Don't ignore behavior that makes you or your other students uncomfortable. Always directly address any student who swears around you. Make sure that the student knows that swearing is not only inappropriate, but disrespectful, as well.

Mistake 5: You overreact to a discipline problem by becoming upset.

Example: Several students did not complete the work that you assigned for homework. When you asked them about it, they told you that they had a major project for another class due at the same time and couldn't get to your work. You became so angry that you not only shouted at the entire class, but you gave twice as much homework to make up for the time that they did not spend on the previous assignment.

Suggestion: Instead of wasting time in anger, take a problem-solving approach to prevent it from happening again. Raising your voice and assigning punishment work will not change the situation. Instead, talk with your students about the importance of communicating with you about their conflicting due dates well in advance of when they are to turn the work in.

Mistake 6: You give too many negative directions, setting an unpleasant tone for your students.

Example: You frequently find yourself telling your students *not* to do something: stop tapping on the desk, stop wasting time, stop daydreaming. . . .

Suggestion: Your students will tune out too many negative remarks—the opposite of what you intend with an emphatic negative command. Instead, make an effort to replace the negatives with positives whenever you can. Instead of a grouchy command to "Stop playing around this instant," replace it with "Get started on your assignment now." Your students will respond more quickly to the positive tone.

Mistake 7: You don't take the time to listen to your students when they are trying to express their feelings about a problem.

Example: Your students are upset over a test question they find unfair. When they try to talk to you, the situation deteriorates until you tell them that you don't want to hear more complaints.

Suggestion: Not allowing students to discuss their feelings is a serious mistake that will only worsen a situation as students grow more frustrated. Encourage students to express their concerns in an appropriate manner and give them chances to do this. When a large group is upset about an issue, you will save time by asking them to write you notes about the problem. You can read the notes later and think about how to respond before you face them again.

Mistake 8: Your lessons are not very interesting and are poorly paced. You find that your students are off task many times.

Example: Many students have finished an assignment and are talking and giggling while the rest of the students try complete the assignment.

Suggestion: Keep your students' attention span at a peak by thinking of your class in fifteen-minute blocks and design activities that can be completed in that amount of time. Your students can be active and not passive learners no matter what the curriculum. Find ways to take a new slant on the material and make it interesting for your students.

Mistake 9: You are inconsistent in enforcing consequences.

Example: You are usually very strict about making students meet their deadlines for projects. However, you decide to let a star athlete have an extra day when his mother writes a note complaining that he didn't have enough time to do the work. Your other students are quick to notice this and complain that it isn't fair. Some of them don't turn in their work on time either.

Suggestion: Make sure that the consequences for breaking a rule are ones that you are comfortable enforcing so that you can be consistent. Make sure that all students know that you intend to be consistent with rules and deadlines.

Mistake 10: You punish one student while overlooking another student's more serious offense.

Example: You reprimand one student for leaving a book bag in the aisle during a test while failing to notice that several other students are cheating on the test.

Suggestion: Take care to assess a situation before you act. Be alert to all that your students do, and be consistent in how you handle misbehavior. The consequences for a misbehavior should be consistently applied to students, and should be in proportion to the misbehavior.

> *"Smile; don't tease. Be serious; don't humiliate. Model; don't imitate."*
>
> —Barbara Knowles, 36 years experience

Why Are Your Students Misbehaving?

Whenever you have to deal with a discipline problem, make absolutely sure before you act that you understand the reason for the behavior that you observe. When you do, several beneficial things will happen.

- Your students will feel less frustration because you allow them to talk about their feelings.
- You will gain an understanding of what caused the problem.
- If there are other causes than what you first noticed, you can act on them.
- You will gain insight into how your students think, feel, and react.
- You and your students have a common ground to discuss other, preferable, choices that they can make in the future.
- You increase the likelihood that you will have prevented this problem from happening again.
- Your bond with your students will be stronger because, even if you enforce unpopular consequences, you have shown them the courtesy of listening and caring about what they had to say.

There are many ways to determine why your students act the way they do. You can be indirect in your approach. Talk to teachers who have taught your students in the past or to parents or guardians. Both can be useful sources of insightful information. You can also check permanent records to find out more about your students' past, home situation, and ability.

Another approach to handling a behavior problem is to interact directly with the student in private. One way that works well with older students is to first have them write out their view of what caused the behavior. When you discuss it with them, you can refer to what they have described to you in writing. Follow these guidelines to make this conversation successful.

- Begin by telling them that you would like to hear their side of the story.
- Listen sincerely and suspend any judgments.
- Keep probing and talking until students have shared what they need to say.
- Make sure that you understand what caused the misbehavior.
- Make it clear that you insist on a mutually respectful relationship.
- Do not rush to punish. Instead, tell a student who has misbehaved that you need to think about what you have learned and you will make a decision overnight.

15 Common Reasons for Student Misbehavior

If you make the effort to determine why your students act the way that they do, you will find that you will benefit by having a clearer understanding of some of the times when your students are going to have trouble staying on task.

Here are some common reasons why students misbehave.

1. They are excited or upset about an upcoming event or holiday.
2. They are having a conflict with a peer.
3. They want your attention.
4. They want the attention of their peers.
5. They finish their work early and want to amuse themselves.
6. Their work is too hard or too easy.
7. They are distracted by something or someone near them.
8. They are worried about something not related to your class.
9. They are upset by something that happened at home.
10. They don't know the procedures or rules.
11. They are embarrassed.
12. They lack the confidence to try for success.
13. They don't feel well.
14. They are exhausted from staying up too late.
15. They are tired of being told what to do.

Take a Problem-Solving Approach

"I warned you never to do that again. Go to the office!" You can probably recall hearing teachers giving angry orders such as this one from your own days as a student. It can happen when teachers lose control of their emotions and react without thinking.

The result of losing your self-control is that you and the child at whom you are directing your anger are both flooded with negative emotions. Even if the situation doesn't escalate into a more serious confrontation, your relationship with that student will still be severely impaired.

Losing control of your emotions and relying only on punishment to effect a change in your students' behavior will not solve discipline problems. *What will stop students from misbehaving is a teacher who takes the approach that misbehavior is a problem with a solution.*

The first step in adopting a problem-solving approach to misbehavior requires that you develop a proactive attitude: refuse to take student misbehavior personally even though you may be hurt, frustrated, and angry. Mentally take a step back and force yourself to become calm if you are upset. Refusing to give in to your first emotional reaction will de-escalate the situation to a more manageable level. You must do this before initiating the action that you want to take.

After you have forced yourself to calm down and control your reactions, you can then complete the rest of the problem-solving process. The following steps will not just help you solve problems, but will prevent further problems.

- Gather information about what happened.
- Define the problem.
- Gather information about the causes from the students who misbehaved.
- Check to make sure that your students understand rules and consequences.
- Tell your students that you will need to take some time to make a decision.
- Ask an administrator or a colleague for advice if you are not sure of the right course of action to take.
- Generate as many solutions as you can.
- Decide on the action that will help students not repeat their misbehavior.
- Decide how you will implement the solution.

Who Can Help?

Not even veteran teachers can single-handedly solve every behavior problem that disrupts their classes during the course of a school year. As a first-year teacher, you are not expected to, either. There is a support network of other adults who can offer you insight and advice when your students misbehave. Turn to them for help. Too often, teachers will not take advantage of this support until a problem is serious enough for an administrator to intervene to assign punishment.

Who can you turn to for help? Before you send a student to an administrator for punishment, try asking these people for their insight.

- Parents and guardians
- Guidance counselors
- The child's other current teachers
- The child's past teachers
- Your mentor
- Assistant principals
- Coaches
- Sponsors of organizations the child may belong to
- Adult friends at school that the child may have
- Special personnel such as social workers or the school nurse

Act Decisively

There are many constructive ways to handle misbehavior that happens in your classroom. Here is a list of some of the most common strategies that other teachers have found to be effective in solving discipline problems, along with explanations of when these strategies might be effective. No matter which approach you choose, you must always act decisively and avoid giving students the impression that you are tenuous about the action you should take to manage bad behavior.

- **Consciously choose to ignore the misbehavior.** First consider the reasons for the behavior and make a choice to accept the behavior as something you can tolerate. Then, anticipate the effects of ignoring the behavior before you choose this technique. Use it when the misbehavior is fleeting and if no other students are affected, such as in the case of briefly daydreaming, getting off to a slow start on an assignment, or tapping a pencil.

- **Delay taking action.** Delay acting when the action that you would take could cause further disruption. For example, if a student is taking a quiz in pencil and the correct procedure is to use a pen, you should delay acting if the student's concentration would be disturbed or if the search for a pen would disrupt other students. Talk to the student about the problem after the quiz is over.

- **Use non-verbal actions.** Moving closer to a student and making eye contact are just two of the non-intrusive interventions that you can use when the behavior is confined to one or two students or when such signals have been agreed upon in advance.

- **Give a gentle reprimand.** Often this will be the only action that you will need to do to end trouble. Move close to the student, and address him or her in a friendly, but businesslike, and firm manner. Word the reprimand in a positive way if possible. Don't allow the student to argue with you or engage your attention further.

▶ **Confer briefly with a student.** Use a brief conference to remind students to stay on task, remind them of a rule, discuss consequences, encourage positive actions, and at other times when you think that a short interaction with a student will solve the problem.

▶ **Move a student's seat.** If you decide to do this, be as discreet as possible by moving several students at the same time or by warning students at the end of class that they will have new seats when class meets again. Use this technique when students are distracted by their immediate environment or by other students.

▶ **Arrange for a time-out room with another teacher.** Arrange this in advance so that at any time you need to send a student to time-out, you can do so with minimum disruption. This technique works well with students who are normally well behaved, but who are upset and need to spend a few minutes out of your classroom to cool off. Be sure that students you send to time out have the materials that they need to complete their class assignment.

▶ **Hold a longer conference with a student.** Schedule this type of conference when there are several issues to be resolved or when the misbehavior is serious. The emphasis should be on determining the causes of the misbehavior and the solution to the problem.

▶ **Have students sign a behavior contract.** When you confer with students, you can formalize the solution to the problem with a behavior contract. Use it to help students acknowledge their behavior and the steps that they must take to correct it.

▶ **Contact a parent or guardian.** If you are having problems helping students control behavior, ask the other adults in their lives to reinforce your efforts. Too often teachers hesitate to do this or wait until misbehavior is serious. Early intervention with a request for help is always a good idea.

▶ **Hold students in a detention.** This is a good time to hold longer conferences with students who need to resolve their behavior problems. Use detention time to create a stronger relationship with a student and work together instead of just as a punishment.

▶ **Arrange a conference with parents or guardians.** If you have tried several interventions for students who persist in misbehavior, including phoning the parents or guardians, and had no success, then you should schedule a parent conference.

▶ **Refer a student to an administrator.** You have to make this choice when you have exhausted all other possibilities or when the misbehavior is serious.

© 2002 by John Wiley & Sons, Inc.

Figure 13.1

HOW TO DETERMINE IF A DISCIPLINE ACTION IS APPROPRIATE

Use this checklist to determine if an action you are considering taking to deal with misbehavior is appropriate and will produce the results you want. You should be able to answer "yes" to all of these questions.

_____ Is the action I want to take consistent with school policy and with my classroom rules?

_____ Can my students anticipate that this will be a consequence of their actions?

_____ Is the action related to the offense?

_____ Is the action fair?

_____ Will my students think that it is fair?

_____ Is the action aimed at preventing future misbehavior?

_____ Have I sought support from other adults?

_____ Does the action address the underlying reasons for the misbehavior?

_____ Is this action a long-term solution to the problem?

Don't Give Up on Your Difficult Students

Of all of the students you will ever teach, the difficult ones are the ones who need you most, because often too many other people have given up on them. All of your students, even your difficult ones, need to be confident of the following facts.

- That you care about them and believe in them
- That it is the misbehavior you don't like, not the student
- That you will never give up on them

Keep in mind that the chief characteristic of children is that they change and grow. Even high school seniors will change dramatically between the first day of school and graduation day. Your chief purpose as an educator is to direct that change and growth so that your students can have productive and peaceful lives.

Experienced teachers have already had the opportunity to observe this change in their students. They have seen kindergartners make the shift from nervous newcomers to confident and eager learners, and awkward teens develop social skills just in time for the prom. Experienced teachers know that the students in their classes after winter break will be very different from the students who entered class on the first day of school.

During your first year as a teacher, you will be able to observe the changes in your students for yourself. Be patient. Even though you know that they will change and grow over the course of the year, it can sometimes be almost impossible to maintain your faith in some of your difficult students. When you find your faith in your difficult students beginning to waver, you must resolve to give them every opportunity to grow and overcome their difficulties.

> *"You need to do what you can to defuse that 'teacher versus student' mentality."*
>
> —Ken Pfeifer, 27 years experience

Dealing with a Difficult Class

Teaching a difficult class can a debilitating experience. This kind of class can turn your determination to help all students succeed into a desire to just make it through one more school day. Fortunately, there are many strategies that you can use to turn a classroom full of smart-alecky, unmanageable, or all-around indifferent students into a class that you enjoy.

What causes a class to be difficult? The reasons are many and varied, and can include any of the following.

- Peer conflicts keep students from paying attention to their work.
- Students may lack goals.

- There may be an unequal distribution in the ability levels of students, causing frustration.

- A negative label given in previous year becomes a self-fulfilling prophecy.

- There may be an unpleasant chemistry between teacher and students.

- There may be an unpleasant chemistry among students.

- The classroom may be too small to comfortably fit all students.

Perhaps the most serious reason that classes can be difficult lies in the way that students regard themselves and their ability to succeed academically. Students who do not believe that they can succeed have no reason to try. Successful teachers with difficult classes have found that they can turn the negative energy in the class into a positive force through persistently communicating their faith in their students' ability to achieve.

While there are many approaches you can take, the strategies listed here can help you turn a difficult class into a successful one.

10 WAYS TO TAKE CHARGE OF THE CLASS

1. From the first class meeting onward, establish that you control the class. Demonstrate that you will regulate the behavior in your classroom for the good of all students.

2. Be prepared. Staying organized is essential when you have a potentially unruly class.

3. Keep the expectations for your class high. Children live up to the expectations of the adults in their lives, so let them know that you expect a lot of them.

4. Smile at your class. If you were videotaped while teaching them, would your body language reveal positive or negative feelings about your students?

5. Call parents or guardians as soon as you can when a problem arises.

6. Work on the noise level every day until your students learn to govern themselves. Teach students which volumes are acceptable and which are not. Establish signals to help students learn to control the noise.

7. Plan activities around your students' short attention spans. Make sure that these activities offer plenty of time for practice and review.

8. Never allow time for students to sit doing nothing but disturbing others. Keep them busy all class period.

9. Stay on your feet and monitor. Students who know that you are watching over them will hesitate before misbehaving.

10. Be clear that you expect your students to do their work well and that you will help them learn to do it.

10 WAYS TO MOTIVATE YOUR STUDENTS TO SUCCEED

1. Have students set goals for themselves at the start of the term and remind them to work towards those goals from then on. This will motivate them to keep trying when the work is difficult.

2. Consider giving them a limited choice of options in how they accomplish their assignments. They will regard this as a sign of your trust.

3. Use non-print media to catch attention. Art and music are just two of the ways that you can manage difficult students more easily.

4. Make sure the work you assign is relevant and meaningful to your students. They will be more eager to get started when they can see a reason for doing the work.

5. Make sure the work you assign is appropriate for your students' ability level.

6. Teach your students study skills and time management so that they can work efficiently and quickly.

7. Consider alternative methods of assessment for your students. For example, giving them frequent short tests and quizzes may make it easier for them to measure their success.

8. Provide a safety net of rules and procedures, but spice up your lessons so your students will find them interesting.

9. Include games in the work that you assign. Games are successful learning tools because they offer variety and activity.

10. Offer incentives other than grades. Students who have never made a good grade may not be motivated by grades. Offer small, frequent, tangible rewards instead, such as stickers, treats, or bookmarks.

10 WAYS TO FOSTER AN ATMOSPHERE OF MUTUAL RESPECT AND COOPERATION

1. Teach your students how to show respect to you and to each other. Stress tolerance of each other's differences as a way to show respect.

2. Model the courtesy you want to see from your students.

3. Praise good behavior as often as you can. Difficult students do not always know when they behave well. If you praise the class for good behavior, you encourage them all to repeat the behavior.

4. Take time to teach and reteach the rules and procedures you want your students to follow.

5. Help your students learn positive things about each other. It will be easier for them to trust and respect each other.

6. Be as specific as you can when telling difficult students what you want them to do.

7. Give them opportunities to help each other. Students who share their knowledge with a classmate will be so busy being productive that they will not have time to disrupt class.

8. Acknowledge the right of individuals in your class. Showing students that you are fair will ease many sensitive situations.

9. Don't threaten. Students should take what you say seriously, but they should not be frightened into compliance.

10. Create a businesslike atmosphere in your class. Get off to a good start and make it evident that doing well is a priority in your class.

The Importance of a Positive Class Identity

Each of your classes will develop its own identity. Some of your classes will pride themselves on being intelligent, others on being creative, and still others on various attributes such as being very talkative or causing a previous teacher to cry or quit. While some parts of this class identity arise naturally, most will come from what teachers tell students about themselves.

The strength of this class identity can be an important factor in what makes a class of gifted students excel even more and a class of slow learners find school overwhelming. If you look back on your own school days, you can probably recall teachers who gave a group you were in a class identity. If you were lucky, you were in a group with an identity that reflected positively on how you thought of yourself.

*"If you have a tough day and spend more time on discipline rather than academics, instead of getting angry, reevaluate your class management.
Go to class the next day determined to recognize only the good behavior."*

—Kim Marie Hogan,
9 years experience

This effect is called synergy. Synergy happens when the whole is greater than its parts. Our nation is founded on this principle. Schools where all teachers follow and enforce the same school rules are strong because of their synergy. And when a group of students has a positive self-image, the synergy can lead students to exceed their original expectations of themselves.

Often a difficult class will come to you with a negative self-image and negative synergy. Sometimes you will find that they have been dragging this negativity around for years. If you can eliminate the negative image and give this class a positive self-image, then you will all reap the rewards of a positive synergy. But this is no easy task. What you must do is make a conscious effort to praise and reinforce their positive group attributes. By doing this, you will promote the group's desirable behaviors and extinguish their negative ones.

Even difficult classes have positive attributes. If a group is very talkative, for example, then you can put a positive twist on this and praise them for their sociability. Further, focus on students' strengths, rather on what they do poorly. For example, because difficult classes often will settle down when handed worksheets that require that they write, you can praise them for their mature efforts to do their work.

To create a positive class synergy, you must find and reinforce the positive attributes of a class. Here's how.

- If you learn that the class has a negative image, let the students know that you disagree with it.

- Observe two things about your class: the way the students interact with each other and with you, and the way that they do their work. Find at least one positive attribute that you can reinforce.

- Begin praising that positive attribute as often as you can. In a few days, you will notice that your students will accept it as truth and will bring it up themselves.

- After your students have accepted that positive class attribute, continue to look for other positive attributes to promote.

- When you notice other positive traits, select one to reinforce and begin the process again. After a few weeks of patient effort, you will have succeeded in giving your class a positive self-image.

Successful Student Conferences

Student conferences can be powerful tools for teachers who want to create a positive discipline climate. There are many times when you will need to confer with your students. You may want to help them work on projects or offer extra assistance after school. You could even offer help when students are working together in a study group.

Student conferences can also be very useful in establishing a positive working environment with a student who has misbehaved. When the two of you can sit down together without the distraction of the rest of the class and work out a solution to the problems that you have been experiencing, you will both benefit.

While holding a successful conference with a student who has misbehaved is not difficult, there are strategies that you can use to guarantee success. The following strategies will be useful when you want to make it clear that you have given much thought to the student's concerns and the ways that the two of you can work together to resolve any problems.

BEFORE THE CONFERENCE:

- Notify the parents or guardians of any students that you intend to keep after school at least twenty-four hours in advance.

- Arrange a time for the conference that is agreeable to you both. Younger students will have to consult their parents for rides home. Be as cooperative about the time as you can.

- Arrange a place to meet that is as free from distractions as possible. Do not confer with students while other students are in the room.

DURING THE CONFERENCE:

▶ Be courteous in your greeting. This will set the tone for the rest of the meeting.

▶ Make the area as comfortable as possible. Offer pen and paper for taking notes and sit side-by-side in student desks or at a table. Do not sit behind your desk.

▶ To protect yourself from charges of misconduct, when you are meeting one-on-one with a student, sit near the door to the room, and make sure that the door is open. If you believe that a conference will be uncomfortable, arrange for a colleague to be in the same room with you and your student.

▶ Be very careful to not touch the student for any reason during a conference. When emotions are heightened, even an innocent pat on the back can be misinterpreted.

▶ Begin the meeting by stating that the purpose of the conference is to work together in order to resolve a problem between the two of you. Avoid rehashing the unpleasant details, name calling, blaming the student, or showing your anger.

▶ Take the initiative by asking the student to tell you why you are meeting. Make sure that you both have a chance to state the problem as you see it. Listen to the student without interrupting. Take notes. Use positive body language to encourage the student to speak.

▶ When you discuss the student's behavior, focus on the misdeed itself and not on your student's negative personality traits.

▶ After the student has spoken, restate the problem in your own words. Make sure that you understand the problem and express your sincere interest in solving it.

▶ Be positive but firm in conveying that it is the student's responsibility to change.

▶ You and your student should brainstorm some solutions. Ask questions such as, How could you handle the situation better? or What could you do instead?

▶ Agree on a plan that satisfies both of you. Make sure that it is simple enough to carry out and that you are comfortable implementing it.

▶ Calmly explain the negative consequences that you will impose if the student fails to carry out his or her part of the plan.

▶ Once again state that you are willing to offer help.

AT THE END OF THE CONFERENCE:

▶ Ask the student if there is anything else that needs to be said. Offer your willingness to listen again.

▶ Be very clear that, now that a resolution has been reached, you will put past misbehaviors behind you and will not hold a grudge.

▶ Thank your student for taking the time for a conference and for deciding to work together. Express your belief that better days lie ahead for both of you.

Behavior Contracts

Whether it's promoting positive behaviors or eliminating negative ones, behavior contracts are one of the most effective tools you have at your disposal. Although there are other types of contracts for various classroom purposes such as daily responsibilities, group contracts, or assignments, behavior contracts are designed to help solve behavior problems.

The types of misbehavior that can be solved most easily by a behavior contract are discipline problems caused by a student's bad habits: not doing homework, talking back, making rude remarks to peers, not cleaning a work area, and many others. They should not be used with students who commit serious misbehaviors or who only misbehave occasionally.

Behavior contracts are effective because they clarify the problem and its solution for teachers and students, and because they help both teacher and student avoid negative emotions and focus on steps to improve a misbehavior. Here's how to use behavior contracts successfully in your class.

- ▶ Find a quiet time and place to talk with your student about setting up a behavior contract. An after-school conference is ideal.

- ▶ Begin with contracts that have very specific goals that can be achieved in a short length of time. Use small, easily achievable steps to encourage success.

- ▶ Start with tangible rewards rather than intrinsic ones so that the child can immediately see the results of improved behavior.

- ▶ Check to make sure the student has a clear understanding of the problem and the solutions to which you both agree. State this agreement explicitly in the contract.

- ▶ Although you may adopt a contact format to meet the needs of your students, you should consider including these items:

  - Name of the student
  - Name of the teacher
  - Beginning and ending dates
  - A statement of the problem
  - Dates when progress will be checked
  - Specific actions to be performed
  - Rewards
  - Consequences
  - Signatures

See Figure 13.2 for a sample behavior contract.

You can also enter into a contract with a parent and a child when the need arises. This is particularly effective in solving homework problems. If a parent is actively involved in the solution to a problem, everyone wins when that parent is involved in creating the contract.

Figure 13.2
Sample Behavior Contract

Contract between _____ and _____
                                Student   Teacher

Date _____

Problem to be resolved: _____

_____

The student agrees to: _____

_____

The teacher agrees to: _____

_____

Dates for checking progress:_____

Rewards:_____

Consequences: _____

The student's efforts to solve this problem will be considered complete when

_____

_____

Student Signature_____

Teacher Signature_____

Put Detentions to Good Use

If your school district allows you to detain students after school, you can use this time productively if you make sure that the purpose of a detention is not to punish, but to resolve problems that the detained students are having in your class. If your goal is to permanently change students' negative behaviors into positive ones, then you should plan detention activities that will help you reach that goal.

Although there are many approaches that you can take when detaining students, the following suggestions will help you make the process easy to manage and effective in preventing future misbehaviors.

"Teach and practice procedures with students so that they know the routines to follow. Take the opportunity to review the steps to any routine when necessary. Students are only human and they forget, too!"

—R.K. Gach, 3 years experience

BEFORE YOU ISSUE A DETENTION NOTICE:

 Take time to learn what your district's policy on student detentions entails.

 Make sure that you have plenty of forms on hand so that you will be able to hand students the notice as they leave class.

 Before you write out a notice, try to prevent the misbehavior. Privately warn students of the rules they may be breaking and of the consequences. No student should be surprised when you issue a detention for misbehavior.

 If your district allows you to and it's convenient for you, consider holding morning detentions.

 Decide what you are going to do if the child refuses to serve a detention. Know your district's policy on how to handle this issue before you have to address it.

ISSUE THE DETENTION NOTICE:

 When you must issue a detention notice, do not write the notice when you are upset or in a hurry. You will appear less than professional.

 When you do write the notice, use a dark pen and write neatly. Make sure that you spell the student's name correctly as well as the names of his or her parents or guardians.

 Be very specific when you write the notice so that the student and the parents or guardians know what has happened to cause the notice. If you use a detention for a third tardy to your class, for example, be sure to state that the student has been tardy two previous times and give the dates and consequences you may have assigned for the previous tardies.

⬧ Be very clear with your students that their parents or guardians must sign the notice before you can allow them to stay. You should never cause a parent or guardian to worry because the child was late coming home from school.

⬧ Because students may take detentions lightly and parents or guardians do not, call home to let parents know that you have issued a detention notice to their child. Alert them that their child will be getting home late and ask for their cooperation in helping the child serve the detention.

⬧ Issue the detention quietly, matter-of-factly, and at the very end of class to avoid embarrassing students or to avoid a scene with an angry student.

⬧ When you issue a detention notice, ask the student to sign a brief statement that he or she has received the notice. Be sure to date it and keep it in your records.

⬧ If a student crumples or tears the notice, continue to be very calm. If the student does not come back for the note and apologize before the end of the school day, contact the parents or guardians by phone at once. You should also lengthen the time of the detention by a few minutes because you will need to discuss this issue with the student.

⬧ Never issue detention notices to a large group of students at the same time. You will appear to have lost control of your class.

⬧ Plan what you want to accomplish with a detained student and how you are going to reach that goal.

DURING THE DETENTION:

⬧ Be careful to protect yourself from being accused of misconduct by keeping the door open at all times when you detain a student. Do not touch the student at all.

⬧ Establish a very businesslike atmosphere. Refuse to tolerate an inappropriate behavior.

⬧ If you have more than one student staying for a detention, do not allow them to sit near each other or to be playful.

⬧ Talk with your students about the problem and how it should be resolved. Have them write out their thoughts before they try to talk with you about the problem. Such writing is not busy work, but a tool to open a helpful dialogue. Try using questions such as these to get your students thinking about why they have been detained and what changes they can make to prevent the problem from happening again.

• What other choices can I make rather than the ones I did?

• What are some appropriate behaviors that I have used in this class in the past?

• What are the reasons that I should change my behavior?

• How can I improve my approach to my work, my classmates, and my teacher?

• What are my goals for this class and how can I achieve them?

AFTER THE DETENTION:

⇨ Make notes about what happened during the detention. Keep a record of the conference and a copy of your students' writing.

⇨ Do not give students a ride home. If a parent or guardian has signed the notice, then transportation is not your responsibility.

⇨ Do not leave a child alone in an empty school. Wait with the student until his or her ride appears.

⇨ Make it clear to any student that you detain that you have high hopes for future behavior improvements and that you will not hold a grudge about past misbehavior.

Referrals to an Administrator

If the discipline process is to be a meaningful one, there must be some recourse for teachers who need assistance with students who are making learning impossible for themselves and others. Usually, this recourse will take the form of an administrative referral.

Referring students to an administrator during your first year as a teacher is, at best, a nerve-wracking experience. The referral process will be much easier for everyone involved when you follow the suggested answers to the questions below.

WHEN SHOULD YOU SEND A STUDENT TO AN ADMINISTRATOR?

There is no question that you should refer a student to an administrator for any of these behaviors.

- Persistent defiance
- Bullying
- Stealing
- Sexual harassment
- Vandalism
- Deliberate profanity
- Bringing weapons to school

- Substance abuse
- Making threats
- Violent behavior
- Truancy
- Cheating
- Persistent disruptions
- Habitual tardiness

HOW CAN YOU MAINTAIN YOUR CREDIBILITY WITH STUDENTS, PARENTS, AND ADMINISTRATORS?

A referral to the office is a serious step to take in the discipline process and should not be taken lightly by anyone involved. To safeguard your credibility, you should follow these five guidelines.

1. Don't send students to the office for minor misbehaviors that you are expected to handle successfully, such as:

- Not doing homework
- Scribbling on desks
- Rude comments
- Infrequent tardiness
- Not working in class

- Non-violent peer conflicts
- Excessive talking
- Chewing gum or eating candy
- Poor work habits
- Inattention

2. Unless a misbehavior is sudden, such as a fight where students have to be removed from the room, administrators should not be surprised to receive a referral from you. When you begin to notice a pattern of misbehavior, make an appointment with an administrator to discuss the problem and to ask for help. When you finally refer a student, the administrator will have a clear understanding of what has happened and what you have done to try to resolve the conflict. By giving administrators this background information, you not only make it easier for them to make the best decisions about how to handle problems, but you also present yourself as a competent educator who can handle most of your problems.

3. When you write a referral make sure that the language you use is as professional and objective as possible. Because many different people will read a referral, including the student and his or her parents, choose language that is behavior-oriented and factual.

4. Call the student's parents or guardians before the end of the day to inform them of the incident and of the referral.

5. Between the time you turn in a referral and the time that an administrator acts on it, speak to the administrator to discuss the problem and to add any details you didn't want to write on the referral form.

HOW CAN YOU AVOID MAKING THE DISRUPTION WORSE WHEN YOU REFER A STUDENT?

- Make sure you have copies of the referral forms on hand so that you will be able to write it quickly and with a minimum of distractions.

- Maintain a student's dignity and privacy in front of classmates. Do not tell the student in front of the other students that you intend to write a referral. Be discreet. This will also help you avoid the possibility of an angry outburst disturbing the other students.

- Remain calm and remind the student of the rules and consequences. Don't threaten or bully a student even if you are angry.

- Students should not be surprised that they are being referred to an administrator for persistent misbehavior. By the time a student needs to be referred to an administrator, you should have intervened several times. If they know the consequences of their actions in advance of taking the actions, they will not be surprised by a referral.

WHAT SHOULD YOU DO IF YOU DISAGREE WITH THE ACTION THAT AN ADMINISTRATOR HAS TAKEN?

If you have been working together with an administrator to prevent the student's misbehavior and to avoid writing a referral, you should know the action that the administrator intends to take when you refer the student. If the administrator's action is different from what you had discussed or not one that you are comfortable with, speak with him or her to find out the reason for the decision. Resist the temptation to publicly criticize the decision.

HOW CAN YOU PREVENT THE MISBEHAVIOR FROM HAPPENING AGAIN?

▶ Learn from your mistakes. Examine the actions that led to the final referral. Determine what other interventions you could have taken early in your relationship with this child to prevent the misbehavior from reaching this final point.

▶ Help students leave the behavior and the referral behind. Make students aware that you view referrals as closure to misbehavior and do not expect further problems.

▶ Continue to use a variety of early interventions to prevent misbehaviors from reaching the referral point.

> *"It has been my experience that most of the teachers who have discipline trouble bring about 90 percent of that trouble on themselves."*
>
> —Ken Pfeifer, 28 years experience

25 Discipline Don'ts

1. Don't waste time trying to prove that you are right and your students are wrong. Instead, work together with your students to solve problems.

2. Don't let a situation strip you of your objectivity or cause you to lose your temper.

3. Don't take student misbehavior personally. Distance yourself emotionally from student misdeeds and remain objective.

4. Don't create problems by tempting your students. Don't leave valuables lying around, don't leave the room unsupervised, and don't allow students opportunities to cheat because you are not monitoring.

5. Don't confront a student in front of the class. Not only will this create a disruption that will upset everyone who watches, but the misbehaving student may act even worse to avoid more embarrassment. Talk to misbehaving students privately whenever you can.

6. Don't force a student to apologize. This will only humiliate the student and is not likely to result in a sincere apology.

7. Don't subtract points from a student's grade because of misbehavior. A grade reflects a student's academic progress, not his or her behavior.

8. Don't touch an angry student. Your innocent touch can be misconstrued.

9. Don't neglect to intervene when a problem is small enough to be handled simply.

10. Don't label students negatively. Their behavior may be bad, but they are not bad people.

11. Don't be too quick to send a student to an administrator. Handle your own problems as often as you can.

12. Don't jump straight to a referral for a pattern of small offenses. Establish a management plan where consequences build in severity as misbehavior continues.

13. Don't assign double negative consequences. Not allowing a student to join classmates at recess and also assigning a detention is an example of a double negative consequence.

14. Don't remain angry at students who have misbehaved. Knowing that you are still angry will not encourage students to behave better after they have made mistakes.

15. Don't reward students for improper behavior. Allowing students to make fun of each other or just rolling your eyes as they do are two ways that you reward improper behavior.

16. Don't attempt to threaten or bully your students into behaving well. It won't work.

17. Don't just tell them to stop; tell them what they must do to be successful.

18. Don't hide a serious problem such as cheating in an attempt to help the student. Involve other concerned adults and follow your school's policy.

19. Don't punish in anger. Calm down and think before you act.

20. Don't assign academic work as punishment. The consequence should match the misbehavior.

21. Don't punish a group of students for the behavior of some.

22. Don't be confrontational. Take a problem-solving approach instead.

23. Don't order an angry student to comply with your demands.

24. Don't bargain with your students to coax them to behave better. Enforce your rules instead.

25. Don't be inconsistent.

Journal Entries to Help You Handle Behavior Problems

▶ What emotions surface in your students and in yourself when students misbehave? How can you cope successfully with these emotions?

▶ What are the lessons that you can learn from student misbehavior? How can you turn a discipline situation into a learning opportunity for yourself and for your students?

▶ What would you do if two students began fighting in your class? How would you stop them? How would you minimize the negative effect on other students?

▶ Look back to the days when you were in the same grade that you teach now. What kinds of misbehavior were common to both school experiences? What kinds are different? Why do you think these similarities and differences exist?

▶ What are the most frequent behavior problems that you have to handle? What strategies do you use? Evaluate the success of those strategies.

▶ Are you ever the troublemaker in your class? How? What can you do to avoid this in the future?

▶ Look at a referral from the point of view of a student and of an administrator. How are their viewpoints similar to yours and how are they different?

▶ What is your greatest skill in handling students with discipline problems?

▶ What are some traits that teachers whose students misbehave frequently share? Do you share any of these traits?

▶ Think of a behavior problem in your class. What are the underlying reasons for the behavior? What did you do well about how you handled the problem? What did you learn about how to handle future problems?

Solutions for Some Widespread Problems

She really had too much to do to just sit and watch someone else teach, but her new principal had insisted that all of the first-year teachers spend time visiting other classrooms and observing other teachers during at least part of their plan periods.

As she settled impatiently into the student desk at the back of the room, she recognized several of her own students. She immediately noticed how differently these students acted for this teacher. They were so quiet, even the ones who were troublemakers in her own classes. Her classes were all noisy ones. Sometimes her students even ignored her until she got angry enough to shout over the noise.

This teacher was really soft-spoken. And the students! They actually stopped talking when he told them to and listened to him when he taught the lesson. They even settled down to their work without having to be told.

She took out a pen and paper and began taking notes. If this teacher had already figured out the noise problem, perhaps he also had answers for some of the other problems she was having.

*E*ven though it may sometimes seem as if your school days are beset with problems unique to a first-year teacher, there are some common problems that experience alone doesn't prevent. The following seven problems fall into this category.

1. Tardiness
2. Absenteeism
3. Excessive noise
4. Crowded classrooms
5. Substance abuse
6. Fighting
7. Harassment

Some Problems That Educators Face

No teacher is immune from the potentially disruptive effects of students who are tardy or absent to class. Most teachers of older students will say that tardiness is the most prevalent discipline problem that they have to manage during each school day. And few teachers have students with perfect attendance. In school districts where attendance problems are serious, the effort and energy that must be spent on managing attendance is enough to have a serious impact on educational opportunities for the students who do attend school regularly.

Two of the problems, excessive noise and overcrowded classrooms, frequently accompany each other. Students who are packed into a small classroom designed for only a few students find it difficult to stay focused on learning, much less remain quiet. Because both problems are partially the result of tight educational budgets and population growth, neither one is going to vanish.

Another problem, student substance abuse, can take many forms. Although you may teach very young children and do not have to deal with student substance abuse problems on the scale that teachers of teens do, the age at which students begin experimenting with illegal substances has become shockingly young. Student substance abuse is an issue that can have a serious impact on any classroom.

The final two problems, fighting and harassment, are ones that have drawn national attention because of highly publicized incidents. When students are harassed to the point that they lash back with weapons, then the need for successful management of these problems is self-evident.

"How to prevent discipline problems: On the first day of school, you should welcome your students and present a set of simple rules that you expect to be followed in your classroom. You should also denote the consequences for each infraction. STICK TO IT. No matter who 'commits the crime,' they suffer the consequence. Once the students see that 'you mean what you say' they will become believers, and will have respect for your convictions, and also see that you are 'fair'... a very important part of disciplining students."

—Marlene M. Stanton, 23 years experience

Figure 14.1

How Would You Handle Some of the Problems Educators Face?

Below you will find three scenarios that involve some of the widespread problems that you may have to cope with this year. How would you handle each of these situations? Jot down your solutions, then review the suggested solutions that follow.

Scenario 1: In Ms. Hahn's sixth grade science class, students often argue with each other about even the smallest things. Name-calling is a daily battle. Sometimes, one student will even hit another one, claiming that the other student hit him first. When Ms. Hahn tries to intervene, the students protest that they are friends and are just "playing around."

Scenario 2: Mr. Baldwin has a class of enthusiastic tenth graders in his life science class. They make it clear that they like his class and the hands-on work that he gives them to do. However, his colleagues are not as enthusiastic. They have complained that the noise from his class, particularly as students are cleaning the lab at the end of class, disturbs their students.

Scenario 3: One of Mrs. Viola's third graders, Nicole, always made good grades without really trying. She is a pleasant and well-liked student. Recently, Mrs. Viola has noticed that Nicole is missing school a lot. Sometimes she comes to school late, as well. Because of her academic skills, Nicole works hard to make up her work and is usually successful. Lately, though, she seems stressed and is having to struggle to keep up.

Suggested Solutions

Here are some suggestions for effectively handling the problems in the three scenarios.

Scenario 1

- Involve students more fully in the assignment so that they don't have time for as much off-task behavior.
- Categorically refuse to accept name-calling or physical abuse in your classroom. Consistently enforce class rules and consequences about treating others with respect.
- Teach students acceptable social skills.

Scenario 2

- Take time to teach acceptable noise levels for hand-on activities.
- Make controlling the noise levels an effort that involves every student.
- Divide the class into two groups at the end, one for clean up duty and one for silent review activities. Teach the clean up crew acceptable ways to work quietly.
- Praise students for their behavior when they make progress in controlling the noise.

Scenario 3

- Contact parents to determine the cause of absences and tardiness. At that point, work with them to help students come to school more often and on time.
- Offer assistance with make-up work because absent students have double the amount of work to do when they have to catch up.
- Determine the underlying causes of student stress and offer assistance and support. Contact other support personnel if necessary.

Problem 1: Tardiness

Very few students can attend school for an entire term without being tardy at least once. There are many reasons to delay their arrival in class, and by the end of your first semester you will have heard many creative excuses. Expect your students to suffer car trouble, traffic, stuck lockers, lost notebooks, arguments with friends, sleepy parents, and mysterious alarm clock failures.

The real reasons for your students' tardiness are not as colorful. Frequently, the reason students are late to class is because they do not see the advantage to being on time. At other times it's because the teacher or the administration has not established or communicated to students the consequences for tardiness. A final reason for student tardiness is that inconsistent enforcement of the consequences leads students to believe that being late to class is not a problem.

Although tardy students are the first to claim that being tardy is not a serious offense and that they are not hurting anyone else, they often seriously underestimate the negative effect of their tardiness. You must raise their awareness of the negative effects associated with their tardiness, which include the following.

- Tardy students cause a disruption no matter how quietly they try to slip into the class. Further, when students see their classmates being allowed to be tardy with no teacher action, then they will take this as a cue that it's okay for them to be tardy, too. The disruptive effect multiplies as more and more students are tardy to your class.

- Tardy students and others affected by the disruption miss instruction when you start your class on time.

- Tardy students set a negative tone in a class. Tardy students are tacitly sending a message to you and other students that the activities that you have planned for them are not important enough for them be in class on time. As a result, the focus in your class will shift from learning to a power struggle between you and those students who are interested in testing the boundaries of your patience.

YOUR RESPONSIBILITIES

- Make it important for your students to be on time to your class. Begin class as soon as the bell rings with an interesting and meaningful assignment.

- You must have a tardiness plan in place and to enforce your procedures for tardiness consistently. Be sure that your plan is in line with your school's policies. Chronically tardy students respond particularly well to a plan with escalating consequences because it forces them to take their actions seriously. Here is a suggested one that you can adapt for your students.

First tardy:	Warning
Second tardy:	Phone call home
Third tardy:	Phone call and ten-minute detention
Fourth tardy:	Phone call and thirty-minute detention

- You must involve parents or guardians if students are tardy more than once or twice in a marking period. This is an especially important step for you to take if the tardy student is late to school and not just late from another teacher's class.

- Most schools have a policy for handling habitual tardiness. At some step in the process, you will be expected to refer the student to an administrator for action. Be sure to do so in a timely fashion according to your school's tardiness procedures.

- Model the behavior you expect. Your students will be very quick to point out your hypocrisy if you are tardy and then reprimand them for the same offense.

MISTAKES TO AVOID

- Never embarrass tardy students with sarcastic remarks such as "Glad you decided to join us." Sarcasm will not solve the problem, nor will it earn you respect; instead, it will make a tardy student even more reluctant to enter the room.

- Don't delay calling home. The second time a student is tardy, you should contact a parent or guardian and enlist his or her support in handling the problem.

- Don't be a pushover for shabby excuses. Refuse to accept excuses that are not legitimate, and enforce the consequences for tardiness.

- Never stop what you are doing and interrogate a tardy student in front of the rest of the class; instead, allow the student to slip into class while you continue giving instruction.

- Don't overlook tardiness or the problem will spread.

- Don't allow students to stand in the doorway before class starts. Students who do this interrupt the smooth start of class as they delay their classmates from getting to their seats and ready for class on time.

- Don't give up on your tardy students. Tardiness is a learned habit that can be broken with persistence and patience.

STRATEGIES THAT WORK

- Define tardiness for your students, and be reasonable in your definition. Most teachers will agree that a student who is inside the classroom but not in a seat is not tardy; others are more particular and insist that a student who is not actually sitting down is tardy. This second definition is harder to justify to your students and to their parents.

- Begin class quickly and with assignments that students will want to do. If necessary, give assignments that you grade at that time so that your students will see a strong purpose for being on time. Make the first few minutes of class as meaningful as the rest.

- The first two weeks of the term are important for establishing the expectations you have for the prompt arrival of all of your students. Make tardiness control a strong priority during this time and you will avoid many problems later on.

- Speak with a tardy student privately to determine why he or she is late to class.

- Be sure that your attendance records are accurate. It is sometimes confusing to stop class and change the absence mark to a tardy mark, but your records must be accurate. When you refer a student to an administrator or when you talk to parents, you must be able to give the dates that tardiness occurred.

- Move a chronically tardy student to a seat near the door to minimize disruptions. When you pass out materials and the student is not present, place materials on the desktop to prevent disruption in case he or she comes late.

- Encourage students to help each other get to class on time. For example, if students are late because they have to make locker trips to get their books, their classmates can remind them earlier in the day to take their books to class. Make solving tardiness a team effort.

- Find out about the background of tardy students. Often their tardiness is the result of a disorganized family life where children are not taught to be punctual.

- Be consistent in enforcing your procedures about tardiness. If students see that you are not comfortable enforcing them, they will not be on time to class.

- Whenever you talk with your students about their tardiness, put the responsibility for their behavior where it belongs—on them. Ask tardy students what steps they plan to take to eliminate the problem. Offer support, but remain firm in your expectations.

> *"Many times students themselves don't understand why they are doing what they are doing."*
>
> —Ken Pfeifer, 28 years experience

Problem 2: Absenteeism

In the last few decades a profound social shift has taken place resulting in an increased demand for educated workers. As the gap between the availability of high-paying jobs for educated workers and lack of jobs available for uneducated workers widens, it is more and more evident that students need to stay in school.

Students rarely become at-risk for dropping out suddenly. Usually a consistent pattern of poor attendance develops from their earliest days onwards. Many factors contribute to a child's poor attendance. For instance, when a family is in turmoil, children find it difficult to attend school. Frequent illnesses can also be a factor, especially with the rise in respiratory illness among very young students.

Another factor that causes some students to miss school is that their families do not value education and do not encourage regular attendance. Further, students who are parents themselves find it almost impossible to overcome the difficulties associated with having a child and attending school. Sometimes older children have to stay home to take care of younger siblings or other family members for various reasons.

It is necessary that you take an active role in encouraging students to attend school regardless of the reason for their absenteeism. Encouraging your students to attend school on a regular basis is one of the most important and most difficult tasks that you will face in your career.

YOUR RESPONSIBILITIES

- Be aware of the attendance patterns of your students. Find out the reasons for a student's absenteeism so you can offer support and assistance.

- When you determine that a student has an attendance problem, don't ignore the problem. It is up to you to help that student in the most appropriate way.

- Students who feel connected to their school, their classmates, and their teachers rarely miss school without good reason. Encourage regular attendance by building a strong relationship with each of your students. Children need to feel that they will be missed if they are not in school.

- Your classroom is a place where students should feel challenged and capable at the same time. If a class is too difficult or not challenging, a student will have no reason to attend.

- Students should know that you disapprove of absence without good reason. Contact parents or guardians of absent students to make sure that everyone involved knows that you believe that it is important for every student to attend school.

MISTAKES TO AVOID

- Don't allow a student to be absent without determining the reason. Ignoring attendance problems will only encourage students to miss more school.

- Don't make it too difficult for students to make up missing work. Arrange times that are convenient for both of you to meet if necessary. Make sure that the child has all of the assignments that he or she missed and has the support that is necessary to complete them in a reasonable length of time.

- Make sure that your attendance records are accurate. If is not always easy to keep up with attendance records, but students need to have an accurate accounting of their attendance all term.

▶ Don't assume that absent students want to miss school.

▶ Don't imply that the next day's work will not be interesting or important. You should make sure that everyone has a reason to attend your class every day.

STRATEGIES THAT WORK

▶ Follow your school district's procedures for reporting and handling attendance. You will need to do this in order to seek assistance for truant students.

▶ Consider sending a letter home after students have missed the third day in your class. Keep a copy of the letter as documentation that you have contacted parents or guardians.

▶ Contact the parents or guardians of students who have excessive absences to work together on the problem. Some parents of older children who may be tempted to skip school may request that you contact them whenever their child is absent. Try to honor this request whenever you can.

▶ Encourage students and their parents to keep a calendar of the days that their children miss school. Some parents do not realize just how often their child is out without a reminder such as this.

▶ Ask counselors to speak to your students who are having trouble with their attendance so that they have a clear picture of their options. Many believe that they can drop out and just pick up a GED certificate, not realizing how difficult the test for the certificate can be.

▶ Pay attention to the work that at-risk students are doing. Design lessons that are interesting, engaging, and achievable. This will benefit all your students, particularly those who have attendance problems.

▶ Some parents or guardians do not value school and do not encourage regular attendance. Make sure that parents of students who have excessive absences understand the importance of regular attendance and the short- and long-term consequences for students who do not attend school.

▶ Talk to students about their absences. If your students are having family problems or social problems, seek help for them. Have them talk to the guidance counselors at your school to enlist their support in maintaining regular attendance.

▶ Make your students aware that their attendance is important to you and to their classmates. Always greet them pleasantly when they arrive in your class and show your caring and concern.

Problem 3: Excessive Noise

Many of your students thrive in a very noisy world. Their lives are full of blaring radios, deafening television shows, earsplitting music, ringing phones, and endless conversations punctuated by excited screams. Unfortunately, your students' tolerance of noise can have a negative impact on the productive and orderly learning environment that you want to promote in your class. No teacher likes having to shout to be heard above the pandemonium in a noisy class—and no teacher should have to.

With the increase in cooperative learning activities and other teaching techniques that allow students to be active learners, classrooms have become much noisier places than they were a generation ago. When the teacher is clearly in control of the situation and when the noise is the result of a well-planned and meaningful activity, noisy classrooms are not a cause for concern.

The problems with noisy classrooms arise from noise that is excessive or that arises from students who are engaged in personal conversation and activities rather than meaningful group assignments. Learning to control excessive noise in your class requires patience and persistent effort.

YOUR RESPONSIBILITIES

- ◗ Although noisy classes are more accepted now than in the past, administrators are very clear in their expectations that noise be the result of productive activities.

- ◗ You must develop ways to control the noise levels in your room.

- ◗ You must teach students how to control their own noise levels.

- ◗ You are expected to be considerate of the teachers around your classroom. Your students do not have the right to disturb other classes.

MISTAKES TO AVOID

- ◗ Never talk over noise or shout to be heard in your classroom. Doing so would only add to the problem.

- ◗ Don't plan group work activities without teaching students how to control the noise level of their groups.

- ◗ You should not try to assume control of a noisy class without enlisting the cooperation of your students. Noise control should be the concern of everyone in the room, not just the teacher.

- ◗ Don't allow noise to get out of control and then try to quiet students. Once students are very loud, you have to take extreme measures to get them to stop being noisy. It's easier to control the noise from the first minute of class.

- You cannot control noise levels effectively from your desk. In order to maintain an orderly and productive classroom, you must carefully monitor your students.

- Don't waste your breath shushing your students over and over. Teach noise control techniques instead.

- Make sure you understand the difference between productive classroom noise and noise resulting from students who are idle or off-task. No complaint about noise is legitimate if you are clearly in control of your class and if all of your students are engaged in learning. Complaints about noise levels that result from students who have nothing to do or who believe that it is acceptable to be loud are legitimate complaints.

STRATEGIES THAT WORK

- Make your students aware of the importance of courteous listening. Teach your students how to listen to you attentively. When you give directions, your students should stop what they are doing and look at you until you are finished speaking.

- Some noisy activities are just not acceptable. Teach your students that it is never acceptable to talk during a movie, talk when you are giving instructions or lecturing, shout at any time, talk during a test or other quiet activity, and talk across the room to classmates.

- When you plan activities that have the potential to be noisy, consider moving to a part of the building where you can't disturb others. Always take noise levels into account when you plan activities for your students.

- Make controlling noise a team effort. Elicit suggestions from your students about how to manage noise.

- Be consistent in enforcing the noise levels that you expect from your students. Set reasonable limits and stick to them if you want students to learn how to manage their own noise.

- Teach students acceptable loudness levels by using distances as measurements. For example, students should find a one-foot voice useful for working in pairs and a three-foot voice useful for working in groups. When you give directions for an assignment, include the noise level that you find most productive in your directions.

- Model the noise level that you want from your students. If you speak softly, your students will follow your lead. If you shout, you will dramatically increase the noise level in your class because students will see this as permission for them to shout, too.

- Establish noise-control signals with your students—a flick of the lights, a mark on the board, a raised hand, and you moving to a certain spot in the room should all signal that students need to lower the volume.

- Many teachers have found playing soft instrumental music as a background a good way to control noise. Students know that they should be able to hear the music at all times and if they can't, then the class is too loud.

"I think it's important to connect to kids because they need to know you care, not just about your subject, but about them as people. They need to feel that they are unique and special individuals, not just warm bodies filling the room."

—Patty Muth, 9 years experience

Problem 4: Overcrowded Classes

Overcrowded classes are common in many school districts because of a boom in population growth and tight school budgets. Rows of mobile classroom units surround many schools while still others have many teachers who "float" from class to class with their materials on a small cart. Even in schools without such visible signs of overcrowding, there are many classes where there are just too many students for anyone to be comfortable. The proliferation of overcrowded classes is especially ironic in light of research studies that show the correlation between small class size and successful student achievement.

Although overcrowded classrooms may be inevitable, the problems associated with them are not. Your attitude is the most important factor in coping with the demands of a large class. Careful planning, strong connections with students, and interesting lessons—not the number of students you are required to teach—are the determining factors in the success of your classroom.

YOUR RESPONSIBILITIES

▶ You are expected to provide the same quality of instruction for a large class as you would for a small one.

▶ You are expected to manage supplies and equipment efficiently.

▶ Student safety is even more of a concern when classes are crowded. You should be aware of the activities that have the potential to be unsafe and successfully manage them.

▶ You still need to create strong bonds with your students to avoid students from being lost in the crowd.

MISTAKES TO AVOID

▶ Don't neglect to enlist your students' help in managing the situation. If you create a team spirit, you will find it easier to manage the challenge of a crowded class.

▶ Don't delay in returning papers. Although keeping up with checking student work is more challenging when dealing with a large class, it's more important than ever to do so. Falling behind will not only cause you more stress, it will also deprive students of the attention and feedback that you have already been forced to spread too thin.

- Don't arrange the furniture so that you can't move around easily.
- Do not allow students to place their desks near a wall where they could vandalize it with graffiti.
- Do not allow students to disrupt class by not following class routines. Routines are especially important in creating an orderly environment in a large class.
- Don't neglect to get to know your students as individuals. Make sure that your students know that you are aware of them as people, not as just faces in the crowd.
- Don't allow small problems to grow into large ones. Monitor, contact parents, teach courtesy, and use other strategies to prevent problems from becoming serious.
- Don't neglect to deal proactively with the noise levels that can accompany a large class.

STRATEGIES THAT WORK

- Monitoring large classes is even more important than monitoring small groups to maintain an orderly environment. Stay on your feet and remain alert.
- Room arrangements are very important in overcrowded classes. Pay attention to traffic patterns and student movement and arrange the furniture in your class to accommodate your students. Make sure that you have enough desks for every student to have a place to sit. Reduce clutter by storing equipment that you are not using.
- A seating chart is necessary to keep everyone on task.
- Be very organized. You will need to make sure that you have enough materials, books, and handouts for every student. Create a seating chart and insist that students adhere to it. Maintain your personal space in the class in an orderly fashion.
- Create and enforce routines for class activities. Teach your routines early in the term and reinforce them as necessary. Students should be able to predict what they are supposed to do in your class even though there are very many students in the classroom.
- Keep student movement to a minimum by encouraging students to dispose of trash at the end of class and sharpen pencils at the start.
- Be alert to the opportunities for cheating that can happen as a result of an overcrowded classroom. Monitor vigilantly during tests and quizzes.
- Stop horseplay at the first sign that it is about to begin. "Just playing around" can quickly escalate into a dangerous situation when there are too many students in the room to maneuver safely.

◗ Speak with every student every day. Greet students at the door and make sure that everyone knows that you are not only aware of them as people, but that you are concerned about them, too.

◗ Create small groups within the larger group to increase students' sense of belonging. When students have partners to support them, they will feel like part of the group instead of just one of many.

◗ A large courteous class is much easier to handle than a small rude one. Insist that all students treat you and each other with courtesy at all times.

Problem 5: Substance Abuse

Students are subjected to a barrage of mixed messages about cigarettes, alcohol, and drugs. On television, they see public service announcements telling them that all three substances can be deadly, yet within the hour those same students can watch programs where substance abuse is taken lightly or, even worse, treated as a cool choice made by grown ups. No wonder so many students are confused about illegal substances and appear to be just biding their time until they can be old enough to experiment.

Many teachers do not have a clear idea about how they can help students resist the lure of drugs and alcohol. They are not sure what to do when students appear in class bragging about a weekend party or reeking of cigarette smoke. Many teachers want to believe that educating students about substance abuse is someone else's job, especially parents and family members. The problem with this assumption is that many families are either unable to cope with the problem or are themselves at the root of the problem.

Educating students about the harsh consequences of substance abuse is one of your most important responsibilities.

YOUR RESPONSIBILITIES

◗ You are expected to know and follow your district's guidelines about student substance abuse.

◗ You are expected to involve other adults to help students as soon as you determine that a problem exists.

◗ You are expected to be a role model and to discourage students from experimenting with illegal substances.

◗ You are expected to be a supportive and caring adult who will help students with substance abuse problems.

MISTAKES TO AVOID

◗ Don't ignore substance abuse problems among your students. This problem does not go away by itself.

▶ Don't overreact. For example, if a student makes a passing mention of a weekend party, don't lecture or notify a counselor. Instead, speak privately with the student about making sound decisions.

▶ Don't ignore your school's policies regarding students with substance abuse problems.

▶ You should not attempt to handle a serious substance abuse problem without involving other adults. If you have a student with substance abuse problems, remember that this problem is a very serious one and needs to be handled with support from all of the adults in a student's life.

▶ Don't forget that you are a role model. Teachers who talk about happy hour or the fun they had at college frat parties will not encourage students to make wise choices for themselves.

▶ Do not lose sight of the fact that students are under-age no matter how old they may seem. It is against the law for students to use tobacco or alcohol or controlled drugs without a prescription.

STRATEGIES THAT WORK

Prevention:

▶ You do not have to spend hours of instruction time teaching students about illegal substances. Instead, when the subject arises, be clear about your position on the issue.

▶ Give your students the facts about substance abuse. By doing this, you will enable them to make wiser choices based on real information rather than the opinions of their friends who may be just as confused as they are.

▶ Many students, and especially younger ones, are simply not aware of the health risks and social consequences of substance abuse. Make sure that they are aware of these as well as the legal penalties.

▶ Your school district probably has programs to help students who struggle with substance abuse. In addition, the guidance counselors at your school are good sources of information about community resources.

▶ Make sure that your students understand the school policies concerning student use of tobacco, alcohol, and drugs and the consequences for violating these policies.

Intervention:

When you notice that a student has violated your school's policies for substance abuse, you should follow these steps to intervene.

▶ Remove the student to the hall and quietly question him or her to determine if a problem does exist.

▶ Don't be tempted to overlook the problem. Immediately and calmly put your school's policies into effect.

- Contact the person at your school designated to handle substance abuse problems and explain the problem as you see it. That person will conduct a search if necessary and involve the child's parents and other appropriate personnel.

- Make sure that the student sees you as a supportive and caring person. Students with substance abuse problems need support and assistance, not blame.

Problem 6: Fighting

Any teacher dreads the signs that a fight is imminent. The potential for serious injury is very real when students set out to hurt each other. And because other students often gather around to encourage the participants, they are also at risk.

After a fight is over, the effects can disrupt classes for the rest of the day. Students do not want to settle down, preferring instead to discuss the fight blow-by-blow. Even worse, a fight often triggers a series of other conflicts as anger and adrenaline run high throughout the school.

In the last few years, there has been a dramatic increase in the numbers of fights at school as students bring conflicts from their neighborhoods to school. Further, in recent years conflicts have been more likely to involve the use of weapons. As an educator, there is much that you can do about the increase in violence by taking a proactive stance.

YOUR RESPONSIBILITIES

- You are expected to know and follow your school district's procedures for handling student fights.

- Your school district will expect you to act quickly to prevent fights by reporting student rumors.

- You should stop students from harassing each other in your presence and to report incidents of bullying to administrators.

- You are expected to keep your students as safe as you can when a fight erupts.

- You are expected to take reasonable measures to stop fights without putting yourself or others in danger.

- You may be expected to provide accurate witness reports and appear in court.

MISTAKES TO AVOID

- Don't try to physically restrain violent students without help from other adults. Teachers who inadvertently hurt students in the course of stopping them from fighting have been successfully sued. Still others have been seriously injured.

- Don't leave the fight area. Send students for help instead.

◗ Don't allow a fight to hinder the rest of the day's instruction. Make an effort to settle students down.

◗ If you are assigned to hall duty, cafeteria duty, or any other extra duty, don't miss it. Be on time and be alert. A strong adult presence deters many fights.

STRATEGIES THAT WORK

Preventing fights:

◗ Teach your students the school-wide policies concerning students who fight at school. Remind them of the severe penalties that they will have to pay for fighting.

◗ Teach students how to mediate peer conflicts. If your school has a conflict resolution program, refer students who are at risk for violent behavior to it.

◗ Make sure your students are aware of their options in a peer conflict situation. They should not have to immediately turn to fighting as a way of resolving problems.

◗ Be alert to the signs that a fight is building: rumors, a higher level of excitement, remarks about what will happen later.

◗ If you suspect students are contemplating fighting, counsel them. Remind them that threatening to fight does not have the serious repercussions that an actual fight does.

◗ If you see that two students are beginning to square off, remind them that there are serious penalties for students who fight. Often students will take this as an opportunity to back down without losing face because they can claim that they do not want to be expelled.

◗ Immediately contact an administrator about the possible fight. Also contact the parents of the students who are threatening to fight.

◗ Make sure all your students are aware of the school policies on weapons and how they can report weapons to an adult.

◗ Teach your students about bullying and sexual harassment. Make sure that they understand the limits that they should observe in how they relate to one another and what they should do if they are themselves bullied or harassed.

◗ Encourage good behavior by refusing to allow students to horse around and insult each other, even in jest. Both horsing around and good-natured insults can quickly turn to anger and violence.

◗ Teach your students that they can be punished for inciting others to fight and for blocking the area so that adults can't get through to stop a fight.

During a fight:

◗ Immediately get help from other adults by sending students. Do not try to restrain or step between students without another adult present.

◗ The safety of all students at the scene is your first concern.

▶ Be very clear with students who are watching the fight that you want them to leave the area or, if the fight is in your classroom, to sit down.

▶ Be very careful how you approach violent students so that no one, including yourself, is injured.

A fight with weapons:

▶ If you hear a rumor that there is a weapon in the building, contact an administrator at once. You should not attempt to handle this situation by yourself.

▶ When a weapon is used during a fight, make sure that other students do not take it. It will be used as evidence. If you can, confiscate it and turn it over to an administrator.

A fight that results in injuries:

▶ Send a student for the school nurse. Deal first with any injured students and then with the other students at the scene. Do not leave the area.

▶ Assist the more seriously wounded students first. Unless you are a trained medical emergency technician, be careful that the aid that you offer does not injure students further.

▶ Protect yourself and others from contact with blood or other body fluids.

▶ If you are even slightly injured, seek medical attention promptly.

"The best thing to do is to take bullies aside and counsel them by trying to understand why they act the way they do. Then explain alternative ways to handle conflict with classmates such as by simply ignoring the person and walking away. Or get students together to discuss the problem encouraging them to say 'I feel . . .'"

—Donna Nelms, 26 years experience

After a fight:

▶ Model the calm response you want from your students. Resume teaching immediately without rehashing the fight or allowing students to do so.

▶ As soon as you can, jot down the details of what happened. As a witness to the fight, you may be called on to remember these details in court, sometimes months after the incident, so be as specific as you can.

▶ If a fight took place while students were under your supervision, contact their parents or guardians so that you can work together to prevent a recurrence.

Problem 7: Harassment

Schools are not always safe places for teachers. Each year thousands of teachers report that they have been insulted and threatened by their students. Some teachers have even had to report that they had been the targets of sexual harassment by their students. And school can be an even tougher place for students. Every month thousands of students report that a classmate has physically attacked them. Still others report that that they have been too afraid to attend school on at least one occasion. These statistics reveal only what is reported to authorities. Far more harassment occurs than is ever reported.

The worst aspect of the problem of harassment is that teachers have been slow to react to complaints from victims. Some teachers seem to feel that victims of harassment bring it on themselves or are overreacting. Many teachers, despite the recent incidents of school violence, are still inclined to overlook harassment. In fact, many first-year teachers are not sure at what point they should intervene.

The first step that you can take to stop this serious threat is to make sure that you understand exactly what harassment is. There are two forms that it can take: verbal abuse and physical abuse. When students are abused physically, teachers are usually quick to respond. Further, as a result of highly publicized court cases involving sexual harassment—both verbal and physical—teachers also tend to take threats and taunts of a sexual nature very seriously and act quickly. Verbal abuse in the form of taunts, rumors, insults, racial slurs, name-calling, and teasing is the most widespread form of harassment, and it is far more likely to be tolerated by teachers. The result of this tolerance is victims who are hopeless and unable to cope with school.

YOUR RESPONSIBILITIES

- You are expected to take necessary steps to prevent harassment by teaching your students about it and by supervising them adequately.

- Be alert to signs that a student is being harassed by others. Act promptly.

- You must know your school's policy about harassment and the way that you are to resolve the situation.

- Because harassment is such a serious offense, you must involve administrators, parents or guardians, and other support personnel according to the guidelines specified by your district.

MISTAKES TO AVOID

- Never ignore the situation. If you observe an incident, no matter how mild it may appear to you, take action.

- Don't make things worse for the victim by unnecessary public humiliation. Be sensitive to the embarrassment that such students feel at being targets and at having to ask for help.

- Don't ever assume that victims bring it on themselves.

- Don't neglect to teach your students about harassment, the forms it can take, the consequences, how to report it, and why they must report incidents to adults.

STRATEGIES THAT WORK

Before an incident occurs:

- Make teaching social skills part of your classroom procedures no matter how old your students are. Some of your students simply do not know which behaviors are appropriate and which are not.

- Strive to build a sense of a teamwork among your students so that they learn to value everyone's contributions to the class.

- Make sure that you promote acceptance by praising students when they are helpful to each other. It is particularly effective when you can label an entire class as helpful so this prophecy can become self-fulfilling.

- Boost the self-esteem of all students, particularly those who may be tempted to harass others as a result of a poor sense of self-worth and those who may be the targets of harassment.

- Make sure students have the basic skills they need to deal with peer conflicts.

- Be aware of the way students treat each other. Listen carefully to what they have to say to and about each other.

- When you notice an act of harassment, act quickly. Stop the abuse at once.

- When you notice that there are several signs of trouble—students have targeted someone for disrespect or a student is having trouble adjusting to school—document them and report your findings to an administrator.

After an incident occurs:

- **Step 1:** Put the school's procedures into action by speaking with an administrator. It is important to prevent more abuse by acting quickly.

- **Step 2:** Meet with the student whom you suspect of harassing the other and ask him or her to tell you about the incident. Then ask for the details in writing. It is important that you not speak with the victim first so that there will be few reprisals for "tattling."

- **Step 3:** Meet with the victim to discuss the incident. Have this student write a report of the incident, also.

- **Step 4:** Support the victim. Often just talking with an adult will help relieve some of the anxiety this child is feeling.

- **Step 5:** Talk with the parents or guardians of both students to let them know what has been reported. They should understand not only what happened, but that there is a school policy about harassment and that the incident has been reported to an administrator. Elicit their support in working with you and the students to prevent further abuse.

- **Step 6:** Work with both students together to solve their differences. The abuser should apologize to the victim. At the end of their conference, both students should have a better understanding of their behavior.

Managing the 7 Most Common School Problems

Although each of the seven problems covered in this section has the potential to disrupt the learning process in any class, there are a number of strategies that you can adopt to manage them successfully. Here are some that have been successfully used by other teachers.

1. **Act quickly.** These problems will not solve themselves if you adopt a "wait and see" attitude. In fact, this particular group of problems requires prompt intervention.

2. **Know what you are supposed to do.** When you deal with problems as potentially serious as these, you need to know what to do. Educate yourself about your district's policies. Find out what steps you are supposed to take.

3. **Be a professional.** Let your actions be guided by your professionalism rather than by your personal preferences. For example, while you may not see the importance of excellent attendance for all students and while loud classes may not trouble you, the professional approach to both of these is to take steps to correct them.

4. **Ask for help.** Because these problems involve serious issues, you need to ask for help from other concerned adults as soon as you see that your initial intervention has not resolved the problem. You must involve parents or guardians, counselors, and administrators as soon as you need their support.

5. **Refuse to be discouraged.** Just because these problems are serious and ubiquitous, you should not give up on finding workable solutions to them. Adopt a "cup-is-half-full" rather than a "cup-is-half-empty" attitude to find success.

6. **Adopt a problem-solving approach.** Work with your students, parents or guardians, and administrators to assist your students and to solve the problem. A positive attitude will help you and your students deal with any of these problems.

7. **Don't let problems affect your relationship with students.** It is sometimes tempting to let disapproval for a student's actions turn into disapproval for the student. You must always separate misbehaviors and the problems they cause from the student who misbehaved. This will not only help you maintain a professional and positive approach in dealing with your difficult students, it is also important for them to know that they are important to you and liked by you even when there are problems.

8. **Remain open to suggestions.** There are many different ways to solve any of these problems. To be successful, you need to keep trying new strategies. The tougher the problem, the more effort you should put into finding new ways to solve it.

Journal Entries to Help You Find Solutions to Common Problems

▶ What proactive attitudes do you currently hold that will help you successfully solve some of the problems that you share with other teachers?

▶ When students are tardy to your class, what excuses do they give? What are the underlying reasons? What can you do to prevent more tardies?

▶ What are some of the causes of absenteeism in your class? What can you do to help?

▶ Is your classroom too noisy? When does the noise get out of control? What can you do to handle this problem?

▶ Are there overcrowded classrooms in your school? How do other teachers manage some of the problems with overcrowding? How do you manage?

▶ What can you do to educate your students about harassment?

▶ What are some of the signs of harassment that you could observe in your students? Which students would be likely victims? Which ones are likely to be abusers? What can you do with this knowledge?

▶ What can you do to educate your students about substance abuse?

▶ What are some of the signs that your students are struggling with substance abuse? What can you do to help?

▶ What steps would you take if a fight were to break out in your classroom? What are you currently doing to prevent violence in your class?

▶ What can you do to settle your students back into a routine after a fight?

The Diverse Classroom

As she sat at her desk looking over the list of her new students, two veteran teachers came in. "You have our students from last year. Let us look at your class roster and we'll tell you all about them," they suggested.

The two experienced teachers went through the list of her students at a dizzying speed, pointing out troublemakers and good students alike. Every student on her list seemed to have a problem and a label. She heard about IEP forms, pregnant girls, neglectful parents, and students who were probably going to drop out just as soon as school started.

Her spirits sank. How could she be expected to teach so many people with so many different needs? As the veteran teachers drifted out of her classroom, she sat looking at the list once more.

I will never allow that to happen to me again, she promised herself. I don't want to find out what I need to know about my students from teachers who want to gossip about troublemakers. I knew that there would be problems. I can handle them.

Gathering up her class lists, she headed off to see her mentor, determined to figure out how she was supposed to handle these new problems.

When you chose to become a teacher, you may have made your decision based on your love of a particular discipline such as math or literature, or you may have chosen education as a career because of an inspiring role model in your past. Although many teachers list these as reasons why they were first attracted to a career in education, they will say that they stay in the profession because of their students.

Today's classrooms are places of intricate diversity. You can expect that your class will include a mixture of students with different ability levels, ethnic backgrounds, family situations, maturity levels, and school experiences. You can also expect that while these differences can create a rich experience for all of your students, they can also present many challenges throughout the year.

Figure 15.1

WHAT DO YOU KNOW ABOUT THE DIVERSE NEEDS
OF YOUR STUDENTS?

Below you will find a brief description of students that you may have in your class. Match the label in the left-hand column with the description in the right-hand column. Even though there will inevitably be an overlap of characteristics among students, the combination of the characteristics in each description should make it possible for you to match them.

Student

Description

1. _____ Has special needs

A. No materials, head down on desk, hostile, reading a novel instead of working, variable performance in different classes, highly involved parents

2. _____ Gifted

B. Inadequate parental supervision, poor reading comprehension, attendance problems

3. _____ At risk for dropping out

C. Pleasant in demeanor, anxious about the quality of work, perfectionist, highly involved parents, hands in incomplete work

4. _____ Pregnant

D. Does not necessarily qualify for special education classes, but does receive other accommodations

5. _____ Repeating the class

E. Distractible, fidgety, disorganized, short attention span

6. _____ Lives in poverty

F. Forgetful, inconsistent, active, demands attention, overreacts

7. _____ Has an attention disorder

G. Distracted, writes notes, sloppy dress, withdrawn, defensive

8. _____ Impulsive

H. Attendance problems, family problems, troubled peer relationships, receives free lunches

9. _____ Has a 504 plan

I. Complains that the work is too easy, already knows the material, self-critical, frequently off task

10. _____ Underachiever

J. Can have a wide range of disabilities, has an IEP, requires special accommodations

Key

*Keep in mind that the descriptions are just snapshots of some of the more obvious characteristics of these students. You may have students identified as any of these types who do not present themselves to you in these ways.

1. **J**—Students with special needs can have a wide range of disabilities from physical impairments to learning disabilities. A plan to address their needs is a document called an Individual Education Plan (IEP).

2. **A**—Gifted students are frequently bored in classes that are not geared for their needs. This frustration can reveal itself in hostility towards teachers and peers. Gifted students also can often have intense interests that they pursue at the expense of class assignments they perceive as not challenging.

3. **B**—Students who are risk for dropping out often have a long-standing pattern of attendance problems. Their parents or guardians may no longer supervise them carefully; some may live with friends or be legally emancipated from parental supervision. Poor academic skills contribute to the problems of at-risk students. A particular concern is their poor reading comprehension skills, which can make almost all school subjects difficult to master.

4. **G**—Girls who are pregnant may be conflicted in their view of their pregnancy because they believe that a baby will solve many of their current problems, while they have some awareness of the difficulties in raising a child. Pregnant girls can sometimes wear overlarge shirts in an effort to disguise their condition as long as possible. Their focus is often not on class work, and this can result in withdrawal from classmates and an increase in notes written to close friends.

5. **I**—Students who have to repeat a grade or a class can be overconfident about what they know. They can recognize material from the previous year and believe falsely that they have mastered it. Their overconfidence and the desire to establish peer relationships can result in off-task behavior. At the same time, students who are repeating are often highly aware of their shortcomings and suffer low self-esteem.

6. **H**—Students who live in poverty lack the material comforts of their peers, causing them much embarrassment. Their peers can be cruel in noting that they don't have fashionable clothes or sufficient materials. Their troubled home lives can exhaust them as can a poor diet. Students who receive free or reduced lunches are obviously students living in poverty.

7. **E**—Many students with an attention disorders find it difficult to stay on task and to remain organized. They can be also be restless and very easily distracted. A short attention span can result in many problems at school, both behavioral and academic.

8. **F**—Impulsive students closely resemble students with attention disorders. They are the students who are too easily excited or annoyed. They are quick to jump out of their seats and to blurt out answers. They demand your immediate attention often enough to frustrate their peers as well as their teachers.

9. **D**—Students who have 504 plans typically do not quality for special education classes, but are eligible for other accommodations based on a disability that impairs their ability to learn.

10. **C**—Students who are underachievers often care very much about their work. In fact, their anxiety about doing it correctly often paralyzes them into not doing it at all, much to the despair of their frustrated teachers and parents. The discrepancy between their ability and their achievement often puzzles the concerned adults in their lives.

Although teachers may often wish for a class of motivated youngsters who are capable of behaving well all the time, experienced teachers know that it is the challenging students who are the most fascinating to teach and whose successes are the most satisfying.

When you look at your class roster, remind yourself that every single one of your students deserves the best instruction that you can deliver every day. When you take this attitude, you will save yourself much needless stress. More than that, you will be able to be the kind of teacher that your students need you to be.

Gifted Students

Gifted students are usually fun as well as difficult to teach. When a lesson interests a gifted child, that student will take the lesson far beyond the boundaries of the material. Gifted students are also a challenge to teach for many of the same reasons. They are impatient with topics that they don't perceive as interesting, and they can be especially impatient with teachers and peers whom they perceive as less than capable.

When you have gifted students in your class, you will have to modify the content of the material or modify the learning process to meet their needs. You can use or adapt the following guidelines for modifying the process and content of your instruction to accommodate the needs of your gifted students.

PROCESS MODIFICATION

- Many gifted students do well with project-based instruction. When you assign a project to gifted students, give a reasonably loose structure and then allow them to take the project as far as they need to.

- Gifted students are self-directed learners. Use this characteristic when you modify the process of learning by allowing them to have a strong voice in how they will accomplish their goals.

- Set a rapid pace for instruction. Gifted students quickly grow bored with the slower pace of undifferentiated instruction.

- Focus on higher-level thinking skills throughout a unit of study because gifted students quickly master the recall and comprehension levels.

- Be as flexible as you can with the amount of time and the nature of the work that you assign gifted students.

- Your gifted students will appreciate and benefit from a multisensory approach to their work.

- Use technology as often as you can. Your students are more than likely to already be proficient at using the equipment and will be able to quickly tap into the resources on the Internet with just a bit of guidance from you.

- Allow gifted students to work together as often as possible. They benefit from being able to bounce ideas off each other.

CONTENT MODIFICATION

- Compact instruction by focusing on the big concepts in a unit of study. Gifted students will quickly grasp the details.

- Provide content that will challenge them to learn and that will appeal to their own interests.

- Use information from a variety of sources and ask students to participate in gathering information. Focus on synthesizing information when you work with gifted students.

- Encourage student input in the selection of material. You may have a general unit of study, but allow students to also study the details that most interest them. For example, you may teach a general unit on space first and then have each student work on a particular part aspect of space such as planets, asteroids, or comets.

- Ask students to not only solve problems, but to formulate their own problems from real-life situations. For example, you could ask students to anticipate and solve the problems that they would experience if they were pioneers or if they were to create a new city.

- Use textbooks as a launching point for further exploration.

- Focus on a depth of content rather than on more content. For example, reading three excellent books on a topic under study is better than asking students to read five books of lesser quality.

- Plan to move instruction out of the classroom whenever possible to study material first hand. Enrich lessons with trips to museums and other appropriate points of interest.

"In the 1960s, a student was placed in my general mechanics class because he could not read. I asked him what he liked to do. He said he liked to mess with motors. He took his diesel tractor motor out and put it in an old pickup truck. This is what he drove to school. In the spring the motor went back in the tractor for spring plowing. Other teachers told me this boy was dumb."

—Edward Gardner, 36 years experience

GIFTED STUDENTS IN A GROUP OF STUDENTS WITH MIXED ABILITIES

- Plan instruction to meet the needs of your gifted learners as carefully as you plan for your other students. Differentiate instruction for gifted students by modifying the content and process of instruction on an individual basis.

- Although allowing gifted students to serve as peer tutors is acceptable, be careful not to overuse this technique. It reinforces what they already know, but it doesn't allow enrichment.

- When working in groups, place gifted students with other high-achieving students.

- Assign a modified assignment as often as you can.

- Work closely with the parents of gifted students to ensure that each child's needs are fulfilled and that frustrations are minimal.

To learn more about teaching gifted students, begin your Internet research with these sites.

www.smu.edu

www.ed.gov/databases/ERIC_Digests

www.kidssource.com

Special Needs Students

Special needs students will be the treasures of your first year as a teacher when you learn to work with them successfully. "Special needs" is a very broad term that encompasses a wide rage of disabilities or conditions.

In years past, most teachers did not see students with special needs in their classes. These students were segregated into special classrooms or centers where they had little contact with the general school population. This practice ended with the "mainstreaming law"—PL94-142. As a result of this law, students who have special needs are now frequently part of ordinary school life.

> "The teacher may provide more scaffolding or prompts for special needs students: a specific list of resources or Web sites, a visual of a teacher-made story board, or examples of past student projects that could be used as a template or guide. For gifted students, you may let them use their talents to do the assigned task in any method they feel would meet the objective."
>
> —Stephanie Mahoney, 24 years experience

You can expect to have many different types of special needs students in your class, from those who need only a slight accommodation to help them learn to those with severe disabilities. How successfully you handle this challenge will depend on your attitude. Along with having a positive attitude, the following general strategies can guide you as you learn to successfully teach your students with special needs.

- Be proactive in dealing with special needs students. Make sure that you understand their specific disabilities and the accommodations that you should make to ensure success.

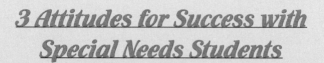

3 Attitudes for Success with Special Needs Students

There are three positive attitudes that can help you as you learn to teach students with special needs.

1. **Special needs students deserve your best effort.** When you take this view, you will be in a good position to help your special needs students. You will be expected to work closely with the special education teachers assigned to help you modify your instruction to meet the needs of every learner in your class.

2. **Accept your students' limitations and help them overcome them.** Although some teachers think that students with special needs, particularly those with disabilities that are not as obvious as others, just need to try harder, trying very hard is not enough to create success for many special needs students. Students who don't understand the work or need help that they are not getting will not be successful no matter how much effort they put forth.

3. **Accept responsibility for your students' success.** Don't think that you will receive extensive additional training to help your students with special needs. You have probably already had extensive training in your content area and in educational methods. Continue to educate yourself regarding how to work well with your special needs students by reading professional literature, researching relevant Web sites, attending workshops, and observing special education teachers as they teach.

▶ Use the resources that are available to you. Study students' permanent records to understand what instructional strategies have worked well in past school years, and contact the special education teacher working with the students in your class to learn specific strategies. Some of the other adults who can help you learn about your students are parents, the school nurse, counselors, and previous teachers.

▶ Talk with each special needs student that you have about his or her concerns. Make it easy for your special needs students to communicate with you.

▶ Make sure that you are sensitive to the needs of each student and anticipate them whenever you can. For example, be sure to seat students with special needs where they can see and hear you without distractions.

▶ There is a great deal of information about students with special needs available to you on the Internet. To learn more about this topic and what you can do to become a successful teacher, try these Web sites.

www.nichcy.org
www.ldonline.org
www.cec.sped.org

INSTRUCTION STRATEGIES FOR SPECIAL NEEDS STUDENTS

In addition to the general strategies, incorporating the following instructional strategies should make it easier for you to help your special needs students be successful.

- Limit the materials that you ask special needs students to manage at once. They should only have the materials that are necessary for the successful completion of a lesson on their desks.

- Limit the number of practice items. For example, instead of fifteen drill sentences, ask students to complete ten instead.

- Consider each student's preferred learning style when you create assignments. Modify an assignment when you can. If you can provide alternative materials, do so.

- Provide prompt feedback when students complete an assignment.

- Limit the amount of written work that you assign special needs students.

- Offer a variety of activities. Change the pace several times in each class so students will find it easy to stay on task.

- Highly structure your classroom routines so students can predict what they are supposed to do. Go over the daily objectives at the start of the class and offer students a checklist to keep them on track all period long.

- Make sure the directions that you give are very clear. Ask students to restate what you want them to do. On written work, use bold type or other changes to set them off from the rest of the text.

- Arrange for extra help for students who are less proficient at reading than other students. If you pair students to read, the more able student in the pair will be able to help the less able one.

- Offer collaborative learning opportunities whenever you can.

- Be generous with your praise when your special needs students do something well.

- Help your students with special needs understand their progress. Set small achievable goals and celebrate together when students reach them.

COLLABORATING WITH SPECIAL EDUCATION TEACHERS

When special needs students were "included" in all classrooms, special education teachers and general education teachers began forming teams to help students requiring special accommodations in inclusion classes. The unique feature of this collaboration is that frequently both teachers are present in the classroom at the same time, and both maintain a joint responsibility for the education of all students in their class.

These collaborative teams of teachers face an important challenge: how to successfully share the duties of the class so that they have common goals regarding delivering instruction, assessing progress, and managing behavior. Research reveals that successful collaboration is highly likely if team teachers see themselves as *equal* partners who are actively engaged in all parts of the teaching process. When collaborative teachers begin to work together, they must realize that they both have expertise in a particular field and that, by sharing that expertise, they can form a strong team to meet the needs of the learners in their shared class.

A typical division of responsibilities is usually as follows.

The general education teacher's responsibilities include:

- Creating activities to teach the content
- Finding and adapting resource material for all students
- Delivering effective instruction
- Meeting the curriculum requirements of all students

The special education teacher's responsibilities include:

- Adapting material to meet the needs of special needs students
- Adapting activities to match the learning styles of special needs students
- Modifing assessments
- Meeting the curriculum requirements of special needs students

What makes it possible for two teachers with different educational backgrounds to work together in a successful collaboration? The primary requirement for a positive working relationship is a commitment on the part of both teachers to work together for the common good of their students. Both teachers should also agree to:

- Plan lessons together
- Follow the same classroom management procedures
- Be dependable team members
- Discuss controversial class events in civil tones and in privacy
- Assume equal responsibility for what happens in class
- Present a united front to students
- Share monitoring duties and maintain an orderly classroom environment for all students
- Share resource materials
- Schedule time to work together on a regular basis

The benefits of a successful inclusion team far outweigh the inconveniences involved in learning to share classroom space and responsibilities. These are some of the most obvious benefits for students.

- More teacher attention
- Prompt feedback
- Higher levels of motivation
- Academic and social success
- Reduced time off task

- Increased appreciation of others' differences
- Increased self-esteem

To learn more about inclusion teams, you can search the Internet. These sites are a good place to begin your search.

www.inclusion.com

www.projectparticipate.org

www.specialed.com

> *"Teaching special needs students is so rewarding and worthwhile. I feel so needed and important to my students. It's a wonderful feeling."*
>
> —Paige Adcock, 4 years experience

WORKING SUCCESSFULLY WITH PARAEDUCATORS

Paraeducators are professionals who assist special education teachers and general education teachers by working directly with students. Paraeducators will often be the people with whom special needs students have the closest contact all day.

Paraeducators can assume a variety of tasks in the classroom depending on the particular needs of their students. As a part of an inclusion team or as teaching assistants in your classroom, the paras that you work with will best be able to help you and your students if you work together well. The following tips will help you and the paraeducators that you work with learn to work together successfully.

- Make sure that you include paraeducators in meetings you have with parents and administrators about students. Paras can often offer special insights about the students they work with.
- Treat paraeducators with professional courtesy at all times.
- Once you determine the strengths and special skills of the paras you work with, tap into those skills to help your students. For example, if you have a para who is excellent at reading aloud, encourage him or her to read to students.
- You should decide together what the para's role should be in various aspects of class. Plan exactly what duties and responsibilities you are both comfortable with and remain flexible to change as the term progresses.
- Anticipate and clarify issues that might cause problems. For example, what kinds of interventions should the para make if students are misbehaving?
- Unless a paraeducator is also a certified teacher, do not leave him or her in charge of the class while you are absent from the room. The law requires that a certified person supervise students.
- Maintain open lines of communication by scheduling time to discuss any problems or concerns that may arise.

To learn more about how to work well with a paraeducator, search these Web sites.

www.ed.gov/pubs/paraprofessionals/profdev.html

www.nrcpara.org

www.para.unl.edu

Students with Attention Disorders

Attention Deficit Disorder (ADD) and Attention Deficit/Hyperactivity Disorder (AD/HD) are two learning problems that make it difficult for students who have those disorders to be academically successful in school without intervention.

If you are not a special education teacher, you will usually be informed at the beginning of the term by a special education teacher regarding which of your students have attention disorders. That teacher will make suggestions about accommodations and will review the student's IEP or Section 540 form with you. Both of these documents will provide detailed guidelines regarding your responsibilities for teaching particular students.

Below is a list of some general guidelines to assist you in teaching students with either attention disorder.

- Enlist support from other professionals and from the parents and guardians of ADD and AD/HD students. These people will be an excellent source of support and advice as you work together to assist students.

- ADD and AD/HD students do not always have effective school-related skills such as note taking or following directions. Take time to show them how to accomplish some of the tasks that other students find easy to do. You will find that they do best when they know how to use planners and follow a course outline.

- Clearly define classroom procedures for ADD and AD/HD students to help them stay on task. Be careful to post rules and schedules. These students will benefit from seeing as well as hearing directions and other information.

- Place these students near you so that you can monitor them unobtrusively and frequently. You should also seat them with their backs to other students so that they will be less easily distracted. Other distractions to consider are doors, windows, computer screens, pencil sharpeners, and other high traffic areas.

- Provide ADD and AD/HD students with extra assistance during transition times. It is not always easy for them to adjust to a change.

- When you give directions, be sure to give them one step at a time. Help them understand that each task is a sequence of smaller steps. Use more than one modality when giving directions so that ADD and AD/HD students can see as well as hear what you want them to do.

- Photocopy parts of the text that they may find particularly difficult and highlight the parts that are most important. Do this to show your ADD and AD/HD students how they can do this themselves to focus on the most important information in the text.

- ADD and AD/HD students usually do well with an audiotape to listen to as they read a selection. You do not have to create these tapes yourself. Contact the publisher of your textbook, a special education teacher in your building, or your state's textbook adoption committee for copies.

- Be as flexible with extra time to complete assignments as you can.

- Learning to use a computer is often a skill that **ADD** and **AD/HD** students find helpful because it enables them to work quickly and competently.

- Peer tutoring is often very helpful for **ADD** and **AD/HD** students to reinforce skills and to share advice about study skills.

- Review frequently to make sure that these students have the basic skills and facts mastered before you move on to the next topic.

To learn more about how you can help students with attention disorders, search the Internet beginning with these sites.

www.addwarehouse.com

www.chadd.org

www.add.org

Students with 504 Plans

A 504 plan is a legally binding document that protects students who have a documented physical or mental disability that limits their ability to learn. Students with 504 plans are students whose disabilities do not have to be addressed by a teacher specifically trained to teach special education students. Instead, 504 plan students have needs that can be successfully addressed with modifications by a general education teacher.

Disabilities that a 504 plan student might have include ADD/ADHD, chronic illness, anger management problems, impaired vision or hearing, obesity, or being wheelchair-bound. While these students do not have impairments that are severe enough to qualify them for special education programs where they would have IEPs, their 504 plans spell out the special accommodations that they must receive. The accommodations that are included in a 504 plan usually include specialized instruction, school-related services (classrooms that are wheelchair accessible or special transportation, for example), or accommodations in the regular education classroom. The most frequent 504 plan accommodations are those that modify regular education instruction to meet the needs of the protected student.

When the school term begins, you will receive copies of the 504 plans that your students have. You may or may not be able to keep copies depending on your school's policies. You will also meet with the 504 plan administrator for your school to discuss each plan and what your specific responsibilities are.

Although each 504 plan is necessarily unique because it is tailored to the needs of the child it protects, the following are several typical accommodations that you can expect to see.

- Preferential seating
- Extended time on assignments
- Extra books or materials
- Reduced amount of practice
- More frequent parental contacts
- Early parental notification when problems arise
- Written copies of notes you may present orally
- Assistance with organizational skills

You must follow the 504 plan exactly. 504 plans are different from other school documents in that if you fail to follow them, the parents or guardians of the child have the right to sue not just the school district, but the *classroom teacher* as well. Even if an accommodation is not one that you are personally comfortable meeting, you *must* make that accommodation. To find out more about how you can help students with 504 plans, search the following Web sites.

www.mindskillspress.com
www.angelfire.com
www.adprima.com.specialed.htm

At-Risk Students

At-risk students are those who are very likely to drop out of school instead of graduate. Because their future success depends on getting as much education as they can, at-risk students depend on their teachers to help them stay in school.

While there are many promising programs and a great deal of support available for most students who are at-risk, there are still too many students who drop out of school. It is very possible that some of your own students will not finish their education. There is little that can discourage a teacher more than to have a promising student see no other way out of a current problem than to give up on an education.

Students can be at-risk for dropping out for many reasons. Here are just a few of the possible contributing factors.

- Family problems
- Poor academic skills
- Substance abuse
- Pregnancy
- Emotional problems
- Chronic peer conflicts
- Repeated failure in school

- Inadequate parental supervision
- Undiagnosed learning problems
- Chronic illness

Even though there are many factors that can contribute to a student's risk of dropping out, there are also many strategies that you can use to assist students who are in danger of not completing their education. These strategies will benefit all your students; however, it is even more important for you to reach out to those who are at-risk. Adapt the following ideas to accommodate the needs of your at-risk students.

▶ Be persistent in your efforts to motivate these students. Don't hesitate to let them know that you plan to keep them in school as long as you can.

▶ Set small goals that will help students reach a larger one. If you can get them in the habit of achieving at least one goal each day, they can build on this pattern of success.

▶ Involve them in cooperative learning activities.

▶ Motivate students to want to be successful by providing them with role models. Invite guest speakers and even have older students talk with younger ones about the importance of staying in school.

▶ Offer open-ended questions so that at-risk students can attempt answers without fear of failure.

▶ Be generous with praise and attention. Often your kind words may be the only ones your at-risk students will hear all day.

▶ Seek assistance from support personnel and family members. Begin with the guidance counselors at your school. It takes many determined adults to change a student's mind once he or she has decided to drop out.

▶ Check on them when they are absent. Call home. Show your concern.

▶ Create situations where these students can be successful. Perhaps they can tutor younger students, mediate peer conflict, or help you with classroom chores. Focus on their strengths.

▶ Connect to these students in a positive way. Make sure that they feel that they are important to you and to the rest of the class.

There is a great deal of research about the factors that cause students to drop out and the best ways to prevent this from happening. To learn more about at-risk students, you can begin your own Internet research with these sites.

www.ed.gov
www.mckinneyisd.net/soar
www.wmich.edu/at-risk

Students Repeating Your Class

Students who have to repeat a class or a grade level often bring some of the negative emotions from the failure into their new class. At first, they may start out full of energy and enthusiasm for the new class, but this positive attitude can fade.

To help students who may be taking your class for the second time or who have to repeat a grade level, you can take a proactive stance that will make the second experience a positive one for both you and the students. Follow these suggestions.

- Be sensitive to the emotional needs of these students. They have already experienced a significant amount of failure and its repercussions. In addition, students who have to repeat a class are worried about making new friends, having others think they are not intelligent, letting their families down, and failing again.

- Don't make unkind or joking references to the past failure even if the students do it themselves. Acknowledge what they say briefly, and then reassure them that your class is a different experience from the first one.

- Help them make new friends by assigning collaborative group members.

- Repeating students often mistakenly believe that merely recognizing the work as something that they did previously is the same as mastering it. Help them to understand that even though they may have seen the work before, a review of the material will make sure that they know it.

"I make students believe they are actually working a job while they are in school. They need to report to work on time and be ready to work. Their report cards serve as paychecks! When students are getting in trouble, they are warned that they are about to get fired. Believe it or not, they don't want to be unemployed."

—Sabrina Smith, 3 years experience

- Design lessons so these students have new material to learn or new ways to learn it. This is especially crucial if you are teaching students who were in your class the previous school year.

- Boost their self-esteem by allowing them to assume an active and helpful role in the class. Repeating students can be excellent peer tutors and are usually adept at running errands and doing other chores.

- If you find that these students dwell on events in the past more than you are comfortable with, hold a conference to work out some of the issues that caused their failures so that they can move forward.

- Monitor their progress carefully to make sure that repeating students stay on task to prevent the cycle of failure from beginning again.

▶ Make sure that these students have frequent written progress checks so that they can see when they are being successful and when they need to work just a bit harder to maintain a good average.

▶ Be generous and specific in your praise so that they can feel good about themselves again.

Impulsive Students

Impulsivity is a learning problem that is easy to recognize in students at any age. Impulsive students act before thinking and have to suffer the consequences of their actions. Impulsive students are often labeled as troublemakers and draw much negative attention to themselves. While many students are impulsive in their behavior occasionally, the chief characteristic of impulsive students is the extreme degree of their actions. Some of their behaviors can include the following.

- Forgetting to do their homework
- Blurting out answers
- Beginning an assignment over and over
- Forgetting class rules or procedures
- Poor anger management
- Hyperactivity
- Mood swings
- Extreme disorganization

Impulsive students require patient and persistent firmness. You can help impulsive students become successful with patience and consistent effort. Your goal with impulsive students is to replace their inappropriate behaviors with positive ones. If you have impulsive students, adapt some of these strategies to help them learn to control themselves.

▶ Be very specific about behavior limits. Impulsive students need clear boundaries and consistent, calm enforcement.

▶ Teach impulsive students how to manage their materials. They often lack strong organizational skills and need your support in learning how to keep up with their belongings.

▶ Talk to the parents and guardians of your impulsive students to enlist their help in promoting a systematic approach to organizational skills. Sometimes a simple technique such as packing up a book bag or laying out clothes at night will help these students develop organizational skills.

▶ Allow only the materials that they need for an assignment on their desks. Discourage them from keeping toys, gadgets, cosmetics, and other distracting items at school.

▶ Monitor carefully to keep off-task behavior to a minimum. Be gentle, firm, and calm with these students when you redirect them.

- If your efforts are not as successful as you would like, hold a conference with the student and work out a behavior contract. Often impulsive students respond well to behavior contracts because they are very specific about which behavior is acceptable and which is not.

- Insist that impulsive students use a daily planner and check it often to make sure that they are using it to organize their lives.

- Structure your lessons so that these students can understand the big picture of what they are to do each day.

- Impulsive students are easily overwhelmed by long-term assignments. Break their work into small manageable steps and monitor their progress on each one.

- Impulsive students are used to receiving negative attention for their behavior. Use positive reinforcement to build their self-confidence and keep them on the right track.

Pregnant Students

More than half a million school-aged girls become mothers each year. The effects of this widespread problem are painful to the girls, their families, the fathers, and to the babies. When a girl becomes pregnant, she finds it almost impossible to stay in school.

When a girl confides to you that she is pregnant, you must maintain a professional distance. While you can offer your support and understanding, there are clear limits to the role that a teacher should assume with students who are pregnant. Your primary obligation to a pregnant student is to be her teacher, not her confidant, and your goal should be to find support to help the student stay in school as long as she can. This means that you should refer her to the trained professionals in your school who knows how to successfully manage student pregnancies. Counselors, the school nurse, and school social workers are all helpful resources. Further, you should encourage the girl to tell her parents or guardians at once. While many girls are afraid of disappointing their parents, it is not your place to usurp their authority when their daughter is pregnant.

Be careful of becoming overly involved in a pregnant girl's concerns. Here are some guidelines to help you deal successfully with pregnant students.

- You may not offer any medical advice, nor are you permitted to assist the student in arranging medical help. If you find that she needs help, arrange for her to speak with the school nurse.

- You can make pregnant girls more comfortable by moving them close to the door so that they can slip out to the restroom. Arrange for a comfortable desk. Often a chair and a table is a more comfortable seating arrangement than a school desk.

- While it is acceptable for a pregnant girl to talk about her pregnancy with you, be careful to maintain your position as a teacher when you talk with her. Don't offer advice about child care or child rearing. Instead, help her stay focused on school concerns as long as you can.

▶ Make it as easy as you can for a pregnant student to make up missed work and to keep up with her class work. A pregnant student is likely to require homebound instruction. Be prompt in getting the work to her and in providing prompt feedback so she can stay on track.

To learn more about how you can handle pregnant students in your class, try these Web sites.

www.ed.gov/pubs/ParentingTeens/chapter

www.reeusda.gov/f4hn/efnep/success-pregnantteens.htm

Students Who Are Underachievers

Few students have the capacity go through all of their school years without having moments when they could have done better. Occasional underachievement is to be expected. The problem with this behavior occurs when it is the overriding pattern of a student's approach to school life.

Chronic underachievement is a problem you will find in many students no matter how old they are or how capable they are. Their parents will be quick to tell you that their children are lazy or just don't try hard enough. The students themselves will also often label themselves in these negative ways.

As you begin to work with underachieving students, you will find yourself calling their parents or guardians often, and you will find yourself frustrated when no punishment that you can devise will solve the problem. In fact, many underachievers will accept punishment as their due.

Chronic underachievement is not just a bad habit. It is often an elaborate defense mechanism that students adopt to protect themselves from their anxiety about failing. Often underachieving students will have parents who are very involved in their lives and who are successful and highly goal-oriented people. Parents of underachievers spend lots of energy trying to understand and help their children.

The problem is compounded when underachievers are gifted students. These students often must live up to their parents' and teachers' high expectations and their own exacting standards and they opt for certain failure instead of trying hard and possibly failing. The contrast between their potential and what they achieve is frustrating for everyone who works with them.

Working with underachieving students can be made less frustrating with a combination of these strategies.

▶ Accept that these students' shortcoming are not the result of laziness, even though they may see themselves as lazy and worthless. Their anxiety levels often paralyze them.

▶ Work together with parents and guidance counselors to create a team of concerned adults, but be aware that over-involvement can sometimes increase a student's anxiety.

- Have extra supplies on hand for the times when an underachiever will forget to bring them to class.

- Be matter-of-fact about assignments. Expect that they will be done and offer extra help and encouragement. If you allow your anger to show or reprimand a student harshly for not completing the work, it will never be done.

- Monitor the student to offer help soon after you make an assignment in class. For many underachievers, the hardest part of an assignment is getting started. Often they will make several starts before giving up.

- Underachievers have a perfectionist approach to their studies that results in incomplete work—the opposite of what they wanted to accomplish. Offer encouragement often.

- Most underachievers have no trouble accepting the criticism that the adults in their lives use to express their disappointment over the years. They tend to use the negative labels to excuse themselves from not working. Don't allow students to give you excuses such as, "I am just lazy" or "I never do well in math."

- Boost their self-esteem by encouraging them to tutor less able students. Often underachievers will do for other students what they cannot do for themselves.

Students Living in Poverty

Over ten million school-aged students in America live in poverty. You don't have to teach in a blighted urban area or a depressed rural one to teach students who are from poor families.

The lives of poor students are often very different from those of their more affluent peers. They cannot look forward to an abundance of presents at Christmas or on their birthdays. Back-to-school shopping is not an exciting time of new clothes and school supplies. Even small outlays of money are significant to students living in poverty; a locker fee, a soft drink for a class party, and a fee for a field trip may all be out of their reach. And because they do not wear the same fashionable clothes as their peers, these students are often the targets of ridicule.

Economically disadvantaged students have a very difficult time succeeding in school. One of the most unfortunate results of their economic struggles is that students who live in poverty often drop out of school, choosing a low-paying job to pay for the luxuries that they have been denied instead of an education.

Despite the bleak outlook for many of these students, there is much that you can do to make school meaningful and a haven for them. You can help your students who live in poverty by implementing some of these suggestions in your class.

- When you suspect that students are being taunted by their peers for their poverty, act quickly to stop it.

- Work to boost their self-esteem by praising their success in school and for positive peer relationships instead of what they own.

- Don't make comments about your students' clothes or belongings unless they are in violation of the dress code. Doing so may underscore the economic disparity among

439

students. In addition, students are often too focused on their belongings and you should avoid reinforcing this focus.

- Be careful about the school supplies that you expect your students to purchase. Keep your requirements as simple as you can for all students.

- Arrange a bank of shared supplies for your students to borrow from when they are temporarily out of materials for class.

- Make sure that you don't require activities that are costly. For example, if you require students to pay to go on a field trip, some of your students will have trouble going on the trip.

- If you notice that a student does not have lunch money, check to make sure that a free lunch is an option for that child.

- Be very sensitive to the potential for embarrassment in even small requests for or comments about money that you make. For example, if you jokingly remark to these students that "there is no such thing as a free lunch," you will embarrass them.

- Be aware that class parties where students are required to bring in food to share are difficult for some students.

- Make it clear that you value all of your students for their character and not for their possessions.

For more information on how to help your economically disadvantage students, try these Internet sites.

www.findarticles.com/cf_dls/m2248

www.students.dsu.edu/barthelc/education.context.html

www.fortnet.org/hcc/issues

Avoid Gender Bias in Your Classroom

Research studies are clear in their results: Boys receive more attention from their teachers and gender stereotyping is a common practice in almost every classroom. Gender bias is one of the most prevalent unconscious attitudes that many people, including teachers, hold.

The problem with gender bias lies in the damage that it causes. For example, many girls do not enjoy mathematics because they see it as a subject suitable for boys. On the other hand, boys who are loud and rude often receive far less substantial punishments than girls who do the same thing because their teachers adopt a "boys will be boys" approach.

You can help yourself and your students understand and mitigate the gender bias in your classroom by raising your awareness and by being as proactive as you can. Here are some strategies that can help.

- Make sure that you communicate the same expectations for academic achievement to both genders. Males and females can be equally capable students in any subject.

- Balance the genders that you use in examples and problems.

- Use language that includes both genders. For example, replace "mailman" with "mail carrier" and "chairman" with "chairperson."

- Make non-traditional situations the norm in your class. For example, when you make a general reference to a job associated with men, such as a pilot, say "she," and when you mention a "woman's job," such as a nurse or secretary, say "he."

- Pay attention to how you give attention. Do you focus more on the males in your class than you do the females?

- Do not allow students to group themselves according to gender. Make sure that you balance genders when you create groups in your class.

- When you have classroom duties, do not assign them along gender lines. Girls can carry things and boys can tidy up a mess.

Celebrate the Cultures in Your Class

One of the most enduring successes of the public school system in America is the variety of cultures that meet peacefully in thousands of classrooms each day. In classroom after classroom, students of all different races and cultural backgrounds study together. At a time when school systems are under relentless attack from many sides, classroom diversity is one of our nation's greatest assets.

Although some people try to narrowly define culture in ethnic or racial terms, a broader definition is more accurate. Every person belongs to a variety of cultural groups delineated by such features as geography, age, economics, gender, religion, interests, or even education levels. If you ignore the cultural differences among your students, you will create strife and tension. Conversely, if you choose to accept and celebrate those differences, you will find those differences a rich resource in your class.

By teaching your students to value their differences, you create a truly global classroom. And by expanding students' appreciation of each other, you will show them how to appreciate the rest of the world.

Here are some general guidelines you can use to incorporate the many cultures in your classroom into a successful unified group.

- Expose your students to a wide variety of cultures throughout the term. By doing this, you will enable them to be more tolerant of each other's differences.

- Make discussing the differences in cultures in your class an important part of what you and your students do together. You can use a few minutes at the start of class every now and then to manage this without losing valuable instructional time.

- Accept that the concerns of a parent or guardian who is not part of your culture may not be the concerns that you have. If you are sensitive to this when you speak with parents, you will find yourself asking questions that will help you determine what their goals for their children are before you attempt to impose your own beliefs.

▶ Stress the importance of an open-minded attitude about people whose beliefs or lifestyles are different from your students. Make sure you model that acceptance yourself.

▶ Promote activities that will increase your students' self-esteem. Students who are self-confident are not as likely to taunt others in order to feel good about themselves.

▶ Even if you have lived in your community all of your life, take time to learn about its various cultural groups. Understanding how these groups are represented in the school system will help you understand your students better.

▶ If students are taught racism or intolerance at home, you will have a very difficult time stopping it in class. Your first step in combating these attitudes is to make your position very clear to your students through what you say and what you do.

To learn more about how to incorporate a multicultural approach to educating your students, explore these Web sites.

www.nameorg.org

www.newhorizons.org

www.curry.edschool.virginia.edu/go/multicultural

Transcend the Differences in Your Classroom

Time after time successful adults who overcome disabilities, prejudice, and other hopeless circumstances have credited their success to the powerful influence that school had on their lives at a time when they needed guidance. Although the circumstances for your students in your school district may not be as grim as for those in disadvantaged areas, there are plenty of students in your class who need nurturing and guidance.

When you create a positive classroom culture for your students, you help them transcend the differences that could divide them. You replace those differences with a classroom culture that supersedes the other cultures in your room and you help your students develop a sense of loyalty and belonging. Students in this kind of classroom see themselves as part of a large and supportive team.

There are many ways to create a classroom culture of mutual support. Begin the process with the strategies in the following list that best fit your students' needs.

▶ Use plural possessive pronouns often. Saying "our" room, "our" books, and "our" desks is much friendlier than saying "my" and "mine."

▶ Post a chart of the good things you notice your students doing in a prominent place in the room. It never hurts to remind them of their successes.

▶ Stress the importance of courtesy as a mark of respect to each other, the class, you, and themselves.

- Encourage students to help each other in understanding their lessons as often as possible. Students who study together or who tutor their peers not only learn the material better, but form a bond.

- Have students work together to make up missed work. Students should be the ones to remind each other to do this so you don't have to nag.

- Involve students in the daily tasks of the classroom such as cleaning up, passing out papers, and running errands.

- Celebrate often. Choose overlooked holidays such as Flag Day as well as students' birthdays and successes.

- Ask students' advice and opinions about school issues. Students often have useful insights on issues that may puzzle you.

- Picking on each other and saying insulting things is an unpleasant habit for many students. Teach your students the importance of saying complimentary things to each other.

- Have a class goal for your students. For example, they might have to work toward improving their behavior so that they can take a field trip. Emphasize what they can do as a group to share in a reward that they all worked to earn.

- Present students with as many real-life problems to solve as possible so they can see the need to work together. For example, if your school's cafeteria has plain, drab walls, your students could organize a project to cover the walls with student-produced murals.

- Display your students' work along with photographs of them working together. This will increase students' sense of pride as well as their sense of partnership with other students.

- Accept your students' help when they offer it. If someone offers to help you carry something or run an errand, accept the offer whenever you can.

Journal Entries to Help You Thrive in a Diverse Classroom

▶ What do you anticipate as your biggest challenge as a teacher in a diverse classroom? How can you rise to this challenge?

▶ What are some of the different cultures in your class? How do they reflect your community? How can you promote awareness and appreciation of these cultures?

▶ Which of your students is obviously different from the others? What problems has that caused? What are the benefits? What is your role?

▶ Do you have any unconscious gender biases that affect the way you treat your students? What steps will you take to ensure that both boys and girls thrive in your classroom?

▶ How can your school improve how special needs students are taught? How can you improve how you teach these children?

▶ Which student population struggles most in your school? What can you do to help?

▶ Which of your students are at risk for dropping out? What can you do to intervene?

▶ Do you pay attention to the special needs of gifted students in your class? What support do you offer them and what allowances do you make for their accelerated learning abilities?

▶ Which of your students may have undiagnosed special needs? What can you do to help?

▶ Which of your students has an attention disorder? What can you do to help this student be successful?

▶ What strengths do you bring to a diverse classroom? What is there in your background that enables you to be a successful teacher?

Stress Management for Educators

It's 8:05. She stands at her mailbox looking over the pile of papers. She finds a phone message marked "Urgent," a list of her students' overdue library books, a reminder notice about the staff meeting after school, and a note from the assistant principal: "Please see me this morning."

She heads off to her classroom. The copier is still down. Today's quiz will have to be oral. Glancing at the clock she sees that she has only eight minutes to write the day's warm-up on the board, turn on the computers, check e-mail, and organize the graded papers she needs to return. Last night, she spent two hours creating three different versions of the test she is supposed to give tomorrow. She is still upset about last week's cheating incident. She wonders if she handled it correctly. Is that why the assistant principal wants to see her?

Tonight she will have to go to a copy shop to photocopy the test if the copier is still down. It will be expensive, but what else can she do? She knew that teaching would be a challenge, but she did not expect it to be so grueling. She sighs. The weekend will be here soon.

Surveys in recent years reveal that teaching is one of the most stressful occupations in America. Teachers face escalating pressures from a society that looks to education to solve the problems of its children. Those same surveys point out the obvious: The members of our profession most vulnerable to the negative effects of career stress are novice teachers.

The negative effects of these intense stress levels often erode a teacher's initial idealism. The result? Burnout. While inexperienced teachers are most at risk, burnout can happen to anyone at any time. It is not a sudden event, but rather an accumulation of stresses that, in time, can turn even the most enthusiastic teacher into a disheartened cynic. In fact, it is the idealistic teacher who is most affected.

Burnout Can Happen to You

How can you tell if you are in danger of burning out? The signs of burnout vary from person to person, but here are some common symptoms.

• Fatigue	• Negativity	• Absenteeism
• Depression	• Sleep disturbances	• Listlessness
• Impatience	• Undereating	• Cynicism
• Defensiveness	• Overeating	• Angry outbursts
• Illness	• Substance abuse	• Low self-esteem
• Alienation	• Impatience	• Blaming others

Burnout begins slowly. The combination of work stresses and inadequate coping skills leads first to exhaustion and then to an increasingly negative attitude. As a teacher struggles to cope, a common mistake is to work longer hours in an effort to fix the problem, which only increases the sufferer's mental, emotional, and physical fatigue. All educators are at risk of burnout. They don't have to be inexperienced or have a difficult schedule or have the worst behaved students in the school. Teachers are all at risk at any time.

Although even the best teachers can experience burnout, it is not inevitable. As a teacher, there are many steps that you can take to prevent stress from having a negative effect on your life and your career. Because this stress is not going to vanish overnight, it is up to you to protect yourself from burnout. No one else can do it for you.

In the rest of this section you will find suggestions that will help you learn to successfully cope with the demands of your profession. You will learn how to avoid the harmful effects of burnout by building a supportive workplace and by taking charge of your own emotional, mental, and physical well being.

Reasons Novice Teachers Can Be Especially Vulnerable to Burnout

New teachers may be vulnerable to burnout for the following reasons.

1. They lack expertise in juggling the daily routines of teaching.
2. They lack a support network.
3. They face the same demands as experienced teachers.
4. They are uncertain about the right action to take.
5. They do not have enough accumulated resource materials.
6. They experience a loss of idealism when faced with classroom reality.
7. They can be assigned the students or classes no one else will take.

Figure 16.1

WHAT DO YOU KNOW ABOUT STRESS MANAGEMENT?

As a teacher, even during just one class period, you are bombarded with demands on your time, energy, and emotions. Class after class, you rush through your workdays coping with obligations and problems. Gradually the stresses can build until they replace your enjoyment and wear away your confidence.

How you decide to manage this stress determines whether or not you can manage your professional life successfully. To begin the stress management process, you should first determine what you already know about stress management.

Below you will find a list of stress management options. Select the ones that you use whenever you face a difficult day at work. Then, check your score to see if your stress management strategies could be more effective.

Whenever I have a difficult day at school, I handle it by:

1. _____ Taking a quick nap
2. _____ Drinking alcohol
3. _____ Sending a heated e-mail about the source of my stress
4. _____ Talking it over with a friend
5. _____ Working even harder
6. _____ Cooking a hearty meal
7. _____ Watching the news
8. _____ Taking a brisk walk
9. _____ Watching two or three hours of television
10. _____ Writing a journal entry
11. _____ Smoking
12. _____ Asking for advice
13. _____ Taking an exercise class
14. _____ Figuring out how to delegate responsibility
15. _____ Talking to my mentor
16. _____ Reading a book
17. _____ Getting up two hours earlier
18. _____ Indulging in a sweet treat
19. _____ Playing with a child or a pet
20. _____ Straightening up my classroom
21. _____ Writing out a plan for tomorrow
22. _____ Turning on some music
23. _____ Meditating or praying
24. _____ Staying up late
25. _____ Doing something creative

Check your rating

If you chose any of the responses explained below, then you are not managing your stress as effectively as you could, and you could be headed for burnout.

2 Alcohol is a depressant. It won't help you solve problems.

3 Ranting and raving may feel good at the moment, but there may be serious repercussions from your angry message. It's better to cool down first.

5 Working harder is a logical response, but one that can lead to more stress and physical exhaustion. Figure out ways to work more efficiently, not harder.

7 Although it is important to be well informed, watching a series of disasters on the news will not relieve your stress.

9 Although this may provide a temporary "escape," becoming a couch potato is not the answer to your work frustrations.

11 Smoking is a serious health concern and is certainly not a solution to your workday difficulties.

17 Sleep deprivation will only compound your stress. You need an adequate amount of sleep in order to do your job well.

18 Sweet treats in moderation are not bad for you. Overindulging is.

24 Staying up late is just as stressful as getting up too early. Your body needs rest.

Figure 16.2
RATE YOUR SUSCEPTIBILITY

Although all people live with stress, it only becomes a problem when it takes over a person's life. Then it is no longer a positive force that keeps a person motivated, but toxic distress instead, leading to burnout.

Use this simple test to determine your susceptibility to distress and burnout. Follow these two-step directions.

1. Carefully consider each statement and determine how it applies to your professional life, and decide how many work days a week you believe each one could apply to you.

2. On the line preceding the statement, place a number from 0 to 5 for the number of school days per week the statement could apply to you.

1. _____ I have enough energy to be an effective teacher.

2. _____ My students are motivated to succeed.

3. _____ I efficiently manage my non-instructional responsibilities: grading papers, planning, reports, phone calls, faculty meetings, duty assignments, conferences, etc.

4. _____ I use effective discipline procedures.

5. _____ I enjoy my students.

6. _____ The people I work with think that I am a good teacher.

7. _____ I make a difference in my students' lives.

8. _____ I control what happens in my classroom.

9. _____ I work with friendly and supportive colleagues.

10. _____ I pay attention to my stress levels and use stress reduction techniques whenever I feel overwhelmed and frustrated.

Add up your total points and multiply them by 2. My score is _____ × 2 = _____.

Here's how you're doing.

90–100	=	A	You're managing stress well.
80–89	=	B	There are some problems at school that you can manage more effectively, but your overall stress management skills are sound.
70–79	=	C	You need to take time to deal with some of the issues that are causing you stress. If you attend to them now, your professional life will be much more rewarding.
Below 70	=	F	You are in danger of burning out. But don't give up. You can avoid burnout if you commit yourself to managing stress. Look at the areas covered in the ten questions to see where you can begin to manage your school responsibilities and your school stress with more ease. Talk to a mentor and seek more support. Read the rest of this section for strategies that can help reduce your stress to manageable levels.

Work Stressors You Can Control

Although there are many problems facing both experienced and novice educators, you can reduce frustration levels when you realize that there are many stresses at school that you can control with just a bit of effort and some creative thinking. Here is a brief inventory of some common problems that you can manage with just a little time, effort, and imagination. You may be struggling with some of these now, while others may be problems you will face in the future. Below each problem you will find a few suggested solutions, as well as space for you to add your own solution.

Problem 1: Unpleasant colleagues with whom you share planning periods

Suggested solutions:

1. Ask your congenial colleagues where they gather to work and make it a point to join them.
2. Avoid joining in negative conversations even if you agree with the complaints.
3. Structure your plan period time so that you accomplish as much as possible.

Your solution: _____

Problem 2: Paperwork that seems overwhelming

Suggested solutions:

1. Use a "To Do" list to manage your school time as efficiently as possible.
2. Keep a supply of the materials you need to manage the work easily: pens, calculator, folders, etc.
3. Prioritize your paperwork so that you complete it on time.

Your solution: _____

Problem 3: An untidy or unappealing classroom

Suggested solutions:

1. Share the responsibility with your students by taking the last two minutes of each class to have them straighten their work areas.
2. Arrange the desks so students are not against the walls. This will discourage graffiti.
3. You do not have to purchase expensive posters or other supplies to make a room appealing. Display your students' work instead.

Your solution: _____

Problem 4: Students who nag about unreturned papers

Suggested solutions:

1. Stagger the due dates for papers that take longer to grade than others.
2. Use rubrics to grade as many assignments as possible.

3. Make a commitment to yourself that you will return all papers to your students within three days.

Your solution: _____

Problem 5: Maintaining a professional image

Suggested solutions:

1. Try to find casual clothing that projects a professional image while allowing you maximum comfort. When you are shopping, find a balance between your desire for casual comfort and your identity as a role model.
2. Meet all of the people in your building with a pleasant smile and a friendly greeting.
3. Keep your personal life private.

Your solution: _____

Problem 6: Parents and guardians who are not as cooperative as you think they should be

Suggested solutions:

1. Be the first to reach out to them. Begin each term with a pleasant and informative introductory letter.
2. Send home positive notes and make positive phone calls.
3. Continue to reach out to uncooperative parents and guardians with positive news as well as requests for help.

Your solution: _____

Problem 7: Students who are not interested in the lessons that you plan

Suggested solutions:

1. Add relevance by relating lessons to your students' interests and goals.
2. Build in plenty of motivation techniques when you plan lessons.
3. Make sure that your students understand how they can benefit from the material you teach.

Your solution: _____

Problem 8: A sense of uncertainty about what you are supposed to accomplish

Suggested solutions:

1. If your district does not have a planned course outline for your subject, use the Internet to research what other districts or states use.
2. Plan large units of study first so that you can see the big picture of what you expect to accomplish.
3. At the start of each term write a personal mission statement that reflects your goals for your students.

Your solution: _____

Work Stressors You Can't Control

In education, as in all professions, there will always be problems that you just can't control. One of the most frustrating aspects of your professional life will be learning to recognize the stressful situations that you can change and those that you can't.

For situations that you can't control, at least during the current school year, the most practical solution is to learn to accept their existence. Determining what you can realistically change and what you can't is a very important step in avoiding burnout. This acceptance does not mean that these problems don't really exist or are not significant. It also doesn't mean that you won't work on them at some time in the future. What it does mean is that you are choosing a mature and healthy approach to your current professional responsibilities.

Your school life will be much easier and more rewarding if you learn to change what you can and accept what you can't. Complete the assessment in Figure 16.3 to help you identify problems that you face in your career as an educator and think about how you will handle them. Take comfort in knowing that other teachers face these same problems, but have adjusted. Focus on what's really important: being the best teacher you can be in spite of the problems you can't solve.

> *"Education is potentially the most rewarding, the most satisfying profession in the world, but you need to understand the extent to which it will occupy your self. You must really want to teach if you are going to do it."*
>
> —Ken Pfeifer, 28 years experience

Figure 16.3

WHICH PROBLEMS MUST YOU CHANGE AND WHICH
MUST YOU ADAPT TO?

The following list identifies common problems many educators face. When you look over this list, place a check beside the ones that apply to your present situation. After you have done this, use the space provided for you to list any other problems that you can recognize as ones that you can't control at this point in your career.

- ☐ Too much will always be asked of teachers.
- ☐ You can't reach every child every day.
- ☐ You are expected to work well with everyone, even very negative people.
- ☐ You will be called on to help students with overwhelming problems.
- ☐ Your students engage your emotions, sometimes to your distress.
- ☐ Even the best supervisors can be overburdened and unsympathetic.
- ☐ No one has limitless energy and time.
- ☐ You will not always be certain about the right course of action.
- ☐ Some parents or guardians will not be supportive of schools or teachers.
- ☐ You will never have enough productive time with your students.
- ☐ Many teachers cope with outdated equipment and texts, overcrowded classes, inadequate supplies, and buildings in need of repair.
- ☐ Not every student will be prepared for the subject or grade level that you teach.
- ☐ The paperwork load is arduous.
- ☐ Surveys show that many teachers and students no longer feel safe at school.
- ☐ School districts may have ineffective discipline policies.
- ☐ There will never be enough available phone lines to contact parents or guardians easily.
- ☐ Standardized tests will not always be an accurate reflection of student achievement.
- ☐ There are hundreds of important policies, procedures, and rules to learn.
- ☐ Teachers will have more homework than their students.
- ☐ You will always want to be a better teacher.

Problems that I am experiencing right now that I can't control:

_____

_____

_____

_____

The First Step: Focus on the Positive

If your mental blueprints tend to be negative ones, you are far more likely to suffer from the ill effects of stress than a person with a positive outlook. A positive person interprets many events as interesting challenges, whereas a negative person will see them as stressful impediments. The positive person will not suffer the ill effects of stress; the negative one will. Fortunately, there are many ways to cultivate a strong positive mindset. Positive thinking is a habit that becomes easier with practice.

20 Positive Thinking Strategies

If you want to protect yourself from the unhappiness of stress and burnout, begin to practice a positive attitude with some of these strategies.

1. Help a student or colleague feel important.
2. Take inventory of your teaching strengths.
3. Quit striving for perfection.
4. Make yourself smile often.
5. Surround yourself with your favorite colors.
6. Keep a running list of your daily successes.
7. When you find yourself obsessing about a problem, STOP.
8. Be generous with compliments.
9. Add more of what enriches you to your life.
10. Ask yourself what it is that you take for granted.
11. Look your best.
12. Make yourself tolerant of others.
13. Practice random acts of kindness.
14. Savor the good things that happen.
15. Spend time on an activity you enjoy.
16. Indulge in a pleasant memory.
17. Tell your students how much you appreciate them.
18. Look for options when you are faced with a problem.
19. Figure out five ways that you are lucky.
20. Make a point of expressing gratitude.

> *"Remember to give yourself personal time."*
>
> —Kelly Mansfield, 2 years experience

25 Other Proactive Anti-Burnout Strategies

Although developing a positive outlook is one of the most effective tools that you have in the battle against burnout, it is not enough. To avoid the damage that burnout can cause, you need to be proactive. You have to prevent the buildup of the small stresses that eventually lead to distress and burnout. Consider some of the following strategies when you create a proactive plan to prevent toxic stress from taking over your life.

1. Place great value on your personal time. Working longs hours every day is a sure path to burnout. You need time to just be yourself.

2. Allow yourself time to make effective transitions from one class to another. This is particularly difficult when you have many classes each day. One way to manage this is by having an opening routine that your students can do independently. This will free you to make the mental, emotional, and physical switch from one group of students to another.

3. Keep a flexible attitude. Get into the habit of looking for solutions instead of dwelling on your problems. If you are open to alternatives, you will be able to assess your options much more quickly.

4. Spend your energy in pursuit of the important things at school. When you are asked to do extra tasks that are too time-consuming, learn to say no. Practice saying, "Thank you for asking. I just can't do that right now."

5. Everyone benefits when you delegate responsibilities. Decide who you want to do a task, clearly explain how you want it accomplished, and then step back and allow the people you selected to get busy.

6. Plan ahead. When you know that you are approaching a tough time at school, find opportunities to solve problems and not just suffer through them. Plan to thrive and not just survive.

7. Don't procrastinate. Resolve to accomplish the items on your "To Do" list before they become a problem. Small problems are less stressful than large ones.

8. Take good care of yourself. Teachers tend to be nurturing people who focus on the needs of others. But to succeed in taking care of others, you must take care of your own needs. Allow yourself time to rest, relax, have fun, exercise, eat well, and socialize.

9. Stop rushing from one responsibility to the next. Slow down. Here are some ways to slow your life down: take time to eat lunch, allow yourself at least ten minutes to relax with colleagues at some point during your day, and use your journal for reflection.

10. Adjust your mindset to accept that you will *never* be free from professional responsibilities during the school term.

11. Take time for frequent self-evaluation. Don't be overly critical, but when you find an area that you can improve, start to work on it. Start small and work on it one day at a time.

12. Plan how you will cope with stress in advance. A good way to do this is to make a plan of stress reduction strategies and keep it on hand for those times when you need to defuse anxiety and distress. You will find Figure 16.4 useful for this.

13. Keep the promises that you make. This proactive strategy will not only enhance your professional reputation, but it will also make your life much easier. Be careful not to over-commit, but when you make a promise, keep it.

14. Avoid unhealthy habits such as overeating, substance abuse, and obsessing. More bad habits will only make your life more difficult.

15. Skip the late night news. Read something humorous or inspirational instead.

16. Plan activities that you and your students can look forward to. Few teachers experience burnout while they are having fun.

17. Learn to pace your instruction to allow for some less intense teaching periods. For example, you should not lecture day after day. Instead, allow your students time for independent work, small group work, or even activities such as viewing films related to the subject under study. Being "on" all of the time will quickly exhaust you.

18. Work consistently to have a well-disciplined class. This will not only save you daily stress, but will benefit your students as well.

19. Add structure to your life. Routines will prevent many problems. For example, if you always place your classroom keys in the same spot in your desk each day, you will avoid the stress of looking for them.

20. Start to put together a network of supportive and positive people who can help you. Being connected to others is an important way to avoid the isolation that often accompanies burnout.

21. Take command of your school life. Establish realistic long- and short-term goals for yourself and then strive to achieve them.

22. Start your day with a clean desk.

23. Keep up with grading papers. Passing back papers quickly will allow you to remediate areas of weakness before they become serious.

24. Finish a task before you begin another. This habit will give you a solid sense of satisfaction that will carry you through the tough times in your day.

25. Think before you act. If you plan your responses to unpleasant situations you will prevent many problems. Situations that you should think about before you act include dealing with incomplete homework assignments, angry parents, defiant students, cheating incidents, tardy students, and other classroom disruptions.

A Dozen Ways to Ease Tension with Laughter

1. Make friends with amusing people.

2. Sign up with one of the many joke-of-the-day sites on the Internet.

3. Read the comics. Cut out some of the ones you like and put them on the bulletin board.

4. Watch a funny video.

5. Learn to value the absurdity in everyday life. Look for the humor in small things.

6. Keep a file of humorous stories, cartoons, riddles, jokes, photos, or other items related to your subject area. Share them with your students.

7. Keep another file of those funny mistakes that your students make.

8. Hang funny posters and photographs near your desk.

9. Check out humorous books from your nearest public library.

10. When times are really stressful, make a joke out of your problems.

11. Learn to tell jokes. You'll be welcomed in the teachers' lounge.

12. Ask your students to share jokes with the class. A shared moment of laughter will do wonders for you and your students.

Create a Collegial Support Group

Even the most experienced teacher can't do his or her job without the support of others. Every successful professional needs a supportive working environment, the benefits of which range from the relief of sharing frustrations to the sharing of insights and practical solutions.

Unfortunately, one of the biggest hurdles that novice teachers face is the lack of this necessary support. The isolation that can accompany a teaching career is especially evident in the first few years as new teachers adjust to their new profession. Being "out of the loop" can be a drawback for anyone, but it is especially detrimental to inexperienced teachers who can benefit most from the support of friendly colleagues.

Look past your department or grade level to see just how many colleagues you really have. Every adult involved in education is a potential source of support: hall buddies, mentors, outstanding teachers, other new teachers, people who teach in other grade levels, even people you meet at conventions or conferences can be part of your professional support network.

Keep the following pointers in mind when you begin to establish your own network of supportive colleagues.

- Don't just associate with the few people near your classroom. Be a friendly person who cheerfully greets everyone in the building. Be unfailingly upbeat and courteous.

- Begin by talking to other teachers whose classrooms are near yours or who share the same planning schedule. Ask teachers who teach the same courses that you do to collaborate with you on various projects that arise during the school year. Perhaps you could even experiment with team teaching.

▶ Invite one or two of the outstanding teachers in your school to come into your classroom to observe you as you teach. Share your concerns with colleagues about what you would like to improve about your teaching performance. Ask for feedback and really listen. Don't become defensive or angry if an observer has something negative to say about your performance.

▶ Organize a study group of your own. A good place to begin is with the other new teachers in the building. Pick a specific topic to study such as classroom management or lesson planning, and elicit advice from each person in the group. Share lesson plans, handouts, computer files, and materials.

▶ Make it a point to listen attentively when other teachers share their ideas. Be careful to associate with teachers who are enthusiastic about teaching or about projects involving their classes. Avoid the complainers who can infect you with their negative attitudes.

▶ When you are with your colleagues, steer the conversation past daily problems to bigger issues. Encourage others to go beyond gripes to share strategies, solve school problems, or advise you of ways to manage your professional responsibilities.

▶ Join professional organizations or subscribe to newsletters, journals, and magazines. When you do, you will develop a new appreciation for your profession, learn new ideas, and develop a new perspective that goes beyond the day-to-day routines of your school life. You will be motivated to try new ideas as well as make important contacts with other professionals.

▶ When you have an opportunity to attend conferences, workshops, inservices, or classes, take advantage of these opportunities. Keep an open mind and spend the meeting time learning as much as you can. Afterwards, talk over what you have learned with your colleagues.

Study Group Success Tips

1. Establish a regular meeting time and place.
2. Follow an agenda to organize your discussion.
3. Be open-minded and willing to listen.
4. Use the meeting time to:

Share insights.	Discuss problems.
Learn new ideas.	Connect with others.
Ask for guidance.	Celebrate successes.
Compare strategies.	
Plan projects and assignments together.	

Turn Problems into Opportunities

Suppose that you've scheduled an important test and on the test date ten of your students went on a field trip as part of another class instead of taking your test.

One response that you could have would be to become angry. You could scold the ten students for choosing the field trip instead of your test. If you chose this response, then your annoyance will cause you even more stress as your ten students react to your negativity. A more productive choice you could make would be to accept that the ten absent students probably didn't have a choice over whether or not to attend the field trip. You can arrange a time to work with them to make up the missed test. You can also use the time with them to discuss the importance of letting you know when they will be absent on a day when a test is scheduled.

By choosing to react in a productive way, you can turn a negative situation such as this one into an opportunity to help students make up their test and learn how important it is to communicate well with their teachers. You can react in a negative way or you can choose to solve a problem.

In every problem at school, even a very stressful one, there are opportunities to change, to learn, to grow, and to solve problems. Instead of viewing your problems as disasters, choose to see them as challenging opportunities.

6 Steps for Turning Challenges into Opportunities

Here is a six-step plan to follow whenever you are presented with a potential disaster that you want to turn into an opportunity.

Step 1: Choose to see a situation as an opportunity instead of as a problem.
Step 2: Take an objective look at all sides of the situation.
Step 3: Look for options by brainstorming as many solutions as you can.
Step 4: Carefully examine your possible solutions. Select the best solution that you can.
Step 5: Set your goals and make a plan to implement the solution.
Step 6: Put your plan into action.

In addition to a formal plan to rethink stressful situations, there are many techniques that will help you manage stress. Some are very easy to put into practice and some will take more time and effort, but your colleagues, your students, and you will all benefit from a positive approach.

Experiment with some of the following techniques to see which ones will help you in your current situation. Discard the ones that don't appeal to you right now and find creative ways to incorporate the ones that will help you balance your life and work responsibilities.

- Ask yourself how realistic you are when you are faced with a tough problem. Are you too optimistic about what you try to accomplish in a single day?

- Make a list of what you can learn from a troublesome situation.

- If your students are disruptive or defiant, refuse to take it personally. The cause of the problem probably has nothing to do with you.

- Stop and ask yourself what you might have done to cause a stressful situation and what you can do to prevent it from happening again. Take the opportunity to learn from your mistakes instead of dwelling on them.

- Ask yourself: Is a career in education causing stress or is it the day-to-day grind? Facing a career with many troubling demands is not easy, but neither are other careers. Before you allow yourself to burn out, carefully consider whether another career will really satisfy your needs.

20 Strategies for an Educator's Tough Times

Having a bad day? Try the following strategies to banish the stress that comes with a bad day at school.

1. Go to your school's media center and escape into a good book or read a newspaper.
2. Talk things over with a sympathetic colleague or mentor.
3. Take a brisk walk around the perimeter of your building.
4. Refuse to take it personally when students are rude or disruptive.
5. Find a quiet spot and practice deep breathing exercises.
6. Slowly count to one hundred before you speak in anger. Still stressed? Keep counting until you feel yourself relaxing.
7. Find a way to laugh at yourself or the situation.
8. If you have too much to do, divide each task into manageable amounts and get busy.
9. Turn on some music.
10. Take a break. Change activities. Do something you enjoy.
11. Brainstorm solutions to the cause of your stress.
12. Eat a healthful snack. Avoid junk food.
13. Acknowledge that you are genuinely upset. Denial doesn't help you solve problems.
14. Plan a pleasant activity that you can anticipate with pleasure.
15. Clear up some clutter. Tidy your desk or your classroom.
16. Shift your activity. Move to another location, if possible.
17. Ask for help.
18. Tackle busy work: grade quiz papers, answer e-mail, anything to be productive instead of paralyzed in negative emotions.
19. Deal with the problems that cause you stress. Don't procrastinate. Cope.
20. Remind yourself once again that today's problems probably won't be important a year from now—or maybe even a week from now.

Figure 16.4
SET GOALS TO REDUCE YOUR STRESS

How can I become more organized and efficient in my daily responsibilities?

Task	Strategy

Which responsibilities can I delegate?

Responsibility	To Whom	When

What productive activities can I add to my life?

_____

_____

What non-productive activities can I eliminate?

_____

_____

What long range plans to enhance my life can I put into effect right now?

_____

_____

How can I make sure I . . .

eat well? _____

sleep enough? _____

exercise regularly? _____

relax? _____

socialize? _____

have fun? _____

have time alone? _____

Figure 16.5
MAP OUT YOUR "TOUGH TIMES" STRATEGIES

Problem	Your Reaction	Your Stress Reduction Strategy

461

> *"Don't be hung up with the sour grapes and bad apples at your school."*
>
> —Edward Gardner, 36 years experience

Use Professional Growth to Prevent Burnout

One of the most important causes of burnout is the uncertainty that novice teachers feel about what course of action to take in many school situations. Fortunately, you have many opportunities to avoid this particular cause of burnout. Growing professionally arms you with the knowledge that you need to make informed and sensible decisions.

Here are a few of the options that you have for professional growth. Plan to take advantage of as many of them as you can.

Read professional literature. Investigate your school's professional library. Chances are good that you will find many useful resources there. In addition to the many books about education that are available to you, many periodicals are helpful to new teachers. Here are some that you should investigate.

Education Week
Suite 100
6935 Arlington Road
Bethesda, Maryland 20814
www.edweek.org

The Reading Teacher
International Reading Association
800 Barksdale Road, P. O. Box 8139
Newark, Delaware 19714
www.reading.org

Teaching K–8
400 Richard Avenue
Norwalk, Connecticut, 06954
www.teachingk-8.com

Mathematics Teacher
National Council of Teachers of Mathematics
1906 Association Drive
Reston, Virginia 20191-9988
www.nctm.org

Instructor Magazine
Scholastic Inc.
555 Broadway
New York, New York 10012
www.scholastic.com

Learning
3515 W. Market Street
Greensboro, North Carolina 27403
www.learningmagazine.com

Use the Internet. There are many wonderful Internet sites for teachers. One of the best ways to take advantage of them is to join a listserve. There are many of these discussion groups available for educators. Here are three that novice teachers will find particularly helpful.

Learning and Instruction	http://listserve@asu.edu
Middle School	www.middleweb.com
Teacher Stress	www.teacherstress.co.uk

Take classes. Many school districts offer courses in conjunction with local colleges. You may even qualify for reduced tuition payments.

Take advantage of inservice opportunities. Attend every workshop and inservice meeting with the purpose of learning something useful. You won't be disappointed if you have this attitude.

Attend conferences. Attend professional conferences and conventions. You will not only learn new ideas, but you can also add to your network of supportive colleagues.

Join professional organizations. Many teachers value the support of professional organizations such as the American Federation of Teachers or the National Education Association. In addition to these, there are many organizations dedicated to specific disciplines. Ask your colleagues for local organizations that they find helpful.

Participate in peer observations. Ask colleagues whose opinion you value to observe you. Pay attention to the feedback from these voluntary evaluations. Also ask if you can observe other teachers and their classes. Many teachers will welcome you.

Evaluate yourself. Set up a videotape or an audiotape and record your lesson. This exercise is an invaluable way to see just how you interact with your students.

The Safety Net of Professionalism

Professionalism means being the very best teacher that you can be every day. When you choose to conduct yourself in a professional manner, you send the message that you are in control of your classroom and yourself, and you earn the respect of your students and colleagues in the process. Although it is not always easy to be a professional educator, especially when you are just starting out, professionalism is one of the best tools that you have to prevent stress.

The following are just some of the professional behaviors that can serve as guidelines to stress prevention.

- Treat your students with respect. Don't be a pushover or play favorites.

- Accept criticism from your supervisors in a calm and professional manner. Do not be defensive. Instead, work to correct the problem.

- Take your workday appearance seriously. Dress comfortably but neatly. Your appearance sends a message to your students that you take your position seriously.

- Greet everyone you meet with a friendly word and a smile. Project an air of confidence and soon you will *feel* confident.

- Become an organized and efficient worker so that you can accomplish all of your paperwork chores.

- Take charge of your classroom with sound discipline policies.

- Be known as a punctual person who does not miss school without a good reason.

- Plan lessons that are meaningful, interesting, and based on your district's or state's curriculum guidelines.

- Never shout at your students. If you are tempted to do this, stop and reassess the situation.

- Admit it when you make a mistake. Ask for help.

- Be careful about what you say and how you say it. Use Standard English. Never allow students to curse in front of you.

- Make sure that the goals you set for your students are attainable and that you give them the skills to reach them.

- Have high expectations for your students. If you want to encourage achievement, you must expect a great deal.

- Take pride in your profession. Share this attitude with your students.

- Follow all school rules.

- Let students know that you care about their welfare. Don't give up on them when things are difficult.

What Students Expect from Their Teachers

Students expect that their teachers will:

Enjoy being with students	Teach the material	Return papers quickly
Use different techniques	Be understanding	Act like an adult
Not be too strict	Keep promises	Be friendly to everyone
Know the subject matter	Offer extra help	Not have favorites
Admit mistakes	Be open-minded	Be enthusiastic
Give students a voice	Maintain order	Dress like a professional
Help with problems	Help everyone succeed	Be organized

---

*"Keep your fresh innocence alive. Don't fall victim
to the negativity of those who no longer seem to be able
to find a bit of good in the world."*

—Dawn Carroll, 4 years experience

Keep Problems in Perspective

One of the most important tools you can have in your burnout prevention plan is to learn how to keep daily problems in perspective. Often in the rush of daily business, problems can seem overwhelming. With the distance that time provides, however, most problems dwindle into insignificance. One of the best ways to keep your problems in perspective is to learn how to turn off the doom and gloom that may be circling in your mind. The next time that you are faced with a stressful problem, take time to consciously convert the negative messages in your mind into positive ones.

Here are some positive messages you can remember to help you get started on the path to keeping today's problems in their proper prospective.

- Today's big problems will not matter a year, a month, or even a week from now.
- Not every day will be perfect. I did the best I can today.
- Other teachers experience the same problems that I do. I can ask for help.
- I am in control of my classroom and my behavior.
- It is unrealistic to think that every student will enjoy my class every day.
- I am learning new skills every day. With time I will find my job easier.

Journal Entries to Help You Manage Stress

- If I could change just one thing about how I handle my workday, what would it be? How would I benefit?
- Which teaching skills can I be confident about at this point in my career? How can I build on these strengths?
- What is throwing my life out of balance? Which problem can I solve first? To whom can I turn for assistance?
- What did I learn today? What new skills have I acquired as a result of a stressful situation?
- What stress-relief actions can I take right now to improve my physical and emotional well being?

Helpful Resources for Teachers

Internet Sites

Advice/Online Forums/Ideas Exchange/Articles/Research

www.teachnet.com
www.school.discovery.com
www.teachervision.com
http://vceps.edschool.virginia.edu
www.worldwidelearn.com
www.learningcompanyschool.com
www.awesomelibrary.com
www.inspiringteachers.com

Education Databases/Links to Other Useful Sites

http://web66.edu
www.askeric.org
www.educationworld.com
www.iloveteaching.com

Helpful Advice for Beginning Teachers

www.positiveparenting.com
www.atozteacherstuff.com
www.mcrel.org/products/noteworthy/noteworthy.barbaram.asp
www.nbpts.org
www.cps.k12.il.us
www.kdp.org

General Lesson Plans

www.thegateway.org
www.encarta.msn.com
www.coreknowledge.org
http://school.aol.com
www.theeducatorsnetwork.com/lessons
www.sitesforteachers.com

United States Department of Education

www.ed.gov

General Classroom Management

www.disciplinehelp.com
www.classroom-management.com
http://education.indiana.edu
www.nea.org

Classroom Management for Middle School

www.middleweb.com

Classroom Management for Secondary School

www.7-12educators.about.com

Online Homework Help for Students

www.homeworkhelp.com
www.kidsclick.org
www.ajkids.com
www.yahooligans.com

Make Your Lessons Dynamic

www.criticalthinking.org
www.fpsp.org
www.teachwise.com
www.utc.edu/teaching-resource-center/critical.html
www.fno.org/toolbox.html
www.mde.state.mi.us/school/materials.shtml
www.nytimes.com/learning/teachers/less

Social Studies Lesson Plans

www.pacificnet/~mandel/SocialStudies.html
www.lcweb.loc.gov/homepage/lchp.html
www.newslink.org

English/Language Arts Lesson Plans

www.ccc.commnet.edu/grammar/index.htm

Mathematics Lesson Plans

http://mathforum.org/teachers
www.gamequarium.com/
www.col-ed.org/cur/math/math53.txt

Science Lesson Plans

www.sierraclub.org/education/
www.csrnet.org
www.physlink.com

Technology in the Classroom

www.iste.org
www.webnovice.com

Gifted Education Ideas

www.gifted-children.com
www.gifted.uconn.edu

Substance Abuse Education

www.acde.org

Students with Special Needs

www.snow.utoronto.ca

Professional Organizations

American Federation of Teachers (AFT)
555 New Jersey Avenue
Washington, DC 20001
1-202-879-4400
www.aft.org
   The AFT is a teachers' union that offers research and assistance with collective bargaining.

National Educational Association
1201 16th Street NW
Washington, DC 20036
1-202-833-4000
www.nea.org

The NEA is the largest national teachers' union. It offers assistance with collective bargaining and provides instructional research to its members.

Association for Supervision and Curriculum Development (ASCD)

1250 N. Pitt Street
Alexandria, Virginia 22315
1-703-549-9110
www.ascd.org

ASCD offers school leaders assistance with curriculum and instruction.

The Master Teacher

Leadership Lane
P. O. Box 1207
Manhattan, Kansas 66505-1207
1-800-669-9635
www.masterteacher.com

The Master Teacher provides assistance with professional development and classroom management issues. The organization also publishes a journal by the same name.

National Board for Professional Teaching Standards (NBPTS)

1900 M Street NW, Suite 210
Washington, DC
1-202-463-3980
www.nbpts.org

This organization has established a system to certify teachers who meet the criteria for a national teacher's certificate.

U. S. Department of Education

600 Independence Avenue SW
Washington, DC 20202
1-800-USA-LEARN
www.ed.gov/free

The Department of Education offers hundreds of free resources and provides links to other helpful Web sites.

Professional Journals

Educational Leadership
Association for Supervision and Curriculum and Development
1250 N. Pitt Street
Alexandria, Virginia 22314
www.ascd.org

Education Week
Scholastic, Inc.
555 Broadway
New York, NY 10012
1-212-343-6100
www.scholastic.com/public/EL/El.html

Instructor Magazine
Scholastic, Inc.
555 Broadway
New York, NY 10012
1-212-343-6100
www.scholastic.com/Instructor

Learning
3515 W. Market Street
Greensboro, NC 27403
www.learningmagazine.com

The Master Teacher
Master Teacher
P. O. Box 1207
Manhattan, Kansas 66505-1207
1-800-669-9635
www.masterteacher.com

Phi Delta Kappan
P. O. Box 8139
Bloomington, IN 47402
www.pdkintl.org/kappan/kappan.htm

Teacher Magazine
6935 Arlington Road, Suite 100
Bethesda, Maryland 20814
1-301-280-3100
www.teachermagazine.com

Books

Abbamont, Gary and Brescher, Antointette. *Study Smart!* West Nyack, NY: The Center for Applied Research in Education, 1990.

Armstrong, Thomas. *Multiple Intelligences in the Classroom*, Second Edition. Alexandria, Virginia: Association for Supervision and Curriculum Development, 2000.

Bigham, Vickie Smith and George D. *The Prentice Hall Directory of Online Education Resources*. West Nyack, NY: The Center for Applied Research in Education, 1997.

Breeden, T. and Mosely, J. *The Cooperative Learning Companion*. Nashville, TN: Incentive Publications, Inc., 1992.

Costa, A. L. *The School as a Home for the Mind*. Arlington Heights, IL: Skylight Press, 1991.

De Fina, A. A. *Portfolio Assessment: Getting Started*. New York: Scholastic, 1992.

Delisle, Robert. *How to Use Problem-Based Learning in the Classroom*. Alexandria, Virginia: Association for Supervision and Curriculum Development, 1997.

Flick, Grad. *ADD/ADHD Behavior Change Resource Kit*. West Nyack, NY: The Center for Applied Research in Education, 1997.

Goleman, Daniel. *Working with Emotional Intelligence*. New York: Bantam Books, 1998.

Gardner, Howard. *Multiple Intelligences: The Theory in Practice*. New York: Basic Books, 1993.

Harwell, Joan. *Complete Learning Disabilities Handbook*, Second Edition. West Nyack, NY: The Center for Applied Research in Education, 2001.

Hunter, Madeline C. *Improved Instruction*. Thousand Oaks, CA: Corwin Press, 1976.

Hunter, Madeline C. *Motivation Theory for Teachers*. Thousand Oaks, CA: Corwin Press, 1996.

Hyerle, David. *Visual Tools for Constructing Knowledge*. Alexandria, Virginia: Association for Supervision and Curriculum Development, 1996.

Mamchak, H. Susan and Steven R. *Teacher's Time Management Survival Kit*. West Nyack, NY: The Center for Applied Research in Education, 1993.

Martin-Kneip, Giselle O. *Becoming a Better Teacher: Eight Innovations That Work*. Alexandria, Virginia: Association for Supervision and Curriculum Development, 2000.

Morgan, Jill and Ashbaker, Betty Y. *A Teacher's Guide to Working with Paraeducators and Other Classroom Aides*. Alexandria, Virginia: Association for Supervision and Curriculum Development, 2001.

Newmann, Dana. *The Complete Teacher's Almanack*. West Nyack, NY: The Center for Applied Research in Education, 1991.

Osborn, Particia. *Reading Smarter!* West Nyack, NY: The Center for Applied Research in Education, 1995.

Stiggins, R. J. *Student-Centered Classroom Assessment*. New York: Macmillian College Publishing Co., 1994.

Taggart, G. L., Phifer, S. J., and Wood, M. *Rubrics: A Handbook for Construction and Use*. Lancaster. PA: Techomic, Publications, 1998.

Index